Early America and the Modern Imagination

To all our colleagues
who endeavor to work in the field of Humanities inquiry and the
creation of new knowledge—despite institutional austerity,
increased workloads, and a rise in anti-intellectualism.

Early America and the Modern Imagination

Rewriting the Past in the Present

Edited by Patrick M. Erben and
Rebecca L. Harrison

EDINBURGH
University Press

Edinburgh University Press is one of the leading university presses in the UK. We publish academic books and journals in our selected subject areas across the humanities and social sciences, combining cutting-edge scholarship with high editorial and production values to produce academic works of lasting importance. For more information visit our website: edinburghuniversitypress.com

© editorial matter and organization Patrick M. Erben and Rebecca L. Harrison, 2025
© the chapters their several authors, 2025

Edinburgh University Press Ltd
13 Infirmary Street
Edinburgh EH1 1LT

Typeset in 11/13 Bembo by
IDSUK (DataConnection) Ltd

A CIP record for this book is available from the British Library

ISBN 978 1 3995 3617 2 (hardback)
ISBN 978 1 3995 3619 6 (webready PDF)
ISBN 978 1 3995 3620 2 (epub)

The right of Patrick M. Erben and Rebecca L. Harrison to be identified as the editor of this work has been asserted in accordance with the Copyright, Designs and Patents Act 1988, and the Copyright and Related Rights Regulations 2003 (SI No. 2498).

EU Authorised Representative:
Easy Access System Europe
Mustamäe tee 50, 10621 Tallinn, Estonia
gpsr.requests@easproject.com

Contents

List of Figures	vii
Acknowledgments	ix
Notes on Contributors	xi

Scripting the Past in the Present: Early America and the Modern
    Imaginary—An Introduction   1
Patrick M. Erben and Rebecca L. Harrison

PART I Graphic Novels and Gaming: New Modalities and Historical Representation

Section Overview   25

1. *Ghost River*'s Restorative Fiction: Prioritizing Indigenous Pasts and Presents   27
Will Fenton and Katelyn Lucas

2. Simulating Sovereignty: Alternative History, Video Games, and the Haudenosaunee   64
Harry J. Brown

3. Learning through Looking: Early American History and Race in Contemporary African American Graphic Novels   84
Oliver Scheiding

PART II Women in Film: Gender, Consent, and Representation

Section Overview   109

4. More Authentic Yet Less Accurate: The Challenges of Depicting Women in Early American Film and TV Adaptations   111
Stacey Dearing

5. "Check her for marks!": Teaching Bodily Consent and
   Autonomy through the Salem Witch Crisis Documents
   and Netflix's *Fear Street: 1666* 132
   Danielle Cofer

6. Sex Education: Teaching Revolutionary Constructs of
   Womanhood through AMC's *Turn* 156
   Patrick M. Erben and Cryslin Ledbetter

PART III Staging the Nation: From Theater to Television

Section Overview 177

7. Performing, Remembering, and Reiterating: Early
   America on Stage 179
   Shira Lurie

8. Aaron Posner's *JQA* as Layered History: Promoting
   Aesthetic-Historical Reflection in a Texas Theatre's
   Production 202
   Sarah Ruffing Robbins

9. *Ted Lasso* and Early American Identity 223
   Anne Roth-Reinhardt

PART IV Grammars of Colonial Violence

Section Overview 251

10. "The Truth is Much Different": Eliza Lucas Pinckney's
    Literary Lives and the (Re)Production of Colonial Violence 254
    Kirsten Iden

11. African Cinema on American Slavery 280
    Steven W. Thomas

12. Epistolary Writing and the Afterlife of Letters from a
    Woman of Color 312
    Lisa Vandenbossche

Index 333

Figures

0.1	John Gadsby Chapman, *Baptism of Pocahontas*, 1840. (Credit: Architect of the Capitol.)	6
0.2	Rioters gather in the US Capitol Rotunda on January 6, 2021 in front of the iconic paintings depicting scenes of American colonization and nation-building, including John Gadsby Chapman's *Baptism of Pocahontas*. (Credit: Saul Loeb / AFP via Getty Images.)	6
1.1	The Turtle Island origin story, as depicted in *Ghost River: The Fall and Rise of the Conestoga*. (Credit: Weshoyot Alvitre. Copyright held by the Library Company of Philadelphia.)	40
1.2	Map showing the locations of ancestral Lenape homelands and the tribal headquarters of the five federally recognized Lenape/Delaware Tribal Nations or First Nations in the United States and Canada. (Credit: Katelyn Lucas.)	47
2.1	Battlefield image from *Warpath*. (Credit: Creative Assembly.)	78
5.1	Shot from *Fear Street Part 3: 1666*. (Credit: NETFLIX.)	147
6.1	Assignment sheet from ENGL 4003: Early American Literature, Summer 2021. (Credit: Patrick M. Erben.)	160
6.2	Pre-reading activity chart. (Credit: Cryslin Ledbetter.)	171
8.1	In-the-round staging drawing Forth Worth audiences into *JQA*'s conversations. (Credit: Evan Michael Wood.)	203
8.2	Stage West's multigenerational, multiracial cast for *JQA*. (Credit: Evan Michael Wood.)	215
8.3	Adams's portrait next to an actor modeling engaged listening to a mid-career Adams. (Credit: Evan Michael Wood.)	218

11.1 *Ceddo*, directed by Ousmane Sembene. (Credit: Janus Films.) 288
11.2 *West Indies ou les Nègres marrons de la liberté*, directed by Med Hondo. (Credit: Ciné-Archives.) 293
11.3 *Sankofa*, directed by Haile Gerima. (Credit: Array.) 299

Acknowledgments

This essay collection started as a collaboration between us in the summer of 2021—when the world was just beginning to emerge from COVID lockdowns and vaccinations were making some limited travel possible again. Nevertheless, our sense of individual and collective scholarly futures was deeply shaken by remote and dual modality teaching, institutional reorganization and austerity measures, canceled conferences, and the loss of the collegial bonding and networking that has always been integral to germinating and developing scholarly projects. Although we had been playing with the idea for this project for a long time, the pandemic brought home to us the renewed urgency of sustaining scholarly and pedagogical conversations with our colleagues near and far. Moreover, the summer of 2020 had seen widespread social justice protests in the wake of the murder of George Floyd, and, in January 2021, the nation was shaken by insurrectionists storming the US Capitol. As social and political norms frayed and the future of democracy was (and very much remains) at stake in the United States and across the globe, we sought to explore the connections between early American precedents, a contested present, and an uncertain future.

The many exciting responses we received to our initial call for proposals filled us with hope, knowing that we were not alone in seeking to interrogate the many uses and abuses of early America in contemporary media, literature, politics, and culture. Thus, we thank the many colleagues who sent us proposals—whether or not we were able to accept them. The presenters at the fall 2021 online South-Atlantic Modern Language Association conference panel and the 2022 American Literature Association panel in Boston—the first in-person conference we attended post-pandemic—further helped us sharpen our vision for the collection and find much-needed feedback and collaboration. Above all, our heartfelt gratitude goes out to the thirteen contributors who worked diligently through numerous drafts and editorial processes and who steadfastly stuck with us, despite a lengthy production cycle. We are especially grateful to Sarah Ruffing Robbins who both championed our collection and facilitated the pitching of our project to the wonderful editorial team at Edinburgh University Press.

At Edinburgh, we especially thank Senior Commissioning Editor Emily Sharp, who quickly embraced our project and believed in its potential despite (or perhaps because of) our unorthodox period-transcending approach to American Literary and Cultural Studies. Emily stalwartly shuttled our proposal through several iterations, commissioned expert reviewers, and helped us secure the coveted publication contract. Our two anonymous peer readers provided us, in several rounds of review, with much-needed critical feedback and particularly ensured that we articulated our project's position within several critical conversations, such as Public Memory Studies. Next, Senior Assistant Editor Elizabeth Fraser navigated our manuscript through the intricacies of the production process with expert skill; we particularly appreciate her patience in explaining UK–US differences in copyright and permission laws and terminologies. Finally, we thank the EUP production team for all of their work along with our copyeditor, Caroline Richards, who contributed a keen eye and sharp attention to formatting, references, and writing conventions.

At our home institution, we would like to thank our former and current chairs, Shelly Elman and Robert Kilpatrick, for supporting our work, particularly during times of budgetary contraction and increased teaching loads. Patrick much appreciates his early American literature students across several semesters—especially his collaborator Cryslin Ledbetter—for validating his pedagogical approaches to connecting early American and contemporary subjects and critical questions. And, both of us remain indebted to Dr. Reiner Smolinski, a gifted teacher and scholar without whom we would never have met nor developed a love for all things early America. Also, we thank our children, Samuel and Ruby, who faithfully tolerated many evenings and weekends of working parental units and who yet always cheered us on with a not so tongue-in-cheek *dann mach es doch*. Finally, we relished the opportunity for the intellectual companionship this project allowed us over several years. We each contributed unique perspectives and skills, but at the end of the day, the project has proven once again that Rebecca is the superior editor of this duo.

Patrick M. Erben and Rebecca L. Harrison

Contributors

Harry J. Brown (PhD Lehigh University) teaches early American literature, Native American literature, literature of the environment, science fiction, and game studies at DePauw University. He has published three books: *Injun Joe's Ghost* (2004) examines Native American hybridity in American writing; *Videogames and Education* (2008) considers the relation between video games and the humanities; and *Golf Ball* (2014), part of Bloomsbury's Object Lessons series, looks at such diverse subjects as empire, trade, advertising, landscape design, sport, and mysticism through the lens of a dimpled polyurethane orb. He has also published recent articles and essays on ethical simulation in video games, Puritan gravestone verse, and Indigenous forms of Christianity. His most recent research explores literary futures in the wake of AI large language models.

Danielle Cofer, an independent scholar, received her PhD from the University of Rhode Island. A specialist in early American literature, Gender and Women's Studies, and the gothic, her teaching and research interests include the Salem witch crisis, popular culture representations of early American narratives, African American literature, and women writers. Her work has appeared in several venues, including *Coriolis: The Interdisciplinary Journal of Maritime Studies* and *ABC-CLIO's Hollywood Heroines: The Most Influential Women in Film History*.

Stacey Dearing is a Teaching Professor of English at Siena College. Her work has appeared in *Early American Literature*, *The Journal of Medical Humanities*, and *Dialogue: A Journal of Mormon Thought*. In 2019, she was an Erikson Scholar in Residence at the Austen Riggs Center in Stockbridge, MA. In addition, she has presented her research to the public in a webinar co-hosted by the Plymouth Antiquarian Society and the Pilgrim Hall

Museum, and through the Austen Riggs Center. She has also presented her research at the Society of Early Americanists biennial conferences, the Society for the Study of American Women Writers conference, the Alden March Bioethics Institute Ethics Grand Rounds at Albany Medical College, and the Austen Riggs Center Grand Rounds. Dearing's essay in *Early American Literature* on Dorothy May Bradford's death and mental health received the 2021 Richard Beale Davis prize.

Patrick M. Erben is Professor of English at the University of West Georgia, where he teaches courses in early American literature, American Romanticism, and Cultural Studies. His work has appeared in journals such as *Early American Literature* and *The William and Mary Quarterly* as well as in numerous edited collections. He is the author of *A Harmony of the Spirits: Translation and the Language of Community in Early Pennsylvania* (2012), which won the Brown Award given by the Young Center at Elizabethtown College. Most recently, he served as editor of *The Francis Daniel Pastorius Reader* (2019), the first book-length presentation of Pastorius's work across genres. Erben is a past president of the Society of Early Americanists and currently serves on the editorial board for *Early American Literature*.

Will Fenton is the creator of Digital Paxton and the editor of *Ghost River: The Fall and Rise of the Conestoga*. Fenton earned his PhD from Fordham University from the Department of English in 2018, specializing in early American literature and the digital humanities. Prior to his current role at the Foundation for the Children's Hospital of Philadelphia, he served as Associate Director of Stanford University's Center for Spatial and Textual Analysis, Program Officer at the National Endowment for the Humanities, and Director of Research and Public Programs at the Library Company of Philadelphia. His writings have appeared in *American Quarterly*, *Early American Literature*, and *The Journal of Interactive Teaching and Pedagogy* and in edited volumes from Modern Language Association Press and Rutgers University Press.

Rebecca L. Harrison is Professor of English at the University of West Georgia where she teaches courses in southern women writers, American literature, film, Gender Studies, and pedagogy. A women's literature specialist, Harrison has published on writers including Eudora Welty, Beatrice Witte Ravenel, and Julia Alvarez, alongside her work on active pedagogical practices. She is the co-editor of the *Eudora Welty Review* and President of the Eudora Welty Society. Her books include *Inhabiting La Patria: Identity,*

Agency, and Antojo in the Work of Julia Alvarez (2013), *Teaching, Pedagogy, and Learning: Fertile Ground for Campus and Community Innovations* (2017), and *Revitalizing Classrooms: Innovations and Inquiry Pedagogies in Practice* (2017).

Kirsten Iden is an Assistant Professor of English at the University of South Carolina Salkehatchie, where she teaches writing and early American literature. Her research focuses on eighteenth-century South Carolina, material culture, and the production of historical narratives. Her previous work on Eliza Lucas Pinckney has appeared in *The Journal of the South Carolina Historical Association*, and she is currently at work on a book project that examines the social, political, and economic significance of Pinckney's textile archive.

Cryslin Ledbetter is a graduate of the University of West Georgia with a bachelor's degree in English. Her role models are writers such as Sylvia Plath, Kate Chopin, and Toni Morrison, and she has a specific interest in linguistics and Southern Women's literature. Ledbetter plans to continue her education in the master's program at the University of West Georgia.

Katelyn Lucas works as the Historic Preservation Officer for Delaware Nation (a federally recognized Lenape Tribal Nation) and manages their extension office in eastern Pennsylvania, Lenape homelands. She is also a PhD candidate in Temple University's English Department, specializing in early American and Native American literatures.

Shira Lurie is Associate Professor of U.S. History at Saint Mary's University. She is the author of *The American Liberty Pole: Popular Politics and the Struggle for Democracy in the Early Republic* (2023). Her writing has been published in *The Journal of the Early Republic*, *The Washington Post*, *TIME*, *The Toronto Star*, and *Inside Higher Ed*.

Sarah Ruffing Robbins is the Lorraine Sherley Professor of Literature at Texas Christian University, where she teaches for the departments of English, Women and Gender Studies, and Comparative Race and Ethnic Studies. She has published ten academic books, including *Learning Legacies: Archive to Action through Women's Cross-Cultural Teaching* (2017), *The Cambridge Introduction to Harriet Beecher Stowe* (2007), and *Managing Literacy, Mothering America* (2004, 2006), as well as several essay collections growing out of grant-supported humanities partnerships. As co-director of "The Genius of Phillis Wheatley Peters," a participatory humanities project launched during the 2023 anniversary of 1773's publication of *Poems* by Phillis Wheatley (Peters), she facilitated a series of in-person and virtual events, development of new teaching resources, a project website, and new scholarly publications. With Andrew Taylor and Linda Hughes, she edited *Transatlantic Anglophone Literatures, 1776–1920* (Edinburgh University Press, 2022), and she led extension of that work into a complementary website on "Teaching Transatlanticism."

Anne Roth-Reinhardt, an independent scholar, currently leads literacy work in St. Paul Public Schools. Her past appointments have primarily been in contemporary and nineteenth-century American literature at the Universities of Minnesota, St. Thomas, and Metropolitan State. Her scholarly research explores the way history is (re)created through the reading of the past in the present, especially through, but not limited to, references to clothing and textiles in eighteenth- and nineteenth-century American historical fiction. She was a 2010 Jay and Deborah Last Fellow at the American Antiquarian Society, and her work has been published in *Common-Place* and *American Periodicals* as well as presented at conferences across the United States.

Oliver Scheiding is Professor of North American Literatures and Early American Studies in the Obama Institute for Transnational American Studies at Johannes Gutenberg University in Germany. His research focuses on print culture and criticism as well as Periodical and Material Culture Studies. He served as editor-in-chief of *Amerikastudien / American Studies*, the quarterly of the German Association of American Studies, from 2010 to 2019. He edited the volume *Worlding America: A Transnational Anthology of Short Narratives before 1800* (2015). Most recently, he contributed book chapters to the *Cambridge History of Native American Literature* (2020) and the *Routledge Companion to the British and North American Literary Magazine* (2022). He served as co-editor of a special issue on Indigenous periodicals published by the journal *American Periodicals* (2023). His new book, *Print Technologies and the Making of American Literatures*, is forthcoming.

Steven W. Thomas is Professor of English and Director of Integrated Learning at Wagner College in New York City. He has published several scholarly essays on eighteenth-century American and transatlantic literature including "The Labor of Regions," which compares the representation of slavery in tobacco, rice, and sugar economies. In 2018–19, he was a fellow at the McNeil Center for Early American Studies, where he examined the representation of Ethiopia in European and American literature from the fifteenth century to the twenty-first century. In 2016, he was a Fulbright Scholar in Ethiopia, where he taught film theory, and he has published numerous articles on the movie industry in Ethiopia, including a textbook chapter for the second edition of *African Film Studies: An Introduction*. In 2017, he co-edited with Srividhya Swaminathan the collection of essays titled *The Cinematic Eighteenth Century: History, Culture, and Adaptation*.

Lisa Vandenbossche is a Lecturer in the Department of English Language and Literature at the University of Michigan. Her scholarship focuses on writing by and about sailors and their families as a nexus between print culture and reform movements in the long eighteenth-century anglophone world. Most recently, her work on reform discourse, travel writing, and women's bodily autonomy has appeared in *ABO: Interactive Journal for Women in the Arts, 1630–1840*, *Women's Studies*, *The Mark Twain Annual*, and *Cultural Economies of the Atlantic World*.

Scripting the Past in the Present: Early America and the Modern Imaginary—An Introduction

Patrick M. Erben and Rebecca L. Harrison

In July 2011, Zabelle Stodola, former president of the Society of Early Americanists, began an extensive thread on the SEA's listserv when she looked for "[c]ontemporary adaptations of early American texts." A host of colleagues chimed in with pairings and groupings they had successfully used in their teaching, ranging from contemporary plays, poems, and novels re-envisioning the Salem witchcraft trials (such as Maryse Condé's *I, Tituba, Black Witch of Salem* and Margaret Atwood's "Half-Hanged Mary") to films reimagining Jamestown, the first permanent English settlement in North America (including the omnipresent Disney princess Pocahontas in the eponymous 1994 animated movie and Terrence Malick's *The New World*, released for the 400-year anniversary of Jamestown in 2007). Stodola subsequently amassed and shared a long list of sources, demonstrating how important transhistorical connections are to early Americanist scholarship and pedagogy.[1] If Stodola's inquiry accentuated a thriving teaching practice in the field of Early American Studies, choosing it as an inspiration and starting point underscores our volume's ethos as well as its critiques.

Teacher-scholars not only leverage the links between early American and contemporary materials to animate student interest in the early period but, more importantly, they recognize the larger explanatory power of such constellations for understanding central issues in early American *and* present-day literature, history, culture, religion, and politics. Yet, critical

---

[1] Stodola's list is accessible via the SEA website's compendium "Teaching Early American Topics" site, created by Edward J. Gallagher and coordinated and updated by Susan Imbarrato: https://web.mnstate.edu/seateaching/Early_American_Adaptations.pdf.

studies pursuing a rigorous analysis of the ways in which the present reimagines the early American past occupy only a small slice of scholarship, even in the burgeoning field of Public Memory Studies. The present volume seeks to begin to fill the void created by the discrepancy between classroom practice and scholarly publishing. As a born-in-the-practice-of-teaching project, *Early America and the Modern Imagination* reverses the usual trajectory of scholarship trickling down to pedagogy by underscoring that teaching has long been ahead of critical work in foregrounding the rescripting of early America in the present. To engage with our students, we inevitably make our personal investment in the contemporary relevance of early American topics visible. Unlike scholarship that distances the positionality of researchers from the subjects and periods studied, our essays make apparent the entanglements of past and present, of scholarly subject and scholarly self.

Among many such entanglements of early American past and present, recent "culture war" controversies about critical race theory, book banning, and reproductive rights (among others) have turned public attention to early American precedents. At the same time, early American tropes enjoy a stunning cachet in popular culture. For example, the immigrant story as key to US nationhood propelled *Hamilton* to phenomenal success, and a cross-cultural romance plot set against the backdrop of settler colonial violence underwrites James Cameron's *Avatar* saga. So, what is the academic response to these phenomena? How can humanities scholarship wield methods of cultural, textual, and historicist analysis to interpret the significance of these transhistorical reimaginings of the early American past?

Early America and the Modern Imagination draws on productive approaches for understanding the social and cultural construction of collective remembrances from the growing field of public memory scholarship. Its practitioners interpret and critique contemporary renderings of the past—ranging from visual media to public celebrations to museums and monuments—as windows into the often contested ways in which societies conceptualize their relationship to history. Yet, Memory Studies have so far generated few scholarly contributions from the field of Early American Studies, in spite of proliferating debates about the colonial and early national periods.[2] Our collection addresses this scholarly gap by assembling an array of essays that investigate how texts, artifacts, and events have rescripted early America as a usable past for contemporary audiences.

---

[2] One of the few studies in memory scholarship focused on early America specifically is Rex and Watson, *Public Memory, Race, and Heritage Tourism of Early America*.

This volume interprets early American themes and their present-day echoes as transhistorical nexuses in order to grapple with the evolving and highly contested import of the American nation's past. *Early America and the Modern Imagination*, at its core, analyzes and critiques appropriations and reworkings of the early American past in contemporary popular culture (from the twentieth century to the present) across a variety of genres, media, and topoi, including literature, film, theater, graphic arts, video games, cultural memory, politics, and education. While scholars have certainly addressed individual contemporary texts or phenomena concerned with early America,[3] no scholarly monograph or critical collection to date broadly traces and theorizes the implications of this early American resurgence. Our contributors employ a diverse range of critical perspectives and scholarly methodologies to interrogate how such texts repurpose early America as a usable past to achieve strategic cultural work—from entertainment to calls for political activism—in the present.

The collection as a whole also argues that deployments of the early American past in contemporary cultural and political discourse too often come untethered from actual texts, histories, stories, and sensibilities. Public debates frequently display a disregard not only for early American literary, cultural, and historical precedents but also the contemporary texts that respond to them, ultimately leading to distortions and even manipulations of popular opinion. Yet our primary project in this volume is not to find and rectify inaccuracies in contemporary engagements with the past or to correct mischaracterizations of such engagements by political detractors. Rather, by gathering scholars well-versed in both early American and contemporary materials and methodologies, *Early America and the Modern Imagination* underscores the academic and larger public significance of finding a nuanced understanding of the dynamic relationship between the past (and its documentary record) and present-day responses as texts requiring rigorous study in their own right. We seek to center the key role that methods of textual, rhetorical, and cultural analysis play in revealing the power dynamics driving contemporary deployments of early America. Such work illuminates the present and the past in a multidirectional approach superseding rigid periodization and disciplinary borders.

By choosing Stodola's assemblage from 2011 as a touchstone for this volume, we ask our readers to question commonplace definitions of history (including literary history) and contemporaneity. Scholarship often shuns

---

[3] For example, Renee Christine Romano and Claire Bond Potter, *Historians on Hamilton: How a Blockbuster Musical Is Restaging America's Past.*

viewing the past through contemporary artifacts because of the fleeting nature of what counts as "present" or "contemporary." Publishers, especially academic presses, fear their publications becoming "dated" and losing their relevance and marketing cachet. As a result, academic publishing shies away from making the intertwining of present and past the subject of rigorous scholarship. And whereas historians are frequently called upon in popular media to interpret current events in light of historical knowledge, Literary and Cultural Studies scholars remain more commonly beholden to strict conceptualizations of what it means to work in "contemporary" or "popular" culture versus past literary periods or movements. Though obsolete in teaching, such a policing of literary periods inhibits critical analysis of early American topoi in the development of thought, feeling, politics, and aesthetics across time. Conflated with the alleged demise of the English major, moreover, Literary and Cultural Studies lose their relevance in the public sphere, where—if properly valued—they could provide indispensable tools for problematizing popular mythologies. Hence, even somewhat older adaptations or rewritings of early American texts and topics on Stodola's list should remain relevant because they allow us to analyze the ways in which powerful cultural and political phenomena such as fear, hate, restrictive gender scripts, exceptionalism and exclusion, and white supremacy and racial hierarchies govern our lives. As Ed Simon aptly states in his review of Abram Van Engen's seminal book *A City on a Hill: A History of American Exceptionalism*, the American public and scholars alike are still obsessed with "the *fiction* that an American origin can be found." Van Engen's book meticulously traces how one such fiction—of the Puritan origins of America—has been constructed and leveraged across time. Our volume's object is not to pinpoint correctly the early American origins of trends in contemporary American culture. Rather, *Early America and the Modern Imagination* asks what more recent stories about early America can show and tell us about ourselves, and what kind of work they are made to do in the present.[4]

---

[4] Ed Simon, "When Perry Miller Invented America: On Abram C. Van Engen's 'City on a Hill.'" For the purpose of our collection, we define "early America" as ranging from pre-Columbian Indigenous worlds through the colonial and early national period (leading up to the Civil War). Contemporaneity, in our study, comprises the period from the mid-twentieth century (circa 1945) to the present in order to highlight that such transhistorical rescriptings are no passing phenomenon but rather an evolving practice of remembering the early American past vis-à-vis changing sociocultural and political contexts. We derive our periodization of "contemporary" from the fields of Literary Studies, History, and Cultural Studies, as our volume draws mainly on contributors and seeks audiences from these disciplines. Yet, the book also foregrounds an awareness of the constructed, malleable, and contested nature of periodization and period boundaries.

One of the unresolved traumata in the psyche of the American public is the insurrection and near-overthrow of American democracy at the US capitol on January 6, 2021. This event reveals what persistent narratives of white supremacy and grievance politics can do. Soon after the insurrection, journalists and scholars seized on the strange constellation of rioters posing for photos in the Capitol Rotunda in front of murals portraying scenes of early American settler colonial conquest that made possible the founding of the US nation state—ranging from John Vanderlyn's depiction of Christopher Columbus's conquistadorial posturing upon his arrival on the island of Guanahaní (1847) to John Gadsby Chapman's *Baptism of Pocahontas* (1840) (Figure 0.1), showing the inception of the young Powhatan woman (whom settlers fashioned as Indigenous royalty) into the regime of British imperialism.[5] Commenting on a photo of men with red hats and black batons in the foreground and Pocahontas in the background, published by the British newspaper *Independent* on January 7, early Americanist Lisa Logan wrote on Facebook (Figure 0.2):

> Here is the money shot for my early American lit survey course, which always begins with origin stories. We look at how the progress of empire is narrated in the Capitol Rotunda paintings. We talk about how these stories continue to shape our ideas about the US. Folks, I give you The Baptism of Pocahontas by John Chapman framed with 21st century terrorists and white supremacists. Survey gold. Too soon?

Along similar lines, Cherokee scholar Joseph Pierce traced the origins of the self-styled "QAnon Shaman" (aka Jacob Anthony Chansley) and his posturing for the camera to Romantic-era portrayals of Native American warriors allegedly ceding sovereignty to white colonizers. Pierce's essay interprets Chansley's horned headdress as evoking a long line of white colonial appropriations of Indigeneity that lay claim to America as land and nation. Other optics captured during the insurrection reflect the linkages between American slavery and white supremacist ideologies encapsulated in Confederate-flag wielding protestors standing in front of a portrait of John C. Calhoun, one of the most strident defenders of slavery in American history (Stanley).

---

[5] Both paintings can be viewed on the website of the Architect of the Capitol. See *Landing of Columbus* (https://www.aoc.gov/explore-capitol-campus/art/landing-columbus) and *Baptism of Pocahontas* (https://www.aoc.gov/explore-capitol-campus/art/baptism-pocahontas).

Figure 0.1 John Gadsby Chapman, *Baptism of Pocahontas*, 1840. (Credit: Architect of the Capitol.)

Figure 0.2 Rioters gather in the US Capitol Rotunda on January 6, 2021 in front of the iconic paintings depicting scenes of American colonization and nation building, including John Gadsby Chapman's *Baptism of Pocahontas*. (Credit: Saul Loeb / AFP via Getty Images.)

Echoing Logan, one might say that lessons in early American iconography revealing the connections between settler and contemporary violence have not come soon enough. The essays in this book, therefore, consistently drive home the crucial need to understand "the differences between *history* and *historiography*" (Simon)—between the past as an elusive set of facts and the past as a continually rewritten sociopolitical and cultural script. But aside from serving as a rich field for classroom analysis, the scenes unfolding in the Capitol Rotunda on January 6, 2021 demand a set of critical tools explaining how and whether memories of an American past rooted in settler colonialism, genocide, slavery, and white supremacy animated the actions of rioters. How, in other words, do images of Pocahontas submitting herself to settler authorities serve as a usable and, in this case, *ab*usable past?

These and similar questions and scenarios are the province of public memory scholarship. Over the past twenty or more years, this field has created an interdisciplinary tool box for interpreting the ways in which societies remember their collective past, transmit historical knowledge, and adapt or refashion the past in textual, visual, and material media in the present. In examining how contemporary cultural artifacts reinterpret and reinscribe the early American past, our project interfaces with this burgeoning field. Public memory scholarship, in the words of Brady Wagoner, "works at the intersection of a community's continuity with the past and innovation for the future" (1). Like Cathy Rex and Shevaun Watson in *Public Memory, Race, and Heritage Tourism of Early America*, our book analyzes "the ways that cultural artifacts and practices are used by various groups to strategically remember parts of the past that are deemed important for the collective to share and pass on" (7).

Early America and the Modern Imagination enters a critical conversation with a range of public memory scholars. Our volume posits that remembering early America involves dynamic processes of construction and reconstruction, engages intersubjective sets of social relationships, and links a spectrum of texts and contexts. Our contributors, however, go beyond memory scholarship's primary focus on the formation of a "collective awareness of sharing some past together" (Rex and Watson 7); they read texts and cultural artifacts as multitudinous agents that contest specific constructions of the past and even disrupt the notion that a foundational, shared memory is possible or desirable. Importantly, *Early America and the Modern Imagination* joins a small group of scholarly works grounding Memory Studies in early America and its contemporary uses. While taking up this banner in their critical collection, Rex and Watson nevertheless acknowledge that "the valuable perspectives of those trained as early Americanists specifically are missing from discussions about public memory of the period in which they specialize" (8). In order to further build on Rex and Watson's momentum, it is first necessary to situate the present volume in the principal concerns and methodologies of Memory Studies.

Public memory scholarship is, in its broadest terms, concerned with the relationship between individual and collective remembering, the effect and instrumentalization of public memory for the construction of communal identity, and the specific mediation of memory through a variety of textual, visual, material (including bodily and performative), and, more recently, digital agents. Central to all contributions in this volume, this interdisciplinary field distinguishes itself from traditional historiography because it always "attends to both, the moment recalled and the moment of remembering. Memory is analyzed as the place and process where past and present interact in instances of individual and communal self-positioning and definition" (Hebel x). Memory scholarship examines the ways in which the transmission of memory in modern and contemporary societies has moved away from the late nineteenth- and early twentieth-century nationalist project of tying memory to heredity—what historian of science Laura Otis has termed "organic memory." The notion that memories are passed on, along with physical/bodily features, through one's ancestors formed the core of racial and ethnocentric definitions of community seeking to efface the always evolving construction and constructedness of modern societies in order to cast one's national and/or racial identity as unalterable and enduring.[6] The key figure in establishing the present field of Memory Studies was the French philosopher and sociologist Maurice Halbwachs, whose 1925 *Les Cadres Sociaux de la Mémoire* and especially its 1992 translation as *On Collective Memory* pioneered the understanding of memory as socially contingent—that is, determined and constructed through social practices and itself constitutive of communal identity. Though subsequently criticized for sidelining individual psychological factors, Halbwachs's belief that "all of one's memories, even those that feel private, are actually collective" has served as the formative

---

[6] Notably, at the beginning of Russia's large-scale invasion of Ukraine beginning in February 2022, Russian president Vladimir Putin was eager to justify his war by contrasting Russian identity and nationhood as enduring and existing since time immemorial and Ukrainian identity as constructed, arbitrary, and mutable. It is the task of public memory scholarship to unveil and analyze the mechanics of such rhetoric and situate it in a range of politically efficacious memory practices.

perspective for the flourishing of Memory Studies. Following Halbwachs, scholarly works that study "social frameworks of memory often serve the purpose of social cohesion and thus are tied to a culturally and historically specific group of people" (Landsberg, *Prosthetic Memory* 8). For public memory scholars, the mechanics, conduits, and processes of this mutually constitutive relationship between memory, culture, and social cohesion becomes a particular point of interest. Udo Hebel sums up, in his introduction to the volume *Sites of Memory in American Literatures and Cultures*, the various foci and approaches of memory scholarship:

> Memory is studied as a *transformative* force in the construction, contestation, and revision of individual and collective identities; memory is investigated as a productive influence in the formation, preservation, and problematization of group coherence; memory is taken as a shaping factor in acts of political legitimization and opposition. [...] Memory is explored as the production of inclusion and exclusion. The politics of memory in differing historical and cultural contexts has moved center stage. (x)

One of the key questions in Memory Studies and for this volume, therefore, is how different avenues for remembering and re-envisioning the early American past have shaped and continue to impact concepts of American culture and identity in the present. As the example of January 6, 2021 demonstrates, however, ways of remembering and recalling the past can very much serve the splintering of social cohesion, as some groups seek to revitalize settler colonial and white nationalist paradigms, while others problematize this fraught inheritance of the early American past. In this volume, several essays demonstrate the necessary intertwining of decolonial and anti-racist narratives of the American past as cornerstones for a more just future.

Early America and the Modern Imagination also joins memory scholars in forging a deeper understanding of the medial transmission and recall of the past in the present. In particular, memory scholars like Alison Landsberg investigate how mass media (film, TV, the Internet) create common "memories" for audiences though they may "share little in the way of cultural and ethnic background" (*Prosthetic Memory* 8–9). Landsberg argues that mass-mediated memories are not premised on a claim of authenticity or "natural ownership" but rather function as what she calls "prosthetic memories" inviting people "to take on memories of a past through which they did not live" (8). Landsberg argues, rather optimistically, that this "prosthetic" form of memory "opens up [...] identities to persons from radically different backgrounds" and "creates conditions for ethical thinking by encouraging people to feel connected to, while recognizing the alterity of, the 'other'" (11, 9). In *Engaging the Past: Mass Culture and the Production of Historical Knowledge*, Landsberg further identifies and studies the "affective" or "experiential mode" in mass culture conveying historical knowledge, which harnesses an emotional and even bodily experience among the public that establishes a direct conduit between "affect and cognition" (3). Landsberg ascribes to modern mass media R.G. Collingwood's characterization of history as "mental reenactment" and, quoting Hans Ulrich Gumbrecht, "the presentification of past worlds" (6, 9). Crucially, Landsberg and other public memory scholars follow Gumbrecht in claiming that film, TV, and other mass media help viewers respond to historical scenarios with both their mental and physical faculties because they wonder how they would have acted in those contexts—ultimately leading to positive pedagogical and even ethical results.[7] Anticipating objections to this theory as naive, Landsberg characterizes the work of her own book and other memory scholarship as focusing on the "*complexity* of being touched by history" (10; emphasis added). Similarly, Renee Romano and Claire Bond Potter's volume *Historians on Hamilton* argues that the blockbuster musical "has the potential to shape how Americans understand the nation's early history" and has further created something like its own public sphere, where "contemporary political debates about partisan politics, race, multiculturalism, and immigration" can play out or be facilitated (6). With Landsberg, Romano, Potter, and others, the contributors in this volume recognize the efficacy of contemporary popular media in cultivating a desire among viewers for a connection to the past. Similar to Romano and Potter, we argue that such scholarly interpretation must go "beyond assessing [historical] accuracy" and study the techniques of historical engagement facilitated by *Hamilton* and similar phenomena. Indeed, "[t]he effect of popular culture on the public mind is a matter of keen interest for historians" (Romano and Potter 8).

Yet the crucial difference between public memory studies and this volume stems from diverging concepts of the role and value of critical and pedagogical scholarship. By and large, Landsberg's "prosthetic memory" and Gumbrecht's "presentification" assume that literary works

---

[7] For a useful overview, see Hans Ulrich Gumbrecht, *Production of Presence: What Meaning Cannot Convey*.

and popular culture artifacts about history are *e*ffective because they are *a*ffective—engaging senses and bodies in the production of meaning and, by extension, historical knowledge.[8] Our volume does not question the significance and power of sensory and affective involvement in historical fiction, film, TV, video games, and graphic novels; rather, *Early America and the Modern Imagination* underscores the key role that careful humanities scholarship, interpretation, and teaching plays in establishing the connection between such affect and cognition. Whereas Landsberg, Gumbrecht, and others believe this relationship to flourish through the virtue of well-written and effective historical media,[9] our contributors demonstrate the potential danger of historical "knowledge" being mediated without the critical and historicist facilitation of expert teaching and scholarship in the humanities. The role of scholarship should not be limited to studying and describing the mechanics by which mass media elicit historical sensibilities.[10] Instead, our contributors demonstrate that humanities scholarship must play an active—perhaps even activist—role in inspecting and debating the relationship between past and present, especially as this reciprocal relationship is impacted and often skewed by contemporary political and cultural prerogatives that intervene, sometimes covertly, in the linkage between affect and cognition. Memory Studies argues that mass culture artifacts have come to replace the "cognitive or intellectual awareness" that used to be ascribed to historical teaching (Landsberg, *Engaging the Past* 10). Yet, as several of our authors cogently demonstrate, the entertainment promulgated by popular contemporary texts such as National Geographic's *Saints & Strangers* (see Dearing, this volume) or Creative Assembly's strategy game *Empire: Total War—The Warpath Campaign* (see Brown, this volume) hardly rises to the level of historical memory.

What our authors and our volume argue is not a rejection of popular culture engagements of the early American past and the significance

---

[8] See Tim Lanzendörfer and Mathias Nilges's useful discussion of the ways in which postcritique, including Gumbrecht's work, minimizes the contributions of literary criticism by promulgating a kind of "academic populism." Our volume and its contributors demonstrate the continuing relevance—nay, necessity—of "critique," especially in interpreting the axis between early America and its contemporary leveraging in popular culture and politics.
[9] Landsberg's *Engaging the Past*, for example, studies closely the TV shows *Deadwood* and *Mad Men* popular in the mid-2010s.
[10] Landsberg, to be sure, reveals a sophisticated interplay between familiarization and alienation—something akin to Berthold Brecht's "Verfremdungseffekt" (alienation effect)—in her analysis of the abovenamed shows.

of these artifacts for mediating a contemporary dialogue between past and present. Rather, *Early America and the Modern Imagination* advocates for studying and deploying transhistorical constellations between past and present. But whereas memory scholarship claims a productive interplay between "privately felt public memories that develop after an encounter with a mass cultural representation of the past, when new images and ideas come into contact with a person's own archive of experience" (Landsberg, *Prosthetic Memory* 19), our collection assumes a more sober stance toward the ability of such artifacts to accomplish a conscious awareness that "one is engaged in this kind of inquiry"—one that connects affective and cognitive faculties (Landsberg, *Engaging the Past* 10). Our volume underscores that scholarship must serve as an active intermediary in facilitating the greater public's understanding of the constructed nature of historical thinking in the present. Perhaps most prominently, the essays by Will Fenton and Katelyn Lucas on the graphic novel *Ghost River* and Oliver Scheiding on contemporary African American graphic novels reveal the work that must be done to fully realize a dialogue about the social and political repercussions of early American rescriptings in the present. Our contributors lean on but distinguish themselves from Memory Studies scholarship; they foreground the indispensable work of modeling and practicing the readerly skills necessary to unpack cultural, historical, literary, and political tropes across time and consciously critique the interplay between affect and cognition in contemporary media about early America. As humanities scholars, we must not abandon the charge to interpret the relationship between the early American past and its contemporary adaptation, retooling, and even abusing. In a cultural and political moment when local and state politicians in the United States remove "divisive topics" from K–12 and even collegiate curricula, humanities scholars should wield critical analysis and pedagogical interventions in order to make the creation, dissemination, and manipulation of public memory a central concern in public culture, rather than retreating from it.

Recent work in Memory Studies that shifts focus to the problem of forgetting underscores the need for the type of critical and pedagogical interventions that contributors in this volume pursue and model. Marc Howard Ross's *Slavery in the North: Forgetting History and Recovering Memory* joins memory scholars in paying attention to the storage of collective memories in "images created by artists, photographs, films and TV shows, books, musical compositions, statues, [. . .] former battlefields, and other sacred sites" (32). Yet Ross's scholarship usefully argues that remembering requires reinterpretation: "The messages found in these cultural expressions are not necessarily enduring, however, and they require active contemporary engagement, interpretation, and accessibility to remain emotionally meaningful, even when they are initially 'set in stone' and intended to be eternal" (32). Ross explicitly shifts the role of scholarship and pedagogy from merely studying how mass media performs memory work to the need for a more active participation in shaping public memory and its cultural utility. "Research over many decades," according to Ross, "shows that the connection between the message sent and the message retained is often weak or nonexistent, even when the message is repeated many times. [. . .] To be retained, media messages require not just reception but social processing and interpretation as well" (47). The need for interpretation undergirds what the contributors in our volume both explicitly and implicitly argue—that the connection between memories and actions are not automatic but shaped to meet the needs of the present. Scholarship, therefore, must examine and make visible the modus operandi of historical forgetting and remembering. The essay by Fenton and Lucas, for instance, goes beyond tracing and interpreting the violence perpetrated by the Paxton vigilantes; the authors focus on the ways in which the graphic novel *Ghost River* privileges the victims of such violence and restores Indigenous knowledge.

Early America and the Modern Imagination also shares with scholars such as Diana Taylor and Marisa Fuentes a central interest in the ways in which different systems of knowledge transmission variably modulate the relationship between past and present. In her focus on Performance Studies, Taylor distinguishes between "the *archive* of supposedly enduring materials (i.e. texts, documents, buildings, bones) and the so-called ephemeral *repertoire* of embodied practice/knowledge (i.e. spoken language, dance, sports, ritual)" (19; original emphasis). Whereas "archival memory" separates "the source of 'knowledge' from the knower," "the repertoire enacts embodied memory" and thus "requires presence: people participate in the production and reproduction of knowledge by 'being there,' being a part of the transmission" (19, 20). The essays by Shira Lurie and Sarah Ruffing Robbins, with their focus on theater, foreground the ways in which embodiment on the stage today produces public spheres for debating both the past and the present. In one way or the other, all of our contributors examine what Taylor calls "scenarios," or "specific repertoires of cultural imaginings" (31). Taylor discusses, as an example, the "scenarios of discovery," which have served across time as "a portable framework [that] bears the weight of accumulative repeats. The scenario makes visible, yet again, what is already there: the ghosts, the images, the stereotypes" (28).

"The scenario," Taylor continues, "structures our understanding," and it "haunts our present, a form of hauntology [...] that resuscitates and reactivates old dramas" (28). The repetitive and evolving nature of early American "scenarios" features in all our chapters—such as the comedic revival of the naive American bumpkin in *Ted Lasso* (Roth-Reinhardt) or the connection between the bodily violations performed in early American witchcraft examinations and the transhistorical operation of sexual assault in Netflix's *Fear Street: 1666* (Cofer). The investigations in our volume, therefore, echo Taylor's questions about the transhistorical functionality of such scenarios: "Why do they continue to be so compelling? What accounts for their explanatory and affective power? How can they be parodied and subverted?" (28).

Scholars like Taylor and Fuentes do not posit that we must leave the traditional archive behind and focus solely on performance for interpreting the ways in which the present rewrites and reinterprets the past. Just as our volume examines a variety of modes and genres through which early America is rewritten and reimagined in the present, Taylor acknowledges no strict separation between the archive and the repertoire for transmitting knowledge about the past to the present: "Since before the Conquest, writing *and* embodied performance have often worked together to layer the historical memories that constitute community" (35; emphasis added). For Fuentes, in fact, the methodology she dubs "reading along the bias grain" specifically requires scholars to face the "epistemic violence" of the traditional archive that silenced enslaved women (8, 5). Rather than rejecting the historical archive for its biases, Fuentes seeks to make visible archival imbalances and, thus, to pursue "a methodological project" that is "concerned with the ethical implications of historical practice" (6). Essays in our collection such as Kirsten Iden's examination of the posthumous lionizing of the South Carolina planter Eliza Pinckney in biographical and popular literature thus examine the traditional archive and its deployment across time. Iden reads "along the bias grain" in order to flesh out the ways in which the hagiography on Pinckney renders invisible the inextricable connections between her widely celebrated introduction of indigo and her privilege and power as a slave holder.

The questions of what we consider an "archive" (ontology) and how we gain knowledge from said "archive" (epistemology) become even more far-reaching when we consider Saidiya Hartman's *Lose Your Mother: A Journey along the Atlantic Slave Route*; here, Hartman herself—her travels in West Africa, her genealogical linkages to slavery—functions as the archive. Since enslavement severed the self from one's history and familial relationships,

Hartman characterizes herself as a "stranger" with "a particular relation to the past":

> If the past is another country, then I am its citizen. I am the relic of an experience most preferred not to remember, as if the sheer will to forget could settle or decide the matter of history. I am a reminder that twelve million crossed the Atlantic and the past is not yet over. I am the progeny of the captives. I am the vestige of the dead. And history is how the secular world attends to the dead. (17)

In our volume, Steven Thomas's essay examines several African films about slavery and the slave trade that anticipated by several decades investigations of the archive and its relationship to the individual and communal embodiment of the history of transatlantic violence in the present by Hartman, Taylor, and Fuentes. Part of the "Third Cinema" project, this group of films, Thomas argues, "interrogates the colonial archive and excavates the experiences, cultures, and lives of enslaved Africans that have been silenced in that archive." Crucially, Thomas's chapter counterbalances recent Memory Studies scholarship with an earlier Africanist perspective on memory recovery that has largely gone unnoticed in US-based scholarship. Thomas builds on the earlier work of Sylvia Wynter and Teshome H. Gabriel, who interrogated "the representational apparatus of the West" by contrasting it with the focus on the "issue of consciousness or memory" in African cinematic texts (Wynter 36), as well as Third Cinema's role as "guardian of popular memory" (Gabriel 53). Attention to African cinema's perspective on the transatlantic inheritance of slavery, therefore, presents an important counterpoint to the often exculpatory portrayal of slavery in Hollywood film.

Other contributors in our volume do not necessarily elaborate a personal journey like Hartman, but they nonetheless examine the myriad ways in which "an imagined past" is also an "existent territory with objective coordinates" (Hartman 9). In Danielle Cofer's essay, this concrete territory is a college campus where the bodily violations hidden away in the historical documents of the Salem witchcraft crisis serve as the compass for exhuming the hushed realities of sexual assault. Or, in Lisa Vandenbossche's essay, the private letters written by Meghan Markle to her father and then ruthlessly dissected in the British tabloid press function as the site upon which colonialist politics of race are once more projected and inscribed. What these and other essays in our collection have in common with earlier work by Hartman and the films of Third Cinema that

Thomas examines is their sharply trained focus on the re-emergence of psychological and historical trauma in the present and the realization that rescripting the early American past is a matter of deep personal and communal significance.

Our analysis of the rescripting of early America in the present finally also demands our attention to the movement from old to new media—a phenomenon that Jay David Bolter and Richard Grusin call "remediation." For Bolter and Grusin, "[w]hat is new about new media comes from the particular ways in which they refashion older media" (15). The old media, in this case, are of course the original texts and representations found in early American literature and culture; our essays in one way or another all study the remediation of early American tropes through new media in the present—through film, TV, video games, graphic novels, and so forth. Applied to our context, Bolter and Grusin's theory reveals the mechanics of remediation involved in reimagining the early American past in the present: remediation allows viewers or readers today to imagine themselves in direct contact with or experience of the real. The concept of "transparent immediacy" at the same time requires that the reader or viewer must become aware of the medial nature of their perception (21). Stacey Dearing's essay on NatGeo's *Saints & Strangers* perfectly exemplifies this logic's operation: the producers of the show explicitly avowed the grittiness of their representation of the Plymouth Pilgrims as the means to achieve a greater sense of authenticity—something akin to immediacy; and yet, granting the viewer an awareness of the artificiality or constructedness of this gritty quality would also produce a heightened sense of aesthetic pleasure. Simply put, while viewers are aware that what they watch is not real, they marvel at how well the medium has achieved such an illusion of reality. For Dearing, however, this effect produces the troubling tendency to take far too great a license with historical truth; remediation, in other words, must be subjected to critical inquiry for the losses or distortions involved in the ways that new media reimagine the old. Harry Brown finds in the video game *The Warpath Campaign* a practice akin to what Bolter and Grusin define as "hypermediacy," a form of remediation where the artist or creator defines "a space through the disposition and interplay of forms that have been detached from their original context and then recombined" (39). Concretely, in the game the Haudenosaunee have seized settler colonial technologies of warfare and now rule a successful in-land empire in North America resisting colonial incursions. Recombining historical attributes of the Haudenosaunee (such as their political savviness in creating a federal civic system that may have influenced the

US Constitution) in a new context and across various game-play options, however, problematically allows hypermediacy to elide historical forces of dispossession, colonization, and forced removal. While players of the game may be "simultaneously aware" that hypermediacy has created "a mosaic" in which "individual pieces" are inserted in a "new, inappropriate setting," they have perhaps not learned about the history of Indigenous resistance and dispossession, in which case hypermediacy has lost its connection to the referent in the past (Bolter and Grusin 47). Nevertheless, in his study of African American graphic novels about slavery and the slave trade, Oliver Scheiding credits remediation with giving readers new perspectives on early traditions in slave narratives—such as the trope of the talking book.

How, in practical terms, should scholars who are working with and through contemporary rescriptings of the early American past handle remediation and hypermediacy? What level of historical contextualization is necessary so that the alterity of the past does not simply disappear and remediation does not become the new reality for viewers and readers? Critical Studies must distinguish the type of remediation that productively makes visible the disjunctures between past and present, old and new media, from manipulations that seek to erase the methods of remediation and thus eclipse, for example, the mechanics of settler colonialist appropriation. Just as John Gadsby Chapman created the *Baptism of Pocahontas* to promote colonization as a salubrious force of civilization and whitewash his immediate context of Native American removal in the 1830s and 1840s, remediation of the media footage of the violence at the Capitol is being released as collages or mosaics portraying rioters as peaceful visitors and engaged citizens.[11] Clearly, remediation of early America in the present requires critical interventions to demonstrate historical continuities and ruptures, while making visible the politics underlying different strategies of remediation.

The work our contributors do across the four sections in this collection, therefore, goes beyond illuminating the present by analyzing its engagement with the early American past. Our volume's chapters demonstrate that new

---

[11] In February 2023, then House Speaker "McCarthy gave then-Fox News host Tucker Carlson exclusive access" to January 6, 2021 footage, which Carlson wielded to "bend perceptions of the violent, grueling siege [...] into a narrative favorable to Trump." In November 2023, the new House Speaker, Mike Johnson, released 44,000 hours of January 6 footage to the public, while obscuring the faces of rioters to protect their identity (Amiri). While billing the release of the footage as an effort to promote transparency, this act of remediation actually obscured agency in the insurrection, just as Chapman's *Baptism of Pocahontas* obscured the American government's agency in the removal of Indigenous peoples during the 1830s and 1840s.

methodologies for understanding the past help redress history's erasures. Retelling the early American past through contemporary modes—such as film and graphic novels—posits imaginative, alternative, and sometimes speculative techniques of storytelling to generate an alternative historical consciousness that seemingly objective historiography has, at times, obscured. Engaging critically and creatively with the stories we tell about early America illuminates the past while simultaneously helping us grapple with the present.

Part I, "Graphic Novels and Gaming: New Modalities and Historical Representation," demonstrates the ways in which remediation can hew innovative avenues for addressing historical erasures. In particular, Will Fenton and Katelyn Lucas center the graphic novel *Ghost River: The Fall and Rise of the Conestoga* (2019) as a significant foray into regenerative storytelling: a reimagining of the brutal murder of the Indigenous Conestoga community in eighteenth-century Pennsylvania from a Native perspective—one that resists elegizing the victims and instead privileges creative concepts of Indigenous survivance. In the second half of the essay, Lucas challenges scholars to engage with descendant communities in ways that respect Native cultural and political sovereignty. As a counterpoint, Harry Brown's essay, "Simulating Sovereignty: Alternative History, Video Games, and the Haudenosaunee," exposes what happens when another new medium—video games—engages in counterfactual imaginaries that replace *Ghost River*'s historically grounded fictionalization with "what if" speculations predicating Indigenous survival on the paradoxical embrace of settler colonial warfare and technologies. By employing interdisciplinary methods of inquiry—literary criticism, game theory, and historiography—Brown's essay underscores the pitfalls of leaving a contemporary engagement of the early American past up to the affective engagement of readers/players with commercially produced artifacts. Rounding out this section, Oliver Scheiding's essay, "Learning through Looking: Early American History and Race in Contemporary African American Graphic Novels," skillfully combines the formal analysis of graphic novels about slavery with a politically inflected argument about the instrumentality of this genre in articulating anti-racist and thus more democratic narratives of American history. In sum, the contributions in Part I underwrite the ability of new media to question seemingly settled narratives of nationhood, while cautioning against a revisionism untethered from historiographic accuracy and plausibility.

Part II, "Women in Film: Gender, Consent, and Representation," takes two approaches to critiquing how TV and film convey ideas and ideologies of early American womanhood for contemporary viewers. Following Gender Studies principles, all three essays demonstrate that women's roles in early America were no less culturally constructed than they are now—thus opening options for interrogating concepts of womanhood across historical periods. Employing reader response theory principles, each essay also wonders how viewers and producers of contemporary representations of early American women frame and challenge notions of authenticity, consent, and sociopolitical participation. To begin, Stacey Dearing's "More Authentic Yet Less Accurate: The Challenges of Depicting Women in Early American Film and TV Adaptations" sees the representation of women in Nat-Geo's docudrama *Saints & Strangers* as a problematic inversion; attempting to create among viewers the sensation of witnessing the "authentic" lives of English Puritan and Indigenous Wampanoag women, the show sacrifices historical accuracy in a way that divests historical figures *and* viewers today of representational and interpretive agency. In Danielle Cofer's "'Check her for marks!': Teaching Bodily Consent and Autonomy through the Salem Witch Crisis Documents and Netflix's *Fear Street: 1666*," Gender Studies and reader response theory converge on an issue that could not be more consequential for collegiate readers—the problem of physical violation. In her pedagogy-centered essay, Cofer traces how reading and responding to historical documents can empower students to interrogate gender identity and sexual safety. Patrick Erben and Cryslin Ledbetter's essay "Sex Education: Teaching Revolutionary Constructs of Womanhood through AMC's *Turn*" similarly posits that today's secondary and collegiate students can productively contend with the political backlash against discussing allegedly "divisive concepts" (including gender identity) by engaging contemporary media representations of Revolutionary-era women and their challenge to patriarchal authority and exclusionary models of political participation.

Part III, "Staging the Nation: From Theater to Television," considers the utilization of theater and TV productions—either directly or indirectly representing early American figures and tropes—for advancing or questioning concepts of US-American nationhood. Theater and Television Studies here intersect overtly with public humanities approaches that examine the impact of cultural artifacts on social and political constellations. Shira Lurie's essay, "Performing, Remembering, and Reiterating: Early America on Stage," specifically applies public memory scholarship to musical theater in order to demonstrate the ways in which actual stage work performs evolving concepts of American political culture across time. For her essay "Aaron Posner's *JQA* as Layered History: Promoting Aesthetic-Historical Reflection in a Texas Theatre's Production," Sarah

Ruffing Robbins specifically attended and studied the productions of a play applying a character study of an early American president (John Quincy Adams) to present-day debates about threats to democracy and the nature of ethical political leadership. Similarly, Anne Roth-Reinhardt's contemplation of Ted Lasso (from the eponymous Apple TV+ show)—a fictional personality exemplifying ethical and unifying leadership qualities and its evocation of the common early American literary trope of the naive, homespun bumpkin—deliberates the double-edged work that cliché tropes of American selfhood do around the world.

In Part IV, "Grammars of Colonial Violence," three scholars wield tools of literary, cinematic, and pop culture analysis to decipher how different modalities—ranging from biography to film to epistolarity—both sublimate and expose various types of violence. In her essay "'The Truth is Much Different': Eliza Lucas Pinckney's Literary Lives and the (Re)Production of Colonial Violence," Kirsten Iden takes to task biographies recovering the contributions of early American women while eliding the complicity of much-vaunted figures like Pinckney in the violence of slavery. The two essays rounding out the collection emphatically stress the methodological necessity of flipping the scholarly trajectory from one that remains beholden to US exceptionalist narratives to one embracing an outside perspective. Specifically, in "African Cinema on American Slavery," Steven Thomas studies the representation of slavery in films from the African "Third Cinema" movement and thus embeds a Film Studies approach within an international critique of Western imperialism. Lisa Vandenbossche, similarly, in "Epistolary Writing and the Afterlife of Letters from a Woman of Color," embraces a transatlantic and transhistorical methodology in linking the movement of letters and racialized bodies across national borders, thus exposing how public and private, legal and pop culture discourses are blended to enable anything—even innermost feelings and familial relationships—to be traded and sold. The connection between violence and language expressed in the section title not only unites these three contributions but links them to the purpose of this collection overall: to demonstrate how a morphology of early American tropes and paradigms allows humanities scholars to strategically expose the linguistic and cultural operation of power across time and a variety of media.

In toto, *Early America and the Modern Imagination* pursues rigorous scholarship in service of the needs of a society seeking a nuanced yet accessible understanding of the past. Its movement from robust considerations of new modalities to investigations that center Gender Studies and the nation in media representations to work that scrutinizes varying grammars of colonial violence thus evidences the volume's purpose and provides a structure for how readers, especially those with particular areas of interest, can best use the volume. The specific case studies in each chapter deliberately pursue a larger public engagement with early America and its contemporary representation. Each essay, in turn, engages central early American topics such as contact, exploration, settlement, and founding specifically by examining the transhistorical bridging pursued in contemporary modalities such as novels, graphic novels, TV series, film, video games, theater productions, and the public opinion marketplace known as social media. Akin to public memory scholars, our contributors fundamentally examine the rhetorical efficacy of such cultural artifacts within social contexts to find how "shared memories [are] leveraged for political and ideological purposes" (Rex and Watson 7). *Early America and the Modern Imagination* harnesses the tools of textual and cultural analysis to foreground the ways in which historical changes are reflected in and reinscribed by transformations in mediality. Our volume, thus, performs critical analyses that will easily transfer to the next show, play, film, novel, or video game about early America that—we are certain—is just around the corner.

Works Cited

Amiri, Farnoush. "Speaker Mike Johnson says he'll make 44,000 hours of Jan. 6 footage available to the general public." PBS Newshour, November 17, 2023, https://www.pbs.org/newshour/politics/speaker-mike-johnson-says-hell-make-44000-hours-of-jan-6-footage-available-to-the-general-public (last accessed November 5, 2024).

Bolter, Jay David, and Richard Grusin. *Remediation: Understanding New Media*. MIT Press, 1999.

Engen, Abram Van. *City on a Hill: A History of American Exceptionalism*. Yale UP, 2020.

Fuentes, Marisa J. *Dispossessed Lives: Enslaved Women, Violence, and the Archive*. U of Pennsylvania P, 2016.

Gabriel, Teshome H. "Third Cinema as Guardian of Popular Memory: Towards a Third Aesthetics." *Questions of Third Cinema*, edited by Jim Pines and Paul Willemen. British Film Institute, 1989, pp. 53–64.

Gumbrecht, Hans Ulrich. *Production of Presence: What Meaning Cannot Convey*. Stanford UP, 2003.

Halbwachs, Maurice. *On Collective Memory*. Translated by Lewis A. Coser. U of Chicago P, 1992.

Hartman, Saidiya. *Lose Your Mother: A Journey along the Atlantic Slave Route*. Farrar, Straus and Giroux, 2007.

Hebel, Udo, editor. *Sites of Memory in American Literatures and Cultures*. Verlag Winter, 2003.

Landsberg, Alison. *Engaging the Past: Mass Culture and the Production of Historical Knowledge*. Columbia UP, 2015.

———. *Prosthetic Memory: The Transformation of American Remembrance in the Age of Mass Culture*. Columbia UP, 2004.

Lanzendörfer, Tim, and Mathias Nilges. "Literary Studies After Postcritique: An Introduction." *Amerikastudien/American Studies*, vol. 64, no. 4 (2019), pp. 491–513.

Logan, Lisa. "January 6 Rioters Posing Capitol Rotunda in Front of Pocahontas Painting." Facebook, January 7, 2021, https://www.facebook.com/lisa.logan.9277 (last accessed January 15, 2024).

Otis, Laura. *Organic Memory: History and the Body in the Late Nineteenth and Early Twentieth Centuries*. U of Nebraska P, 1994.

Pierce, Joseph. "The Capitol Rioter Dressed Up as a Native American Is Part of a Long Cultural History of 'Playing Indian.' We Ignore it at Our Peril." Artnet, January 17, 2021, https://news.artnet.com/art-world-archives/native-capitol-rioter-1937684 (last accessed November 5, 2024).

Rex, Cathy, and Shevaun E. Watson. *Public Memory, Race, and Heritage Tourism of Early America*. Routledge, 2022.

Romano, Renee Christine, and Claire Bond Potter. *Historians on Hamilton: How a Blockbuster Musical Is Restaging America's Past*. Rutgers UP, 2018.

Ross, Marc Howard. *Slavery in the North: Forgetting History and Recovering Memory*. U of Pennsylvania P, 2018.

Simon, Ed. "When Perry Miller Invented America: On Abram C. Van Engen's 'City on a Hill.'" *Los Angeles Review of Books*, February 5, 2023, https://lareviewofbooks.org/article/when-perry-miller-invented-america-on-abram-c-van-engens-city-on-a-hill (last accessed November 5, 2024).

Stanley, Tim. "The Art of Insurrection: What the US Capitol's Paintings Tell Us about the Pro-Trump Mob." *Telegraph*, 12 January 2021, https://www.telegraph.co.uk/art/artists/art-insurrection-us-capitols-paintings-tell-us-pro-trump-mob/#:~:text=The%20beauty%20of%20congressional%20art,of%20white%20men%2C%20some%20of (last accessed November 5, 2024).

Stodola, Zabelle, editor. "Contemporary Adaptations of Early American Texts/Authors/Topics." EARAM-L: The Society of Early Americanists Listserv, https://web.mnstate.edu/seateaching/pedagogy.html (last accessed November 5, 2024).

Taylor, Diana. *The Archive and the Repertoire: Performing Cultural Memory in the America*. Duke UP, 2003.

Wagoner, Brady. *Handbook of Culture and Memory*. Oxford UP, 2018.

Wynter, Sylvia. "Africa, the West and the Analogy of Culture: The Cinematic Text after Man." *Symbolic Narratives/African Cinema: Audiences, Theory and the Moving Image*, edited by June Givanni. British Film Institute, 2000, pp. 25–76.

PART I

GRAPHIC NOVELS AND GAMING: NEW MODALITIES AND HISTORICAL REPRESENTATION

Section Overview

The first section of this collection hones in on Indigenous and African American graphic novels, gaming, and the ways in which these modalities engage with and transform historical representation. In Chapter 1, **Will Fenton** and **Katelyn Lucas** lead off this grouping with **"*Ghost River*'s Restorative Fiction: Prioritizing Indigenous Pasts and Presents,"** which examines the graphic novel *Ghost River: The Fall and Rise of the Conestoga* and the possibilities of restorative storytelling via cross-cultural collaborations. This piece documents both the creation process behind the graphic novel and its analytical potential, ultimately evidencing how "restorative effort is in many ways also a decolonial effort, in the sense that the graphic novel seeks to decenter settler colonial privilege and perspectives both in the historical record and in the processes of authorship and publication." In this way, Fenton and Lucas argue for the "necessary extension of that work, acknowledging both the successes and limitations" of such projects "to ensure that it is not an isolated example but rather builds ongoing conversation about how to create more reciprocal representational collaborations with Native communities ... thus, reaffirm[ing] the need for the kind of restorative archival and representational work *Ghost River* does and the vital collaborative processes underpinning it."

Chapter 2, **"Simulating Sovereignty: Alternative History, Video Games, and the Haudenosaunee"** by **Harry J. Brown,** tackles the tricky problem of history and Indigenous representation in interactive gaming and counterfactual inquiry. Brown reads imaginary histories of the Haudenosaunee in Kim Stanley Robinson's novel *The Years of Rice and Salt* as well as the video game *Empire: Total War—The Warpath Campaign* in relation to actual Indigenous resistance. This chapter contends that these contemporary counterfactual representations show a problematic revisionism and theme of abuse: that the survival of Indigenous peoples succeeds only through "the adoption of settler technologies and strategies." This model of assimilatory resistance opposes one of the defining elements of Nativist resistance in early America, Brown argues, which "affirm[ed] the value of traditional tribal culture and lifeways" and "reject[ed] European cultural supremacy." The alternative histories portrayed in *Warpath* and *The Years of Rice and Salt*, he writes, "create the false dilemma of assimilation versus extermination and falsely resolve it by posing cultural compromise or surrender as the only viable response to genocide." "This thesis of history as a perpetual arms race" reaffirms settler colonialism, Brown states, and "its exercise of the technology of conquest ... defers meaningful understanding of the role of the Haudenosaunee in the formation of the American republic."

Oliver Scheiding closes out the first section in his move to African American visual storytelling in Chapter 3: **"Learning through Looking: Early American History and Race in Contemporary African American Graphic Novels."** Scheiding's piece deftly examines the relationship between texts, images, and history in his exploration of graphic novels by writers and graphic artists, such as Kyle Baker and Rebecca Hall, and "the ways in which their visual-verbal texts investigate the problem of collective histories and life stories," where the form of graphic storytelling and its contemporaneity enhances a Black archive "for theorizing democracy and Black citizenship." "Though separated from the immediate effects of slavery by over 150 years," he writes, "African American graphic novels such as Baker's *Nat Turner* (2008) or Hall's *Wake: The Hidden History of Women-Led Slave Revolts* (2021), signify on and reconstitute the past to intervene in the enduring legacies of slavery and race that haunt the present." As Scheiding demonstrates, these artists complicate established racist visual archives in ways that help both Black and non-Black audiences to better appreciate the multiple and heterogeneous traditions African American writers inaugurated and revised. "Scripting the past into the present, both the novels' material potential related to the visual page arrangement and the importance of the 'gutter'—that is, the untold in the space between the panels that makes the reader supply the missing action," he contends, "disturb a 'reading' of history as a linear movement toward transparency and away from ambiguity."

1

Ghost River's Restorative Fiction: Prioritizing Indigenous Pasts and Presents

Will Fenton and Katelyn Lucas

As one of the oldest colonial institutions in America, the Library Company of Philadelphia is an improbable host for a Native American graphic novel. Founded by Benjamin Franklin in 1731, the Library Company's early shareholders were almost exclusively landholding white men, and the institution's most significant expansion of the eighteenth century followed the accessioning of James Logan's library in 1792. Many of those nearly 3,000 volumes would have been purchased with profits from lands in the Upper Delaware and Lehigh valleys that had been seized from the Lenape peoples, signed into law by Governor Logan under the Walking Purchase of 1737, whose ratifying deed is known to have been fraudulent.[1] It was in the Library Company's "Logan room," surrounded by volumes from the Loganian library, below the gaze of Thomas Sully's oil painting of a youthful James Logan, that scholars and Native American artists met in August 2018 to produce a graphic novel that would not simply illustrate a dark chapter of colonial history but reinterpret it from the perspective of Indigenous victims, survivors, and their kin.

The Logan room meeting concretized tensions embedded in the graphic novel *Ghost River: The Fall and Rise of the Conestoga* (Red Planet Books and Comics, 2019). How can colonial institutions, and those who

---

[1] Sometimes termed the "Walking Purchase Hoax," this incident was repeatedly referenced by Lenape peoples as a reason for their siding with the French in the Seven Years' War during negotiations with proprietors and representatives from the Friendly Association. Fifty-eight manuscripts related to the Walking Purchase were recently acquired and digitized by the Huntington Library, Art Museum, and Botanical Gardens; those documents have been added to *Digital Paxton* (http://digitalpaxton.org/works/digital-paxton/walking-purchase-collection).

work for or with them, critically re-examine their histories with partners who have been excluded, effaced, or actively displaced by those very institutions? Seated in a space furnished with the bounties of colonization, every contributor confronted the discomforts of the undertaking. Historical advisor Daniel K. Richter, Director of the McNeil Center for Early American Studies, acknowledged the ugliness of the history that the creative team sought to reinterpret. Cultural advisor Curtis Zunigha (Delaware Tribe of Indians), co-director of the Lenape Center, warned of the risks of taking on such a project. Author Lee Francis 4 (Pueblo of Laguna) expressed his concerns about telling the stories of an Indigenous community to which he did not belong. And artist Weshoyot Alvitre (Tongva) questioned what source material, if any, she could use to recover the voices of a lost people. The next two years of collaboration would include many moments of discomfort and uncertainty as the creative team and advisors sought to navigate the conceptual and practical challenges of sharing a story of a people whose cultural memory had not been systematically collected or preserved and whose kin had been displaced across North America.

This essay uses the graphic novel *Ghost River* as a case study with which to engage the possibilities and limitations of Native and non-Native collaboration for restorative storytelling in historical fiction. In the first half of this essay Will Fenton, editor of *Ghost River*, provides an overview of the historical basis of the project: the Paxton or Conestoga massacres and ensuing pamphlet war, as well as the collaborative creation process behind the graphic novel. In the second half of the essay, Katelyn Lucas analyzes *Ghost River* from her position as a non-Native scholar specializing in Native American literatures to understand how the graphic novel works as a restorative historical representation by centering Lenape worldviews and humanizing its Native characters. This section also offers Lucas's reflection on the challenges of Native literary collaborations informed by her experience working for Delaware Nation—one of the multiple federally recognized Lenape Tribal Nations—as a Tribal Historic Preservation Officer. After interrogating the critical entanglements *Ghost River* reveals between Native literary representation, cultural agency, and real-world practices of tribal sovereignty, this essay concludes by offering some insights from Lucas and Fenton concerning possible solutions to these challenges.

The bifurcated structure of this essay—from context and documentation to assessment and prescription—enacts the principles of reciprocity that Indigenous peoples have asked of predominantly white cultural heritage institutions. At the recent biennial conference of the Society of Early Americanists (June 8–11, 2023), panelists at a forum titled "Leveraging

Academic Resources for Indigenous Communities" stressed the importance of ensuring that decolonization work is ongoing, including assessment and reassessment of that work. For example, land acknowledgments have become a popular starting point for academics and institutions to begin to recognize the Tribal Nations whose lands they are occupying. But Native scholars and tribal government representatives are increasingly having to emphasize that land acknowledgments require majority-white settler colonial rooted institutions to further educate themselves by building reciprocal relationships with Native partners to ensure that these acknowledgments are not simply performative. This sort of collaborative reciprocal work requires careful planning and implementation: leaders must integrate steps that meaningfully address long-standing Indigenous distrust of academic institutions. But vitally, it also asks non-Native leaders to imagine a different temporality of labor and scholarly production, one that accepts that restoring relationships with Native communities—be it through a land acknowledgment or a graphic novel—is not a one-off exercise, but an ongoing iterative process without a decisive end point. That structure of labor and production abrades against the very terms of grant funding, premised on achieving specific outcomes and outputs within a carefully delineated period of performance, the support of which enabled *Ghost River*. With that funding exhausted, this essay seeks to sustain that difficult work by following up, engaging the complexities, challenges, and institutional constraints to tribal consultation, and imagining structural possibilities to supporting new collaborative work.

The Paxton Massacres and Pamphlet War

Nearly a decade of intercontinental war had exposed profound tensions between European empires, colonists, and Native peoples across North America. The Treaty of Paris, signed in February 1763, may have concluded the Seven Years' War (1756–63) and brought a precarious peace to the North American colonies, but across the trans-Appalachian West, the ceasefire collapsed almost as soon as it began. That spring, a group of disparate Native peoples united behind the Ottawa chief Pontiac and staged a series of attacks on colonial forts in defiance of British military expansions across the Great Lakes. Those battles came to the Pennsylvania borderlands with the Siege of Fort Pitt and Fort Bedford later that summer.[2]

---

[2] For a thorough account of these material conditions in North America, see Daniel K. Richter, *Trade, Land, Power: The Struggle for Eastern North America*.

A hundred miles west of those attacks, a group of former militiamen from the Paxtang township, just outside what is today the capital of Pennsylvania, plotted revenge. Their target was Conestoga Indiantown to their east, home to a small heterogeneous community of unarmed Native peoples from different Tribal Nations in the region, but primarily known for being the last distinct community of Susquehannock people. There was little reason for the Conestoga people to earn the ire of the Paxtang militiamen. The Conestoga had remained neutral throughout the Seven Years' War, and most of the twenty inhabitants at Conestoga Indiantown were "praying Indians"; they had Christian names, wore Christian dress, and spoke English. The parents traded woven baskets. The children played with the children of settlers.[3] The Conestoga and their neighbors shared Conestoga Manor, a plot of land that had been set aside for them by their "brother Onas," William Penn, at the founding of the colony of Pennsylvania.

That changed in December 1763. In two massacres, the first at Conestoga Indiantown, and a second two weeks later at Lancaster, a mob of at least fifty "Paxton boys" murdered the last twenty residents of Conestoga Indiantown.[4] Their attacks were intended for public consumption: the Paxton vigilantes burned Conestoga Indiantown to the ground, desecrated the bodies of six victims, and committed their violence in daylight. Two days after Christmas, the mob attacked the Lancaster jailhouse, where the remaining Conestoga had been taken for protection. There, they murdered and scalped six adults and eight children in the courtyard behind the

---

[3] Details derived from Lancaster resident Rhoda Barber's account of her childhood at Conestoga Manor are available at the Historical Society of Pennsylvania. The memoir traverses the writer's life in Lancaster County (1726–82), with descriptions of migration and settlement, trade with Native peoples, and several pages dedicated to the massacre of the Conestoga in 1763. Barber's memoir—highly personal, fragmented, and composed at some historical distance (1830)—and the oral histories documented on *Ghost River* (https://ghostriver.org/more-information/circle-legacy/) gesture toward a wealth of social historical materials that texture and problematize printed narratives traditionally collected or preserved by colonial institutions. The introduction to the 2018 WMQ/EAL (*William and Mary Quarterly/Early American Literature*) forum on Native American Literary Studies usefully posits a series of methodological and institutional changes to center Native peoples' intellectual, literary, and material histories (Mt. Pleasant et al.).

[4] These vigilantes had been trained and armed through a voluntary militia in Paxtang during the Seven Years' War. (Due to Quaker resistance to a colonial militia, Pennsylvania featured a patchwork of local, voluntary militias.) Owing to their town of origin (Paxtang), political allies popularized the name "Paxton boys" in the ensuing pamphlet war. *Ghost River* studiously avoids this euphemistic moniker, which continues to endure today, and instead refers to the vigilantes as either "vigilantes" or "murderers."

jail. The Pennsylvania government responded with alarm, fearing renewed violence across the colony. Unable to shuttle 140 neighboring Moravian Indians (Lenape converted by Moravian missionaries[5]) to New York, Governor Penn reluctantly accepted the refugees into Philadelphia.[6]

The following month, a mob of several hundred Paxton vigilantes marched on Philadelphia to "inspect" the refugees under the protection of the Penn government. The marchers were stopped six miles north of Philadelphia by a militia and delegation led by Benjamin Franklin. They ultimately disbanded without violence. None of the leaders would face punishment for the murders they had committed in Conestoga and Lancaster. But before they left, they published their grievances in a pair of pamphlets that would reshape Pennsylvania settlement policy: away from treaty-making and accommodation and toward a more bellicose policy of Indigenous dispossession. The Paxton pamphlets, "Declaration" and "Remonstrance," sparked a new war, one that would be waged in print in the public sphere (Smith and Gibson). In many ways, Pennsylvania's first major pamphlet war, the 1764 Paxton pamphlet war, was not so different from today's social media skirmishes. With pamphlets cheap and quick

---

[5] The Lenape are the Indigenous peoples whose homelands encompass what are now eastern Pennsylvania, New Jersey, Delaware, and parts of New York and Maryland. Many of the Lenape Tribal Nations today also refer to themselves as Delaware, though this is the term European colonists forced on them. Historically there was not a singular "Lenape Nation," but rather many related communities across their homeland region who shared Lenape culture, family ties, and language dialects (Munsee in the north and Unami in the south), but had different leaders or sakimaòk, though they would often convene with elders and matriarchs for important political decisions which would affect all Lenape people. Today there are five separate sovereign federally recognized Lenape Tribal Nations across the U.S. and Canada as a result of their forced removal from their homelands: Delaware Nation, Delaware Tribe of Indians, Stockbridge Munsee Community, Munsee-Delaware Nation, and Eelūnaapèewii Lahkèewiit or Delaware Nation at Moraviantown. Historically, the Lenape peoples' neighbors to the north were the Haudenosaunee or Six Nations, as well as the Susquehannock who inhabited central Pennsylvania after migrating from Haudenosaunee territory. The Conestoga Indiantown was known for having the last distinct community of Susquehannock people; while the Susquehannock do not exist as a separate Tribal Nation today, they have descendants in other Tribal Nations.

[6] In contrast to the pamphlets and political cartoons that circulated in 1764, these Moravian Indians were not housed within the city of Philadelphia. They were first held at Province Island and later relocated, with the threat of the approaching Paxton mob, to the barracks in Northern Liberties. This synopsis is drawn from Jack Brubaker's detailed accounts of the attacks at Conestoga Indiantown and Lancaster in *Massacre of the Conestogas*.

to produce and disseminate, pamphleteers used the medium to anonymously and pseudonymously assail political opponents, wage unfounded ad hominem attacks, and circulate misinformation. The Paxton debate, which accounted for about one fifth of the colony's printed material that year, ensnared the colony's pre-eminent statesmen, including Benjamin Franklin, Governor John Penn, and Hugh Williamson, who would later sign the U.S. Constitution (Olson 31). At stake was much more than the conduct of the Paxton men. Pamphleteers used the debate over the Paxton vigilantes to stake claims about peace and settlement, race and ethnicity, and religious conflict and affiliation in pre-Revolutionary Pennsylvania. Pamphlets were written as dialogues and epitaphs, poems and songs, satires and farces, flourished with evocations of "CHRISTIAN WHITE SAVAGES" (Franklin 27), troops of "Dutch Butchers" (Dawkins), and Quakers "thirsting for the Blood" of their adversaries (Dove 10).

While many researchers have explored the Paxton pamphlet war through John Raine Dunbar's scholarly edition, *The Paxton Papers* (1957), much of the debate falls outside the twenty-eight pamphlets he edits. There are dozens of alternative editions, answers, and responses to the pamphlets identified by Dunbar, many of which include engravings, artworks, and other forms of materiality that cannot be examined through textual transcriptions alone.[7] Perhaps most importantly, scholars who rely upon the Dunbar edition have tended to prioritize printed materials—pamphlets and to a lesser extent broadsides and political cartoons—inadvertently reinforcing colonial and cosmopolitan biases. Much of the Paxton debate happened outside Philadelphia printers, and researchers seeking to reckon with the massacre's geographic, ethnic, and class complexities must engage manuscript collections that give voice to the borderlands settlers and Indigenous peoples at the center of the tragedy.

Digital Paxton (digitalpaxton.org), a digital collection and critical edition co-sponsored by the Library Company of Philadelphia and Historical Society of Pennsylvania, serves as the scholarly impetus and archival basis of the graphic novel *Ghost River*. The digital collection features a diverse range of materials that traverse some two dozen libraries, archives, and cultural heritage institutions, including documents that might be deemed colonial (letters between colonial authorities), Native (letters and artworks from Native peoples to colonial authorities), or hybrid (treaty minutes and

---

[7] Notably, author Lee Francis 4 embedded one of those political cartoons, *An Indian Squaw King Wampum Spies* (Claypoole), in the graphic novel *Ghost River* (35), a scene discussed below.

letters transcribed by Native trading partners). While the 3,000 pages of documents available in *Digital Paxton* represent a richer array of materials, voices, and perspectives than are available in *The Paxton Papers*, researchers confront undeniable archival silences, particularly from the Conestoga people at the center of the Paxton massacres. Such gaps, silences, and erasures, borne of centuries of colonial collecting priorities, reveal the limits of a strictly archival project.

But what if readers could imagine a perspective on the Paxton massacres that, given the loss of the Conestoga people, cannot be retrieved? What if, instead of telling a story about the Paxton vigilantes, researchers sought to tell a story about the Conestoga—their fortitude and their formative role in the history of colonial Pennsylvania? Here, the scholarship of Saidiya Hartman and Marisa Fuentes informed both the values and methods of *Ghost River*. The project charter cites Hartman's notion of "critical fabulation" as a means to creatively imagine what might have happened, "to imagine what cannot be verified ... to reckon with the precarious lives which are visible only in the moment of their disappearance" (12). Fuentes' scholarship informed much of the project's methodology. Noting that "the archive conceals, distorts, and silences as much as it reveals" (48), Fuentes posits a counter-method: "reading along the bias grain" in order to "stretch" archival fragments and "accentuate the figures ... who are a spectral influence" in those official records (78). The Black, feminist epistemology that Hartman and Fuentes pursue in Africana Studies proves remarkably useful in Native American Studies and this project specifically, where Native voice is almost invariably mediated through the records of settler colonists, be they enemies (in the case of the Paxton vigilantes or their political bedfellows) or ostensible allies (in the case of Quaker diplomats or Moravian missionaries). Stretching those records to imagine what might have been demands a different scholarship, simultaneously critical and imaginative, introspective and collaborative.

Ghost River, the Graphic Novel

The graphic novel *Ghost River: The Fall and Rise of the Conestoga* enlists new investigators to reinterpret the primary and secondary source materials available in *Digital Paxton*. Rather than asking a scholar to lead the project in consultation with Native advisors, *Ghost River* inverts the hierarchy, enlisting scholars to support Native authors and artists to drive the project. Before securing funding for the project, the editor traveled to Albuquerque in 2017 to attend Indigenous Comic Con, then in its sophomore year, to meet potential artists, authors, and publishers and gauge interest in the project. At first, the response was skeptical: Native artists are accustomed to being hired to either bless completed works or illustrate someone else's vision. However, when artists came to understand that they would lead the project, many expressed interest. One artist in particular had a unique investment in artistically engaging historical materials: Weshoyot Alvitre (Tongva).[8]

Upon Alvitre's recommendation, the editor scheduled a meeting with the organizer of the conference, Lee Francis 4 (Pueblo of Laguna). After browsing some of the primary source materials available in *Digital Paxton*, Francis expressed interest in not only writing but also publishing the graphic novel, should it secure funding. As an author of graphic novels, trained scholar and educator who regularly taught at the University of New Mexico, owner of the only Native comic bookstore in the country (Red Planet Books & Comics), and C.E.O. of an eponymous publishing company, Francis understood the Native American comics world better than just about anyone else because he had helped to create it. He had also worked closely with Alvitre on other comics, which would enable the two to easily traverse the layered processes of scripting, thumbnailing, penciling, inking, coloring, formatting, and printing.

When the project was funded in 2018 by The Pew Center for Arts & Heritage, the editor sought out historical and cultural advisors to support Francis and Alvitre in their work. He had little difficulty enlisting support from scholars and their institutions, including leadership from the Smithsonian National Museum of the American Indian, Gilder Lehrman Institute of American History, Free Library of Philadelphia, and the McNeil Center for Early American Studies at the University of Pennsylvania. Academics immediately understood it as a public humanities project. Recruiting Native stakeholders proved more fraught. As all of the federally recognized Lenape Tribal Nations reside far from Philadelphia—a point that Lucas will explore in greater detail—the editor could not feasibly visit all the Nations to introduce himself and the project in the time available. Moreover, his

---

[8] At the time, Alvitre was working on several projects that translated historical events into graphic art. She had recently partnered with the Smithsonian National Museum of the American Indian to illustrate a national educational initiative entitled Native Knowledge 360°. She was also actively collaborating with Elizabeth LaPensée (Anishinaabe), Assistant Professor at Michigan State University, on an educational game, *When Rivers Were Trails*, which would use the familiar structure of Oregon Trail to retell the displacement of the Anishinaabeg during the 1890s.

emails and cold calls to Delaware Nation and Delaware Tribe of Indians went unanswered.

It was not until the editor contacted Curtis Zunigha, the Delaware Tribe of Indians' Director of Cultural Resources at the time, that a response was finally received. Zunigha was understandably skeptical of the undertaking. After several conversations and independent access to the primary source materials and grant application, Zunigha agreed to serve as advisor to the project. Even then, however, he joined in an "unofficial capacity," using his personal email address and stressing that he was doing so outside his affiliation with Delaware Tribe.[9] As he put it, going through the tribal council would exceed the project timeline, and there were no guarantees that his participation would be approved at the end of that deliberative process.

Even in that "unofficial" capacity, Zunigha proved instrumental to securing further Native support. He provided Francis with the Turtle Island origin story that opens the graphic novel, and he connected the editor with Elizabeth-James Perry (Wampanoag), who created a small wampum belt that was integrated into a Library Company exhibition that celebrated the publication of the book. Perhaps most importantly, he introduced the editor to MaryAnn Robins (Onondaga), Executive Director of the Circle Legacy Center (a Lancaster-based non-profit organization dedicated to supporting and empowering First Nations Peoples of the Americas), which contributed enormously to the development of the graphic novel. The Circle Legacy Center includes participation from some federally recognized tribal citizens as well as individuals who self-identify as Seneca, Cayuga, Munsee, or Lenape. Many of its members have lived in the region for generations, commemorated the Paxton massacres inside their community, and mapped the sites of Conestoga Indiantown. Their investment in the people and place at the center of the narrative helped to

---

[9] In all official documentation, Curtis Zunigha is listed as Co-Director of the Lenape Center, a New York-based non-profit that promotes the Lenape homeland (Lenapehoking) by working with arts and cultural heritage organizations on related programs, exhibitions, and land acknowledgment ceremonies. Despite his "unofficial" status on the project, Zunigha was instrumental not only in facilitating consultation with the Circle Legacy Center but in developing the graphic novel. Readers will find his insights implicitly and explicitly referenced in the annotated script (https://ghostriver.org/script/). His contributions were significant enough that Alvitre and Francis agreed to integrate him in the graphic novel as the Native elder who interprets the Benjamin West painting (45–7).

humanize colonial history and ground Francis and Alvitre as they began work on the graphic novel.

The editor wrote several complementary activities into the grant that were intended to both deepen and document the collaborative process behind the graphic novel. These included a national Teacher Seminar, co-sponsored with the Gilder Lehrman Institute of American History, which granted early access to the book to thirty-five schoolteachers who developed lesson plans to support classroom adoption (July 28, 2019–August 2, 2019); a public art exhibition at the Library Company that placed Alvitre's artwork into conversation with the institution's historical materials (November 11, 2019–August 25, 2020); a documentary film that captured the collaborative process behind the graphic novel (ghostriver.org/about/video); a digital edition to bolster access to the text (ghostriver.org); and three convenings of the creative team and advisory board at various stages of the development process.

The first meeting of the creative team and advisory board in August 2018 offers some insights into the centrality of place to the collaborative process. Before the graphic novel had a title, a story, or any sense of artistic direction, the group convened to finalize the project charter and conduct a series of site visits. In addition to compelling the group to grapple with the challenges of the project—as embodied in the Logan room meeting—these field trips laid the foundation for the next two years of collaboration. The team met advisors and explored primary source materials in the archives of the Library Company, American Philosophical Society, and Lancaster Historical Society, toured a longhouse at the 1719 Museum, and visited the sites of the Conestoga Indiantown and Lancaster jailhouse (now the Fulton Theater). They visited Native community members from the Circle Legacy Center at a Mennonite church for a potluck and gift exchange. They bought pretzels and went to a Phillies game. While some of these activities might seem tertiary to the research project, they are vital to any long-term collaboration because they create space for reflection and the cultivation of trust that underwrites complex projects.

After the first day of site visits, the team agreed that the graphic novel should not simply eulogize the Conestoga people. Certainly, the Paxton attacks were massacres. However, despite their transformative effects on Pennsylvania settlement policy, the erasure of Conestoga Indiantown is not the whole story. Nor was it, as scholars have traditionally treated it, the genocide of the Conestoga. Long before the Paxton mob staged its attack, many Conestoga people had intermarried, moved west, or simply left Indiantown. The Paxton vigilantes may have succeeded in murdering the last of the residents at Indiantown, but ancestors have endured, and continue to endure today.[10] To acknowledge that truth is to reject the passivity of the eulogy and to reckon with one's own agency and obligation to right historical wrongs.

Francis lit upon the title on the bus ride back from Lancaster to Philadelphia. *Ghost River* pays homage to the river upon which Susquehannock peoples lived and took their name. During the visit to Lancaster and Millerstown, the van crisscrossed the Susquehanna, the same river that the Conestoga would have fished and bathed in centuries ago. As a recurring metaphor in the text, the Susquehanna provides a visual correlative to the journey the reader takes with the graphic novel, shuttling forward and backward in time, from the raising of the first longhouses in the early 1500s to the team's 2018 field trips, from William Penn's treaty-making in the 1670s to the Paxton violence of 1763. The subtitle of the text—"The Fall and Rise of the Conestoga"—encompasses these tensions. *Ghost River* acknowledges a historical record scarred by violence and betrayal; it also elevates resilience and renewal grounded in contemporary acts of commemoration, reflection, and recommitment.

This essay seeks to stage an analytic recommitment that turns from *Ghost River* as a project completed to *Ghost River* as an object of study and an invitation for future work. In the next sections, Lucas takes the essential next step of considering the difficult work of extending the collaborative process described in the first half of this essay. Using *Ghost River* as a case study, she will consider the intricacies of and challenges to more extensive consultation, including the vital importance of tribally specific awareness, sovereignty, and support systems.

Reading *Ghost River* as Restorative Fiction

The history of the Conestoga massacre is rarely contemplated outside small groups of scholars despite its significant implications for ongoing colonization in the northeast and for the Native Nations who survived this settler violence. *Ghost River* in many ways rescripts this little-known historic incident into a usable form for a general audience to understand how settler

---

[10] Conestoga Indiantown was known for housing the last distinct community of Susquehannock people but was also likely comprised of people from different Tribal Nations in the region, primarily from the Six Nations. Multiple Tribal Nations today claim relation to the Susquehannock and/or Conestoga as their closest living descendants, since their communities would have had frequent interactions and family relationships.

colonialism continues to shape conversations about social justice, historiography, and democracy today. Among scholars who have written about the Conestoga massacre, few have attempted to meaningfully acknowledge the Conestoga's perspective or the Moravian Indians' role in this story as part of a living history. The Moravian Indians are related to today's federally recognized Lenape Nations. Brubaker's *Massacre of the Conestogas* notes that there were surviving Conestoga people believed to have living descendants in some of the Six Nations today, mainly the Seneca (160). Yet, scholars have rarely considered consulting with these contemporary Tribal Nations or seeking their participation in analyses of this history—another form of ongoing settler colonial erasure. This is why, as Fenton indicates, an important motivation behind reinterpreting this particular event was to elevate these previously marginalized perspectives on this story. The Native creators and advisors of *Ghost River* sought to both recover historic Native voices and to emphasize the vitality of contemporary Native oral histories and cultures with this project. Facing a paucity of Indigenous archival records, the creators of *Ghost River* integrated current first-person Indigenous perspectives on the massacre in both the construction process and narrative itself to address this void. Developed in consultation with Lenape and other tribal cultural advisors as well as historians, librarians, curators, and archivists, *Ghost River* sought to ensure an historically and culturally sensitive representation of the Indigenous peoples at the center of this incident. The result is a uniquely collaborative piece of literature, which chose to emphasize Lenape representation.

The following sections of this chapter discuss how *Ghost River* works as a piece of "restorative" Indigenous historical fiction by centering living Lenape worldviews over settler colonial ones and endowing its Conestoga characters with humanity to restore a sense of their presence to the historical record which largely effaced them. Thus, this restorative effort is in many ways also a decolonial effort, in the sense that the graphic novel seeks to decenter settler colonial privilege and perspectives both in the historical record and in the processes of authorship and publication. Notably, the choice was made to classify *Ghost River* as a graphic novel or a piece of historical *fiction*, as opposed to a non-fiction graphic history or visual documentary. Certainly, much of the dialogue between the Conestoga people in the graphic novel had to be imagined due to the lack of their voice in the settler colonial historical record, which speaks to the reasoning behind this classification. Yet, the narrative and its imagery are rooted in archival records, meticulous historical background research, critical scholarship, and contemporary contributions from living tribal citizens—not so different from the work which would underpin non-fiction texts. Furthermore, *Ghost River* also portrays multiple real moments from the text's creation process featuring the author, illustrator, and editor themselves as well as other contributors, speaking to its additional non-fiction value in some regards. To recognize the restorative work *Ghost River* initiated as ongoing, the next few sections perform the necessary reassessment of the successes and limitations of *Ghost River*'s "non-fictive" collaborative process, and its "fictive" literary effort to rescript Native representation into this historiography. The latter half of this essay discusses how *Ghost River* serves as a valuable model for scholars seeking to develop their own restorative (fiction or non-fiction) Indigenous history projects, owing to its representational techniques, collaborative process, and the usefulness of the graphic form for liberating narratives from traditional settler colonial historiographic structures. But it also reveals that there is more work to be done to improve reciprocity, equality, and respect for tribal sovereignty in collaboration and consultation processes for Lenape representation.

Centering Lenape Worldviews

One of the primary ways that *Ghost River* restores Native representation is by centering Lenape worldviews throughout the text. This act heeds the call of Native scholars to acknowledge tribal specificity in order to refute both settler colonial erasure and the homogenization or generalization of Native cultures. Craig S. Womack's *Red on Red: Native American Literary Separatism* speaks to this issue, asserting that "Native literature, and the criticism that surrounds it, needs to see more attention devoted to tribally specific concerns" (1). That is, Tribal Nations need to be understood as distinct sovereign entities with their own specific cultures, histories, and governmental concerns, which can be very different from those of other Native Nations. Womack argues that Native literatures should always be situated and interpreted within the context of their cultural/historical specificities, though his point is still often unaddressed in contemporary Native literary studies.

Ghost River notably does center tribally specific worldviews—largely Lenape worldviews—in order to restore a sense of accurate and living presence to the peoples who resided at Conestoga Indiantown, as well as the Moravian Indians involved in this historical event. *Ghost River* does not begin with a conversation about the Paxton vigilantes or the political climate of eighteenth-century Pennsylvania; it begins with an iconic image that depicts the Lenape origin story of Turtle Island (Figure 1.1), provided

Figure 1.1 The Turtle Island origin story, as depicted in *Ghost River: The Fall and Rise of the Conestoga*. (Credit: Weshoyot Alvitre. Copyright held by the Library Company of Philadelphia.)

by Lenape advisor Curtis Zunigha (Francis 4, 12–13).[11] While reinterpreting the historical record of the Conestoga massacre may be the primary aim of *Ghost River*, the graphic novel intentionally begins prior to this history, emphasizing that Indigenous peoples existed prior to European contact. Alvitre's illustration of the Great Turtle who grew Turtle Island from the Lenape origin story also depicts actual Susquehannock petroglyphs still visible along the Susquehanna River in the background, orienting the narrative

---

[11] There are multiple variations of this Lenape origin story, as with any oral tradition, both among the different Lenape Tribal Nations and in recordings from historic non-Lenape authored ethnographies. This example partly demonstrates the complexity of attempting to achieve tribally specific representations of Lenape or any Indigenous worldviews, as individuals may or may not agree on a singular representation of an oral story, historical event, or cultural tradition. This example also provides additional credence to the questions raised in the third subsection about how and who to consult or collaborate with to create adequate Lenape representations.

in place and concretizing both Lenape and Susquehannock claims to the land prior to contact (12–13). Thus, *Ghost River* centers Lenape (and in this instance also Susquehannock) worldviews by immersing readers in tribally specific oral history, cultural symbology, and spatial-temporal frameworks immediately upon entering the story. Louis Netter and Oliver Gruner have reflected on the unique utility of the comic or graphic novel form for historiography: "[P]oetic imagery, metaphor and myth need not be distractions from, or distortions of, facts. Such features provide a framework within which these facts become significant, vital and living" (516). Within *Ghost River*, the Lenape origin story, which is typically conveyed solely through oral tradition, can be accompanied by culturally significant imagery that reaffirms their Indigenous claims to their homelands and histories since time immemorial. The graphic novel certainly invites participation from Native and non-Native readers alike in witnessing this living culture and history. But importantly, the Lenape origin story resituates the forthcoming historical events on Native terrain first and foremost, prioritizing the history of the Conestoga massacre as "significant, vital and living" for the Lenape and other Tribal Nations today who have survived settler colonial genocide and all too often been ignored by the historical record.

As the narrative of *Ghost River* unfolds, additional artwork integrates Lenape-specific symbols and artifacts which embody Lenape worldviews. For example, the primary plot-driving symbol in the text is that of the wampum belt, through which readers experience the first massacre at Conestoga Indiantown (Francis 4, 32–3). Possessing significant political, cultural, and economic meaning to the Lenape and other northeastern Native Nations, wampum serves as a powerful symbol connecting the Conestoga massacre to a broader transhistorical Indigenous nexus of broken treaties, colonial violence, and dispossession, the consequences of which are still felt in the present. Specifically, *Ghost River* inserts the Treaty of Shackamaxon wampum belt, which features two people holding hands, lying on the ground after the first massacre (34). This particular belt was supposedly gifted to William Penn by Lenape Chief Tamanend to represent the friendship treaty they established upon his arrival to claim Pennsylvania as an English colony in 1682—a history which is also referenced later in the graphic novel (43). The belt is depicted two more times in the text: as broken and bloody after the second massacre and made whole again in the concluding images where the creators of the graphic novel reflect on the land of the Conestoga today (59, 65). Through the repetition of the Shackamaxon wampum belt, *Ghost River* establishes it as a foundational, tribally specific Lenape "document" that stands up equally to the settler colonial paper record which has traditionally been privileged in scholarship. In this manner, the Shackamaxon belt serves as an omnipresent reference point that interweaves the Lenape past, present, and future. A similar reference point is the Lenape language. Before the remaining Conestoga are massacred inside the Lancaster jail, *Ghost River* depicts them offering a prayer, transcribed in both Lenape and English (54–5).[12] These examples of Lenape language and wampum both function as significant tribally specific symbols of Lenape culture that also invoke a temporal orientation essential for understanding how the Lenape worldview is centered in the graphic novel.

In multiple occasions in the text, *Ghost River* blends the Lenape past and present, which can also be understood as an Indigenous-centered framework useful for decentering linear settler colonial temporality. Fenton explains in the introductory material to *Ghost River* that the structure of the graphic novel "serves to make the past present ... carrying the reader backward and forward between past and present ... moments chafe against our very sense of historical time" (6). Similarly, in the "Script Notes" included at the end of the text, Lee Francis 4 expresses that "one of the things about this whole work was that it felt like it couldn't be told in a linear style ... Native and Indigenous stories are not entirely linear in their tellings, they are cyclical and contextual" (97). Here, Francis hints at the plethora of Native-authored scholarship and traditional knowledge indicating that many Indigenous cultures' conceptions of time are distinct from Western linear ones, often described as cyclical.[13] Mark Rifkin coined the term "settler time" as

---

[12] This prayer was taken from the contemporary *Watch Over Us Every Day (Prayer)* given by Nora Thompson Dean (Delaware Tribe of Indians) at the dedication of the Delaware Room at the Bartlesville Public Library History Room on November 20, 1974.

[13] Native scholars have been writing about their conceptions of temporality for decades prior to Mark Rifkin's work. Many of the works of Vine Deloria Jr. from the 1970s have endured as seminal texts of Indigenous Studies and Native metaphysics in particular. He claims in his 1979 book, *The Metaphysics of Modern Existence*, that the idea of an ultimate chronological temporal structure is "uniquely Western" (25). Some of Paula Gunn Allen's scholarship from the 1980s and 1990s aligns with Deloria Jr.'s assertions (though her work was not without criticism). Allen exposed the problematic temporal characterization of Native cultures as static by Western thought, stressing the need to assert the more dynamic or cyclical understandings of Indigenous realities (*Symposium* 174). She also argued that Native literatures are often structured "achronologically" to more effectively relate their "beliefs based on ceremonial understandings" as opposed to Western preferences for chronological time (*Sacred Hoop* 149). While being wary of Allen's tendency to generalize the diverse array of Indigenous temporalities as all sharing a cyclical or non-chronological structure, it is worth noting that countless other scholars have since explicated similar understandings across a breadth of Native literatures (see Blaeser; Cousineau; Dunston; Gagne; Gemein; Hume; Martin).

a shorthand for the Western linear temporality enforced by settler colonial hegemony. His 2017 book *Beyond Settler Time: Temporal Sovereignty and Indigenous Self-Determination* offers a hermeneutic for understanding Indigenous representations of time as a practice of self-determination that he terms "temporal sovereignty" (2), in opposition to the ongoing oppression of settler time, which depicts Native peoples as either purely historic or "primitive" people outside of Western modernity, or "insert[s] [them] into a present defined on non-native terms" (vii). Applying Rifkin's framework, *Ghost River*'s representation of an Indigenous conception of temporality can be understood as restorative and decolonizing through the enactment of temporal sovereignty. *Ghost River* establishes a cyclical model of history through various Lenape references that disrupt settler time by interconnecting the Conestoga and Lenape past with the Lenape present. The aforementioned insertion of a modern Lenape prayer (54–5), the recurrence of the Shackamaxon wampum belt, and moments of metacommentary which embed the novel's creators and collaborators into the graphic novel itself (38–41), all disrupt the linear settler-directed narrative of the Conestoga massacre. Through these examples, *Ghost River* blends references to the Lenape past with a shared present in which author, editor, artist, and thus also the reader grapple with how to interpret the past and their responsibility to it. While aspects of these non-linear representations have origins in Indigenous traditions, it is also worth noting that Michael Cromer and Penney Clark argue that graphic novels by their very nature offer "as part of [their] constellation of sources ... a textual and visual reworking of traditional linear narratives," which is especially useful for teaching history (583). Thus, *Ghost River* leverages the affordances of both Indigenous frameworks and graphic medium to restore tribally specific representations of Native peoples that refute both settler colonial generalizations and the imposition of settler time.

Humanizing Native Representation

Ghost River also functions as restorative storytelling through visual depictions of Indigenous peoples that actively refute dehumanizing portrayals found in historical documents and the stereotypes that circulate in contemporary popular culture. The Conestoga people in the graphic novel are drawn with great attention to detail, especially compared to the Paxton murderers, who are in contrast roughly sketched, blacked out, or backgrounded (Francis 4, 30–1, 56–9). Instead of dehumanizing Native peoples with inaccurate or stereotypical depictions as popular culture has all too often done, *Ghost River* imparts humanity through a breadth of emotions in their representations (which is simultaneously denied to the Paxton murderers) to assert the injustice and inhumanity of the violence done against them. In other instances, as in the illustration of the second massacre at the Lancaster jail, the artwork combats the glorification of violence against Indigenous peoples by refusing to portray the murders in realistic or brutal detail, which would arguably sensationalize or perpetuate the trauma of the historical event. Instead, Alvitre depicts the murdered Conestoga bodies as bloody wampum beads in the snow, which again centers Lenape traditions and resituates the event as a continuation of colonial injustice embodied in the unbraided Shackamaxon belt (Francis 4, 59).

Ghost River also demonstrates that there is a temporal component to humanizing Native representation. Applying Gerald Vizenor's foundational work on Native "survivance" alongside Rifkin's work helps reveal the link between humanizing Native representation and temporal sovereignty. Vizenor promotes representations of Native survivance in literature, which embody "an active sense of presence" or "the continuance of Native stories," in opposition to dehumanizing narratives which promote only Native absence, tragedy, or victimhood (vii). Representations of Native survivance, therefore, can be understood as restorative akin to representations of temporal sovereignty. Both suggest Native peoples must depict their survival as cultures and Nations in the present, and/or their temporal worldviews as coexistent with settler colonial modernity, in order to fully refute settler time and dehumanizing settler stereotypes of Indigenous peoples. To apply this notion to *Ghost River*, the graphic novel invokes survivance in its final image, which connects the Lenape past and present by depicting a group of contemporary Native people standing among the trees and looking down upon readers—a nod to the trees on Turtle's back from the Lenape origin story (Francis 4, 70). This image of Native people as living people with enduring connections to their ancestors, to their homelands, and to their oral histories, refutes settler time and the dehumanizing stereotype of "Vanished Indians." Through the representation of living Native people within this historical narrative, *Ghost River* restores Native presence to settler accounts of the Conestoga massacre, which either marginalized Native memory of the event by privileging settler Revolutionary-era politics or misrepresented the Conestoga as tragic victims without descendants or contemporary kin—both of which perpetuate Native absence.

Ghost River's restorative storytelling also conveys survivance and temporal sovereignty by representing Native people as intellectually active agents in the past and present. In one scene, a Moravian Indian woman confronts a colonial official about an actual political cartoon, *An Indian Squaw King Wampum Spies* (Claypoole), published in the aftermath of the massacre. She holds up the cartoon and protests its racism and misogyny: "We read, sir. Know our bible well, sir. We know the words you speak and how you show who we are ... This is what you think of us? We are savages? Wanton women?" (36). In the appendix to *Ghost River*, scholar Judith Ridner observes:

> [I]n a war sparked by violence against Indians, it is surprising how absent or misrepresented the Conestogas were in these discussions. Few texts acknowledged the Paxton murders. Instead, most works, including political cartoons, either denied the Conestogas' agency by portraying them as helpless dependents of the colony and its Quaker merchants, or by stereotyping them as either cunning, half-naked savages or hatchet-wielding warriors. (Ridner qtd. in Francis 4 et al. 76)

This scene corrects stereotypical historiography by restoring humanity and intellectual agency to Native participants, acknowledging that they were literate and actively protested the historical injustices done to them. Similarly, in another scene readers encounter a contemporary Native educator (intended to depict consulting Delaware Tribe of Indians citizen Curtis Zunigha) explaining the Treaty of Shackamaxon to patrons viewing a famous Benjamin West painting, which glorified and in many ways fictionalized this treaty. The Native educator explains: "The lens of western history has to be woven with traditional memory ... That's what's missing from these 'historical' documents—the voices of our people" (47). This quote establishes a temporal continuation of Native people as intellectually engaged agents and embodies *Ghost River*'s restorative project: to weave Indigenous memory and presence back into settler colonial narratives of the Conestoga massacre and restore agency to the people themselves—both in the past and in the present.

Lenape Sovereignty and Challenges to Collaboration

Perhaps the most important takeaway from Native-authored scholarship for projects seeking to rescript the past or elevate Native voices in historical records is the responsibility to work directly *with* the Native peoples who live the consequences of these histories. Jace Weaver, Craig S. Womack, and Robert Warrior, in their foundational work of Native critical theory, *American Indian Literary Nationalism*, call for "non-Natives who study and write about Native peoples [to] do so with respect and a sense of responsibility to Native community" (Weaver et al. 11). They argue that Native literary representation and interpretation should be a collective process "which takes seriously Native sovereignty and survivance, [and] has indigenous self-determination at its core" (73) and assert an inherent responsibility of Native narratives to accurately represent the Nations they write about (Womack 120). But what does acknowledging such responsibilities look like in the practice of crafting historical fiction? Does *Ghost River* model the type of methodology and collective or collaborative process that Weaver, Womack, and Warrior encourage? *Ghost River*'s editor intentionally addressed many of these responsibilities through the employment of an Indigenous author, Lee Francis 4 (Pueblo of Laguna), and artist, Weshoyot Alvitre (Tongva), as well as the addition of Lenape consultant Curtis Zunigha (Delaware Tribe of Indians) and other advisors throughout the creation process. However, if representation of tribally specific Lenape voices, culture, and worldview was a primary objective of this project, is collaboration with only one Lenape representative sufficient?

Despite the editor's efforts to achieve greater collaboration, the only Lenape Tribal Citizen consulted in *Ghost River*'s creation process was Curtis Zunigha (Delaware Tribe of Indians), which leaves multiple other federally recognized Lenape Tribal Nations lacking consultation on the project. What it means to have "sufficiently" accurate or inclusive representation is, indeed, a highly debated and relative concept, along with the question of what constitutes an acceptable tribal representative or consulting cultural authority. But these questions are necessary to interrogate as part of this chapter's effort to understand how or why the work of *Ghost River* is ongoing. Ultimately, even if *Ghost River* does not achieve a fully "sufficient" Lenape representation, it serves as an invaluable model for unpacking the complicated stakes and questions surrounding projects of this nature, hopefully inspiring further and fuller collaborative Native representations in the future. Through *Ghost River*'s example, this section will identify what is at stake in failing to consult with all the Tribal Nations with ties to a project representing their histories and cultures, and/or in choosing to consult with individual tribal citizens or self-identifying individuals versus federally recognized tribal leadership. This section will also explore how *Ghost River*'s process speaks to the responsibility of scholars, Native and non-Native alike, to navigate these questions and work together to begin to address the institutional constraints and barriers hindering the success of collaborative representation projects.

Ghost River serves as an ideal case study to apply some of these questions, not only because it is one of few examples of Native and non-Native collaborative historical fiction, but also because it is largely a project of Lenape representation. In many ways, the Lenape are one of the most difficult Indigenous peoples to represent and/or engage in representations because of their particularly complicated history with settler colonialism which resulted in five sovereign Lenape Tribal Nations based outside of their homelands, some even in different countries. This sort of situation will not always bedevil collaborative efforts for Native representation; many Native Nations have only one recognized governing entity, if not located in their original homelands, often closer to them than the Lenape nations are today. But *Ghost River*'s undertaking necessitated engagement from Native and non-Native scholars and tribal representatives from geographically diffuse entities, many of whom are not situated in the vicinity of where the Conestoga massacre took place or even in Lenape homelands (Figure 1.2). As such, *Ghost River* engaged in some of the most complicated critical entanglements between representation, cultural agency, and tribal sovereignty for displaced Tribal Nations, illuminating the pitfalls and need for reciprocal protocols for those seeking to engage in collaborative projects rescripting Native histories. In order to unpack these entanglements, it is first necessary to situate *Ghost River*'s process within the tribally specific context of the federally recognized Lenape Tribal Nations and their citizens today—a context which is

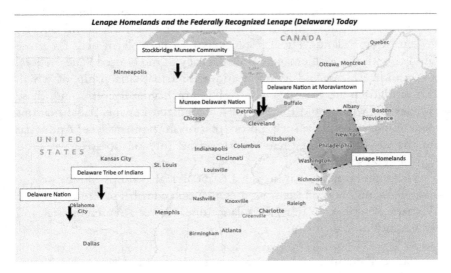

Figure 1.2 Map showing the locations of ancestral Lenape homelands and the tribal headquarters of the five federally recognized Lenape/Delaware Tribal Nations or First Nations in the United States and Canada. (Credit: Katelyn Lucas.)

significantly different from the experiences of many other Tribal Nations and individuals.

As a result of decades of repeated broken treaties, settler colonial violence, and dispossessions which heightened after the 1737 Walking Purchase, the Lenape people were forced to leave their homelands. Despite fragmentation as a result of forced removals, multiple governing bodies or council fires of the Lenape people maintained their sovereignty, as evidenced by the many treaties their leaders signed before they were finally able to settle where their tribal governments are based today. In the United States, Delaware Nation, Delaware Tribe of Indians, and Stockbridge Munsee Community are the only federally recognized sovereign Lenape Tribal Nations. In addition, Eelūnaapèewii Lahkèewiit (Delaware Nation at Moraviantown) and Munsee-Delaware Nation are both recognized Lenape First Nations in Canada. While these Tribal Nations all operate as separate governing entities today, they still recognize each other as relations, and their leadership often collaborate on issues that affect all Lenape peoples. One such issue often provoking a collective response from Tribal Nations across the continent, including multiple of the Lenape Nations, is the increase of contested claims to Native identity and nationhood. Multiple of the federally recognized Lenape Tribal Nations have issued resolutions that they do not work with or recognize any relation to the "state recognized" or otherwise non-federally recognized groups which claim Lenape identity or nationhood and operate in Lenape homelands. These resolutions may raise alarm bells for those familiar with the problematic colonial legacy of the United States' federal recognition process and its implications for tribal citizenship, of which Native Nations are of course also well aware, having lived through these policies. So why would the federally recognized Lenape Tribal Nations feel compelled to make such a proclamation in the first place? And what are the implications of these proclamations for collaborative work on Lenape representation?

These proclamations from the Lenape Tribal Nations illuminate the entanglements between Native representation and tribal sovereignty. Craig Womack describes an inherent relationship between representation and sovereignty in *Red on Red*:

> Native literature, and Native literary criticism, written by Native authors, is part of sovereignty ... While this literary aspect of sovereignty is not the same thing as the political status of Native nations, the two are, nonetheless, interdependent ... The ongoing expression of

a tribal voice, through imagination, language, and literature, contributes to keeping sovereignty ... defined within the tribe rather than by external sources. (14)

And Womack is certainly not the only one to advocate for control over representation as an essential part of protecting tribal sovereignty. Kim TallBear, renowned author of *Native American DNA: Tribal Belonging and the False Promise of Genetic Science,* has said in response to the issue of what she calls white claims to Indigenous identity: "they stole our children, they've stolen our lands, now they have stolen our representation" ("Playing Pretendian" 18.26). She notes how tribal identity and sovereignty are weakened by

> people [claiming Native identity] who have no lived experience as Native people, when they rise through the ranks ... as spokes-people for indigenous issues and history without having lived those lives, they theorize in ways that do not protect our communities, they produce knowledge and artwork ... that are not actually coming from Indigenous lives and standpoints. ("Playing Pretendian" 17.50)

These scholars demonstrate how the efforts of Tribal Nations to define their representation from within is vital to tribal sovereignty and self-determination. However, there is no consensus on what exactly constitutes an authentic lived Native experience or identification, or on who can rightfully claim agency over Native representations. Amidst this uncertainty, decisions made by unassuming scholars on who to consult with as authorities in representing Native histories or cultures can carry significant weight in authorizing said individual's or group's claims to Native identity. This essay aims not to deter scholars seeking to engage in collaborative representation, but to instill in them a healthy degree of caution in light of the issue of contested claims to Native identity.

While stemming from a long history of settler colonizer appropriations of Native cultures since contact, the issue of contested claims to Native identity seems to be amplifying in the twenty-first century. Native scholars have been publishing on this issue at least since the late twentieth century (see the works of Rayna Green, Elizabeth Cook-Lynn, Richard Allen, Cornel Pewewardy, and Philip J. Deloria's foundational *Playing Indian*). But the issue is gaining traction among scholars writ large with significant recent publications working to advance this topic (see the works of Circe Sturm, Darryl Leroux, Kim TallBear, and Joanne Barker). An academic conference titled

"Unsettling Genealogies: A Forum on Pseudo Indians, Race Shifting, Pretendians, and Self Indigenization in Media, Arts, Politics and the Academy," hosted by Michigan State University in March 2022, created a platform for Native and non-Native scholars alike to expose and address the systemic issue of contested claims to Native identity in academia and beyond. Furthermore, incidents of academics being challenged on their claims to Native identity are attracting increasing attention from mainstream media.[14] A recent NPR Code Switch podcast episode entitled "Playing Pretendian"—a play on Philip J. Deloria's text—even focused on this issue, offering a useful summary of the critical debate surrounding contested claims to Native identity through the example of Justin Brake, a Newfoundlander whose family decided to claim Mi'kmaw ancestry in his late twenties. Brake's story should be prefaced with the caveat that the histories of First Nations and their battles over recognition in Canada are different from the histories of federal recognition in the United States. But it is worth discussing Brake's story in more detail because his personal revelations about claiming Native identity illuminate some of the similar harmful logics underpinning non-federally recognized claims to Lenape identity.

In the "Playing Pretendian" podcast, Brake details his journey to understand his family's proclaimed Native ancestry, which stems from an intermarriage between a Mi'kmaw woman and a British settler living in Newfoundland in the late 1700s. Debates over Mi'kmaw identity heightened in 1972, when activists founded the Native Association of Newfoundland and Labrador, eventually renamed the Federation of Newfoundland Indians (FNI), which claimed to represent the Indigenous peoples of these places. In 2008, the FNI negotiated with Canada for the establishment of a band to which "FNI members from communities across western and central Newfoundland would be eligible to apply for enrollment," which would become the Qalipu Mi'kmaq First Nation affirmed by the Indian Act in 2011 (Brake).[15] Brake's family applied and were accepted into this new Qalipu Nation. But the Qalipu's controversial enrollment criteria were met with lawsuits and significant backlash from the long-standing

---

[14] Examples include University of Saskatchewan professor Carrie Bourassa (Leo), Dartmouth College professor Susan Taffe Reed (Keeler), and Andrea Smith who has held positions with multiple universities (Patel; Viren; Russell). The identity of prolific author Joseph Bruchac who has claimed to be Abenaki has also been called into question (Churchill).

[15] "Mi'kmaw" and "Mi'kmaq" are different forms of the same word. See https://novascotia.ca/museum/mikmaq/?section=spelling for further information.

recognized Mi'kmaq Grand Council and Assembly of Nova Scotia Chiefs, who issued formal denouncements of the Qalipu as illegitimate. They also criticized Canada's intervention in determining who qualifies as Mi'kmaq as an infringement on their rights to self-determination.[16] As a result of this criticism, Brake began to question some of his family's justifications for claiming this identity and sought answers by speaking with Mi'kmaw elders and community members. Circe Sturm observed a similar phenomenon in her 2010 study of Cherokee identity, *Becoming Indian*, which discusses claims to Native descendancy or identity apart from citizenship to existing recognized Tribal Nations as "race-shifting" (4–8). Joanne Barker in her book *Red Scare* names this same phenomenon "the kinless Indian" (70). Sturm also participated in the same podcast as Brake, explaining that "most of the people who are engaged in this process of claiming [Native identity] think that they are reclaiming" ("Playing Pretendian" 13.53). But the problem with their logic is that an individual with a potential Native ancestor many generations removed, amidst many more primarily non-Native ancestors, does not necessarily hold an inherent claim to that Native ancestor's tribal identity, culture, or citizenship, especially if that individual has no past or present connection to the existing recognized Tribal Nation to which their ancestor supposedly belonged. Ultimately, Brake concludes he does not have a right to claim Native identity, deciding that "Qalipu's creation without the involvement of the rest of the Mi'kmaw Nation ... represented a questionable way to right past historical wrongs" of Canada's erasure of its Indigenous peoples (Brake).

Brake's journey to understand the implications of his family's claims to Mi'kmaw identity elucidates the problematic logic underpinning many other non-recognized groups' claims to Native identity today. Brake references Sturm's work as well as Darryl Leroux's 2019 book *Distorted Descent* on self-identified "Indigenous" organizations operating in Quebec to demonstrate that non-recognized groups claiming Native identity often share a "common belief rooted in colonialist race-based logic that having an Indigenous ancestor or having 'Indian blood' is a paramount factor of Indigeneity" (Brake). Leroux explains that this logic often stands "to benefit white people at the expense of Indigenous peoples" and obscures the greater complexity of Indigenous understandings of belonging and citizenship (29).

---

[16] See the Mi'kmaq Grand Council's "Statement to United Nations Special Rapporteur Anaya" dated October 14, 2013 (http://www.eskasoni.ca/uploads/newsletter/Sante-Mawiomi-Statement-to-UN-Special-Rapporteur.pdf).

Barker similarly argues that acceptance of invented or contentious claims to Native identity enables colonizers to revise their history and be "absolved of responsibility for any benefit from or complicity with state violence against Indigenous people by suggesting that, all along, they were in fact, if in secret, the Indigenous" (71). Consequently, many have argued that these claims are serious threats to Indigenous rights to sovereignty and self-determination, including Barker (71), TallBear ("Comments"), Leroux (28), Metis and Mi'kmaw leaders (Brake), and others. Brake further explains that "it is the epitome of white privilege to be able to get your hands on documents that show you have Indigenous ancestry and say 'that makes me Indigenous.' That's very dangerous and that's not something [he's] interested in being a part of" ("Playing Pretendian").

Of course, not all individuals self-identifying as Native have come to the same conclusion as Brake. It is worth noting that there are many reasons why some Native people with legitimate relation to existing recognized Tribal Nations may or may not be enrolled citizens of said Tribal Nation. As Kim TallBear has pointed out, it is important not to conflate "white-coded Natives," and/or those who may have been distanced from but have living family in community who they can or are trying to reconnect with, with identity frauds ("Comments"). Brake's story illustrates the dangerous logic underlying more tenuous claims to Native identity without lived relation or connection to long-standing federally recognized Tribal Nations, which many individuals claiming Lenape identity fall under. Many individuals across Lenape homelands claim, typically based on family lore, that they may have had a Lenape ancestor many generations removed who married a European settler and stayed behind "in hiding" while the governing bodies, cultural leadership, and majority citizens of the Lenape Tribal Nations were forced out by settler colonial violence and dispossessions. Multiple non-federally recognized groups have coalesced around these claims in more recent decades in Lenape homelands, making further claims to their own nationhood apart from connection to the displaced federally recognized Lenape Tribal Nations. Because these non-recognized groups cannot meet the citizenship requirements set by the federally recognized Lenape Tribal Nations, they circumvent and undermine their sovereign citizenship processes by instead proclaiming themselves to be Lenape cultural authorities and nations. A major criticism from federally recognized Lenape is that even if individuals might have distant Lenape descendancy, they historically relinquished Lenape citizenship by accepting and benefiting from United States citizenship and non-Native privilege for generations (long before the Indian Citizenship Act of

1924) and escaping many of the settler colonial governmental oppressions that the federally recognized Lenape were subject to.

To dismiss the debate over non-federally recognized claims to or appropriations of Native identity as merely infighting over identity politics would be reductive and imprecise, considering the substantial threat identity fraud poses to tribal sovereignty and its material and legal consequences for society at large. Non-recognized groups claiming Native identity have drawn down significant resources that would otherwise be available for federally recognized Tribal Nations. Deborah Dotson, President of Delaware Nation, is quoted in a 2021 NBC News article referencing how non-recognized groups claiming Lenape identity "compete with us for grants. They receive donations. The state will give them tax breaks" (Brewer and Ahtone). The same article cites a 2012 Government Accountability Office report which "found that over a four-year period, 26 of the 400 nonfederally recognized tribes it identified had been awarded over $100 million in government funds" (Brewer and Ahtone). Ultimately, though, the importance of federal recognition and tribal sovereignty is not about money. It is in large part about holding the U.S. and other Nations accountable for enforcing sovereign rights from treaties they made with the leaders of Tribal Nations—treaties which non-federally recognized groups claiming Lenape identity did not sign. Yet some non-recognized groups claiming Lenape identity today seek to perform their own political actions such as signing "treaties" with local government officials and organizations to try and legitimize themselves as nations.[17] Shawnee Chief Ben Barnes has called groups like this "parasites on the system," specifically condemning their attempts to sign treaties, asserting that only "nations [can] negotiate treaties between themselves" and that "descendancy status is not a conveyance of political status" (Brewer and Ahtone). Sovereignty and federal recognition are also about Tribal Nations self-determining and upholding their own citizenship requirements and governance over their citizens and their homelands. Unrecognized groups claiming Lenape identity in Pennsylvania specifically have publicly criticized the state for not recognizing any tribes within it. Such criticisms obscure the fact that federal recognition supersedes any other level of acknowledgment, rendering

---

[17] The non-profit organization calling itself the "Lenape Nation of Pennsylvania" is an unrecognized group claiming Lenape identity and nationhood which repeatedly performs "treaty signings" and continues to receive resources and attention from a number of institutions and organizations in the eastern Pennsylvania region despite protests from the federally recognized Lenape Tribal Nations (Gregg; Holland; Iplenski; Witkowski).

the idea of state recognition unnecessary. Delaware Nation, Delaware Tribe of Indians, and Stockbridge Munsee Community already are acknowledged as the sovereign Tribal Nations from eastern Pennsylvania and the rest of Lenape homelands, and they already have been consulting at the federal government-to-government level for the management of their homeland region. Thus, at least for the Lenape Tribal Nations, state interventions in determining who is or is not Lenape are typically considered offensive subversions of their sovereignty. The utility of federal recognition has in many ways been reclaimed and redefined by Tribal Nations today. Delaware Nation and Delaware Tribe of Indians, for example, removed blood quantum from their citizenship requirements in favor of lineal descendancy to increase enrollment and eradicate colonizer legacy interventions into their self-determination. Delaware Nation also voted to remove the BIA (Bureau of Indian Affairs) from their constitution. But the federal recognition process still functions for them as a flawed but necessary tool with which to define and enforce their own citizenship requirements and sovereignty today. Doubling down on the federal recognition process, their self-determined citizenship requirements, and refusing to work with non-federally recognized groups or individuals is one of the few ways Tribal Nations have been able to combat fraudulent appropriations of their identity and culture.

Returning to *Ghost River*, understanding the especially complicated relationship between Lenape sovereignty and representation that accompanied the graphic novel's efforts crystallizes some of the challenges facing collaborative projects of restorative Native storytelling. Fenton's discussion of the development process behind *Ghost River* details how he attempted to reach out to representatives from the other federally recognized Lenape Tribal Nations to advise on the project, but that Curtis Zunigha was the only one to respond. This is not uncommon. The Tribal Historic or Cultural Preservation departments (which all federally recognized Tribal Nations have as part of their government offices) often have to filter these sort of collaboration requests in lieu of specific staff designated for this purpose and tend to be overworked, understaffed, and sometimes unable to respond in a timely manner when the more pressing duties of running a sovereign nation have to take priority. Tribal representatives might also be understandably hesitant to respond to or participate in such projects due to the long history of non-Native scholars stealing or appropriating Indigenous knowledge and/or simply seeking Native "stamps of approval" as opposed to engaging in meaningful consultation. Scholars also face their own temporal, financial, and institutional constraints that limit their ability to collaborate. It might be that only advanced or tenured faculty possess the flexibility and security to put projects on hold while they await responses from their tribal partners, especially where multiple Tribal Nations are involved. Furthermore, the situation of displaced Tribal Nations poses real challenges to place-based historical work. Fenton alludes to the need for placed-based engagement, gesturing to how the potluck with the Circle Legacy Center, tour of the longhouse, and site visits helped Alvitre and Francis feel more connected to the people and places they sought to reinterpret. Many individuals living in eastern Pennsylvania—especially with long-standing generational ties to the region and its history, Native or not—undoubtedly have valuable perspectives to contribute to representations of these histories. However, decisions to collaborate with or prioritize local voices (especially those attempting to speak on behalf of Lenape peoples) without consulting the removed federally recognized Lenape Tribal Nations whose homelands and histories are being represented, undermines the sovereignty of those nations and furthers their erasure. As *Ghost River* did not include all of the federally recognized Lenape Tribal Nations in consultation, it may not be received as "restorative" storytelling by all of the Lenape Tribal Nations or Lenape citizens who were not consulted on its creation. But to some extent, is this not the case with any project of literary representation? Or, to re-engage a question posed earlier in this essay, how much consultation is ever sufficient? How can we measure the efficacy of consultation if neither Tribal Nations nor scholars have established a consensus about how to initiate, perform, and structure cross-tribal, collaborative work? While this essay alone cannot offer concrete answers, it concludes by entertaining some of these questions for ongoing discussion.

Structural Challenges Demand Structural Solutions

Ghost River was led by a diverse group of well-intentioned collaborators who made a good faith effort to balance the ethical and practical considerations of Tribal consultation. However, the challenges that accompany consultation are real and structural, and they demand engagement from larger entities—federally recognized Tribal Nations, U.S. federal institutions, universities and other academic, cultural, and historical organizations—with the resources and networks to develop, document, and disseminate best practice. As long as individuals are asked to navigate Tribal governance structures on their own, they are likely to either err in consultation or simply avoid performing this vital restorative collaborative work, especially with extremely displaced eastern Tribal Nations like the Lenape. The latter outcome ought to be unacceptable for both scholars and Tribal Nations alike as it would leave important stories untold and divert resources and opportunities to reclaim agency over their representation away from Tribal entities. Moreover, there are serious limitations to the work Tribal Nations can do on their own to address some of these problems. While the federally recognized Lenape Tribal Nations can pass resolutions asserting their sovereignty and denouncing what they consider to be fraudulent groups, their ability to legally enforce these resolutions beyond their own citizens and federal partners is tenuous at best. As one possible solution to help address public confusion about consultation and non-recognized claims to Native identity, the Cherokee are putting the impetus on museums, media, legislatures, and other institutions to pass their own resolutions requiring that "distinction be made between those ... who are citizens of [the] federally-recognized governments and those who are claiming Cherokee heritage, but who are not recognized by tribal communities/governments as 'Cherokee'" (Hunter). Other Tribal Nations and scholars are working on publicizing comprehensive lists of historians, authors, and other academics who are enrolled citizens of their respective Nations, to facilitate the distribution of contact information and encourage consultation and communication with recognized citizens. The Lenape Tribal Nations do not necessarily have readily available or publicized lists like this. However, inquiries can always be sent to their cultural and/or historic preservation offices (whose contact information is provided on their tribal government websites), which can provide this sort of information upon request. In addition, many Tribal Nations and museums are developing collaborative curation models to institute protocols for how museums should be consulting with Tribal Nations and working within pre-existing tribal approval systems. These models could likely be adapted for other types of scholarly collaborations.

Another possibility to address some of the broader questions about collaborative representation might be to create interstitial organizations situated inside and across Tribal Nations to guide non-Natives seeking consultation. In the case of Lenape peoples, such an organization might resemble a transnational "Lenape Press" which would support communication and engagement across all five of the federally recognized Lenape Tribal Nations on projects of collaborative representation. While some Tribal Nations already have dedicated and successful tribally run presses[18],

---

[18] For an example, see the Chickasaw Nation's tribal press which has received numerous awards (Chickasaw Press).

this is not yet the case for any of the Lenape Tribal Nations. A unifying "Lenape Press" could facilitate consultation requests from scholars for projects of literary representation or historiography by centralizing designees from each of the Lenape Tribal Nations who can distribute corresponding documentation guidelines, timelines, and best practices to carry out collaboration according to tribal approval processes. A "Lenape Press" could also provide a structure to empower Lenape citizens across the five federally recognized nations to more easily create and widely distribute their own narratives without having to navigate through colonial frameworks or institutions. Of course, such an undertaking would require external resources to support staffing, convene stakeholder meetings, create protocols, and build infrastructure, and the benefits of such an initiative might not be realized for years to come. However, were such an organization situated within the federally recognized Lenape Tribal Nations actually established, it would not only advance collaborative, restorative storytelling. It would also, finally, begin to shift the balance of power back toward the very Tribal Nations that have borne the worst effects of dispossession.

Make no mistake; a Lenape Press, which might align with Native American and Indigenous Studies' advocacy for more collaboration and engagement with tribal communities in all stages of scholarship, would not be without criticism. Scholars continue to critique such collaborative approaches to historiography and other scholarship, usually because of the inconveniences or practical complications they pose, but sometimes also by problematically questioning the prioritization or value of contemporary Native contributions. For example, in his controversial 2020 review of Lisa Brooks's *Our Beloved Kin* and Christine M. DeLucia's *Memory Lands*, David J. Silverman argued that some Native scholars have failed to "apply the same scrutiny to their Native sources" as they do to the Western/settler colonial historic record (521). Silverman further suggested that perhaps Native Studies' "decolonizing agenda does not permit such nuance" in acknowledging "the darker sides of the Native past" amidst what he claims is their effort to recast "history in the interest of modern sensibilities" for Indigenous communities (527). Silverman's criticism is symptomatic of recurrent settler colonial logics which condemn presentism as a means to thwart efforts to reprioritize tribal sovereignty, agency, and survivance both today and in our understandings of the past. To insinuate that Native scholars writing within decolonial agendas cannot understand their own histories with nuance or will not engage in complex or holistic representations of their ancestors ignores vast swaths of Indigenous Studies scholarship which does exactly that. And to suggest that the perspectives and concerns of Tribal Nations and citizens today are not valuable in understanding their past perpetuates the same settler colonial logic of settler time, consigning Indigenous peoples to a stagnant past disconnected from their surviving communities today. These enduring and damaging settler colonial logics are precisely what decolonial agendas seek to expose, and which *Ghost River* intentionally worked against in its efforts to collaborate with and prioritize the agency of Native voices to create a more accurate and holistic representation of history.

Ghost River represents the restorative possibilities of critical, collaborative scholarship and the unique affordances of the graphic novel. As this essay demonstrates, *Ghost River* tells the story of the Conestoga massacres using settler historical records and engaging tribal citizens in order to reintegrate their perspective and create a more inclusive and complex historical narrative. The book also shows its own work, integrating the research process into the narrative, revealing scholarly and tribal consultations in the annotated script, and elevating contemporary Native oral histories in the digital edition. This piece serves as a necessary extension of that work, acknowledging both the successes and limitations of this project to ensure that it is not an isolated example but rather builds ongoing conversation about how to create more reciprocal representational collaborations with Native communities. This chapter thus reaffirms the need for the kind of restorative archival and representational work *Ghost River* does and the vital collaborative processes underpinning it. But equally critical is interrogation of those processes to expose the weight that scholars carry in their decisions on when or how to consult with Native peoples in their projects. The reality is that well-intentioned attempts at inclusive collaborations often still fail to consult with all appropriate tribal communities and frequently skirt acknowledgment of the more complex issues underpinning consultation, tribal sovereignty, and representation. By openly engaging these issues, this piece seeks to further *Ghost River*'s decolonizing methodologies: supplementing its restorative Native representations, refusing to paper over the ongoing violence of settler colonialism, and decentering settler colonial privilege in the creation and consultation process. As the recurring voiceover reminds readers—"History is complicated. Violence is simple"—the tragedies settler colonialism inflicted upon the Conestoga people are central to the narrative, but they do not efface Native survivance today. Rather, they underscore the value of prioritizing living Native presence and agency in rescripting their own histories.

Narrative is the engine behind *Ghost River*'s decolonial work. In the introduction to the volume, Fenton writes, "Whereas a visual history might dwell on historical actors and incidents, a graphic novel allows us to particularize and humanize, to entertain different ideas of temporality, and to forge new connections across time and space" (6). *Ghost River* explores the extent to which what has been shapes what is and what can be. In practical terms, the narrative mobilizes the form of the graphic novel to draw continuities between the Native past and present. *Ghost River* restores associations between surviving Native kin with the historical Conestoga victims (24–6). It rescripts the settler narrative of the Conestoga massacre through Native worldviews and record-keeping systems, such as the wampum belt (32–3). And it refutes settler mythologies like the "Vanishing Indian" stereotype and Benjamin West's representation of William Penn's "peaceable" kingdom by casting Lenape elder Curtis Zunigha within a living legacy of Native protests to these narratives (46–8). As much as these scenes serve to advance a more holistic historical narrative in the form of historical fiction, they also honor the project's debt to living Native peoples whose perspectives have all too often been ignored. Despite the violence, dispossession, and displacement of settler colonialism, Tribal Nations have endured, and they are quick to remind anyone who cares to listen: "we are still here."

Works Cited

Allen, Paula Gunn. "The Sacred Hoop: A Contemporary Indian Perspective on American Indian Literature." *Symposium of the Whole: A Range of Discourse Toward an Ethnopoetics*, edited by Jerome Rothenberg and Diane Rothenberg. U of California P, 1983, pp. 173–87.

——. *The Sacred Hoop: Recovering the Feminine in American Indian Traditions*. Beacon Press, 1992.

Allen, Richard L. "My Great-Grandmother was a Cherokee Princess and my Great-Grandfather was Chief John Ross or Sequoyah or Somebody like that, I can't remember . . ." Paper presented to the Five Civilized Tribes Intertribal Repatriation Committee, Sulphur, Oklahoma, November 16, 1995.

Allen, Richard L., et al. "Stealing Sovereignty: Identity Theft, the Creation of False Tribes." Paper presented at Sovereignty Symposium XX, Oklahoma City, Oklahoma, May 30–31, 2007.

Barber, Rhoda. *Recollections written in 1830 of life in Lancaster County 1726–1782 and a History of settlement at Wright's Ferry, on Susquehanna River*. 1830, Historical Society of Pennsylvania, Philadelphia. Manuscript.

Barker, Joanne. "The Kinless Indian: Terror as Social (In)Stability." *Red Scare: The State's Indigenous Terrorist*. U of California P, 2021.

Blaeser, Kimberly M. "Sacred Journey, Poetic Journey: Ortiz Re-turning and Re-telling from the Colonized Spaces of America." *Simon J. Ortiz: A Poetic*

Legacy of Indigenous Continuance, edited by Susan Berry Brill de Ramirez and Evelina Zuni Lucero. U of New Mexico P, 2009, pp. 213–31.

Brake, Justin. "KTAQMKUK." *Maisonneuve: A Quarterly of Arts, Opinion, & Ideas*, June 29, 2021, https://maisonneuve.org/article/2021/06/29/ktaqmkuk/ (last accessed November 6, 2024).

Brewer, Graham Lee, and Tristan Ahtone. "In Texas, a group claiming to be Cherokee faces questions about authenticity." NBC News, October, 27, 2021, https://www.nbcnews.com/news/us-news/mount-tabor-indian-community-texas-indigenous-rcna3746 (last accessed November 6, 2024).

Brubaker, Jack. *Massacre of the Conestogas: On the Trail of the Paxton Boys in Lancaster County*. The History Press, 2010. Chickasaw Press. Chickasaw Nation, 2006, https://chickasawpress.com/about.aspx.

Churchill, Chris. "Is Joseph Bruchac truly Abenaki?" *Times Union*, September 30, 2023, https://www.timesunion.com/churchill/article/churchill-joseph-bruchac-truly-abenaki-18391772.php#:~:text=Bruchac%2C%20in%20turn%2C%20says%20he,author%20believes%20had%20Native%20heritage (last accessed November 6, 2024).

Claypoole, James. *An Indian Squaw King Wampum Spies*. 1764, Library Company of Philadelphia. Political cartoon.

Cook-Lynn, Elizabeth. "Meeting of Indian Professors Takes Up Issues of 'Ethnic Fraud,' Sovereignty, and Research Needs." *Wicazo Sa Review*, vol. 9, no. 1 (1993), pp. 57–9.

Cousineau, Diane. "Leslie Silko's *Ceremony*: The Spiderweb as Text." *Revue française d'études américaines*, no. 43 (1990), pp. 19–31.

Cromer, Michael, and Penney Clark. "Getting Graphic with the Past: Graphic Novels and the Teaching of History." *Theory and Research in Social Education*, vol. 35, no. 4 (2007), pp. 574–91.

Dawkins, Henry. *The Paxton Expedition*. 1764, Library Company of Philadelphia. Political cartoon.

Deloria, Philip J. *Playing Indian*. Yale UP, 1998.

Deloria Jr., Vine. *The Metaphysics of Modern Existence*. Harper & Row, 1979.

Dove, David James. *The Quaker Unmask'd: or, Plain Truth: Humbly address'd to the Consideration of all the Freemen of Pennsylvania*. Andrew Steuart, 1764.

Dunbar, John Raine, editor. *The Paxton Papers*. Springer, 1957.

Dunston, Susan L. "Physics and Metaphysics: Lessons from Leslie Marmon Silko's *Ceremony*." *Arizona Quarterly: A Journal of American Literature, Culture, and Theory*, vol. 66, no. 4 (2010), pp. 135–62.

Fenton, Will. Introduction. *Ghost River: The Fall and Rise of the Conestoga*, written by Lee Francis 4 and illustrated by Weshoyot Alvitre. Red Planet Books and Comics, 2019, pp. 4–6.

Francis 4, Lee. *Ghost River: The Fall and Rise of the Conestoga*, illustrated by Weshoyot Alvitre and edited by Will Fenton. Red Planet Books and Comics, 2019.

Franklin, Benjamin. *A Narrative of the Late Massacres, in Lancaster County.* Franklin and Hall, 1764.

Fuentes, Marisa. *Dispossessed Lives: Enslaved Women, Violence, and the Archive.* U of Pennsylvania P, 2016.

Gagne, Karen M. "Falling in Love with Indians: The Metaphysics of Becoming America." *CR: The New Centennial Review*, vol. 3, no. 3 (2003), pp. 205–33.

Gemein, Mascha N. "'Branched into All Directions of Time': Pluralism, Physics, and Compassion in Silko's *Ceremony*." *Leslie Marmon Silko: Ceremony, Almanac of the Dead, Gardens in the Dunes*, edited by David L. Moore, Bloomsbury, 2016, pp. 57–78.

Green, Rayna. "The Tribe Called Wannabee: Playing Indian in America and Europe." *Folklore* vol. 99, no. 1 (1988), pp. 30–55.

Gregg, Cherri. "Members of Lenape Nation of PA Invite Public to Sign Treaty of Renewed Friendship." CBS News Philly, August 16, 2014, https://philadelphia.cbslocal.com/2014/08/16/lenape-nation-of-pennsylvania-members-invite-the-public-to-sign-treaty-of-renewed-friendship/ (last accessed November 6, 2024).

Hartman, Saidiya. "Venus in Two Acts." *Small Axe*, vol. 12, no. 2 (2008), pp. 1–14.

Holland, Jake. "Lenape Nation of Pennsylvania to Host Treaty Signing in Easton." Lehigh Valley Live, January 2, 2019, https://www.lehighvalleylive.com/easton/2018/08/lenape_nation_of_pennsylvania.html (last accessed November 6, 2024).

Hume, Kathryn. "Gerald Vizenor's Metaphysics." *Contemporary Literature*, vol. 48, no. 4 (2007), pp. 580–612.

Hunter, Chad. "Resolution Passes for Entities to Refer to Cherokees by Enrollment, Affiliation." *Cherokee Phoenix*, February 9, 2022, https://www.cherokeephoenix.org/culture/resolution-passes-for-entities-to-refer-to-cherokees-by-enrollment-affiliation/article_56f627f8-88f3-11ec-8bf9-6f19a9725340.html (last accessed November 6, 2024).

Iplenski, Maureen. "Lenape Nation, Temple Community Sign Treaty to Preserve Native American Culture." *The Temple News*, August 21, 2018, https://temple-news.com/lenape-nation-temple-community-sign-treaty-to-preserve-native-american-culture/ (last accessed November 6, 2024).

Keeler, Jacqueline. "Susan Taffe Reed: Dartmouth's Dolezal?" *Indian Country Today*, September 13, 2018, https://ictnews.org/archive/susan-taffe-reed-dartmouths-dolezal (last accessed November 6, 2024).

Leo, Geoff. "Outrage Brewing after U of S and CIHR Support Professor Who Falsely Claimed to Be Indigenous." CBC News, October 31, 2021, https://www.cbc.ca/news/canada/saskatchewan/saskatchewan-cihr-indigenous-outrage-professor-1.6232177 (last accessed November 6, 2024).

Leroux, Darryl. *Distorted Descent: White Claims to Indigenous Identity.* U of Manitoba P, 2019.

Martin, Calvin. "The Metaphysics of Writing Indian-White History." *Ethnohistory*, vol. 26, no. 2 (1979), pp. 153–9.

Mi'kmaq Grand Council. "Statement to the United Nations Special Rapporteur Anaya." October 14, 2013, http://www.eskasoni.ca/uploads/newsletter/Sante-Mawiomi-Statement-to-UN-Special-Rapporteur.pdf (last accessed November 6, 2024).

Mt. Pleasant, Alyssa, et al. "Materials and Methods in Native American and Indigenous Studies: Completing the Turn." *The William and Mary Quarterly*, vol. 75 no. 2 (2018), pp. 207–36.

Netter, Louis, and Oliver Gruner. "Steal This History: Historiography, the Sixties, and the Comic." *Rethinking History*, vol. 21, no. 4 (2017), pp. 506–28.

Olson, Alison. "The Pamphlet War over the Paxton Boys." *The Pennsylvania Magazine of History and Biography*, vol. 123, no. 1/2 (1999), pp. 31–55.

Patel, Vimal. "Prominent Scholar Who Claimed to Be Native American Resigns." *The New York Times*, August 27, 2023, https://www.nytimes.com/2023/08/27/us/uc-riverside-andrea-smith-resigns.html (last accessed November 6, 2024).

Pewewardy, Cornel. "So You Think You Hired an 'Indian' Faculty Member? The Ethnic Fraud Paradox in Higher Education." *Indigenizing the Academy*, edited by Angela Cavendar Wilson and Devon Abbott Mihesuah. U of Nebraska P, 2004, pp. 200–17.

"Playing Pretendian." Code Switch Podcast from NPR, January 26, 2022, https://www.npr.org/podcasts/510312/codeswitch (last accessed November 6, 2024).

Richter, Daniel K. *Trade, Land, Power: The Struggle for Eastern North America*. U of Pennsylvania P, 2013.

Rifkin, Mark. *Beyond Settler Time: Temporal Sovereignty and Indigenous Self-Determination*. Duke UP, 2017.

Russell, Steve. "When Does Ethnic Fraud Matter?" *Indian Country Today*, September 12, 2018, https://ictnews.org/archive/russell-when-does-ethnic-fraud-matter (last accessed November 6, 2024).

Silverman, David J. "Living with the Past: Thoughts on Community Collaboration and Difficult History in Native American and Indigenous Studies." *The American Historical Review*, vol. 125, no. 2 (April 2020), pp. 519–27.

Smith, Matthew, and James Gibson. *A Declaration and Remonstrance of the Distressed and Bleeding Frontier Inhabitants of the Province*. William Bradford, 1764.

Sturm, Circe. *Becoming Indian: The Struggle over Cherokee Identity in the Twenty-First Century*. SAR Press, 1967.

TallBear, Kim. *Native American DNA: Tribal Belonging and the False Promise of Genetic Science*. U of Minnesota P, 2013.

———. "Identity Is a Poor Substitute for Relating: Genetic Ancestry, Critical Polyamory, Property, and Relations." *Routledge Handbook of Critical Indigenous*

Studies, edited by Brendan Hokowhitu, Aileen Moreton-Robinson, Linda Tuhiwai-Smith, Chris Anderson, and Steve Larkin. Routledge, 2020.

———. "Comments on Indigenous Citizenship in the Academy, 1 Year Later." Invited lecture at the First Nations University of Canada Second National Indigenous Citizenship Forum, March 21, 2022.

Viren, Sarah. "The Native Scholar Who Wasn't." *The New York Times Magazine*, May 25, 2021, https://www.nytimes.com/2021/05/25/magazine/cherokee-native-american-andrea-smith.html (last accessed November 6, 2024).

Vizenor, Gerald. *Manifest Manners: Narratives on Post-Indian Survivance*. U of Nebraska P, 1999.

Weaver, Jace, Craig S. Womack, and Robert Warrior. *American Indian Literary Nationalism*. U of New Mexico P, 2006.

Witkowski, Wayne. "Supervisors Sign Treaty With Lenape." *Pike County Dispatch*, July 20, 2023, https://www.pikedispatch.com/.

Womack, Craig. *Red on Red: Native American Literary Separatism*. U of Minnesota P, 1999.

Zunigha, Curtis. Lenape cultural advisor, external reader, and program participant. 2018–20.

2

Simulating Sovereignty: Alternative History, Video Games, and the Haudenosaunee

Harry J. Brown

Beginning in 1778, the Mohawk war chief Joseph Brant led a string of raids against American settlements in Pennsylvania and New York, allying themselves with Tory rangers in the hope of stopping American westward expansion. The attacks drew the attention of Congress and George Washington, who issued a genocidal order to General John Sullivan in May 1779:

> The expedition you are appointed to command is to be directed against the hostile tribes of the Six Nations ... The immediate objects are the total destruction and devastation of their settlements, and the capture of as many prisoners of every age and sex as possible. It will be essential to ruin their crops now in the ground and prevent their planting more ... You will not by any means listen to any overture of peace before the total ruinment of their settlements is effected. (Washington)

In August 1779, Sullivan led an army of 3,000 men into Haudenosaunee territory. The defenders skirmished and fled, leaving Native settlements along the Susquehanna, Cuyahoga, and Genesee Rivers unprotected. During the subsequent campaign, Sullivan burned houses and cornfields, razed orchards, and drove families into refuge.

The memory of Sullivan's campaign remains vital for the Haudenosaunee Confederacy. On their tribal website, the Onondaga Nation publish Washington's letter to Sullivan, as well as the address by the Seneca chief Cornplanter to Washington upon his election to the presidency:

> When your army entered the country of the Six Nations, we called you Hanadagá•yas [Town Destroyer]: and to this day when that name

is heard our women look behind them and turn pale, and our children cling close to the necks of their mothers. Our counsellors and warriors are men, and cannot be afraid; but their hearts are grieved with the fears of our women and children, and desire that it may be buried so deep as to be heard no more. (Onondaga Nation, "US Presidents: Hanadagá•yas")

Since 1790, the Haudenosaunee refer to the United States President by the title of "Town Destroyer," earned for posterity by Washington.

In 1988, a Congressional resolution acknowledging the influence of the Haudenosaunee Confederacy on the United States Constitution intensified an ongoing debate among historians about the role the People of the Longhouse played in the formation of American democracy, aside from acting as a strategic nuisance to the Town Destroyer. In 1991, historians Donald A. Grinde, Jr. and Bruce E. Johanson declared the Haudenosaunee an "exemplar of liberty" and credited them as our immediate forebears in the "evolution" of democracy. In 2005, Charles C. Mann popularized the idea in the *New York Times*:

> So vivid were these examples of democratic self-government [from colonial Indian histories] that some historians and activists have argued that the [Haudenosaunee] Great Law of Peace directly inspired the American Constitution ... Historians have been reluctant to acknowledge this contribution to the end of tyranny worldwide. Yet a plain reading of Locke, Hume, Rousseau and Thomas Paine shows that they took many of their illustrations of liberty from native examples.

Mann suggests that through a long process of osmosis settler governments adopted an Indigenous political culture, built on equal representation, shared leadership, and a system of checks and balances among the different tribes and clans constituting the confederacy.

The Haudenosaunee Confederacy acknowledges their historical influence of democracy in their online statement:

> While many debate the validity of the claim that the Constitution of the Haudenosaunee Confederacy was a model for the United States of America's Constitution, much evidence leads us to believe that the U.S. Constitution developed by Benjamin Franklin and Thomas Jefferson was indeed influenced by the Haudenosaunee Confederacy.

They proceed to identify parallels between Haudenosaunee and United States government models and discuss the historical basis for the connection in a series of interactions between Haudenosaunee and colonial leaders, including Benjamin Franklin.

In light of this developing consensus among both white and Indigenous scholars, the attempt by American forces to exterminate the Haudenosaunee during the American Revolution poses the morbid irony of an incipient nation committing genocide against the same people who purportedly inspired its governing framework. As the Sioux historian Nick Estes notes, the troops who participated in Sullivan's campaign received as compensation titles to captured Haudenosaunee lands. On the one hand, Grinde, Johanson, and Mann tell us that the founding of the United States was a gift of the Haudenosaunee. On the other hand, Estes writes: "the founding of the United States was a declaration of war against Indigenous peoples" (91). With these two origin stories, American democracy bears the conflicted legacy of having destroyed the prototype for the system of government it hoped to perfect. This conflicted legacy has opened significant gaps in our current understanding of the Haudenosaunee in the national narrative.

Counterfactual History and Procedural Rhetoric

Counterfactual history, in the form of fiction and video games, has sought to fill these gaps with fantasies of resistance and sovereignty. While some historians dismiss counterfactual inquiry as an ahistorical diversion, it nonetheless poses fundamental and useful questions about historical contingency and causality. Rather than showing us the shape of things to come, as science fiction proposes to do, alternative history shows us the shape of things that might have been, and in doing so compels us to examine more closely those moments in the past that created our own world. What if Washington had not issued his order to Sullivan? What if the Haudenosaunee had succeeded in halting American expansion on the colonial frontier? What if European colonization had never happened in the first place? By constructing a virtual past and granting the player agency within it, video games, for example, have become the ideal medium for interrogating contingency and thereby making implicit arguments about the past.

At the same time, counterfactual analysis, whether mediated in a video game or an alternative history novel, confronts us with a paradox. How can we learn about what happened by studying what did not happen? Historical fiction, films, and video games routinely inscribe imagined events into the historical record, but scholars and educators have a more stringent obligation. In fact, some historians argue that counterfactual analysis constitutes an irresponsible form of revisionism. As Richard J. Evans, a historian with a moderate view, suggests: "History in the end is and can only really be about finding out what happened and what was, and understanding and explaining it, not positing alternative courses of development or indulging in bouts of wishful thinking about what might have been" (14). At the same time, others recognize an inherent value in the method. William H. McNeill says:

> There is [a] serious intellectual kernel behind the game [of counterfactual inquiry], for there are events ... that did make quite an extraordinary difference in what followed. And by drawing attention to such occasions and wondering out loud how different the world would be, contingent, surprising, unpredictable aspects of the human past can become obvious to most readers. (21)

In his introduction to *Virtual History*, a collection of counterfactual essays, Niall Ferguson offers a defense and rationale:

> Firstly, it is a *logical* necessity when asking questions about causation to pose 'but for' questions, and to try to imagine what would have happened if our supposed cause had been absent ... Secondly, to do this is a *historical* necessity when attempting to understand how the past 'actually was' ... as we must attach equal importance to all the possibilities which contemporaries contemplated before the fact, and greater importance to these than to an outcome which they did not anticipate. (87)

Video games representing the past have compelled historians to scrutinize the fundamental methods underlying their discipline. While they carry, in Evans's view, "extremely severe" limitations as a means of representing the past, they also represent a powerful pedagogical innovation, in terms of their unique ability to evoke empathy and to consider events from multiple perspectives, as Ferguson claims. In assessing the value of counterfactual history, Allan Megill draws a useful distinction between "exuberant" and "restrained" methods of inquiry. Like historical fiction, Megill suggests, exuberant counterfactual history freely rearranges chronology or intentionally ignores certain aspects of the past in the interest of telling a good story. Restrained counterfactual history, on the other hand, "involves an explicit canvassing of alternative possibilities that existed in a real past" (Megill 17). In Megill's frame, popular renderings of counterfactual Haudenosaunee history, including video games and alternative history novels, veer too far toward the "exhuberant."

The Warpath Campaign expansion of Creative Assembly's strategy game *Empire: Total War* (2009) represents a more "exuberant" approach. At the outset, the game offers players control of one of five Indigenous factions, including the Iroquois Confederacy, and invites them to resist the expansion of colonial powers in North America. When playing as the Haudenosaunee, victory entails the reconquest and defense of the Iroquois tribal homeland. The game drops the player right into that pivotal moment in colonial history, when European empires, Indigenous tribes, and an emergent United States contended for dominance in North America.

In my own campaign as the Iroquois Confederacy in *Warpath*, I start in a precarious position on the eastern Great Lakes in 1783, just a few years after the Sullivan campaign. As the game tells me, I am pinched between my Huron rivals and the emergent United States, with whom the Haudenosaunee remain "at odds" for their support of the British during the War of Independence. Under the leadership of Red Jacket, my "Head of State," I guide the Haudenosaunee to a glorious resurgence under the banner of the Longhouse, forming early alliances with the Huron and Plains tribes, pushing back the French along the St. Lawrence River, and finally marching to reclaim Indigenous control of Massachusetts, New York, and Pennsylvania. By 1815, the previously besieged Confederacy has built its own empire of Great Iroquoia, reaching from Lake Superior to the Chesapeake, and I crown my conquest by building a longhouse in the charred rubble of Independence Hall. I won, I think.

Kim Stanley Robinson's alternative history novel *The Years of Rice and Salt* (2002) imagines a more complex destiny for the Haudenosaunee with a much wider historical and geographical scope. Robinson begins with the counterfactual proposition that the Black Death killed ninety-nine percent of Europe's population in the fourteenth century, effectively removing the whole of Western civilization from world history. As Robinson's imagined history progresses, Chinese and Islamic cultures colonize the globe. In the alternative seventeenth century, a Chinese armada on its way to invade Japan is blown off course into the Pacific, where they ride prevailing currents to the western coasts of North and South America. The Chinese name the new lands Yingzhou, or "Ocean Continents." In Robinson's alternative vision of the discovery of the New World, the sequence of conquest begins in much the same way as it did following Columbus's landing in the West Indies. The Chinese make friends with some Indigenous tribes and skirmish with others, spread smallpox, take a captive, whom they train as a translator and cultural intermediary, and finally return home weak and weary, but determined to return in force. In subsequent years, the Chinese establish a colonial foothold in the West and stand poised to extend their empire over all of North America.

Robinson's alternative history takes another sharp turn, however, when a Ronin samurai, an exile from a later, successful Chinese invasion of Japan, flees to Yingzhou, makes his way east across the Plains to the Great Lakes region, and becomes Fromwest, an adopted chief of the Haudenosaunee. Fromwest embraces the Haudenosaunee as his new nation, praising their egalitarian society as "the best system of rule ever invented by human beings" (376). Robinson imagines Fromwest as a revolutionary figure, a samurai superman who decides on his own that he will turn back the continental advance of the Chinese empire. At a festival to celebrate his chieftainship, Fromwest warns the Haudenosaunee of the threat of the Chinese, who, he prophesies, will subject them to harsh, imperial rule unless the Haudenosaunee form a greater league with all the tribes of "Turtle Island" to resist foreign invasion. Fromwest's prophetic warning has immense historical impact. While the Chinese maintain their colonies in the West, and Islamic colonies spread on the east coast of Yingzhou, the Haudenosaunee League maintains control of the wooded heartland of North America into the modern era and evolves over centuries into a world power. As Robinson's imagined past stretches into an imagined future, the Haudenosaunee system of government becomes the model for a global confederacy of nations, much as historians like Grinde and Johanson surmise that it was the model for the framers of American democracy.

Rousing as these anti-colonial counterfactual histories are, their inquiries about contingency quickly become unrestrained narratives having little to do with the historical reality of colonization and genocide. In my simulation of Haudenosaunee resurgence in *Warpath*, the prospect of an Indigenous tribe adopting the imperialist policies of European nation states leads me beyond the realm of counterfactual historical inquiry and into fantasy. As one reviewer of the game remarks: "Drilled formations of medicine men, Native chiefs overseeing road-building programs and struggling to control settler unrest in ex-colonial settlements ... there are moments when *Warpath*'s theme-abuse is almost comical" (Stone). Even from the perspective of a player only casually interested in the intellectual stakes of historical representation, this "comical" approach to colonial history subverts the purpose of counterfactual history and poses the ethical quandary of "theme abuse."

Ian Bogost's concept of "procedural rhetoric" affords us a way to understand this problem of theme abuse beyond its surface appearance of "comical" historical inaccuracy. In *Persuasive Games*, Bogost defines procedural rhetoric as "the new type of persuasive and expressive practice" at work in video games and related media artifacts: "*Procedurality* refers to a way of creating, explaining, or understanding processes. And processes define the way things work: the methods, techniques, and logics that drive the operations of systems ... *Rhetoric* refers to effective and persuasive expression. Procedural rhetoric, then, is a practice of using processes persuasively" (2–3). He says further that procedural rhetoric is "the practice of authoring arguments through processes ... [I]ts arguments are made not through the construction of words or images, but through the authorship of rules of behavior, the construction of dynamic models" (29). Game play following from an encoded set of rules constitutes one such "dynamic model," and "persuasive games," Bogost explains, are simply "videogames that mount procedural rhetorics effectively" (46). Bogost applies his theory of procedural rhetoric to the spheres of politics, advertising, and education, though it proves equally useful for historical games, which encode rules for historical processes and, in doing so, make implicit arguments about the past. In this sense, the theme abuse in *Warpath* constitutes a more serious problem than unrestrained inaccuracy. Even as the game spins fantasies of decolonization, it procedurally reinstates the terms and outcomes of colonization, arguing that the survival of Indigenous peoples follows from the adoption of settler technologies and strategies. This notion of resistance through assimilation contradicts the essential message of Indigenous resistance movements of the eighteenth and nineteenth centuries, which affirm the value of traditional tribal culture and lifeways and explicitly reject European cultural supremacy, technology, and the market economy, as embodied in firearms, trade goods, and whiskey.

Warpath and *The Years of Rice and Salt* create the false dilemma of assimilation versus extermination and falsely resolve it by posing cultural compromise or surrender as the only viable response to genocide. In this sense, these alternative histories resist attempts to reconsider the influence of Indigenous forms of democracy in the present, as Grinde, Johanson, and Mann propose to do. Rather, they argue for a nihilistic solution to historical injustice and oppression: not equitable government but instead an equitable distribution of gunpowder and steel, as if the only possible response to Sullivan's destruction of Haudenosaunee towns was the Haudenosaunee destruction of colonial settlements. This thesis of history as a perpetual arms race does not represent a critique of settler colonialism so much as a procedural reaffirmation of its exercise of knowledge and technology in pursuit of conquest and further defers meaningful understanding of the role of the Haudenosaunee in the formation of the American republic.

Indigenous Cultural Resistance

Historically, nativist movements differed from more common Indian rebellions. Rather than acting locally with a single tribal interest, they attempted the unification of disparate tribes against the common threat of settler encroachment. In 1763, the Odawa war chief Pontiac attacked Detroit and other English settlements in the Ohio country, demanding for his people better provisions and supply of gunpowder and ammunition for hunting. In his speech before he laid siege to Detroit, recorded by Francis Parkman, Pontiac represents his act not as an attempt by the Odawa to secure fair treatment from an English outpost, but rather as the first strike in a larger war between nations: "It is important, my brothers, that we should exterminate from our land this nation, whose only object is our death ... When I visit the English chief, and inform him of the death of any of our comrades, instead of lamenting, as our brothers the French used to do, they make game of us" (330).

During the War of 1812, the Shawnee war chief Tecumseh achieved greater success than Pontiac did in creating intertribal alliances, causing some of his followers to see him as an Indian messiah, and his American nemesis, William Henry Harrison, to describe him as "one of those uncommon geniuses which spring up occasionally to produce revolutions and overturn the established order of things" (Sugden 215). In a famous speech to the Osage tribe, attributed to Tecumseh by John Dunn Hunter, a white captive, the Shawnee war chief called for a continental war of resistance in terms more bloody than Pontiac's:

> Brothers,—The white men despise and cheat the Indians; they abuse and insult them; they do not think the red men sufficiently good to live.
>
> The red men have borne many and great injuries; they ought to suffer them no longer. My people will not; they are determined on vengeance; they have taken up the tomahawk; they will make it fat with blood; they will drink the blood of the white people. (46)

Both *Warpath* and *The Years of Rice and Salt* appear to take their cues from Pontiac's and Tecumseh's widely anthologized calls to arms. In *The Years of Rice and Salt*, Fromwest delivers an oration that echoes Pontiac and Tecumseh, beginning with a description of the relentlessness of the Chinese in their conquest of Japan and the exhortation to his new countrymen that "the Hodenosaunee [sic] were the first people I had heard of who might be able to defeat the invasion of the Chinese" (Robinson 375). Like Pontiac, he urges a unified front and war against the invading foreigners: "You must live as if you are already dead! Live as if you are warriors already captured, do you understand? The foreigners on the coast must be resisted, and confined to a harbor town, if you can do it. War will come eventually, no matter what you do. But the later it comes the more you can prepare for it, and hope to win it ... Certainly we must try, for all the generations that come after us" (380).

In *Warpath*, the player realizes Tecumseh's vision of reconquest in the role of Seneca chief Red Jacket (Sagoyewatha), the Iroquois "Head of State" in the years after the Sullivan campaign. Historically, Sagoyewatha signed the Treaty of Canadaigua with the United States in 1794, ceding a large part of Seneca territory while also protecting part of the tribal homeland in western New York. In the game, however, Sagoyewatha dispenses with negotiations and, sooner or later, wages a new war against the Americans. The game introduces the Iroquois as "masters of irregular warfare: appearing from the undergrowth, striking at their targets, and disappearing again as quickly as they arrived." Initially lacking in technology and firepower, the Iroquois compensate "with guile, cunning, and ruthless brutality when on the warpath" (*Empire*). While the player receives no stirring exhortation from Red Jacket in the style of Tecumseh, they are prompted nonetheless to violent action against both their colonial and tribal neighbors. With a good strategy, the player, as Sagoyewatha and the Haudenosaunee, leads a campaign that not only secures the ancestral lands in Iroquois, Algonquian, and Ohio territory, but also, like Fromwest's inspired war bands, seizes a new empire encompassing New France, New York, Pennsylvania, Maryland, and the Huron, Michigan, and Indiana territories.

At this point, we might surrender to the fantasies that *The Years of Rice and Salt* and *Warpath* conjure. While the grand scope of these visions far exceeds those of Pontiac and Tecumseh, they nonetheless partake in their anti-colonial struggles for sovereignty. Fromwest's oratory plausibly derives from the words of the Odawa and Shawnee war chiefs, and a different version of Red Jacket might have plausibly rejected the Treaty of Canadaigua and lifted his tomahawk against the Town Destroyer once more—except when we account for the cultural and religious dimensions of Pontiac's and Tecumseh's visions, which alternative histories of Haudenosaunee resistance erase. In the wake of American victories over Indian resistance in the Revolution and the War of 1812, a new type of nativist movement emphasized cultural resistance rather than armed resistance as the most viable model for Indigenous sovereignty, expressed through the formation of spiritual communities, bonded by traditional beliefs, rather than military alliances dedicated to war against the foreign invader.

Neither *The Years of Rice and Salt* nor *Warpath*, for example, contains a figure like the Lenape prophet Neolin, "the Enlightened," whom Anthony F.C. Wallace describes as "one of the religious messiahs" who "were beginning to appear among the disintegrating Indian communities on the frontier" in the mid-eighteenth century, as tribal sovereignty gave way to economic dependency (117). From the Cuyahoga River near Lake Erie, Neolin proclaimed his vision of the Creator, the "Master of Life," who commanded Indian people to give up the wickedness of white influence, including liquor, guns, tools, and linen clothes. Wallace cites the prophecies of Neolin as a significant part of a "concatenation" of events that "set the woods aflame" and gave popular credence to the "conspiracy" that made Pontiac famous and feared. The same Indians who traveled widely to hear Neolin speak also joined with Pontiac, who converted to Neolin's doctrine and adapted it as a "supernatural sanction" for his anti-colonial campaign (Wallace 115).

In the same way, Tecumseh did not succeed solely by the force of his personality or his cunning military strategies. Just as Pontiac's rebellion gained momentum from the prophesies of Neolin, Tecumseh's War found its religious purpose in the teachings of Tenskwatawa, a brother to Tecumseh who declared himself a prophet and, like Neolin, professed the rejection of white ways and a return to tribal practices. Prior to his awakening as the "Shawnee Prophet," Lalawéthika, the drunken "Noisemaker," seemed to personify the broad disintegration of tribal cultures as a result of the rum trade. Like Neolin a generation earlier, Tenskwatawa claimed that he had communed with the Great Spirit, who urged Indian people to cleanse themselves of white cultural influence and return to the old values and customs. Tenskwatawa promised that those who cast aside "wealth and ornaments" would, after death, "find their wigwam furnished with everything" in the spirit world. The Shawnee and other Indian people should cease domesticating cows, pigs, and sheep and return to the hunt, and they should hunt not with guns but with bows and arrows, as their ancestors did. They should grow corn and beans, and gather maple sugar, and they should give up metal tools for cooking and cultivation, and use wood and stone implements, as their ancestors did (Edmunds 37).

This movement toward cultural decolonization continues with Handsome Lake, brother to the Seneca chief Cornplanter and a companion to Pontiac during the siege of Detroit in 1763. In a series of teachings called "The Code of Handsome Lake," the Seneca prophet describes a vision in which the Devil reveals to Columbus all the riches of the New World. Columbus may claim these riches, Lucifer promises, if he delivers five gifts to the people living there: playing cards to "make them gamble away their wealth and idle their time," money to "make them dishonest and covetous," a fiddle to "make them dance with their arms about their wives and bring about a time of tattling and idle gossip," rum to "turn their minds to foolishness," and a diseased bone containing a "secret poison [to] eat the life from their blood" (Parker 18). His vision reflects his acute recognition that the rum trade, combined with the long-standing dependence on European tools and weapons, left the Haudenosaunee in a state of social debilitation and complete dependency on European trade. He urges the renunciation of all of these deadly vices, as well as a new respect for the sanctity of the family and a revival of traditional Haudenosaunee ceremonies. Like Neolin and Tenskwatawa, Handsome Lake grasped the correlation between the dependence on European goods and technology and the loss of Indigenous sovereignty.

John Sugden suggests that the closely shared message of Handsome Lake, Tenskwatawa, and Neolin represents a widespread "prophetic tradition" that exhorted a return to tribal lifeways and flourished among the Lenape, Odawa, and Shawnee (120). Estes, likewise, explains that each of these successive prophets "built upon the messages of the others by calling for pan-Indigenous resistance" founded not only through armed struggle, as *Warpath* and *The Years of Rice and Salt* have it, but also through the rejection of "colonial occupation." Culture rather than conquest grounds their "common desire for Indigenous liberation" (125).

Simulating Sovereignty

The importance of Handsome Lake, Tenskwatawa, Neolin, and the many other unnamed religious leaders appearing in dispersed Indigenous communities in the eighteenth and nineteenth centuries points to the most significant rupture between the historical struggle for Indigenous sovereignty and the simulated sovereignty in *Warpath* and *The Years of Rice and Salt*. By ignoring the cultural and religious dimensions of settler conquest and Indigenous resistance, these fantasies push the Haudenosaunee on a historical trajectory opposite that exhorted by Neolin, Tenskwatawa, and

Handsome Lake and stand in sharp contradiction to the models of sovereignty defined by Indigenous leaders in the present, finally culminating in obvious theme abuse.

In Robinson's novel, the Haudenosaunee system of social organization binds individuals both to other members of their nation and to other members of their clan among the other nations, ensuring both equality among the different tribes that comprise the League, as well as an unbreakable peace and loyalty among them. Fromwest tells his adopted tribe: "I have seen how this system of affairs brings peace to your league. It is, in all this world, the best system of rule ever invented by human beings" (376). This perfectly just system, imagined as the artfully interwoven "warp and weft" of Haudenosaunee nations and clans, stands in opposition to the imperial, autocratic systems of the Chinese and Muslims, which sustain not peace but perpetual warfare; not equality, but the enslavement of the smaller nations by the greater ones. Fromwest tells the Haudenosaunee council: "Everywhere else in the world, guns rule. Emperors put the gun to the heads of sachems, who put it to the warriors, who put it to farmers, and they all together put it to the women, and only the emperor and some sachems have any say in their affairs" (375). These two competing political philosophies, the matriarchal "warp and weft" and the patriarchal empire where "guns rule," define the realpolitik of Robinson's alternative world, with the Haudenosaunee system, centuries later, restoring order to the world after a catastrophic war between the great empires of China and Islam. At the conclusion of his oration to the Haudenosaunee, Fromwest, like the nativist prophets, describes a millennial vision:

> All the nations on this island are your will-be brothers, your will-be sisters ... They will join you if you are their elder brother, showing them the way forward. Struggle between brothers and sisters will cease, and the league of the Haudenosaunee will be joined by nation after nation, tribe after tribe ... I see what will happen in the time to come ... All the world's people will stand before the Haudenosaunee and wonder at the justice of its government. (386–7)

For Robinson, Grinde and Johanson's "exemplar of liberty" becomes the path to world peace.

The problem with Robinson's utopian vision lies in the Haudenosaunee's assimilation of the technologies and military strategies of Chinese and Islamic settlers as the pathway to sustained sovereignty and peace. Rather than preaching a revival of past traditions, Fromwest counsels the

Haudenosaunee to close the technology gap between themselves and the colonizers by adopting their superior technologies of industry and war. He teaches the Haudenosaunee to mine iron ore, smelt alloys, and make their own guns, giving the Confederacy the technological means to protect their destiny. While Fromwest resembles actual nativist leaders in his vision of pan-tribal unity, Robinson's imagined model of resistance suggests that a community faced with conquest can maintain sovereignty not through affirmation of its own beliefs and practices, as historical nativist movements had proposed, but rather through the selective, aggressive assimilation of foreign technology and practices.

By offering players an active role in anti-colonial resistance, *Warpath* invites players to confirm Robinson's counterfactual thesis of cultural and military assimilation. Although the game does not feature a savior character with advanced knowledge, it still compels the player to adopt a strategy similar to the one proposed by Fromwest by giving the player the role of Indigenous military leader and empire builder. To this end, the game introduces a unique mechanic to the *Total War* series, allowing the player controlling one of the Native factions to capture settler technology and to repurpose it for anti-colonial warfare, much as Fromwest counsels the Haudenosaunee to do. The game compels the player to re-enact the history of conquest and colonization, though wearing the graphical and narrative skin of Indigeneity. For white players, that is, most of them, imagining themselves in the guise of nativist saviors offers a further promise of a false redemption from history. We might feel a little less guilty about occupying Native land if we can take imaginary vengeance against the Town Destroyer.

Warpath incorporates Fromwest's program of militarized assimilation into its procedural logic. While Indian factions cannot, on their own, develop settler technology and weapons, they can capture them through the conquest of colonial settlements. Capturing a colonial "Gunsmith," for example, opens a technology tree that allows the player to develop "Ironworking," "Improved Ironworking," "Powder Making," and, ultimately, "Cannon Casting." The textual prompts accompanying each new technology provide the play with alternative historical rationale that resonates as a procedural version of the political philosophy and war strategy that Fromwest offers the Haudenosaunee. For "Ironworking," *Warpath* explains:

> Being able to work metal well makes the manufacture of weapons a quicker, easier process. As America becomes home to an increasing number of European settlers, gunpowder weapons have become widespread. It is therefore useful for native nations to manufacture and

maintain guns for themselves, instead of relying on trade with foreigners for weapons. Ironworking is a new practice for many, but vital if the tribes are to survive.

Just as Fromwest promises, mining, smelting, and incipient industry soon lead to "Improved Ironworking":

> New ironworking allows the manufacture of small arms, reducing the upkeep costs of gunpowder-armed units. Mastering the craft not only frees a tribe from relying on Europeans for iron goods, but also ensures a guaranteed supply of metal and weapons in times of trouble. The introduction of guns has dramatically altered warfare: the best way to keep [up] is for a nation to own and control their own means of making firearms.

Finally, little guns and better guns lead to big guns and "Cannon Casting":

> This technology allows the small-scale production of artillery, and reduces the upkeep costs of firearm-equipped units. Cannons are a most destructive force indeed, but not a brave and noble way of fighting! But, as enemies have cannons, only a foolish tribe would not seek to protect their land and people. The strength of the tribes may be in stealth and surprise, but a new weapon of such power demands new ways.

While we might conceive of an alternative Red Jacket leading frontier skirmishes against American homesteaders and militias in retaliation for Sullivan's campaign, we need a stronger tolerance for theme abuse to conceive of Haudenosaunee regiments unleashing a thundering artillery barrage against the bulwarks of Boston, New York, or Philadelphia.

In *Warpath* as in the imperialist world order imagined in *The Years of Rice and Salt*, "guns rule," and even with their more enlightened and humane form of government, the Haudenosaunee need the technology and weaponry to defend it against those who, as Fromwest warns, would "put the gun to their heads." The textual prompts in *Warpath* offer the player the same advice. While Neolin, Tenskwatawa, and Handsome Lake counseled against firearms and European trade, the game pushes us procedurally in the opposite direction, encouraging us to pursue "Gun Dealing" as the only viable path to sovereignty:

> Trading with outsiders means you can give your warriors firearms, when you cannot make them. A tribe that fails to keep pace with an

enemy risks leaving itself vulnerable to attack ... Hard bargaining can get you many guns, until the tribe's smiths can learn the necessary skills ... A people without guns ran the risk of destruction by enemies armed with the new weapons.

Soon, however, you no longer need to rely on a costly weapons trade, especially when you develop "Powder Making":

> Learning to make gunpowder cuts the cost of recruiting gun-armed units. The ability to create gunpowder means that a tribe no longer depends on supplies from fickle European traders. The tribe can therefore give muskets to more of its warriors, because they can be used, not just carried as clubs. Bullets are less of a problem, as they can be cast by any competent smith, and many gunpowder weapons come with bullet mounds as part of their accoutrements. But the availability of powder remains key: make that, and there are few limits to your power.

Here is the essential message: with muskets, bullets, and powder, "there are few limits to your power." As procedural rhetoric, the game guides the player much as Fromwest counsels the Haudenosaunee in *The Years of Rice and Salt*, toward the construction of an industrial war machine that will enable them not only to resist but to conquer (Figure 2.1).

Figure 2.1 Battlefield image from *Warpath*. (Credit: Creative Assembly.)

Although strategy games like *Warpath* are symbolic and simplified models of the past, limited or biased in their perspective, and marred by inaccuracies and omissions, so too is a history textbook. But video games posing questions about the historical process do not free historians to neglect events, lest we treat history itself like a game. We should not dismantle the historical record, in other words, without knowing how to put it back together again. At their worst, video games might become vehicles for historical myopia, denial, or false suasion, procedural expressions of what Eve Tuck and Wayne K. Yang, in "Decolonization Is Not a Metaphor," call "moves to innocence" (1). *Warpath*, for example, moves us to absolution from the colonial past by affording us a counterfactual cloak of Indigenous identity and resistance. The procedural argument in the game compels us to conquer and build an empire, suggesting that conquest is the necessary and inevitable purpose of civilization and obliterating the difference between "colonization" and "decolonization." The game offers no alternative to constant warfare, nor does it illuminate the differences between the imagined past and the real past, nor does it teach very much about Indigenous culture or the colonial encounter. In terms of their political and cultural objectives, the Haudenosaunee seem much like the Huron, Plains tribes, and Pueblo—and, for that matter, much like England, France, and the United States. Whether we play as Indigenous or colonizer, we raze settlements to fill our treasury and expand our rule over continents and oceans. Sagoyewatha becomes, like Washington, the "Town Destroyer": an instance of theme abuse that verges on obscenity.

Plausible Sovereignty

Video games can never serve as a faithful representation of events as they occurred, and, in fact, should not attempt to do so. For historians like Ferguson, their value rests not in their ability to simulate what happened but rather how things happen, the procedural nature of history, and the contingency of events. Ferguson argues for a "restrained" approach to counterfactual history that avoids theme abuse by working with "plausible" or "probable" historical alternatives:

> We solve the dilemma of choosing between a single deterministic past and an unimaginably infinite number of possible pasts. The counterfactual scenarios we therefore need to construct are not mere fantasy: they are simulations based on calculations about the relative probability of plausible outcomes in a chaotic world ... That narrows the scope

for counterfactual analysis down considerably. Moreover, we can only legitimately consider those hypothetical scenarios which contemporaries not only considered, but also committed to paper (or some other form of record) ... [I]t renders counterfactual history practicable. (85)

What might Ferguson's "plausible" and "practicable" approach look like in a different version of *Warpath*? For one thing, the Haudenosaunee "warp and weft," so cherished by Robinson and historians of democracy, might replace the implausible Iroquois "Head of State" and "cabinet." Perhaps, also, the procedural rhetoric of the game would not compel the assimilation of settler technologies as a precondition for survival. Finally, the strategic options and goals of the Iroquois Confederacy should include neither the annihilation of other Indigenous factions nor the expansion beyond traditional Haudenosaunee lands, which contemporaries like Sagoyewatha never plausibly considered.

We should also consider "plausibility" and "practicability" with respect to the living presence of the nations represented historically in the game. Currently, the Haudenosaunee Confederacy defines its sovereignty plainly:

> Like the individual states of the United States, each member nation of the Haudenosaunee retains the authority to govern its own internal affairs. Within the framework of the Great Law and its own specific laws, each individual nation reserves the right to adjudicate internal disputes, pass laws for the welfare of their own community, assess fees, regulate trade and commerce, control immigration and citizenship, oversee public works, approve land use, and appoint officials to act on its behalf. Every member of the Haudenosaunee has the authority to defend its citizens against internal and external dangers and to advocate for the peaceful resolution of conflict and the equitable distribution of collective resources. (Onondaga Nation, "Sovereignty").

The Onondaga understanding of sovereignty does not include for "Ironworking," "Powder Making," and "Cannon Casting," but rather emphasizes the "peaceful resolution of conflict."

Beyond these necessary statements, earned by centuries of resistance, the Ojibwe writer David Treuer suggests that contemporary Indigenous people embody sovereignty not only in political, religious, or educational practice but also as "the aura of dignity conferred by seeing oneself as belonging to a sovereign people, as having rights that adhered to and derived not from the largesse of government but from continuation of their cultures, community, and polity" (402). Treuer gives personal expression to this "aura of dignity" derived from culture and community in a recollection from his childhood, when his mother taught him the traditional practices of ricing, berry picking, sugaring, and snaring rabbits. "Why bother?" Treuer asks. He was going to go to college and find a good job in the city. He calls back the voice of his mother: "*I was also going to make sure you knew how we lived, how we lived off the land. That way, no matter what happened out there in the bigger world, you'd know how to take care of yourself back here, on the rez. You'd be able to feed yourself*" (388). Her words evoke those of Tenskwatawa, who counseled the Shawnee that traditional practices of sugaring, planting, and hunting were "how to take care of yourself" in the face of cultural absorption.

For Treuer, knowing "how we lived" contains the essence of sovereignty:

> I see in my mother's actions and attitudes something I surely didn't see then—one of the less visible effects of Indian empowerment and sovereignty in the 1970s and 1980s, which came to fruition in the 1990s. Sovereignty isn't only a legal attitude or a political reality; it has a social dimension as well ... To believe in sovereignty, to let it inform and define not only one's political and legal existence but also one's community, to move through the world imbued with the dignity of that reality, is to resolve one of the major contradictions of modern Indian life: it is to find a way to be Indian and modern simultaneously. (388–9)

Treuer offers us a model of cultural sovereignty more plausible in its resonance with historical Indigenous resistance—embodied by figures like Neolin, Tenskwatawa, and Handsome Lake—than the counterfactual fantasies of *Warpath* and *The Years of Rice and Salt*. When simulations of sovereignty set aside dimensions of community and culture, deny "how we lived," and assimilate to the systems of settler colonialism, they also set aside responsibility toward the people they represent, particularly as living Haudenosaunee bear witness to fantasies appropriated from their past in popular culture.

In celebrating the formative role of the Haudenosaunee Confederacy in American democracy, historians like Grinde, Johanson, and Mann, publicly boosted by congressional resolution, risk whitewashing the colonial past with the illusion of peaceful intercultural collaboration. On the other hand, the Onondaga, alongside the other Haudenosaunee nations, insist that any acknowledgment of the Haudenosaunee contribution to American democracy must be accompanied by the parallel acknowledgment of the American contribution to Haudenosaunee destruction: the Sullivan campaign, George Washington's legacy as "Town Destroyer," and the history of settler colonialism as a whole. Failing to make this complete acknowledgment erases historical memory and soothes settler guilt. In the same way, counterfactual Haudenosaunee histories like *Warpath* and *The Years of Rice and Salt* not only offer "exuberant" flights from the recorded and remembered past, as Megill argues, but also reinstate the violent ideologies that the study of history has worked to expose and scrutinize. They do not interrogate historical genocide with questions of contingency, or "what might have been," so much as they naturalize it with the deterministic procedural logic of "what must be." Or, as Fromwest plainly teaches, "guns rule."

Works Cited

Bogost, Ian. *Persuasive Games: The Expressive Power of Videogames*. MIT Press, 2007.

Edmunds, R. David. *The Shawnee Prophet*. U of Nebraska P, 1983.

Empire: Total War—The Warpath Campaign. Developed by Creative Assembly, Windows, Sega, 2009.

Estes, Nick. *Our History Is the Future: Standing Rock versus the Dakota Access Pipeline, and the Long Tradition of Indigenous Resistance*. Verso, 2019.

Evans, Richard J. "Telling It Like It Wasn't." *Historically Speaking: The Bulletin of the Historical Society*, vol. 5, no. 4 (2004), pp. 11–14.

Ferguson, Niall. *Virtual History*. Basic Books, 1997.

Grinde, Jr., Donald A., and Bruce E. Johanson. *Exemplar of Liberty: Native America and the Evolution of Democracy*. American Indian Studies Center, U of California P, 1991.

Haudenosaunee Confederacy. "Influence on Democracy." https://www.haudenosauneeconfederacy.com/influence-on-democracy/ (last accessed November 8, 2024).

Hunter, John Dunn. *Memoirs of a Captivity among the Indians of North America*. Longman, 1824.

Mann, Charles C. "The Founding Sachems." *The New York Times*, July 4, 2005, https://www.nytimes.com/2005/07/04/opinion/the-founding-sachems.html (last accessed November 8, 2024).

McNeill, William H. "Counterfactuals and the Historical Imagination." *Historically Speaking: The Bulletin of the Historical Society*, vol. 5, no. 4, 2004, pp. 21–22.

Megill, Allan. "The New Counterfactualists." *Historically Speaking: The Bulletin of the Historical Society*, vol. 5, no. 4 (2004), pp. 17–18.

Onondaga Nation. "Sovereignty." https://www.onondaganation.org/government/sovereignty/ html (last accessed November 8, 2024).

———. "US Presidents: Hanadagá•yas." https://www.onondaganation.org/history/us-presidents-hanadagayas/#:~:text=Since%20that%20day%2C%20the%20Haudenosaunee,%E2%80%A2yas%20%E2%80%93%20The%20Town%20Destroyer. html (last accessed November 8, 2024).

Parker, Arthur C. *The Code of Handsome Lake, the Seneca Prophet*. SUNY Press, 1912.

Parkman, Francis. *The Conspiracy of Pontiac and the Indian War after the Conquest of Canada*, vol. II. Little, Brown, and Company, 1894.

Robinson, Kim Stanley. *The Years of Rice and Salt*. Bantam Books, 2002.

Stone, Tim. "*Empire: Total War—The Warpath Campaign* DLC Review." GamesRadar, November 4, 2009, https://www.gamesradar.com/empire-total-war-the-warpath-campaign-dlc-review/ (last accessed November 8, 2024).

Sugden, John. *Tecumseh: A Life*. Henry Holt, 1997.

Treuer, David. *The Heartbeat of Wounded Knee: Native America from 1890 to the Present*. Riverhead, 2019.

Tuck, Eve, and Wayne K. Yang. "Decolonization Is Not a Metaphor." *Decolonization: Indigeneity, Education and Society*, vol. 1, no. 1 (2012), pp. 1–40.

Wallace, Anthony F.C. *The Death and Rebirth of the Seneca*. Vintage, 1969.

Washington, George. Letter to Major General John Sullivan, May 31, 1779. Founders Online, National Archives, https://founders.archives.gov/documents/Washington/03-20-02-0661 (last accessed November 8, 2024).

3

Learning through Looking: Early American History and Race in Contemporary African American Graphic Novels

Oliver Scheiding

Touring several museums around the United States since 2019, the exhibition "Arts and Race Matters" illustrates the power of African American visual art in reinterpreting the past. Being the first major retrospective of Robert Colescott's artistic work, his satirical paintings expose the viewer to racist stereotypes of Black people and the inherent racial bias of American history, politics, and culture. Colescott parodies the masterpieces of national art like Emmanuel Leutze's *Washington Crossing the Delaware* (1851). His repaintings of historical events challenge the viewer to consider the legacy of racism and inequality in American national mythology and the visual imagination on which it is built. Likewise, his 1986 series "Knowledge of the Past is the Key to the Future" comments on the absence of Black subjects in Western (art) history. Colescott's Black visual storytelling interweaves past, present, and future. His graphic stories suggest that American racial injuries are ineradicably linked to the nation's myth of discovery and its origins in colonial conquest.

Colescott's work highlights the collectivity of African American expressive culture in revisioning the past to make sense of the present and looking forward to the future. In the context of Black visual storytelling, this chapter is about the relationship between texts, images, and history specific to Black graphic novels. Literary and cultural critics emphasize the unique ability of the graphic novel as a literary form to address questions of historicity, cultural hierarchy, and race.[1] Rather than a simple illustration of original texts, a graphic novel is a way of visual storytelling in

---

[1] See Kunka; Rodriguez; Parr; Stein "Lessons" (620–56); and Wanzo, esp. chapter 2.

book-length form in which each picture tells a story. In contrast to definitions like "visual slave narratives" (Neary 3), superhero comics (Menn and Glaser 149–50), and graphic memoir (Chute, "Space" 195–8), the advantage the novel possesses over these labels as a work of art and human document is the "generic flexibility ... to lay out the kinds of fluid subjectivities" (Spires 30) and to engage culture through literary expression. Moreover, the graphic novel enhances the Black archive of writing and print culture. Black print culture understood as "a civic and textual act" not only provides spaces for theorizing democracy and Black citizenship but experiments with form to imagine alternative histories and political participation (Spires 30, 21). Moreover, the graphic novel establishes a tightly knit visual archive of paratextual and intertextual layers. Its palimpsestic fabric materializes history and dismantles "the representational logic in US culture," challenging its racial frameworks and taste regimes (Wanzo 95). African American graphic novels refigure the tales of literacy-as-freedom in a visual form to imply an alternative to that literacy tradition, the alternative of visuality.

The chapter explores current graphic novels by African American writers and graphic artists like Kyle Baker and Rebecca Hall and the ways in which their visual-verbal texts investigate the problem of collective histories and life stories. It considers the legacies of race and representation and asks how African American visual storytelling energizes African American literature by engaging with and revising "a historical archive of racist visualization" (Chaney, *Graphic Subjects* 73). Though separated from the immediate effects of slavery by over 150 years, African American graphic novels such as Baker's *Nat Turner* (2008) or Hall's *Wake: The Hidden History of Women-Led Slave Revolts* (2021) signify on and reconstitute the past to intervene in the enduring legacies of slavery and race that haunt the present. In Kyle Baker's case, it is Thomas Gray's 1831 bestselling account of Nat Turner's slave conspiracy allegedly told from the perspective of the rebel leader. Baker's graphic novel remediates a white print culture and "unsettles the unidirectionality of the white subject gazing on a black object" (Neary 3). Rebecca Hall voices the histories of women-led slave revolts in early eighteenth-century New York and on board the slave ship *Unity* in 1770. To demonstrate what public accounts do not tell us, Hall writes against the archive. Influenced by what Saidiya Hartman has coined "critical fabulation," Hall's curation of texts, images, and visuals weaves together the personal, the experiential, and the historical reawakening of the stories of Black women's resistance ("Venus" 1–14). Both writers and their graphic works test the limitations of objectivity and how it changes through acts of learning. They create histories that can appear impossible, when we consider what happened and what would have happened had things gone differently. Their re-envisioning of the past is "not just to teach us something new, but to teach us how the very shape of our knowledge could be different" (Stein, "Present Waver").

Kyle Baker's graphic art and the collaborative work of Rebecca Hall, the graphic artist and illustrator Hugo Martínez, and Sarula Bao's caption lettering and typefaces echo what Christina Sharpe calls "wake work" (17). In her book *In the Wake: On Blackness and Being*, Sharpe traces the legacy of slavery in four chapters: "The Wake," "The Ship," "The Hold," and "The Weather." Together, these chapters metaphorically describe the cycle of Black life. The chapter "The Hold," for instance, not only refers to the past and the Middle Passage that kept human beings in the hold of the ship but also mirrors the present situation of Black life being now in the hold of an incarceration system, racial profiling, and police violence. For Sharpe, "to perform wake work" means to explore "forms of Black expressive culture ... representing the paradoxes of blackness within and after the legacies of slavery's denial of Black humanity" (14). Likewise, the visual storytelling in both novels demonstrates that "living in the wake means living in the history and present of terror ... as the ground of the everyday Black existence" (15).

Scholarly attention focuses upon a medium incorporating both textual and visual discourses, demonstrating how it melts these somewhat competing aesthetics into a coherent narrative (Wanzo 1–30). The "crossbreeding of illustration and prose" (Witek 5) that characterizes the use of narrative images can be best illustrated by Kyle Baker's single-panel cartoon entitled "Happy Independence Day!" published on his website on July 2, 2007 ("Independence Day").[2] Baker's cartoon depicts Thomas Jefferson seated inside his home while writing the famous line from the Declaration of Independence: "[w]e hold these truths to be self-evident, that all men are created equal." Meanwhile, in the background, an enslaved child is pressing himself against the window and pleading, "Daddy, I'm cold," while slave masters whip other enslaved people in the fields behind him. Baker's satiric commentary on race and American history is obvious, but I would argue that his cartoon also makes a comment about the use of graphic narrative form in responding to historical events. The parody's

---

[2] To view this image, see https://concret67.livejournal.com/photo/album/322/?mode=view&id=7703.

self-reflective stance is especially evident through the way in which the division of windowpanes visually resembles the panels of a comic's page, inviting the audience to read the section like a comic within a larger panel—a page that reveals a narrative about the drama of slavery that Jefferson ignores.

The irony in this cartoon is the blending of text and image. The text, coming from a well-known historical document, is rendered false by the evidence outside the window, which, other than the brief dialogue, "Daddy, I'm cold," is depicted through cartoon images. Baker uses the powerful imagery in the background to question the "truth" of the written historical record. The cartoon undercuts the myth of equality established in the Declaration of Independence by exposing it to the historical truth of slavery. It highlights the ironic relationship between image and text: words and pictures blend to achieve a meaning of which neither is capable without the other.

Using this example as a frame for reading visual-graphic interventions into dominant modes of storytelling about race, this chapter will focus on the Black graphic novel's "contemporaneity" (Osborne 11). The British philosopher of modern and contemporary art Peter Osborne uses the term to explain new forms of historical time engulfed in "the *act of conjoining times*" as it can be found in present-day artwork (17; original emphasis). He proposes that art has "more to tell us about the changing structure of historical experience than might be supposed" (11). Osborne distinguishes between an historicist meaning of chronological time that presents history as a sequence of events flowing from the past into the present, frequently understood in terms of periodization and advancements of knowledge, and Søren Kierkegaard's "sametimeness" (17). Kierkegaard combines one's own present and the experience of the past as something present and not as something in the past. In terms of contemporary visual-graphic art, a good case in point are the drawings of the African American printmaker, painter, and silhouettist Kara Walker. According to one critic, Walker's disjunctive and collage-like historical portrayals of Black suffering and death "make pain legible not by relegating it to a comfortable past, but by making it palpable in the present" (Berger 583). Likewise, contemporary African American visual narratives consist of specific affective dynamics to achieve "sametimeness." The dynamics themselves consist of different formative histories that serve as contributing elements of the graphic novel's affective arrangement understood as specific "material-discursive formations" (Slaby 5). Baker's and Hall's powerful visual retellings of the hidden histories of slave revolts and their depictions of Black women and men involved in them lure readers into a position that provides opportunities for attachment and immersive experiences.

The inky darkness of the pages and the monochrome black-and-white pencil sketches affect the reading process and the reader's collaboration in conjoining times. Critics highlight the novels' multimodal dimension in which "the reader-viewers become the auditors of an absent community of the ancestral dead, whose pictorial monologues cry out for our affective response in the present" (Chaney, "Slave Memory" 296). The books' visual-graphic textures of black color establish what Courtney Baker calls an "ethics-based look," or a learning through looking (*Human Insight* 4). In the context of a racist visual imperialism and a colonial archive that keeps history's record frequently obscure, *Nat Turner* and *Wake* amplify history. Both texts have a gravitational pull and emotional impact on the reader's attention. Their drawings rich with shadows, expressiveness, tonal nuance, and atmosphere bring the stories of Nat Turner and the women-led slave revolts affectively into the present. Official reports on slave revolts and the mass-produced stereotypes of Black inferiority repeatedly rely on a white supremacist gaze targeting human beings in a web of racism. Conversely, Baker's and Hall's imagery arouses collective and personal racial memories, stereotypes, and persistent prejudices. Looking at the co-temporality of past and present, their graphic novels build a spatial ontology of historical mediation. In doing so, their graphic portrayals of Black anguish and the horrors of slavery "provide a common language of humanity" (Hartman, *Scenes* 18). They transform and alter the ways Black and white people see each other. Their visual storytelling affords "a crucial education about the self and what it means to be human" (Baker, *Human Insight* 7).

In reference to the history of racial disparity and injustice, the novels include frightening execution scenes showing how white people act out brutal fantasies against people of color. In such moments, the visual storytelling reflects upon what critics call "the *spectacle* of Black death" (Wilderson 225; original emphasis). Guy Debord reminds us that "spectacle is not a collection of images but a social relation among people mediated by images" (ch. 1). Debord's theory of the society of the spectacle addresses visibility and the impact of images on everyday lives. In the context of enslavement and the images it heralded, visibility is asymmetric, transmitting a representational history privileging a heroic white iconography. Both graphic novels disrupt the spectacle of a racist visual archive. The power of their graphic imagery puts forward a complex route to witness the "burden of history" and its persistence in the present-day United States (White, "Burden" 111).

(Re-)Mediations of History

Current scholarship in the field of Visual Studies proposes that Black graphic novels foreground "representation as mediation" (Neary 5). As such, they accentuate "the forces that produce and transmit images of enslavement and their authenticating infrastructures" (5). Infrastructures are the material and organizational structures and facilities needed to operate a society (Fielder and Senchyne 7–8). Apart from an entrepreneurial and legal dimension, the infrastructures of enslavement in cultural terms include a national print sphere, information technology, and art industry "authenticating" and mediating blackness within a (visual) rhetoric of white supremacy. Baker's and Halls' visual storytelling challenges the "authenticating infrastructures" of the white archive and its supremacist structures keeping historical records incomplete. While both writers burrow into the archive of enslavement, they bring to life the hidden facts of an excluded past.

Kyle Baker's graphic novel re-envisions the 1831 Southampton insurrection. The "official" documents tell us that on a Sunday evening in late August of 1831, Nat Turner met six associates and began to enter local houses and kill the white inhabitants. Over the next thirty-six hours, they were joined by other enslaved individuals and free Blacks, and they killed numerous men, women, infants, and children. It took the local militia two days to capture, kill, or disperse the insurgents. Nat Turner alone escaped and was caught in the immediate vicinity two months later. While in jail waiting to be hanged, he was interviewed by Thomas Gray, a lawyer who had previously represented several other defendants charged in the uprising. Gray was aware of the intense interest and the commercial possibilities of its originator's narrative. His extensively edited pamphlet *The Confessions of Nat Turner* appeared in 1831 and turned into an immediate bestseller.

Many writers have attempted to represent the Southampton uprising, most notably William Styron in his 1967 Pulitzer Prize-winning novel *The Confessions of Nat Turner*. Styron's novel ambitiously attempts to find creative inspiration from the "original" jail confession Turner gave to Thomas Gray. Both Gray's 1831 pamphlet and Styron's rewriting remain touchstones for heated debates. While earlier Black writers refuted Styron's depiction of Turner as a sexually disturbed figure, recent biographies and biopics retrace Turner's life as "the most famous, but least known person in American history" (Greenberg 3). Kyle Baker's graphic narrative contributes to the growing cultural responses to this legendary Black leader. *Nat Turner* was first released in 2005 in four installments as a self-published weekly mini-series, only to be collected as a graphic novel of the same name three years later. *Nat Turner* has been unanimously praised by critics as an important new contribution to the African American tradition of slave portraiture.

Like the initial mini-series, the book-length version is divided into four chapters accompanied by numerous subtexts such as excerpts taken from Gray's pamphlet, a number of paratexts, such as Gray's original title page, Baker's preface, footnotes, a bibliography, as well as numerous period illustrations. The story of Nat Turner is told in four chapters: Home, Education, Freedom, and Triumph. The first section is almost entirely wordless, illustrating how Turner's family was taken from Africa in chains, showing the horrors of the Middle Passage, and how the families were torn apart and sold as slaves in the United States. In the second chapter, we meet Turner himself and experience his "education" in the context of the violent and merciless environment of chattel slavery. From the second chapter onwards, the rest of the book is a hybrid that overlaps Baker's graphic storytelling with key passages borrowed from Turner's confessions as they appear in Gray's pamphlet.

The novel's literariness is also given emphasis by the book's black-and-white print and expressive charcoal and pencil graphics. The book foregrounds the material possibility of the medium by using a wide range of chromatic nuances within black and white contour drawings demonstrating that neither black and white nor color are monolithic concepts. Baker's monochromatic storytelling with its almost sepia-toned wash highlights the paradigmatic value of non-color in creating a social poetics based on visuality. The visual devices are accompanied by Baker's cartoon-style drawings, giving the whole text a narrative rhythm that drives the reader's pace through the book.

In the first section, Baker offers a series of images that communicate in a particularly effective way the dehumanizing strategies that whites used to maintain control over Blacks in the early stages of American slavery. On board one of the slave ships sailing the Middle Passage, a mother gives birth to a baby but dies as she lies chained to a wooden berth in a hold crowded with her fellow slaves. The man lying next to her sees one of the white slavers toss her body overboard and realizes, while he clutches her baby to his chest, that these men feel no more sympathy for her than do the sharks that follow the slave ships. The pivotal moment of the section comes when the man suddenly breaks away from a line of chained enslaved people on the deck and runs for the side, determined to throw the baby over so he can join the mother and thus escape the fate that awaits the rest of them. In the first panel of a visually arresting four-page arc, Baker portrays the baby, his dark body perfectly centered in mid-air among a group of desperately clutching white hands, falling down toward a shark waiting in the water below. Two white faces are visible as well, grimacing in triumph as they grab one arm. The following panels illustrate the thesis of the entire book: Baker portrays the baby dangling by one arm from a white hand, at the mercy of both the men above and the hungry shark, its gaping maw filled in a solid black, waiting below. All seems lost until, driven mad by his own desperation, the baby's temporary guardian struggles free and bites the white hand that holds the baby, releasing him into a painful but short-lived death. The next image shows a close-up of the baby, turned completely upside-down as he falls.[3] This final full-page image draws the reader's attention to the baby's absolute blackness, represented in silhouette against the sky, in contrast to the shark's white teeth and pale skin. The close-up visualizes the exploitative relationship that the white slave traders established to ensure their profit.

Such close-ups correspond to narrative shortcuts that feature the discourse of particular groups. Slavery's capitalistic basis is featured in a scene in which one of the white slavers shouts to another white man, and the word balloon contains only the dollar sign: "$!" (35). Therefore, the Black man's decision to sacrifice the baby to the sharks rather than chancing the unpredictable horrors of slavery provides a key historical context for Nat Turner's insurrection and for the books writing not only history, but also writing race. In his seminal book *The Slave Ship: A Human History*, Marcus Rediker retraces this context showing what he calls the "ship factory" that produces both labor and "race." Rediker proposes that

> [a]t the very beginning of the Middle Passage, captains loaded on board the vessel a multiethnic collection of Africans, who would, in the American port, become "black people" or a "negro race." The voyage thus transformed those who made it. War making, imprisonment, and the factory production of labor power and race depended on violence. (10)

Near the end of Baker's graphic history, the heretofore rectangular panels begin to disappear, replaced by individual images of axes, blood splatters, body parts, guns, people, and houses signifying the atrocities of both slavery

---

[3] To view this image, see https://www.researchgate.net/figure/Kyle-Baker-Nat-Turner-2008-It-has-become-easier-for-African-parents-to-see-their_fig3_319668917.

and the rebellion itself. Nat Turner's narrative is not one of superheroism but evolves from the horrors fostered by the slave trade that gave direct rise to the horrors of the rebellion. It also suggests through Baker's narrative images that this story is a story of many more people than just Nat Turner.

To immerse the reader in re-experiencing past events, Baker's graphic art mimics the "trope of the Talking Book" that is central to slave portraiture in the African American literary tradition (Gates, *Signifying* 127–69). Henry Louis Gates's discussion of African American literature posits the importance of literacy and textuality that cause a parodic intervention of one voice into another, as white literate texts are echoed in Black writing. It is also closely linked to the "function of signifyin(g)" as a textual strategy of revision and "repetition with a signal difference" (xxxiii). In addition, Baker's novel embodies the trope of the Talking Book on a formal dimension. Baker's text itself becomes a talking book which spells out a Black graphic aesthetic responding to the limitations of the privileged form of literacy prevailing in readings of the African American tradition.

The trope of the Talking Book frequently refers to a scene in African American slave narratives in which the enslaved individual puts his ear to a book, in most cases the Bible belonging to his white master, in order to hear it speak. In his autobiography, published in 1789, Olaudah Equiano tells of his amazement regarding the European practice of reading:

> I had often seen my master ... employed in reading; and I had a great curiosity to talk to the books, as I thought he did; and so to learn how all things had a beginning: for that purpose I have often taken up a book, and have talked to it, and then put my ears to it, when alone, in hopes it would answer me; and I have been very much concerned when I found it remained silent. (ch. III, 68)

Equiano's signed portrait published in his *Narrative* shows him with the open Bible resting in his lap. He commends himself to his readers as a reader of the Talking Book, and the Book itself is depicted in his possession and poised to "speak," that is, open to him and to his readers.

Following Gates, critics have frequently argued that reading is to co-opt literacy for the cause of freedom. Gates concludes that "literacy was to be found the sole sign of difference that separates chattel property from human being" (*Signifying* 165). Enhancing Gates's emphasis on literacy, Baker's text remediates the trope of the Talking Book within the visual narrative of the graphic novel. According to Jay Bolter and Richard Grusin, remediation describes the process of inserting one medium into another medium, for instance, the textual into the visual. Through visuality, remediation offers a new perspective on the historical tradition of the Talking Book, allowing the reader to reinterpret the older form of the idea against the "preoccupations of contemporary media" (Bolter and Grusin 21). The process of remediating the traditionally textual representation of the Talking Book to the visual language of graphic novels highlights concerns specific to the Black graphic form. These concerns range from such themes as representing the very racial dichotomy of master and enslaved person (a difference maintained through access to reading), applying the trope's interest in competing forms of literacy (oral versus written), to understanding current debates around visual and textual literacy. Other concerns demonstrate how textual narratives define and encompass individual narratives and experiences within the African American tradition. Remediation becomes even more recognizable through metafictional allusions within the visual narrative. The graphic representation of the trope adds to the novel's metafictional dimension. The trope becomes remediated into the story, inserted within the narrative, while also calling attention to how the narrative loops back on itself. Visually remediating the trope of the Talking Book allows Baker to create his own visual "signifyin(g)" by focusing on the increased importance of visuality over literacy.

Baker considers the role of reading and visual images through a frame narrative that remediates an instance of the Talking Book. Opposite the title page, and beginning the entire novel, an image of two eyes peering into a bright white book serves as a paradigm for the novel itself. Given Baker's interest in promoting "reading," especially of forgotten Black historical figures and their stories, this image establishes the major thematic concern of the novel, namely liberation through reading. But it also signals Baker's remediation of the trope of the Talking Book. Baker invites his reader to become the person featured in the image, a young Black child ostensibly reading in the night because that is the only free time to be had, using reading to overthrow the debilitating effects of slavery. The Black child gains control of the bright white book, symbolizing an attempt to control the foundational text of white racial difference. As it is widely known, literacy was used by slave owners to establish and maintain the superiority of whiteness. Within this visual context, however, Baker presents an image of subversion, a moment when one individual dismantles the system of slavery through the simple act of reading.

The opening image is counterbalanced by another scene in the final chapter of the text. After his hanging, Turner's body is brutally destroyed by white figures. His body becomes fractured, each limb and body part separated from the other (198). Even through this ordeal, Turner's spirit remains in the form of a book. A white man, making his way to bed and the promise of a tomorrow with one less Black threat present, places a book on a side table (199). The man's slave, knowing the man will not return for the book, disappears with it into the darkness of a solitary room; a line of printed text reveals the book to be a copy of Gray's *The Confessions of Nat Turner*. This sequence provides the image found on the title page, creating a cyclic structure that perpetuates Turner's story as a relevant and viable narrative to overcome the "psychic hold of slavery" (Crawford 151). "Outlawing the teaching of slaves to read or write," as Baker muses in his preface, serves white supremacy to suppress any kind of Black expression (7). Given the endurance of racism in the new millennium, Baker's remediation of the Talking Book extends itself into telling the story of America as "disgorge" (Berlant).[4] Not knowing whether it comes "out of my mouth, his mouth, your mouth," the idea of storytelling as disgorge does not pour itself out into another confession of the oppressed, but rather disgorges stories that show the reader how racism and dehumanization work (Rankine 63). In other words, Baker's graphic work of restorative witness is itself an act of resistance.

    The inclusion of a period print of the 1835 cylinder press within the graphic representation of Turner's death furthers the confluence of visuality and the Talking Book within Baker's history. The reprinted image that separates the brutal mutilation of Turner's body from the white slave owner casting aside Turner's confession represents a technology that has greatly facilitated the print and graphic revolutions that since the 1830s gave rise to the text as a "visual medium" (Baker 6). The embedded image of a nineteenth-century cylinder press which allowed the blending of visual and verbal content in print implies that the reproduction of Turner's words inverts the ripping apart of his physical body. The image also suggests that Turner's struggle lives on and goes beyond the limitations of the physical body as well as the literate white text.

---

[4] In her interview in the arts magazine *Bomb*, Claudia Rankine refers to William Turner's masterpiece of Western art *The Slave Ship* (1840). Both Turner's painting and a "*Detail of Fish Attacking Slave* from *The Slave Ship*" (Rankine 164; original emphasis) appear in the closing pages of her book *Citizen*, an anatomy of racism that combines words and images. Referring to the "elite world" of Western cultural production, Rankine concludes: "The book ends with Turner's *Slave Ship*, because it seemed funny that those trips across the Atlantic would have us disgorging still. Maybe the disgorge is a form of storytelling" (Berlant). She further explains that it is a collective form of storytelling blurring the boundaries of fiction and non-fiction.

Visual Storytelling and Historical Imagination

Wake is a hybrid piece of visual storytelling. Part autobiography, part historiography, mixing lettering and drawing, the book unfolds an epic of Black women's resistance. In ten chapters, the book jumps between the Black Atlantic's past and Hall's research as a historian who is "hunting down the past ... to tell these stories," as she writes in the prologue titled "Atlantic Ocean 1770" (Hall). The juxtaposition of drawings depicting the slave ship's brutal reality and Hall's own role as a historian brooding over files, books, and slave ship logs turn both narrator and reader into time travelers and co-authors spiraling down the deep waters of the slave trade to upwell the horrible truths about the capture and enslavement of Africans brought to the New World. Each chapter gives profound insight into the reality of rampant violence and the ironies of interracial relationships, using writing and drawing to save lives. Hall's story power is not about telling but about "revealing that which has been concealed by time, custom, and by our trained incapacity to perceive the truth" (Ellison 229). Realizing the discriminatory practices of the federal "justice system" and her minor role in it, the opening chapters trace the narrator's decision to quit working in New York's legal profession and to become a historian (Hall ch. 1 "Coming Home"). Working on her dissertation on race and gender, Hall conducts research in numerous archives in the United States and England. While studying "every story about slave revolts," she discovers references to Black women who were found guilty as rioters (Hall ch. 2 "Dom Regina vs. Negro Slaves"). To make their stories come alive, Hall realizes that she "must read the documents against the grain, assuming there are any documents to be found at all" (Hall ch. 4 "Sarah or Abigail"). In the court records of New York's municipal archive, she encounters the names of four Black girls who are briefly mentioned in between the lines.[5] Already, the book's prologue foreshadows the names of two Black female figures, Adono and Alele, otherwise known only as "Woman No. 4" and "Woman No. 10" (Hall ch. 8 "The Insurrection Cargo"). As her research will reveal, both play a prominent role during the slave revolt on board the *Unity* in 1770. The official ship's log states that "*A Woman No. 4 of Captain Moneypenney's Purchase Died Mad*" since her "*Views ... in ye Insurrection*" were "*disappointed*" (ch. 8; original emphasis). Naming them, giving them voices, and portraying their heroic deeds bring to the surface the lives of

---

[5] To view the image, see https://themillions.com/2021/05/panel-mania-wake-the-hidden-history-of-women-led-slave-revolts.html.

the two Ahosi women warriors, a military corps of women in the service of the West African kingdom of Dahomey.[6] Throughout the book, Hall is driven to find out "[w]ho were these women? What were their stories?" Trying to fill the gaps and solving the riddle of the women's disappearance, Hall decides to apply "a measured use of historical imagination in order to reconstruct a story" (Hall ch. 2 "Dom Regina vs. Negro Slaves").

The statement appears on a two-page spread that yields two images of New York City in a mirage-like manner. The upper part of the horizontal panel displays Manhattan's east side with its modern architecture. As the reader's eye runs down the page, the waters of the East River show a mirror image revealing the earlier Dutch colonial harbor front—a reminder of the city's involvement in the Atlantic slave trade. To rotate history's reconstruction around present and past events, the book's chapter structure relies on visual-graphic hinges. The establishing shot on the following page shows a street panorama, dated "New York 1712" (Hall ch. 3 "Some Hard Usage"). It exposes a Black female servant seen from behind as she walks among white city dwellers along the waterfront landing toward a slave market. Creating visual arcs coupled with panels on the previous page, panel zooms and splash pages re-enact the hidden history of women-led slave revolts. The book's visual storytelling and layout mirror R.G. Collingwood's approach to reconstructing history (231–302). Since past actions do not have real existence at the point in time in which

---

[6] The release of the 2022 movie *The Woman King* (dir. Gina Prince-Bythwood) sparked a debate about slavery and the Kingdom of Dahomey and the movie's depiction of the women warriors, also called Agodjie. Venerated as wives of the king, their privileged status was given expression by also naming them Ahosi. Critics find fault with the movie's treatment of Dahomey as an anti-slavery kingdom. Focusing on two female soldiers, Alele and Adono, Rebecca Hall renders a more nuanced history of the West African nations' involvement in the European slave trade. At the background of their enslavement stands the expansion of the Oyo empire (1300–1835). The Oyo subjugated the Dahomey and relied heavily on the slave trade throughout the eighteenth century. In *Wake*, the Dahomey female warriors Adolo and Alele share the fate of soldiers in colonial wars who become war captives and were sold into slavery. While the Agodjie were mentioned in late nineteenth-century French colonial records, Hall suggests that earlier "documentation shows that there were women warriors involved in these wars, women from many different nations and ethnic groups fighting to protect their villages from slave traders throughout West Africa" (Hall ch. 8 "Insurrection Cargo"). Retelling the entangled history of the "Trans-Atlantic Slave Trade" and how it turned into a dehumanizing force altering the history of West Africa, the lives of the two female soldiers promote a history from below that extends to these women, restores their agency, and challenges historiography; on the Kingdom of Dahomey see Hall ch. 9, "All Water Has Perfect Memory."

they are studied, historians imagine the thoughts and motivations of people involved in past events. However, as Collingwood writes, the constructivist approach is neither fictitious nor unreal, but constrained by space and time as well as the evidence gathered from the sources. Hall bridges the gaps in what the sources tell her. What she fills in can be seen in the visual re-enactments of events that occurred in New York in 1712 (Hall ch. 3 "Some Hard Usage") and in the Kingdom of Dahomey in 1769 (Hall ch. 9 "All Water Has a Perfect Memory"). As a historian, Hall also acts like a lawyer, placing authors and historical documents on the witness stand. Interrogating the sources, she shakes testimony and raises critical questions about the given evidence. At one time, she begins to rely on "new digital technologies" used by "quantitative historians ... to study big-picture-historical trends" (Hall ch. 8 "The Insurrection Cargo"). After having collected data on more than "36,000 slave ship voyages," they conclude that "[t]he more women onboard a slave ship, the more likely the revolt" (ch. 8). Given the historians' bias against Black women's active role in history, they simply dismissed their findings "as some kind of statistical fluke" (ch. 8). Hall's web of imaginary construction is set between these findings and her own conclusions drawn from the reality on board the slave ships. Given the fact that Black women were frequently sexually abused, she concludes that they were more mobile and thus had "access to weapons to plan and initiate revolt," as in the case with Adono and Alele (ch. 8).

The book's final section contains two double pages. One of the two-page spreads shows the slave ship *Unity* ploughing the seas. Following the trade route of the Middle Passage, the ship carries human "cargo" across the Atlantic Ocean. The flames on deck signal the slave revolt that had occurred on board in June 1770. The burning ship signals the unbroken human will to resist slavery. At the rear of the ship and out of the wake's churning water comes a clenched fist, an emblematic reference to Black power both in the past and present. The raised fist holding an Ahosi woman warrior's spear targeting the ship's stern belongs to Alele. The drawing evokes Toni Morrison's haunting verses in *Five Poems* (2002). In one of the poems, "I Am Not Seaworthy," the reader finds these private lines that bear witness to the horror of the Middle Passage and the enforced voyage in the slave ship's dark hull:

> I had a life, like you. I shouldn't be riding the sea.
> I am not seaworthy.
> Let me be earth bound; star fixed
> Mixed with sun and smacking air. (ll. 3–6)

The concluding spread shows the full and active body of Alele upwelled from the ocean's depth and catapulted to the surface holding a spear in an attack mode, hissing the words "[f]or the Future!" The book's closing image morphs the kinesthetic dynamic of Alele's body with the illustrator's propulsive graphic marks and the writer's empowering words. The visual storytelling gives the entire book the quality of becoming. Despite the dismal and horrible experiences of slavery, it charges the drawing with the possibility of an alternative state of being and a fresh lens through which to experience history, and "to go back and retrieve our past" (Hall ch. 10 "Ancestry in Progress"). According to Hall, "this is ancestry in progress, and it is our superpower" (ch. 10).

Materializing History and the Artifacts of Race

In her astute article "Comics as Literature? Reading Graphic Narratives," Hillary Chute maintains that graphic narratives are "productively self-aware in how they 'materialize' history" ("Comics" 457). Graphic novels offer a bridge between textual and visual narratives, two crucial modes for African American writers plagued by the legacy of visual representations of race and slavery.[7] From the earliest images of so-called Black savages cataloged by painters to the iconic stamps of runaway slaves used in antebellum broadsides, visual images have been used to delimit the potential humanity of Black slaves in the imaginations of European and white American audiences. Black artists and writers, nearly from the beginning of colonization, have resisted these delimiting images, finding empowerment and liberation through the manipulation of visual discourse.

As the contemporary graphic novel often focuses on issues of history and memory, many critics have cited the potential of the graphic form to foreground the contemporary struggle to maintain viable material archives in the age of ever-increasing information. Jared Gardner, in *Projections*, demonstrates how graphic novels assume a liminal space as archives of popular culture. In this sense, one could argue that the graphic novel is about making the present aware of its own archive.

Such densely referential texts as Kyle Baker's *Nat Turner* and Rebecca Hall's *Wake* recognize the value of sources beyond text showing the close relationship between visual storytelling and the archives of material history.

---

[7] For a comprehensive survey of the mass production of racist stereotypes in the U.S., see Henry Louis Gates, Jr., *Stony the Road*, esp. chapter 3.

Baker's text ends with one of the most well-known visual icons of slavery. The final page reproduces the image of the slave ship *Brooks*, first drawn and published by a group of Plymouth abolitionists in November 1788. Likewise, in chapter seven, "England and the Slave Trade," Hall reproduces the storage plan of the "British Slave Ship Brookes under the REGULATED SLAVE TRADE" (ch. 7; original emphasis).[8] The *Brooks*, built in 1781, had a long life as a so-called slaver, making ten successful voyages over almost a quarter of a century, carrying more than 6,000 slaves to North America. The *Brooks* represented the miseries of the slave trade more fully and graphically than anything else the abolitionists would find. The result of their campaign in Philadelphia, New York, and London was the broad dissemination of an image of the slave ship as a place of violence and horrific death. Baker's incorporation of an image of the *Brooks* describes a "violence of abstraction" (Redicker 12), or what Toni Morrison calls the "unspeakable thing unspoken" ("Unspeakable 161") that has plagued the study of the slave trade from its beginning. Frequently balance sheets, graphs, and tables have rendered abstract, and thereby dehumanized, the reality of slavery and comforted those involved in the slave trade. Remediating this visual archive, the slave ship demonstrates not only the truth of what one group of people was willing to do to others for pecuniary gain, but also how they managed to hide the reality and consequences of their actions (that is, Turner's and Alele's insurgency) from themselves and from posterity.

Baker's *Nat Turner* and Hall's *Wake* respond to the numerous visual and written legacies of race and slavery embodied by the image of the slave ship. The first chapter, "Home," and Hall's prologue contain full-page frames which symbolize stories of the people whose lives were shaped by the slave trade. In *Nat Turner*, the four miniature panels, containing a waxing quarter moon, a full moon, a waning quarter moon, and total blackness, indicate the passing of at least one month (33). This figurative shortcut is repeated throughout the book numerous times; it suggests that the atrocities of that period continued in a monotonous cycle, with no hope of relief. The background relates to it in a documentary-like fashion depicting a schooner, especially popular among North American merchants, and an illustration of a slave transport in Africa. The background imagery paints an ambivalent reality. It refers to both the transatlantic slave trade and slavery *within* Africa. The novel's bibliography

---

[8] To view the *Brooks* image, see https://www.loc.gov/pictures/resource/cph.3a34658/; Hall's spread is available as part of a preview at https://www.amazon.com/Wake-Hidden-History-Women-Led-Revolts/dp/0241523559.

includes, for example, the 2003 biography of Francis Bok, a Dinka tribesman who was held as a slave for ten years in South Sudan.

Wake's final chapter evokes another ambivalent reality about the nation's progressive self-idealization in the context of the "afterlife of slavery" (Hartman, *Lose Your Mother* 6). The large panel zoom-out that opens chapter ten, titled "Ancestry in Progress," shows Hall and the Black women whose stories she has told throughout the book posing on one of the eagle heads at the Chrysler Building gazing out of the city.[9] Martínez's panel layout not only remediates the Bible's topos of the high place (Deut. 34.1), but it also echoes the iconic image of the four continents as women stand on a cliff that provides them with a bird's-eye view over the Atlantic coastline and allows them to glimpse the country's western land. The allegorical cover illustration was printed in *Frank Leslie's Illustrated Historical Register of the United States Centennial Exposition, 1876* to herald America's progress.[10] The maidens, Asia and Africa, appear in descending order. They are guided by the British-American sisters foreshadowing the Anglo-Saxon supremacy that is to crown the world. Columbia's inviting gesture pointing to the west signals America's future role as the new promised land. *Wake*'s re-enactment serves less as the fulfillment of the nation's progressive dream but rather reminds the reader that New York's vision as the haven of mankind is based on the Atlantic slave trade. Built with African granite along with Moroccan marble, the Black women's presence on top of the Chrysler Building turns the city into a site of memory that brings together the voices of a Pan-African ancestry. Maya Angelou's quote—"[b]ringing the gifts that my ancestors gave, I am the dream and the hope of the slave"—and the chapter's reference to Zap Mama's 2004 album of the same name envision "a new way of appreciation" for Blackness and being, despite the apparent setbacks in racial progress (Zap Mama "Intro").

Both texts thus illustrate that European, African, and American societies still live with the multiple legacies of slavery and race. The faceless female body in Baker's *Nat Turner* ultimately functions as a causal link between the slave trade and the transformation of Africans into "black people." The visual narrative highlights the narrative insufficiency of subtexts such as Gray's, and others, and "speaks" the real human cost of slavery. Likewise, one of the final two-page spreads shows Hall walking through New York's

---

[9] To view this image, see https://interminablerambling.medium.com/retrieving-history-in-rebecca-hall-and-hugo-mart%C3%ADnezs-wake-a5ece2073078.

[10] To view this image, see https://www.pafa.org/museum/collection/item/frank-leslies-illustrated-historical-register-centennial-exposition-1876.

empty Grand Central Station while rays of light streaming through the windows illuminate episodes of racism in American history. At the end of her own "wake work," she concludes: "[w]e are haunted. Haunted by slavery and its legacy. Our country lives in the afterlife of slavery" (ch. 10 "Ancestry in Progress"). Baker's and Hall's graphic books blend the elliptic form of comics narration with symbolic images that go beyond the mere pictorial resonance of the graphic book's monochromatic drawings. Scripting the past into the present, both the novels' material potential related to the visual page arrangement and the importance of the "gutter"—that is, the untold in the space between the panels that makes the reader supply the missing action—disturb a "reading" of history as a linear movement toward transparency and away from ambiguity.

Contemporary African American graphic novels entrench a "strategic presentism" that demolishes "a set of racial protocols from the inside" (Neary 3). Baker and Hall call the reader's attention to the gaps, silences, and traumas that exist in the cracks of history and the way in which they are kept alive in the present, shaping Black people as the other. In doing so, both authors give fresh meaning to stories about slavery and the history of the Middle Passage as it can be found in the earlier works of Arna Bontemps (*Black Thunder: Gabriel's Revolt*, 1936), Robert Hayden ("Middle Passage," 1945), Maya Angelou (*Still I Rise*, 1978), Toni Morrison (*Beloved*, 1987), and John Edgar Wideman ("Nat Turner Confesses," 2018). Baker's and Hall's visual narratives conjure an elusive history enacting the tension between absence and presence, loss and survival, oppression and resistance. However, they do not render a mere representation of the past, but rather rely on a meta-historiographical mode of critical fabulation to disclose the fabrications of history. Baker's *Nat Turner* challenges the genre of nineteenth-century slave confessions as a retrospective narrative penned and authenticated by white authors fueling the racial fantasies of a "superior majority" (7). Frequently considered as ethnographies of crime and criminal justice, these accounts destroyed "the slave's mind," as Baker writes (7). He holds that the accompanying infrastructures of "outlawing the teaching of slaves to read and write" had been "more effective than whips and guns" (7).

Extending Baker's visualization, *Wake*'s graphic imagery reinterprets the past through the collaborative work of the illustrator's hand and the writer's wording. To illustrate the formative trajectories of Black subjecthood, *Wake*, for instance, amalgamates lettering and typography.[11] Hall's

---

[11] To view the image, see https://themillions.com/2021/05/panel-mania-wake-the-hidden-history-of-women-led-slave-revolts.html.

thoughts and the Black women's voices appear in hand-drafted letters in captions and dialogue balloons. Sarula Bao's uneven lettering expresses the emotive and intimate quality of the utterances among the vanquished. In contrast to the expressive pen-drawn letters, the italicized roman typefaces of the archival documents reflect a print culture that preserves the "history written by the victors" (*Wake* ch. 2 "Dom Regina vs. Negro Slaves"). *Wake* unveils the redolence of history and the ever-present white supremacy. While Baker's drawings function as a make-over of Gray's earlier account and reassess Nat Turner's revolt from a second author's point of view, *Wake* is a metahistory. It follows a synecdochic emplotment (White, *Metahistory* 29–38) in which Hall's autobiography (part for the whole) and her becoming a professional historian morph with her forensic research uncovering the crimes against Black women as well as humanity. Both books proffer drawings for racial self-realization. To disinter the buried memories of atrocity and pain, they rip the veil drawn over a terrible reality. The vivid storytelling implores the reader to take stock of a painful past and its implications in the present. Despite fundamental disagreements over the role of slavery in American history, brought to light by the 1619 Project (2019) and its reframing of the nation's beginning, *Nat Turner* and *Wake* teach lessons of empowerment and agree on the necessity of an essential rereading of history which acknowledges the role African Americans play in the realization of freedom and liberty.

Both writers emphasize the unique ability of the graphic novel as a literary form to address questions of historicity, cultural hierarchy, and race. Graphic novels such as Baker's *Nat Turner* and Hall's *Wake* not only enhance the canon of African American literary history, but also complicate our understandings of what constitutes raced texts and Black authors' audiences so that both Black and non-Black people can better appreciate the multiple and heterogeneous traditions African American writers inaugurated and revised. Moreover, in a climate of extreme cultural wars, Baker's and Hall's graphic novels remind their readers that "[t]he language of race developed in the modern period and in the context of the slave trade" (Hartman, *Lose Your Mother* 5). Given the present moment when so many people refuse to see what is right in front of them, their graphic novels pull readers "into environments outside the pages" (Morrison, "Invisible Ink" 350). Their rescripting the past into the present reminds the reader that the (graphic) novel is a place to continue the "American conversation," as Tommy Orange writes (81). In a country steeped in "slave labor" and "genocidal bloodshed," Orange claims that "reading books is a good place to start thinking about and understanding people's stories you aren't familiar with, outside your comfort zone and experience" (81). Avoiding rigid dualisms, Hall and Baker address the need for a renewed understanding of literary politics to reorient and activate the reader, and, in doing so, to retain the future-oriented and critical push of narrative fantasy and fiction.

Works Cited

Baker, Courtney R. *Human Insight: Looking at Images of African American Suffering and Death*. U of Chicago P, 2015.

Baker, Kyle. "Happy Independence Day!" *Kyle Baker*, July 2, 2007, https://concret67.livejournal.com/photo/album/322/?mode=view&id=7703.

———. *Nat Turner*. Abrams, 2008.

Berger, Maurice. "The Site of Memory: Kara Walker Drawing." *Kara Walker: A Black Hole is Everything a Star Longs to Be: Drawings 1992–2020*. JRP Editions, 2020, pp. 575–85.

Berlant, Lauren. Interview with Claudia Rankine. *Bomb* 129, October 1, 2014, https://bombmagazine.org/articles/claudia-rankine/ (last accessed November 8, 2024).

Bolter, Jay David, and Richard Grusin. *Remediation: Understanding New Media*. MIT Press, 1999.

Chaney, Michael A. "Slave Memory Without Words in Kyle Baker's Nat Turner." *Callaloo*, vol. 36, no. 2 (2013), pp. 279–97.

Chaney, Michael A., editor. *Graphic Subjects: Critical Essays on Autobiography and Graphic Novels*. U of Wisconsin P, 2011.

Chute, Hillary. "Comics as Literature: Reading Graphic Narrative." *PMLA*, vol. 123 no. 2 (2008), pp. 452–65.

———. "The Space of Graphic Narrative: Mapping Bodies, Feminism, and Form." *Narrative Theory Unbound: Queer and Feminist Interventions*, edited by Robyn Warhol and Susan S. Lanser. Ohio State UP, 2015, pp. 194–209.

Collingwood, R.G. *The Idea of History*. 1946. Revised edition. Oxford UP, 1994.

Crawford, Margo N. *What Is African American Literature?* Wiley Blackwell, 2021.

Debord, Guy. *The Society of the Spectacle*. Black and Red, 1970.

Ellison, Ralph. "The Art of Romare Bearden." *Going to the Territory*. Vintage, 1986, pp. 227–38.

Equiano, Olaudah. *The Interesting Narrative and Other Writings*. 1794. Introduction and notes by Vincent Carreta. Penguin, 1995.

Fielder, Brigitte, and Jonathan Senchyne. "Introduction: Infrastructures of African American Print." *Against a Sharp White Background: Infrastructures of African American Print*. U of Wisconsin P, 2019, pp. 3–26.

Gardner, Jared. *Projections: Comics and the History of Twenty-First-Century Storytelling*. Stanford UP, 2012.

Gates, Henry Louis, Jr. *The Signifying Monkey: A Theory of Afro-American Literary Criticism*. Oxford UP, 1988.

———. *Stony the Road: Reconstruction, White Supremacy, and the Rise of Jim Crow*. Penguin, 2020.

Greenberg, Kenneth S. *Nat Turner: A Slave Rebellion in History and Memory*. Oxford UP, 2003.

Hall, Rebecca. *Wake: The Hidden History of Women-Led Slave Revolts*. Illustrated by Hugo Martínez and lettered by Sarula Bao. Simon & Schuster, 2021.

Hartman, Saidiya. "Venus in Two Acts." *Small Axe: A Caribbean Journal of Criticism*, vol. 12, no. 2 (2008), pp. 1–14.

———. *Lose Your Mother: A Journey Along the Atlantic Slave Route*. Farrar, Straus and Giroux, 2007.

———. *Scenes of Subjection: Terror, Slavery, and Self-Making in Nineteenth-Century America*. Oxford UP, 1997.

Kunka, Andrew J. "Intertextuality and the Historical Graphic Narrative: Kyle Baker's Nat Turner and the Styron Controversy." *College Literature*, vol. 38, no. 3 (2011), pp. 168–93.

Menn, Ricarda, and Tim Glaser. "Graphic Realities Comics as Documentary, History, and Journalism." Report on the Conference "Graphic Realities: Comics as Documentary, History, and Journalism." Justus-Liebig-University Giessen/International Graduate Centre for the Study of Culture (GCSC), February 22–23, 2018. *DIEGESIS: Interdisciplinary E-Journal for Narrative Research/Interdisziplinäres E-Journal für Erzählforschung* 8.1, 2019, www.diegesis.uni uppertal.de/index.php/diegesis/article/download/339/545.

Morrison, Toni. *Five Poems*. Illustrated by Kara F. Walker. Rainmaker Editions, 2002.

———. "Invisible Ink: Reading the Writing and Writing the Reading." *The Source of Self-Regard: Selected Essays, Speeches, Meditations*. Alfred A. Knopf, 2019, pp. 346–50.

———. "Unspeakable Things Unspoken: The Afro-American Presence in American Literature." *The Source of Self-Regard: Selected Essays, Speeches, Meditations*. Alfred A. Knopf, 2019, pp. 161–97.

Neary, Janet. *Fugitive Testimony: On the Visual Logic of Slave Narratives*. Fordham UP, 2017.

Orange, Tommy. "What Novels Can Teach Us." *Time Magazine*, vol. 192, no. 18 (2018), pp. 81.

Osborne, Peter. *The Postconceptual Condition: Critical Essays*. Verso, 2018.

Parr, Jessica. "Teaching Trauma: Narrative and the Use of Graphic Novels in Discussing Difficult Pasts." *The Junto: A Group Blog on Early American History*, July 14, 2015, https://earlyamericanists.com/2015/07/14/teaching-slavery-the-use-of-graphic-novels-in-discussing-difficult-pasts/ (last accessed November 8, 2024).

Rankine, Claudia. *Citizen: An American Lyric*. Penguin, 2014.

Rediker, Marcus. *The Slave Ship: A Human History*. Viking, 2007.

Rodriguez, Jacqueline. "The Graphic Novel as Argument: Visual Representation Strategy in Kyle Baker's *Nat Turner*." *Inquiries Journal*, vol. 13, no. 2 (2021), www.inquiriesjournal.com/a?id=1875.

Sharpe, Christina. *In the Wake: On Blackness and Being*. Duke UP, 2016.

Slaby, Jan, Rainer Mühlhoff, and Philipp Wüschner. "Affective Arrangements." *Emotion Review*, vol. 11, no. 1 (2019), pp. 3–12.

Spires, Derrick R. *The Practice of Citizenship: Black Politics and Print Culture in the Early United States*. U of Pennsylvania P, 2019.

Stein, Daniel. "Lessons in Graphic Nonfiction: John Lewis, Andrew Aydin, and Nate Powell's *March* Trilogy and Civil Rights Pedagogy." *Journal of American Studies*, vol. 55, no. 3 (2021), pp. 620–56.

Stein, Jordan Alexander. "The Present Waver: On 'Wake: The Hidden History of Women-Led Slave Revolts." *Los Angeles Review of Books*, September 17, 2021, https://lareviewofbooks.org/article/the-present-waver-on-wake-the-hidden-history-of-women-led-slave-revolts/ (last accessed November 8, 2024).

Wanzo, Rebecca. *The Content of Our Caricature: African American Comic Art and Political Belonging*. New York UP, 2020.

White, Hayden V. "The Burden of History." *History and Theory*, vol. 5, no. 2 (1966), pp. 111–34.

———. *Metahistory: The Historical Imagination in Nineteenth-Century Europe*. Johns Hopkins UP, 1973.

Wilderson III, Frank B. *Afropessimism*. Liveright, 2020.

Witek, Joseph. *Comic Books as History: The Narrative Art of Jack Jackson, Art Spiegelman, and Harvey Pekar*. UP of Mississippi, 1989.

Zap Mama. "Intro." *Ancestry in Progress*. V2 Records, 2004.

PART II
WOMEN IN FILM: GENDER, CONSENT, AND REPRESENTATION

Section Overview

Part II brings depictions of women and early American history on screen to the fore. In Chapter 4, **Stacey Dearing's "More Authentic Yet Less Accurate: The Challenges of Depicting Women in Early American Film and TV Adaptations"** opens this segment with a nuanced examination of the distortions of early American women in contemporary film and TV representations of frequently mythologized events in American history, such as the sailing of the *Mayflower* and the founding of Plymouth Plantation. Specifically, Dearing investigates the branding of the series versus the portrayal of white and Indigenous women in the National Geographic docudrama *Saints & Strangers*, given that the show capitalizes on a form of historical authenticity while nonetheless eclipsing historical accuracy and cultural differentiation. Dearing argues that historical "truth" and cliché tropes of early American founding moments are repackaged in a grittier exterior that may feel more authentic but ultimately reinscribe the marginalization of women—especially Native women—for a modern audience. She states, "[r]ather than telling a true, unsanitized version of the *Mayflower* and the colonization of Patuxet, *Saints & Strangers*," despite its branding by NatGeo, "is participating in a long tradition of telling a revisionist origin story of the English colonies in New England," one that "obscures [an] imperialist lens, masking the ways in which the series perpetuates the erasure of Native cultures" and women. *Saints & Strangers*, Dearing concludes, seems to be more about "getting the 'spirit' of the story right," a problem that fails to recognize "that the story's alleged spirit is not static; it changes based on who is telling the story and why," a problem further exacerbated by the powerful scope and influence of contemporary media that impacts how the past is archived in the experiences of those in the present.

Moving squarely to pedagogy in Chapter 5, **"Check her for marks!" Teaching Bodily Consent and Autonomy through the Salem**

Witch Crisis Documents and Netflix's *Fear Street: 1666*" by **Danielle Cofer** presents practical strategies for teaching college students apathetic toward the textual documents surrounding the 1692 Salem witch crisis by linking this historical event to the recent Netflix show *Fear Street: 1666* as well as contemporary concerns about bodily consent and threats of bodily violation. Cofer's piece showcases a series of cleverly constructed case studies that move students through considerations of bodily autonomy in its intersection with class, race, marital status, and social power that impact both bodily and narrative control. Her approach demonstrates how analyzing the contemporary pop culture text alongside Salem witch crisis documents centers the persistent problem of sexual assault and consent in current U.S. culture, while tracing the central features of this debate—especially women's agency and bodily autonomy—back to the colonial period. "[T]his act of tracing connections," Cofer maintains, "opens up tense, at times discomforting, yet productive conversations that we can collectively engage in as a classroom community in order to challenge the social and cultural climate of silence which persists around assault."

Cryslin Ledbetter and **Patrick M. Erben** round out this section in Chapter 6 with their turn to **"Sex Education: Teaching Revolutionary Constructs of Womanhood through AMC's *Turn*."** This chapter links revolutionary period contestations of womanhood—especially in Judith Sargent Murray's essay "On the Equality of the Sexes"—to the cunning inversions of gender roles in the fictionalized portrayal of George Washington's spy ring in *Turn* and the current backlash against gender fluidity and women's reproductive rights. As a double-layered pedagogy essay, "Sex Education" first introduces Erben's college-level triangulated assignments encouraging students to interpret early American textualities and discourses in conversation with contemporary artifacts and sociopolitical debates. Such constellations, according to Erben, grant students "multiple access points for examining the ways in which gendered power and disenfranchisement operate transhistorically." With a close focus on the *Turn* character Anna Strong, Ledbetter—a former English education student—deploys Strong's covert spying activity as a didactic guide for the ways in which public school educators must now develop stealth approaches for engaging secondary students in critical analysis of allegedly divisive topics. Ledbetter's pedagogical reflections and high school lesson plan demonstrate how the detour via Murray's essay and the show *Turn* allows "students to question seemingly stable assumptions about womanhood, gender, and sexuality in contemporary discourse."

4

More Authentic Yet Less Accurate: The Challenges of Depicting Women in Early American Film and TV Adaptations

Stacey Dearing

American origin stories, such as the sailing of the *Mayflower* and the establishment of the English settlement of Plymouth on Wampanoag land at Patuxet, have considerable cultural power. Innumerable stories of the men of the *Mayflower* have been told in multiple media, spanning from romantic poetry, short stories, and novels to film and TV.[1] In recent years, a few prominent Native American men have received more attention in adaptations about the *Mayflower* and Patuxet/Plymouth, such as Ousamequin, commonly known as Massasoit (Pokanoket Wampanoag), Tisquantum (Patuxet), Samoset (Abenaki), and Hobbamock (Pokanoket Wampanoag). Yet few stories are told about the women of the *Mayflower* and even fewer about the Native American and Indigenous women, or *Ninnimissinuok*, who inhabited the land soon to be occupied by English settler colonists (Bragdon xi).[2] Men tend to be the main characters in *Mayflower* stories, while women are relegated to the background. Ethel J.R.C. Noyes notes this disparity in the foreword to her 1921 history of the female passengers of the *Mayflower*, observing that "[h]istory has dwelt long and minutely upon the Pilgrim Fathers and their great adventure, but has passed over

---

[1] Even framing the story as that of Plymouth erases the Indigenous inhabitants by elevating the English perspective. Film and TV adaptations almost exclusively refer to the *Mayflower* or Plymouth in their titles; I do my best in this essay to recognize the sovereignty of the Native people who lived at Patuxet prior to European contact.

[2] *Ninnimissinuok* is "a variation of the Narragansett word" for people and "connotes familiarity and shared identity" and can be used to refer to Native people of southern New England (Bragdon xi). I also use the term "Algonquian" to refer to the Native people of southern New England, as this term is commonly used to refer to Nations that use Algonquian languages.

the women with a generalization and occasionally a tribute. Even their contemporaries had but little to say about them" (Noyes 5). Indeed, few historical and fictional works focus on recovering the women of the *Mayflower* or Native American women, about whom the so-called Pilgrim Fathers wrote even less.[3] Due to the dearth of archival records about these women, much of what is "known" about the Indigenous and English women in what we now call Massachusetts consists of highly romanticized fictional narratives developed by writers in the nineteenth century such as Nathaniel Hawthorne, Henry Wadsworth Longfellow, and Jane Goodwin Austin. These authors' tales shaped both Native American and Pilgrim women in the cultural imagination for generations.

Unfortunately, the lived experiences of the women in 1620 have only become more cloudy as docudramas and TV specials increasingly, and inaccurately, build on the legacy of those nineteenth-century texts to portray the "true" story of the *Mayflower* and the colonization of Patuxet/Plymouth.[4] The limited roles afforded to women in these stories matter because of the role mass media plays in creating shared public memories of the past. Alison Landsberg argues that film and TV make "particular memories more widely available, so that people who have no 'natural' claim to them might nevertheless incorporate them into their own archive of experience" (Landsberg, *Prosthetic Memory* 9). Landsberg persuasively argues that film and TV can create prosthetic memories, and that these memories can be useful when they make "memories and identities" accessible "to persons from radically different backgrounds" (11). On the surface, some adaptations of the *Mayflower* story appear to be engaged in making the cultural memory of Plymouth

---

[3] Few texts focus exclusively on the women of the *Mayflower*. Some that do are: Annie Russell Marble, *The Women Who Came on the Mayflower* (1920), Ethel J.R.C. Noyes, *The Women of the Mayflower and Women of Plymouth Colony* (1921), and, more recently, Sue Allen, *In the Shadow of Men: The Lives of Separatist Women* (2020). Caleb Johnson's *Mayflower History* website also includes a page on the "Women of Early Plymouth." For information on the limited role of women in the extant historical records, see María Carmen Gómez-Galisteo, "'But That I Be Not Tedious': Women's Role, Representation, and Lack of Relevance in *Of Plymouth Plantation* by William Bradford." Women are mentioned in many of the general histories of the *Mayflower*, at least to some degree. Dorothy May Bradford has garnered more attention from scholars due to the (debunked) rumors about her death; for an overview of those claims, see my piece in *Early American Literature*, "Remembering Dorothy May Bradford's Death and Reframing 'Depression' in Colonial New England."

[4] Annette Lamb defines a docudrama as "a film that adheres closely to known historical facts. Where possible, the dialogue includes the actual words spoken as recorded in primary source documents" (46).

more inclusive, as most recent versions do include more female characters, ostensibly to make the story accessible to a wider audience. The problem, however, is that most *Mayflower* adaptations seem determined to remember women in very limited ways. Female characters in such representations serve as ideal vessels for "based on a true story" adaptations about this period because they exist in the historical record and are, therefore "real," but so few concrete details are recorded about them that they can become whatever the filmmakers want them to be. As a result, characters based on these women are grounded in a form of authenticity, and yet the specific known details of their lives—courtships, marriages, friendships, deaths, and so on—are embellished to create narrative drama. Indigenous women are often completely excluded from the story—a version of the "vanishing Indian" trope—or are limited to extras silently populating the background of village scenes.

Analyzing female characters in *Mayflower* adaptations reveals the ideological assumptions—intentional or not—of filmmakers. There are many adaptations I could have chosen for my analysis, as myths and stereotypes are pervasive in film and TV adaptations of early American stories. The few women of the *Mayflower* who appear as named characters have been portrayed on screen primarily as stereotypes such as demure maidens, goodwives, and/or shrews.[5] In fact, some female characters, such as Mary Brewster, are portrayed as diametrically opposed stereotypes in competing versions of the story.[6] In this essay, I use female characters in National Geographic's mini-series *Saints & Strangers* (2015) as a case study of how Eurocentric stereotypes of women permeate adaptations of early America.

---

[5] Without fictional additions, the story of the *Mayflower* tends to be fairly bland and does not make great TV/film. To liven up the plot, early adaptations such as *The Plymouth Adventure* (MGM, 1952) or *Mayflower: The Pilgrims' Adventure* (CBS, 1979) prioritize interpersonal relationships, such as the alleged love triangle between John Alden, Priscilla Mullins, and Miles Standish popularized in Longfellow's poem *The Courtship of Miles Standish* (1858). These versions perpetuate a vision of Priscilla Mullins as "the damsel Priscilla, the loveliest maiden of Plymouth" and seem unable to imagine her as anything else (Longfellow ln 148). Similarly, multiple adaptations, including *The Plymouth Adventure* (1952), *Desperate Crossing: The Untold Story of the Mayflower* (History Channel 2006), and *Saints & Strangers* (National Geographic 2015), amplify the notion that Dorothy May Bradford suffered from melancholy and took her own life in December of 1620—a myth created by Austin in her short story "William Bradford's Love Life" (1869).

[6] Mary Brewster is presented as a nagging shrew in Encyclopedia Britannica Films' *The Pilgrims* (1955), but then is depicted as the unquestioningly loyal wife who would do anything—including lie to agents of the King—to protect her husband in *Mayflower: The Pilgrims' Adventure* (1979).

I selected *Saints & Strangers* because it is one of the most recent adaptations as of this writing and because the producers chose National Geographic specifically for its brand identity of accuracy and rigor. It matters that *Saints & Strangers* adopts a dubious mantle of authority while actually portraying many highly fictionalized characters and events because doing so obscures the ideological choices that shape the series.

The advertising campaign for the series, which largely focused on the ominous phrase "The Mayflower is Coming," went to great lengths to invoke authenticity, including the development of a full experiential component described by Brian Everett, VP of Creative Design for National Geographic Partners, as "a 1620s Pub recreation in NYC. The experience featured a custom menu from Chef April Bloomfield as well as activities & games from the time period" (Everett). The recreation of a 1620s era pub—an odd choice that further complicates the series' depiction of the "real" considering Plymouth did not have a pub in the period the show depicts—is the most extreme example of how *Saints & Strangers* as an entire production engages in what Hans Ulrich Gumbrecht calls "'the presentification of past worlds' orchestrated by 'techniques that produce the impression (or, rather, the illusion) that worlds of the past can become tangible again'" (qtd. in Landsberg, *Engaging* 9).[7] Additional art and promotional materials for the series used the taglines "The True Story" and "The Real Story of the First Thanksgiving" (Rebus; Everett). The official description of the series on the National Geographic YouTube trailer is a bit more nuanced, describing the series as "a story that goes beyond the familiar historical account of Thanksgiving, revealing the trials and tribulations of the settlers at Plymouth Plantation" (National Geographic). Further, as we will see, executive producers Grant Scharbo and Gina Matthews framed the series in promotional interviews as telling the story as accurately as possible.

The claims in the promotional materials that the series presents the "true" or "real" story incorrectly imply that there is a single true story that remains definitive across time and culture. Landsberg effectively cuts through such claims, reminding us that "filmic narratives are always to some extent shaped by the economic logic of the industry and the ideological pressures and concerns of their moment of creation. That film could somehow reveal the

---

[7] Landsberg clarifies that the use of presentification in historical film and TV projects "is not about locating the 'meaning' of historical objects but rather about 'mak[ing] us imagine how we would have related intellectually and with our bodies, to certain objects (rather than ask what those objects 'mean') if we had encountered them in their own historical everyday worlds'" (Landsberg, *Engaging* 9).

past in a transparent, unbiased manner—as opposed to creating a representation of it—is itself pure fantasy" (*Engaging* 2). Claims that *Saints & Strangers* portrays an inherently "true" or unbiased adaptation of *Mayflower* history conceals any liberties taken with the story and reinforces the often invisible power structures that enable a storyteller, regardless of the medium, to don the mantle of "truth-teller."

While it may be easy for viewers to recognize how the highly romanticized *Mayflower* films of the 1950s to the 1980s embellish the known facts, more recent iterations employ more sophisticated methods to depict ostensibly "authentic" stories. It can be especially difficult for viewers to parse truth from fiction when filmmakers intentionally, and incorrectly, suggest that their versions are historically accurate. Susan Bordo describes the increasing challenge of determining accuracy in docudramas as

> the post-Oliver Stone, postmodern problem: In our media-dominated, digitally enhanced era, people are arguably being culturally trained to have greater difficulty distinguishing between fact and fiction. If the created reality is vivid and convincing enough (whether a flawless, computer generated complexion or a spin on events), it carries authority; that's the way advertisers and politicians want it. The movies, which are often extremely attentive to historical details, creating a highly realistic texture for the scaffolding surrounding the actions of the characters, make it even harder for audiences to draw the line. (Bordo n.p.)

Even the titles can be confusing. *Desperate Crossing: The Untold Story of the Mayflower* (History Channel, 2006) was originally subtitled *The True Story of the Mayflower* before being revised to the *Untold* story (IMDB, "Desperate Crossing"). Presumably some of what the program claims was "untold" was excluded by earlier iterations because it conflicted with the claim to be "true." *Saints & Strangers* epitomizes these tensions, particularly in its portrayal of female characters.

Though the show claims to present a highly realistic version of the female characters in the Plymouth/Patuxet story, it ultimately conflates "accuracy" and "authenticity" with a vague notion that the show looks or feels true, the "texture" Bordo references.[8] By blurring accuracy and

---

[8] Kathryn Florence emphasizes the importance of "feeling true" as a marker of authenticity in heritage tourism as well, noting that visitors to Indiana's Feast of the Hunters' Moon and other historical re-enactment sites "come for the *feeling* of authenticity, not the stipulation of accuracy" (Florence 76; original emphasis).

authenticity—meaning correct in detail, factual, and/or genuine—with fictionalized elements for entertainment value, *Saints & Strangers* glosses the many plot elements based on speculation that comprise virtually all of the content involving female English and Native American characters. Authenticity in *Saints & Strangers* seems to be about getting the "spirit" of the story right, rather than presenting only the facts. Yet Dallen J. Timothy and Stephen W. Boyd remind us that authenticity, when it comes to historical re-enactment or adaptation, is "a subjective notion that varies from person to person depending on one's own social conditioning" (qtd. in Florence 75). The problem, then, is that the story's alleged spirit is not static; it changes based on who is telling the story and why.

Upon first viewing, *Saints & Strangers* certainly presents an aesthetic of accuracy, particularly in its sets and costumes.[9] The series prominently features Native people, who even speak "Western Abenaki, a dialect similar to what the pilgrims encountered when they arrived in America" (Landry). Reviewers such as Maureen Ryan commented favorably on the authenticity of "the sets and costumes" which "give a realistic idea of what the initial Pilgrim settlement was like" (Ryan). Upon closer examination, however, it becomes clear that the series' primary claim to accuracy is based on presenting a darker, more *Game of Thrones*-esque tale of the founding of Plymouth colony than on portraying an historically accurate plot. Googling the show brings up many reviews highlighting the program as "gritty," "grim," "thorny," "raw," "unsentimental," and "real" (Bauder, Berkowitz, Rivera, and Stuever). Many reviewers observe that the show is trying to tell "the Pilgrim story in a grim, more accurate way" (Stuever) or that it attempts to show "a side of Thanksgiving that isn't taught in schools or known by most Americans" (Berkowitz). Most reviewers seemed to agree that the show succeeded in the "grim" and "gritty" categories, but they were far more mixed or negative in their assessment of the show's historical accuracy.

---

[9] Gone are the most obvious inaccuracies such as using a printing press on the *Mayflower* to save the ship during a storm (*Plymouth Adventure*); gone is the overly romanticized love triangle between Priscilla Mullins, John Alden, and Captain Myles Standish (*Mayflower: The Pilgrims' Adventure*); and gone are the more glaring anachronisms such as calling the Pilgrims "Bible-thumpers" (*Mayflower: The Pilgrims' Adventure*). The *Oxford English Dictionary* dates the term "Bible-thumper" to 1923 ("Bible-thumper").

And yet, accuracy was, ostensibly, one of the producers' primary goals for the program.[10] The filmmakers cultivated the series' ethos in large part by relying on primary sources and by partnering with National Geographic. According to David Bauder's review,

> [Grant] Scharbo and his wife, Gina Matthews, were making the project as a short-run series for NBC when that network backed out a year ago [2014]. They made a deal with National Geographic, *an affiliation the producers believe will enhance the film's legitimacy*. National Geographic pressed for historical accuracy, even hiring an expert to teach actors the Abenaki language used in the film. (Bauder; emphasis added)

Series writer Seth Fisher reiterated the relationship between the series' alleged accuracy and its home at National Geographic, telling Indie Wire, "National Geographic is the perfect place—a place that values accuracy and wants to set the precedent for getting it right. Ultimately, we always sided with history, and what we see on screen is very well-documented and supported" (qtd. in Berkowitz). National Geographic is a well-established brand known for its high-quality educational content; schools regularly show National Geographic programs, and the company's website includes lesson plans and student activities related to the *Mayflower* story. The ethos of National Geographic enabled the producers and writers to claim the mantle of authentic truth-teller while glossing the series' many liberties or inaccuracies, particularly those relating to female characters.

In order to include prominent female characters in the *Mayflower* story at all, *Saints & Strangers* follows earlier adaptations in speculatively filling the gaps left in documents such as *Mourt's Relation* (1622), *Good News From New England* (1624), and "Of Plymouth Plantation" (completed 1651).

---

[10] Not everyone involved in the production believed that they were telling a true story. In an interview with GQ, Vincent Kartheiser, who plays William Bradford, acknowledges the challenges of dramatizing Dorothy May Bradford's life, in particular, stating: "But you've got to understand, there will be some dramatic shifts, there always will be ... Because all we can do is link the dots. There are going to be spaces where we don't really know—like whether my wife jumped, or slipped off the edge. We don't know, so we're going to have to make a choice. You can leave it vague, but at a certain point, you're going to have to connect those dots. As an actor, as an entertainer, you have to say it's entertainment first and foremost" (qtd. in Rivera). Kartheiser might believe he is creating "entertainment first and foremost," but that intention may not be clear to all viewers considering the larger discourse around, and branding of, the series.

Part of the issue with this adaptation is one of historiography, as the production team's research seems to have clouded rather than clarified the narrative. According to executive producer Grant Scharbo, "[o]ur goal was to tell the true story ... The problem is that the story has been sanitized to such a degree that no one knows the real story" (qtd. in Bauder). Scharbo's apparent belief in the existence of a "real story"—and, paradoxically, also in its inaccessibility—is illuminating, as is his implicit definition of "realness." In part, he is stating a fact: there is no inclusive, complete history of Plymouth that satisfies modern curiosity and sensibilities. More importantly, Scharbo's claim that "no one knows the real story," or that unnamed people or forces have sanitized the history until it is incomprehensible contradicts the show's own marketing. Yet instead of engaging deeply with modern historiography to critically examine gaps in the primary record, to untangle competing accounts about Plymouth/Patuxet, or to complicate the notion of a single truth, Scharbo instead conflates "unsanitized" with the "real story." One wonders what he even means by "sanitized." Perhaps he is referring to how neat and clean the Pilgrims are portrayed in earlier iterations. Perhaps he is alluding to how many adaptations whitewash some of the more problematic actions taken by the Pilgrims, including looting graves and stealing corn from Wampanoag homes. Perhaps he means "romanticized," which carries a very different connotation than "sanitized." While Scharbo's meaning, unfortunately, is unclear, the reality is that "unsanitized" does not necessarily mean historically correct.

Despite Scharbo's and Fisher's claims that the series is telling the previously unknowable real tale of the Pilgrims, in fact, the *Saints & Strangers* production team joins other filmmakers in using a philosophy best articulated by Ebony Elizabeth Thomas: "[F]or the purposes of storytelling, it is less important that myths are true than that they feel true" (Thomas 74). *Saints & Strangers* may feel truer than previous adaptations to a twenty-first-century, mainstream American audience in part because it is "unsanitized." The characters get dirty. Their behavior is sometimes uncouth. Women are harassed. Native American homes are looted. The camera filters cast the world as grim and dim. But the series' aesthetic of "unsanitized" history does not mean the story in *Saints & Strangers* is factual, even if viewers perceive the series as looking or feeling "realer" than earlier versions. The problem with relying on feelings over facts is that feelings are subjective. Different stories feel real to different people at different times.

Debates about the series feeling accurate versus being accurate followed the production from the start. Alysa Landry published an article in *Indian Country Today* in December 2015 titled "How 'Saints & Strangers'

Got it Wrong: A Wampanoag Primer" that details inaccuracies with the production from a Native American perspective. Landry includes a quote from Jessie Little Doe Baird (Mashpee Wampanoag), "cofounder of the Wôpanâak Language Reclamation Project and vice chair of the Mashpee Wampanoag Tribe," who walked away from a consulting role on the project in part because of the stereotypical and culturally inaccurate portrayals of Native people. Little Doe Baird reflected of the series, "[w]hen we talk about relationships, especially cross-cultural and race relations, it really is important to get things right ... When you dramatize a set of events, it's one thing. But to change the facts is dangerous because people watching it take it as fact" (qtd. in Landry). Of the many cultural and linguistic inaccuracies in the show, Linda Coombs (Wampanoag Tribe of Gay Head Aquinnah), director of the Aquinnah Wampanoag Cultural Center, who also walked away from the project, directly rebuts the executive producers' claim that "no one really knows the true story" of Plymouth, arguing, "[i]t's completely irresponsible telling of history ... This is one of the most well-documented parts of history, but it is distorted [in *Saints & Strangers*] for the purposes of sensationalism" (qtd in Landry).

After receiving these criticisms, National Geographic doubled down. The company maintained that the series is accurate, without clarifying the producers' ideological framework or defining how they measure the "truth" or "accuracy" of the story. Nor did National Geographic's spokesperson recognize the power dynamics at play between Native American critics and the creators of the series—something Landry identifies. Landry writes:

> By criticizing National Geographic, the Wampanoag communities are taking on a global organization that prides itself on "integrity, accuracy and excellence." In a statement responding to the criticism, Christopher Albert, senior vice president of communications and talent worldwide for Nat Geo, defended the film. "National Geographic Channel is very proud of 'Saints & Strangers' and *the great lengths our producers went to portray the time period as accurately as possible.*" (Qtd in Landry; emphasis added)

Albert's comments illuminate who gets to decide if an adaptation is accurate. In this case, that power lies not with the four Wampanoag communities, or Wampanoag experts, but with Scharbo, Matthews, Fisher, and National Geographic. Albert and National Geographic reinforce the claim that the series is accurate without addressing issues such as the show's use of stereotypes in its portrayal of Native American and female characters.

Saints & Strangers consistently imagines Wampanoag and English women in predictable and stereotypical ways, primarily as love interests, wives, and mothers. All of the women are depicted either as subservient to men or as almost exclusively focused on child-rearing or household labor. The plots of the few unmarried women in the story—mainly Priscilla Mullins (Meganne Young) and Elizabeth Tilley (Jessica Sutton)—center on their respective courtships and end once they couple with an appropriate male love interest. Other English women with speaking roles, such as Dorothy May Bradford (Anna Camp) and Elizabeth Hopkins (Natascha McElhone), largely converse on topics revolving around their identities as wives and mothers. Dorothy May Bradford speaks the majority of her lines to her husband William, for example, and the content consists of traditional "women's concerns." Approximately fifty percent of her dialogue is about her son John and her distress over leaving him in Europe, about Elizabeth Hopkins's childbirth and Dorothy's role in aiding Elizabeth's labor, and/or about caring for children on the ship. By focusing on a few reductive stereotypes for female characters, *Saints & Strangers* flattens them to the point where the women could be interchangeable. As such, their depiction is not an "authentic" representation of each woman's lived experience; rather, it limits them to a few specific tasks that fall under the label of "women's work" and fills in the unknowns of their personal relationships with patriarchal assumptions of female subservience. By suggesting that the series is "true" through the brand affiliation with National Geographic, the show obscures these patriarchal assumptions, presenting them not as one way to view the story, but as the most accurate version of the story.

The flat depiction of women becomes even more apparent with the addition of Kaya (Bianca Simone Mannie), a Pokanoket Wampanoag woman loosely based on the wife of Hobbamock (Tatanka Means), a Pokanoket *pniese* who lived among the English for a time. Hobbamock's wife is mentioned in both Edward Winslow's *Good News From New England* and William Bradford's "Of Plymouth Plantation," though neither records her name (Winslow 64; Bradford 98–9).[11] Kaya's presence

---

[11] It is unclear why they chose the name Kaya. She is the only female Indigenous character with a name in the series; the other female Native American characters are credited simply as "Massasoit's 1st wife" (Amrain Ismail-Essop) and "Massasoit's 2nd wife" (Iman Isaacs), and "Old Woman" (Wilma Pelly) (IMDB "Saints & Strangers").

in the series is a departure from previous adaptations, in which Wampanoag women almost always work silently in the background. What initially seems like a revelatory choice—to raise a Wampanoag woman to prominence—is undermined by the fact that Kaya's character is underdeveloped and appears to be included *pro forma* for the sake of diversity and representation.

The idea that a version of the *Mayflower* story must be more inclusive of marginalized perspectives and characters is not a neutral choice. The diverse representation in *Saints & Strangers* reflects current ideologies about how to adapt history, a position that is widely understood, if not always appreciated, by the viewership. A quick skim of the comments on the series' trailer on YouTube, for instance, shows anxiety and sometimes anger about the inclusion and portrayal of Native people on the show. One commenter succinctly summarizes the issue: "Can you people please shut up? It's National Geographic in 2015, they're obviously going to show the story from both [N]ative and European perspectives" (KonguZya). That a version of the *Mayflower* story must include Native American perspectives is not, of course, "obvious." The commenter's assertion reflects the twenty-first-century progressive expectation that historical adaptations tell more than just white, male stories. One way to achieve greater representation is by including a female Native American character in a speaking role, so the filmmakers created Kaya. Unfortunately, her character consists of many stereotypes. Her arc, such as it is, is one of replacing her initial hostility toward the interlopers with a trite sense that the Wampanoag and English could get along if they just got to know each other.

To that end, Kaya and Elizabeth Hopkins develop an uneasy acquaintance in the second episode of *Saints & Strangers*, a relationship that lets the filmmakers promote a theme of acceptance and cross-cultural bonding based on their vision of universal female experiences rooted in a European patriarchal worldview. Even though the women share an initial skepticism toward each other and view the other as a potential threat to their respective families and cultures, in TV odd-couple fashion, they come to find that they have more in common than they imagined. The problem is that there is a significant lack of imagination on the part of the series when it comes to depicting how, exactly, these two women might have bonded. Essentially, it comes down to husbands/patriarchy, kids, and cooking. They are wives and mothers who complete domestic tasks; that is the full extent of the bond this program imagines for women across divides of race, class, religion, and geography.

Food preparation serves as the first site of cross-cultural bonding. In one scene, Elizabeth comes across Kaya, who is singing while preparing a meal. Kaya ceases her song as Elizabeth approaches.

> E. Hopkins: You don't have to stop singing. You have a lovely voice. Please sing. [pause] You don't like being here. You, or rather you don't, you don't like us being here. Hey, I don't like us being here either. I only came because my husband has something to prove in this world. He promises that all our troubles are worth enduring. I suspect you've been told similar tales.
> Kaya: [Speaking Abenaki] Why do you bother? We do not understand each other. My husband wishes me to be friends with you but I have nothing to say. I'm only here because this is where Massasoit has placed him. I go where he goes, I live where he lives, I do as he wishes. So here we are. Your words fall on my ears empty of meaning, but still ... I answer you. (Episode 2, 13:02–15:20)[12]

At this point, Kaya looks confused at her own participation in this conversation. Though presented as a dialogue, communication is not actually occurring, in that neither woman understands the other. Only Kaya acknowledges this reality when she says: "why do you bother? We do not understand each other." In the scene, she cannot understand her own motivation for speaking to Elizabeth because this conversation exists not for the characters but for the benefit of the viewers, the only people with access to subtitles who can comprehend their discourse in full.

The dynamic between the two women begins to soften when Elizabeth asks what food Kaya is preparing. Their body language, facial expressions, and vocal tone become more comfortable as they start to build a shared vocabulary:

> E. Hopkins: What are you, what are you working at? What, um, what is it?
> Kaya: Nasaump.
> E. Hopkins: Nasa ... nasaump?
> Kaya: Nasaump.

---

[12] Note on transcriptions: I transcribed the dialogue from all of these programs myself and consulted subtitles and online transcripts where possible or appropriate. Insertions in brackets describing actions, settings, or tone are entirely mine, and provide context for each scene or line of dialogue.

E. Hopkins: Is it food? Food.
Kaya: Food. Yes.
E. Hopkins: Yes? You know 'yes.' [very surprised] That's good!
Kaya: [Chuckles]
E. Hopkins: Nasaump. Food. Yes.
Kaya: Yes. (episode 2, 13:02–15:20)

When they try to communicate and learn a few words, their scowls and tense facial expressions transform, as they smile and laugh. Kaya's brief resistance to her husband's desire that she befriend the English thaws as they share a brief moment of humor and realize a shared commonality: food. The giggling toward the end of the conversation is the only way this scene resolves Kaya's hostility toward the English, which largely disappears after this scene.

Considering that this is an entirely fictionalized conversation, it is telling that the bond the filmmakers imagine between these two women is their subservience to their husbands and to male leaders—a shared experience that the viewer becomes privy to, but that neither woman in the scene fully understands. As I note above, the cultural and linguistic divide is only bridged for viewers with the luxury of subtitles. The resolution between the characters is therefore unconvincing, as Kaya and Elizabeth cannot understand that their desires are subordinate to their husbands' as they must "go where he goes," "live where he lives," and "do as he wishes." Patriarchy, according to *Saints & Strangers*, is universal and transcends the language barrier.

Indeed, the filmmakers seem unable to imagine Elizabeth and Kaya not having identical social roles or Wampanoag society not following the norms of European patriarchy. Puritan society "rested on a firm hierarchy of male authority," in which "English women's status was defined primarily by the men to whom they were bound, by birth to their father's rank, and by marriage, to their husband's" (Brooks 33, 34). In contrast, Algonquian women such as Kaya had very different social roles and duties, a reality that frequently confused Europeans. Wampanoag women engaged in different kinds of labor for their communities, including "cultivat[ing] communal fields," and were not, as were their English counterparts, "confined in [their] work to the domestic household and kitchen garden" (Brooks 34). Not only did Algonquian communities including the Wampanoag incorporate a greater variety of social roles for women, they did not subscribe to the English concept of coverture, meaning "the common law idea that during marriage a husband's authority and legal identity covered his wife's"

(Stretton and Kesselring 3). Algonquian women had rights and authorities independent of their marriage status (Brooks 43).

By not seriously engaging with how Kaya's life and values were different from Elizabeth's, *Saints & Strangers* is not telling the "true" story. Instead, it is participating in a long history of "underplaying" and "denying" the crucial role of women among the *Ninnimissinuok* (Bragdon 50). The filmmakers' decision to deny the series' ideological framework, particularly around its vision of a universal female experience, masks the many ways the show perpetuates a Eurocentric narrative that erases the lives and cultures of Native American women.

The series only once offers a brief glimpse of the alternative social roles available to Algonquian women, later in episode 2 when Kaya takes on a diplomatic mission to Massasoit. I say brief because the show quickly undermines her agency by reframing her actions to better fit a Eurocentric understanding of women's roles. The scene comes as the Englishmen start to worry about Tisquantum/Squanto's trustworthiness (Kalani Queypo). In the series, as Kaya's son, Wematin (Nahum Hughes), gains fluency in English, he starts to reveal inaccuracies in Squanto's translations. Wematin's alternative translations suggest that Squanto may be manipulating all parties for his own advantage. Unsure of what to do—and aware of their acute dependence on Squanto's knowledge—William Bradford (Vincent Kartheiser), Stephen Hopkins (Ray Stevenson), and the other male leaders of Plymouth decide to send Kaya to see if Massasoit (Raoul Max Trujillo) remains their friend or if he has become an enemy as Squanto claims. After Kaya solemnly wishes her son farewell, Elizabeth Hopkins expresses concern for Kaya and Wematin as a fellow mother:

> W. Bradford: May your journey be a swift and safe one.
> E. Hopkins: How can you send a defenseless woman to do a man's work?
> W. Bradford: I beg your pardon?
> S. Hopkins: Hold your tongue, now. Now, she's off to confirm what is true and what is false ... Whether Massasoit is a friend or an enemy.
> E. Hopkins: And what if he's an enemy? What, does he let her wander back to live amongst the English villains? Or does he burn her alive, leaving her husband captive and her poor boy an orphan?
> S. Hopkins: That's enough!
> E. Hopkins: [To Kaya] I will watch over Wematin for you. He will be safe with me. I swear it. (Episode 2, 43:42–44:28)

Even though Kaya's character still cannot speak or understand much English, after Elizabeth declares her intention to protect Wematin, Kaya embraces her, placing their foreheads together to convey mutual understanding. The two women seem to bond, mother to mother, over a desire to protect their children—a desire that overcomes the limitations of language.

Kaya's journey to see Massasoit highlights a prominent, historically documented, and oft-overlooked action by a Native American woman in 1622.[13] However, the significance of her role is undermined by the fact that Elizabeth calls out her mission as "men's work" that is inappropriate, if not dangerous, for a "defenseless" woman. The fictional addition of Elizabeth's and Kaya's bond over their children emphasizes Kaya's importance not as a leader but as a mother, a choice that forecloses an interesting possibility: the real-life woman Kaya is based on could have been a type of diplomat. If the filmmakers had wanted to seriously consider Kaya as a leader, they could have drawn on the history of female *sachems* in New England. According to Lisa Brooks,

> in Algonquian communities and languages, the title "*saunk-skwa*" was commonly applied to women leaders like Warrabitta and Weetamoo, as equals to their male relations. They were the "rock women" on whom entire communities relied. These titles contain the most important role that *sôgemak* and *sôgeskwak* played. They were not ruling "kings" and "queens," but rather ambassadors, "hard-bodied" diplomats who traveled to other nations, carried their community's deliberate decisions, communicated effectively and persuasively with other leaders, and traveled swiftly to return the wider deliberations home. (34)

Considering the scene is already incorporating fictional elements, the filmmakers could have used this moment as an opportunity to explore the cultural differences between Kaya and Elizabeth by recognizing the valuable role women played as equals in Algonquian society. Instead of exploring how "women's work among the Ninnimissinuok profoundly shaped the social relations, political structure, and ideology of their societies," this scene diminishes Kaya, limiting her agency within a Eurocentric, patriarchal vision (Bragdon 51). The danger to her character is not that the mission is risky for a diplomat, but that she might not return to her son.

---

[13] The scene builds on a historically documented experience, portraying both the English's and Wampanoag's growing suspicion of Tisquantum, as well as Hobbamock's unnamed wife's reconnaissance mission to Massasoit (see Winslow 64; Bradford 98–9).

Her value, then, is in her role as Wematin's mother, not in her role as an emissary to Massasoit.

While including a female Native American character appears progressive, closer examination suggests that Kaya exists for the sake of representation and not to authentically represent the experience of Hobbamock's wife. The show settles for surface-level claims of a universal female experience that relies on essentialized notions of wife and motherhood rather than engaging in a deep and authentic exploration of Kaya's and Elizabeth's cultures and gender roles. Doing so allows the program to quickly move past the fear and anxiety each feels toward the other. The alleged bond between Kaya and Elizabeth ultimately whitewashes the imperialist power dynamics at play in Plymouth. It also whitewashes the Eurocentric framework that shapes the entire series. The filmmakers' claims that they are telling the most accurate story possible obscures this imperialist lens, masking the ways in which the series perpetuates the erasure of Native cultures.

Rather than telling a true, unsanitized version of the *Mayflower* and the colonization of Patuxet, *Saints & Strangers* is participating in a long tradition of telling a revisionist origin story of the English colonies in New England. Like George Bancroft and other historians of the early Republican period, writers of the so-called American literary Renaissance, including Hawthorne, Longfellow, and Austin, created American origin stories that served particular political and ideological agendas. Thomas King (Cherokee) notes the cultural potency of origin stories, observing that "within creation stories are relationships that help to define the nature of the universe and how cultures understand the world in which they exist" (King 10). Origin stories of the United States are potent, ideologically inflected stories. Many nineteenth-century texts "telling the story of America" established myths to validate the new American nation state (Lepore 9). Bancroft's efforts to date the "founding of America" to Columbus's voyage in 1492, for example, served to provide the young United States with a far longer and more impressive history, effectively making America, on paper, "three centuries older than it was" (Lepore 10).

Similarly, Pilgrim stories became immensely popular in the nineteenth century, particularly in the post-Civil War colonial revival that began in the 1870s (Gyure). In the nineteenth century, Pilgrims became a focus for American origin stories and myth making. As Kelly Wisecup argues, editors in the nineteenth century reimagined Edward Winslow's *Good News from New England* (1624) "as a founding text of the American nation and its history. In this way, they presented the Plimoth (*sic*) colonists as proto-U.S. Americans, despite the fact that this identity was unimaginable to the colonists" (14). The *Mayflower Compact* (1620), signed in the wake of the *Mayflower*'s arrival far north of their intended destination in the Virginia colony, was later reimagined as a proto-Constitution, thereby providing an extended pedigree not only to the nation, but to the political ideology that formed the basis of American government.[14]

Saints & Strangers, like these earlier iterations of the *Mayflower*'s journey, is not telling the true story. Instead, it is another version of the narrative that reflects the ideological views—and limitations—of its creators. Analyzing how the series portrays female characters is one way to parse the filmmakers' ideology. In this case, the series' goals include creating a dark, dirty, despairing setting that they believe will feel "real" to twenty-first-century viewers who have grown weary, if not suspicious, of the so-called "sanitized" version of the *Mayflower* story. The creators acknowledged the social pressure to include diverse perspectives and characters but ignored critiques from the very Native communities they sought to represent. The writers and producers also neglect to grapple with the power structure provided by Hollywood and National Geographic that enabled a set of largely white filmmakers to decide upon the "true" story. Viewers should be skeptical of any historical adaptation claiming the mantle of authenticity, particularly when it is so cagey about its own ideological framework, and so vague in its definition of what makes their version of the story the "real" story.

When adaptations such as *Saints & Strangers* rely on female stereotypes, they contribute to a larger erasure of genuine female experiences in American history—an erasure that is not limited to film and TV. Representation is not achieved by inserting generic female characters into pop culture adaptations, nor by whitewashing important cultural differences between Native American and English characters. To build on the argument of high school student Micaela Wells, the stories we tell in history curricula—and, I would add, in pop culture adaptations—"[reflect] our societal values" and by excluding women's lived experiences, these sources are "perpetuating ... the idea that women are comparatively worthless. Worse, it's sending the message to girls that their stories and accomplishments don't matter" (Wells). As my analysis of depictions of women in

---

[14] See for instance Encyclopedia Britannica Films' 1955 short film *The Pilgrims* (20:42–21:10). Francis J. Bremer provides a succinct summary of how the *Mayflower Compact* came to be seen as "a fundamental stepping-stone in the development of democratic processes in America" despite the fact that "[m]ost scholars have concluded that this document does not exemplify the criteria by which they determine what is or is not a constitution" ("Mayflower Compact").

Saints & Strangers shows, merely including underdeveloped female characters, whether English or Native American, in historical adaptations flattens them, reducing complex people, whole genders, and entire Indigenous Nations to stereotypes. Such portrayals create multiple layers of problems because stereotypes, by definition, are inaccurate. Substituting fake experiences as the "real story" implies that the historically documented real stories and real accomplishments of historically marginalized groups do not matter or cannot be recovered. What seems to matter most is that the stories *feel* true—at least to the storytellers.

Acknowledgments

Many thanks to Kirsten Iden Lindmark, Karen Sonnelitter, Abram Van Engen, Marion Rust, Joy A.J. Howard, Rebecca Harrison, and Patrick Erben for your support of this project and for providing feedback on drafts. Thank you also to Kari Halloway Miller, Donna D. Curtin, and Anne Mason for facilitating a virtual webinar for the Pilgrim Hall Museum and Plymouth Antiquarian Society featuring a selection from this essay. Thank you always to Sarah Symans and John Raymond for your indefatigable excellence with interlibrary loans, without which so much of my work would not be possible.

Works Cited

Allen, Sue. *In the Shadow of Men: The Lives of Separatist Women*. Edited by Caleb Johnson, DomTom Publishing, 2020.

Austin, Jane Goodwin. "William Bradford's Love Life." *Harper's New Monthly Magazine*, June 1, 1869, pp. 135–40.

Bauder, David. "TV Movie 'Saints & Strangers' Offers a Grittier Version of the First Thanksgiving." *The Orange County Register*, November 22, 2015, https://www.ocregister.com/2015/11/22/tv-movie-saints-strangers-offers-a-grittier-version-of-the-first-thanksgiving/ (last accessed November 11, 2024).

Berkowitz, Jeremy. "National Geographic's 'Saints and Strangers' Cast on Trying to Tell the Real Thanksgiving Story." *Indie Wire*, November 12, 2015, https://www.indiewire.com/2015/11/national-geographics-saints-and-strangers-cast-on-trying-to-tell-the-real-thanksgiving-story-54368/ (last accessed November 11, 2024).

"Bible-thumper, n., slang" *OED Online*, Oxford UP, December 2021, www.oed.com/view/Entry/18605 (last accessed November 11, 2024).

Bordo, Susan. "When Fictionalized Facts Matter." *The Chronicle of Higher Education*, May 6, 2012.

Bradford, William. *Of Plymouth Plantation, 1620–1647*. Edited by Samuel Eliot Morison. Alfred A. Knopf, 2016.

Bragdon, Kathleen J. *Native People of Southern New England, 1500–1650*. U of Oklahoma P, 1996.

Bremer, Francis J. "Mayflower Compact." *American Governance*, edited by Stephen Schechter, et al., vol. 3, Macmillan Reference USA, 2016, pp. 256–8.

Brooks, Lisa. *Our Beloved Kin: A New History of King Philip's War*. Yale UP, 2018.

Dearing, Stacey. "Remembering Dorothy May Bradford's Death and Reframing 'Depression' in Colonial New England." *Early American Literature*, vol. 56, no. 1 (2021), pp. 75–104.

Desperate Crossing: The Untold Story of the Mayflower. Directed by Lisa Quijano Wolfinger, starring Nicholas Asbury, Christopher Haas, and Keith Bartlett. The History Channel, 2006.

Encyclopedia Britannica Films. *The Pilgrims*. 1955. Produced by John Barnes, YouTube, October 25, 2021, https://www.youtube.com/watch?v=oI0AhHGrH9M&ab_channel=NealSehgal (last accessed December 22, 2021).

Everett, Brian. "Saints & Strangers." Brian Everett, https://brianeverett.tv/Saints-Strangers (last accessed November 11, 2024).

Florence, Kathryn. "At the Table or On the Menu at Indiana's Feast of the Hunters' Moon." *Public Memory, Race, and Heritage Tourism of Early America*, edited by Cathy Rex and Shevaun E. Watson. Routledge, 2022, pp. 68–85.

Gómez-Galisteo, María Carmen. "'But That I Be Not Tedious': Women's Role, Representation, and Lack of Relevance in *Of Plymouth Plantation* by William Bradford." *Clepsydra*, vol. 6 (2007), pp. 59–72.

Gyure, Dale Allen. "The Colonial Revival: A Review of the Literature." *Colonial Revival in America: Annotated Bibliography*, University of Virginia. 2003, http://colonialrevival.lib.virginia.edu/ (last accessed November 11, 2024).

IMDB. "Desperate Crossing – The True Story of the Mayflower." Internet Movie Database, 2022, https://www.imdb.com/title/tt0493146/ (last accessed November 11, 2024).

———. "Saints & Strangers Full Cast & Crew." Internet Movie Database, 2022, https://www.imdb.com/title/tt4705002/fullcredits/?ref_=tt_cl_sm (last accessed November 11, 2024).

Johnson, Caleb. "Women of Early Plymouth." Caleb Johnson's Mayflower History, 2020. http://mayflowerhistory.com/women (last accessed November 11, 2024).

King, Thomas. *The Truth About Stories: A Native Narrative*. U of Minnesota P, 2003.

KonguZya. Comment on "Saints & Strangers Trailer National Geographic." YouTube, 24 September 2015, https://www.youtube.com/watch?v=TdP8y916SHs (last accessed November 11, 2024).

Lamb, Annette. "Fact to Fiction: The Truth behind Movies Based on True Stories." *Teacher Librarian*, vol. 46, no. 5 (June 2019), pp. 46–52.

Landry, Alysa. "How 'Saints & Strangers' Got it Wrong: A Wampanoag Primer." *Indian Country Today*, September 13, 2018, https://ictnews.org/archive/how-saints-strangers-got-it-wrong-a-wampanoag-primer#:~:text=At%20another%20point%20in%20the,care%20of%20the%20lost%20child. (last accessed Noveber 11, 2024).

Landsberg, Alison. *Engaging the Past: Mass Culture and the Production of Historical Knowledge*. Columbia UP, 2015.

———. *Prosthetic Memory: The Transformation of American Remembrance in the Age of Mass Culture*. Columbia UP, 2004.

Lepore, Jill. *These Truths: A History of the United States*. W.W. Norton, 2018.

Longfellow, Henry Wadsworth. *The Courtship of Miles Standish*. Project Gutenberg, 2018, https://www.gutenberg.org/files/57417/57417-h/57417-h.htm (last accessed November 11, 2024).

Marble, Annie Russell. *The Women Who Came in the Mayflower*. The Pilgrim Press, 1920.

Mayflower: The Pilgrims' Adventure. Directed by George Schaefer. Starring Anthony Hopkins, Richard Crenna, and Jenny Agutter. CBS, Syzygy Productions, 1979.

National Geographic. "Saints & Strangers | National Geographic." YouTube, November 3, 2015, https://www.youtube.com/watch?v=ID2i6-LUl2I (last accessed November 11, 2024).

Noyes, Ethel J.R.C. *The Women of the Mayflower and Women of Plymouth Colony*. 1921. Gryphon Books, 1971. Hathi Trust, https://babel.hathitrust.org/cgi/pt?id=uva.x000474782&view=1up&seq=10&q1=dorothy (last accessed December 2, 2021).

Plymouth Adventure. Directed by Clarence Brown. Starring Spencer Tracy, Gene Tierney, Van Johnson and Leo Genn. Metro-Goldwyn-Mayer Studios, 1952.

Rebus, Dima. "'Saints & Strangers' National Geographic 2015." *Behance*, December 7, 2015, https://www.behance.net/gallery/31880733/Saints-Strangers-National-Geographic-I-2015 (last accessed November 11, 2024).

Rivera, Joshua. "Vincent Kartheiser Is Damn Near Unrecognizable in His First Big Post-Mad Men Role: In Which the First Thanksgiving Gets a Gritty Reboot." *GQ*, November 21, 2015, https://www.gq.com/story/vincent-kartheiser-first-thanksgiving (last accessed November 11, 2024).

Ryan, Maureen. "TV Review: 'Saints & Strangers.'" *Variety*, November 19, 2015, https://variety.com/2015/tv/reviews/saints-and-strangers-vincent-kartheiser-review-natgeo-1201638374/ (last accessed November 11, 2024).

Saints & Strangers. Directed by Paul A. Edwards and starring Anna Camp, Vincent Kartheiser, Ron Livingstone, and Kalani Queypo. National Geographic, November 2015.

Stretton, Tim, and Krista J. Kesselring. *Married Women and the Law: Coverture in England and the Common Law World*. McGill-Queen's UP, 2013.

Stuever, Hank. "In 'Saints & Strangers,' a Noble Attempt to Tell Thanksgiving's Grimmer Truths." *The Washington Post*, November 20, 2015, https://www.

washingtonpost.com/entertainment/tv/in-saints-and-strangers-a-noble-attempt-to-tell-thanksgivings-grimmer-truths/2015/11/20/116c36e0-8f31-11e5-baf4-bdf37355da0c_story.html (last accessed November 11, 2024).

The Pilgrims: A Documentary Film by Ric Burns. Directed by Ric Burns American Experience Films, 2015.

Thomas, Ebony Elizabeth. *The Dark Fantastic: Race and the Imagination from Harry Potter to the Hunger Games*. New York UP, 2019.

Wells, Micaela. "Opinion: In my Advanced High School History Class, It's as if Women Didn't Exist." *The Washington Post*, January 1, 2022, https://www.washingtonpost.com/opinions/2022/01/01/advanced-placement-history-textbook-women/ (last accessed November 11, 2024).

Winslow, Edward. *Good News From New England by Edward Winslow: A Scholarly Edition*. Edited by Kelly Wisecup. U of Massachusetts P, 2014.

Wisecup, Kelly. "Introduction." *Good News from New England by Edward Winslow: A Scholarly Edition*, edited by Kelly Wisecup. U of Massachusetts P, 2014, pp. 1–50.

5

"Check her for marks!": Teaching Bodily Consent and Autonomy through the Salem Witch Crisis Documents and Netflix's *Fear Street: 1666*

Danielle Cofer

It can be difficult to entice present-day college students to engage with early American texts as students often describe the language in such texts as dense, unfamiliar, or even the dreaded *boring*. In my teaching experience, I have encountered very few college students who are eager to close read the historical documents collected in Richard Godbeer's *The Salem Witch Hunt: A Brief History with Documents* (2018). While this text in particular contextualizes the various testimonies and examinations of women accused of witchcraft in seventeenth-century Salem, Massachusetts, students explicitly state that the reading is "boring," and they find it difficult to stay immersed in the texts due to the language and diction, as well as unfamiliar religious and historical references and allusions. Yet, these same students are also intrigued by contemporary depictions of seventeenth-century witches, such as those depicted in the third installment of Netflix's widely popular slasher trilogy series *Fear Street Part Three: 1666* (2021).[1] In spite of their enthusiasm for popular culture's take on the Salem witch trials of 1692, few college students dedicate as much fervor to reading the actual narratives presented in the historical documents from the event that I typically assign in American literature courses. In this chapter, I discuss the strategies I use in the classroom to invite students to challenge a powerful fear present in early America, a fear that remains ever-looming in our contemporary moment: the threat of bodily violation.

While I have used variations of this approach specifically in a special topics course focused on the Salem witch crisis, as well as in an upper-division

---

[1] Referred to as *Fear Street: 1666* throughout.

"American Literature before 1865" course, I share a number of practical strategies that can help educators broach difficult discussions on the subject of consent in the classroom to meet the needs for varying environments. Ultimately, teaching popular culture representations that refer back to the setting of early America alongside early American texts provides students with a specific framework, critical analytical tools, and the historical context necessary to situate and interrogate the complementary as well as contrasting ways bodily consent has been persistently problematized in American literature since, and before, the nation's inception. Analyzing the third installment of Netflix's *Fear Street: 1666* alongside Salem witch crisis documents creates new ways to identify the persistence of the problem of sexual assault and consent with roots we can trace back to the development of the nation. As such, this act of tracing connections also opens up tense, at times discomforting, yet productive conversations that we can collectively engage in as a classroom community in order to challenge the social and cultural climate of silence which persists around assault.

Dual Problems: Back Thenness and Discomfort

Students constitute a large segment of the TV-watching audience, and they are often well aware if not highly intrigued by depictions of seventeenth-century witches in contemporary TV and film media. This interest is reflected in the popularity and acclaim for the third installment of Netflix's widely popular new slasher trilogy series *Fear Street: 1666*, which focuses on a curse established in the fictional seventeenth-century town of Shadyside. Another Netflix hit series, *The Chilling Adventures of Sabrina*, is set in fictional Greendale in the twenty-first century, and it also heavily references and alludes to Salem of the 1690s. While early America is an alluring setting for popular TV series, in an early American literature survey course it can still be challenging to get students invested and engaged in looking at pieces of American literary production from the seventeenth-century, even when the students are English majors. As Russell Reising outlines in his account of pedagogical approaches to teaching early American literature, "the teacher of early American literature needs to make some complicated initial decisions" (259): in a periodized course covering some of the nation's earliest literature, should one focus on one central theme, take a genre-based approach, or center the discussion of the texts around gendered or ethnic relations during the time period? Or should one take a completely different approach? Reising provides several approaches educators ought to consider, ultimately offering a rationale for some of the reasons to "begin with an investigation of American Puritanism and then demonstrate some of its most important issues, ideas, themes, styles, and metaphors throughout the eighteenth-century and into the earliest decades of the nineteenth" (260). For Reising, issues and themes in colonial American literature such as rigid hierarchies and Puritan theology continued to be prevalent in the minds of writers into the nineteenth century (261). Furthermore, he highlights the necessity of contextualizing an important cultural tension, one that I have also found many students struggling with—distinguishing the difference, but also seeing parallels, between twenty-first-century American culture and early American culture shaped by a Puritan belief system.

I use the term "back thenness" to describe a default rhetorical strategy that I find students often refer to when they feel a disconnection between twenty-first-century American culture and early American culture. Students will sometimes pivot to describing motive, meaning, or even symbolism in early American documents as being alien, removed from their own lived experience due to its back thenness, as if the past is a sort of vacuous abyss completely detached and removed from our current moment. Texts, social issues, and cultural conflicts that predate the contemporary moment become relics of a past that is entirely severed from modern-day experience when relegated as such. One danger of such a strategy is that it inhibits critical thinking. Often, students see this strict separation as proof of teleological progress from back then to now. In order to break out of this reductive pattern, I guide students to use a comparative approach to see that the conflicts that we will interrogate throughout the class are ongoing social problems whose origins extend far into the colonial period of the nation. *Fear Street: 1666* has representations of early American women whose demands for consent—or whose consent comes in the form of queer coupling—lead them to suffer from violence. Thus, students begin to see that the early American period and our current moment are not two dramatically disparate realities.

In addition to comparing the cultural conditions in time periods, we also consider and compare "interpersonal pairings," as Reising refers to them, or relationships, which he describes as ensnared in "rigid hierarchies definitive of Puritan[ism]" (261). Understanding hierarchy requires students to compare the subject at the top of the hierarchy as opposed to the bottom. Throughout his course, Reising invites students to consider the ways that these Puritan hierarchies "recast all interpersonal pairings (husband and wife; parent and child; master and servant) as sublunar versions of the dominant God human relationship" (261). He also adds that "in a problematic extension of these hierarchies, Puritan beliefs commonly scorned intellectual and cultural ambition among women, frequently defining intellectual women as freaks or mentally ill" (261). Drawing on this categorization of intellectual women fits in quite nicely with an understanding of some of Salem's most problematized figures, such as Bridget Bishop, Sarah Good, and Tituba, among others.[2] Moreover, the Puritan gendered hierarchy, believed to be instituted by God, casts any women who challenged or occupied a role besides wife and mother as "servants of Satan" (Godbeer 12). The characters Sarah Fier and Hannah Miller in *Fear Street: 1666* complicate this hierarchical demonization by showing how patriarchal Puritanism sought to enforce violent power over women who demanded bodily autonomy, while also providing the imaginative possibility of an escape from those conditions in their story world.

By honing in on the fact that the gender dynamics and tensions regarding sex, sexuality, and consent in seventeenth-century Salem are operating in the gender and racial regimes that permeate twenty-first-century American culture, students are better able to map out and identify the ways in which intellectual and ambitious women are still scorned in U.S. society today. More generally, popular culture representations can also garner enthusiasm and excitement from students who initially struggle to invest themselves in texts; they can then find resonating relevance in that which they see as too far removed from their own time period and twenty-first-century interests.

Yet the important and extremely sensitive topic of the ways in which these women's bodies served as sites of violation and punishment due to their challenging of and non-conformity with Puritan gender roles can create discomfort for students. Critical conversations about bodily autonomy and the necessity for consent in the college classroom environment are just as important today as they have ever been; yet, discussions about bodily violation, coercion, sexual assault, or even using the word "rape" are often regarded as taboo. As a result, it becomes difficult to navigate conversations about these sensitive topics in a safe and welcoming manner

---

[2] Bridget Bishop was accused and tried for witchcraft, becoming the first person to be executed in the Salem witch crisis on June 10, 1692 (Breslaw, *Witches* 359). Sarah Good and Tituba were two of the first three women to be accused of practicing witchcraft in Salem. Good was hanged on July 29, 1692 (Games 176). Tituba, who was an enslaved woman, was accused of witchcraft and confessed to the charges. She eventually recanted her confession and was freed from prison when an unknown person paid her prison fees (Games 176).

that leads to productive understanding of the text and multiple viewpoints in the classroom setting. Jennifer Hirsch and Shamus Khan, in *Sexual Citizens: A Landmark Study of Sex, Power, and Assault on Campus*, argue that conversations about consent are critical and need to be ongoing. Many students understand and have knowledge of "the legal standard of affirmative consent," but they also hold a "cognitive dissonance, as they describe their own consent practices, which they know to be suboptimal" (116).[3] There is a discomfort in talking about consent in the classroom because these conversations often entail students acknowledging that they do not always thoroughly ask for consent, even if they understand the import and need to receive direct and clear consent. A lack of consent, and more specifically a lack of seeking affirmative consent, is a cultural problem that needs to be confronted in a safe manner. Close reading the Salem witch trial documents with a focus on identifying violations of consent and the consequences of a broader cultural acceptance of such allows an opportunity for us as educators and students, in the safe space of the classroom, to examine these early instances of violation so as to break the social curse of sexual assault as a sanctioned violation in our time and place. Throughout this essay, I discuss ways to examine the difficulty in understanding the language in original Salem documents as well as the difficulty in understanding gendered and sexualized violence and assault. The Salem witch crisis documents and the topic of bodily consent are two topics that require delicate, careful, and meticulous unpacking and confrontation, and they need to be handled with care.

The topic of consent is prevalent to varying degrees in campus discussions and usually couched within the ambiguous category of campus safety and security, or in the prevalent rhetoric of personal control and responsibility that permeates campus orientation primers on sexual assault. However, an approach that speaks to the larger cultural climate allows for the normalization of sexual violence, and the discounting of clear, affirmative consent is necessary to prevent assault from happening. Hirsch and Khan ask the question: "[W]hat if prevention work did more to address the social context that makes rape and other forms of sexual assault such a predictable element of campus life?" (xii). Using early American texts alongside popular culture references allows for more pointed examinations of how consent remains a long-standing problem in American culture, one that we

---

[3] Hirsch and Khan also engage in more nuanced discussions on how these "suboptimal" practices of consent seeking are also impacted in different ways by race, ethnicity, gender identity, sexuality, and other social identities. See pp. 115–35.

often avoid addressing because of the sensitivity of the subject. The early American literature classroom becomes an opportune space to show that the "social context" contributes to sexual assault.

How I Address Both Issues

Using the popularity and appeal of contemporary popular culture as a hook to get students enthusiastic about the general subject of persecuted witches, I also draw from Donna Freitas's book *Consent on Campus: A Manifesto* and Alison Gulley's *Teaching Rape in the Medieval Literature Classroom: Approaches to Difficult Texts* to develop a framework for some pedagogical approaches that address both problems—a lack of interest in the subject matter of early American Salem witchcraft trial documents and broaching difficult conversations about the threat of sexual violence. Freitas and Gulley both see the classroom as an opportunity to do more than encourage academic growth and development; educators are also "necessarily engaged in the cultivation of the whole person" (Gulley 8). Following Gulley, teaching college students about difficult topics like sexual assault connects the classroom sphere with the world outside the space of the college campus. Freitas further argues for the university's responsibility for engaging students to work for the "common good," which necessarily entails confronting the reality of sexual assault (149). The role of the literature classroom in this pursuit of the "common good" and enriching the "whole person" is that texts about sexual violence and consent can act as springboards "to a difficult conversation, offering us a means for talking about a subject without revealing ourselves directly in the process" (Freitas 151). Literature and media about witches and witchcraft allow this space and distance from the subject of consent since these figures are associated with the supernatural. Therefore, students can engage with sensitive topics regarding sex, sexuality, and violence pertinent today through the buffer of the past and of fictional stories—even if they draw on historical events.

Witchcraft remains a major topic of interest for students, and in the American consciousness more generally, as does our collective tendency to look for a scapegoat for larger societal problems. As such, I use this interest in women witches threatened by and subjected to violence as a means to consider the ways women's bodies are represented as not deserving protection or autonomy when they have been designated as scapegoats. To engage students with enthusiasm, I show a PowerPoint that introduces them to a host of well-known pop culture representations of Salem witches, such as the Sanderson sisters in the film *Hocus Pocus,* Sabrina Spellman from

The Chilling Adventures of Sabrina, Lily Colson in *Assassination Nation*, and Agatha Harkness in the Marvel series *Wandavision*. I also invite them to add their own examples of witches in TV and film, or I ask generally if there are other depictions of witches in media that they can list even if they fall outside the parameters of being defined as Salem witches specifically, inviting and encouraging participation from all. After gathering a list, I ask them to think critically of any connections they see between the large number of witches in popular televisual media. I project and ask them to answer leading questions such as: Why do you think there are so many recent films and TV series centered on witches and/or Salem right now? What do witches represent historically, but also in our current social and cultural climate? Why do popular audiences still find depictions of Salem and witches intriguing or enthralling nearly four hundred years later?

Using their responses to the priming activity, we create a cluster, free-word association of all witch content. I also tell them that we will watch the third installment of Netflix's *Fear Street: 1666* as a reward for getting through reading the primary documents. The promise of taking a break from reading historical documents to watch a contemporary series appears as less rigorous work for some students, but the work we do with the series is certainly robust and arguably more demanding as they are required to close read scenes as well as offer a comparative analysis between it and the Salem witch crisis documents. This approach allows me to assert two necessary expectations: the import of comparative work and the value of finding synergy between the historical documents and the televisual media.

Following the screening of *Fear Street: 1666*, we return to the text with a close read of Richard Godbeer's introduction, which contextualizes the religious, social, and cultural milieu of the period and outlines some of the most important tensions leading up to the Salem witch crisis. I contextualize the difference between spirituality and religious beliefs in seventeenth-century and twenty-first-century America, clarifying that Puritan belief dictated that every occurrence that happened in the natural world was believed to be a direct result of God's will. Puritans thus understood extraordinary events such as eclipses, comets, catastrophic fires, epidemics, or issues with childbirth to be imbued with supernatural significance.[4]

Furthermore, I situate the way Puritan examination of one's own place in the world could also be conceived of as a gendered ontological question.

---

[4] See chapter 2 of David D. Hall, *Worlds of Wonder, Days of Judgment: Popular Religious Belief in Early New England*.

While Puritan ministers did not blatantly assert that women were more inherently evil than men, Elizabeth Reis draws attention to the fact that colonists believed that women's bodies were physically weaker than men's bodies; thus, "the Devil could more frequently and successfully gain access to and possess women's souls" (Reis 110). In addition, the concern that women's bodies were more compliant vessels more easily susceptible to becoming "unfit and unworthy" was also not a belief held exclusively by Puritan men (38). Puritan women often internalized these beliefs and, in turn, accused other women of contamination and possession or attacked their own moral character as a result of their investment in the patriarchal Puritan views of womanhood.[5]

After discussing gender roles, we contextualize the texts within the tensions between Puritans and the Indigenous people whose land Puritans settled, leading to tensions between the two communities. I invite students to consider the significance of the fact that many of the accusers were recently orphaned as a result of "Indian" attacks. Dislocated and often pushed further south, many of the orphaned accusers found themselves newly integrating into the homes of their distant family members, some of whom had taken them in out of obligation and often expected these orphans to serve them as a form of repayment. Farmland and the resources associated with the farmland had also been greatly destroyed in "Indian" attacks; thus, many of the young accusers during the witchcraft trials were sharply aware of their vulnerable position as young women who had no dowry and bleak marriage prospects.[6] When we consider the ways that these orphans were burdened by the weight of displacement, resentment, and paralyzing fear, in addition to the subsequent guilt for indulging in these negative emotions, students can more easily consider the possible motives for witchcraft accusations. Tragic circumstances such as being orphaned or losing one's family and home thus aligned certain people in seventeenth-century Salem with a lower class that, when paired with being women, positioned them as social outcasts. This Puritan logic of class and gender makes it clear how powerful members of the community deployed these social casts to implicate the marginalized as witches, such as in the documents based on Sarah Good, one case study we critically analyze in class.

---

[5] Reis further offers that Puritan men were more capable of distinguishing a difference between their sinful deeds and a sense of their own identity apart from those deeds, whereas Puritan women often conflated the two categories.

[6] See Richard Godbeer, *The Salem Witch Hunt*, and Carol Karlsen, *Devil in the Shape of a Woman*.

Assignment #1: Sarah Good

Through Discussion Board posts, I ask students to express all initial reactions to the documents that they read in reference to Sarah Good before we have a chance to discuss them in class.[7] Anachronism is invited as I encourage "hot takes." Students are given instructions to use their positioning as twenty-first-century outside examiners to comment on anything they find odd or provocative, allowing them to feel less self-conscious about their understanding of the documents. This permission also leads to students revealing some of their initial biases as well. Students often comment on the fact that Good smokes a pipe, an activity they did not imagine women engaged in at that time. Other students hyper-focus on the cows and the strange descriptions of the livestock suddenly becoming bewitched whenever Sarah Good is not allowed to take up residence in someone's barn for the night. In Judge Hathorne's examination of Sarah Good, she is described as walking away and "muttering a psalm" (Godbeer 70); some students have pondered which psalm she might have muttered. Others have asked: Isn't it strange that she is accused of hopping on and off her horse three times? Why is that significant? Once I gather all of their reactions and preliminary observations, we collectively sift through their responses together in class and spend some time situating Sarah Good in her own time and place with more proper context.

As I project the historical documents on screen in class, I remind them of Sarah Good's story. She was the daughter of a once wealthy innkeeper.[8] After her father died, Sarah did not inherit his property or his wealth; rather, a man her mother married took over the fortune. Sarah married Daniel Poole who was formerly an indentured servant, but he died and left her his debt. Her second husband, William Good, could not maintain his work as a weaver and laborer, so both were left homeless and reliant on assistance from local residents for food and shelter. Sarah became known in town as a bitter outsider, beggar, a nuisance for her fellow neighbors, and someone who directly criticized her fellow townspeople for contributing to her declining fortunes (Godbeer 68). As the arrest warrant indicates,

---

[7] Sarah Good's importance within the history of the Salem witch trials lies in that she was one of the first to be accused of witchcraft, as a result of which she was subsequently found guilty and hanged.

[8] For this assignment, students look at the arrest warrant issued for Sarah Good, Salem magistrate John Hathorne's interrogation of Good, as well as the included testimonies levied against Good by various citizens in Salem, and Good's death warrant. See Godbeer, pp. 68–80.

Good was detained under "suspicion of witchcraft... thereby much injury done to... all of Salem Village" (qtd. in Godbeer 70). Her status as a poor, housing insecure woman whom the town viewed as an ingrate, and her constant need for charity and handouts from the community set her apart as a social pariah, making her an easy target for accusation.

We then return to close read some of the testimony used as evidence against Sarah Good to consider how power over who gets to control women's bodies comes to complicate understandings of consent and who is given the authority to give consent. For example, we examine William Good's testimony that "the night before his wife was examined, he saw a wart or teat a little below her right shoulder which he never saw before," and Samuel and Mary Abbey's claim that Sarah Good "hath behaved very crossly and maliciously to them and their children calling their children vile names and threatening them often" after they had kicked the Goods out of their home (Godbeer 73, 78).[9] The Abbeys also add that their cows were suddenly ailed, which led them to confirm Sarah Good was indeed a witch. Samuel Sibley, speaking the most directly to bodily violation, testified that Elizabeth Hubbard saw Sarah Good "upon the table... with all her naked breast and barefooted [and] barelegged," leading Hubbard to dismiss Good as a "nasty slut" and that she would "kill her" (Godbeer 80). Here, the notion of a woman willing to consent to the exposure of her own body marks her as a "slut," echoing the contemporary rhetoric of slut-shaming often hurled at women today who take control of and consent to their own sexual promiscuity or the exposure of their own bodies. Good's seeming willingness to display her nude body, whether true or not, signals her own control over her body, which is interpreted as antithetical to the proper femininity instituted by Puritan gender scripts. I press students to think about what these testimonies are telling us about the importance of women's bodies, how "goodness" or "badness" for women is assessed through an understanding of the exposed body and through an understanding of behavior and language.

I then ask several framing questions to have them close read the document: Why is William Good's description of what he claims to see on Sarah's body prioritized over Sarah Good's own testimony about her innocence? What does this say about a husband's control over his wife's body in Puritan society, and what does this say about women's rights or lack thereof to insist upon consent and bodily autonomy? Why is it important to note

---

[9] The Abbeys once allowed Sarah and William Good to live in their home.

that Sarah Good insults and poses a threat to children specifically? And, how do resources—and *lack* of resources, more specifically—factor into our understanding of Sarah Good as an embattled or embattling Puritan woman?[10] In using this assignment on the Sarah Good documents, students can build on our initial conversations to create a framework upon important themes of vulnerability, consent, and bodily autonomy in the Salem witch trial documents to draw parallels with our contemporary text.

Fear Street: 1666

In her book *Consent on Campus: A Manifesto*, Donna Freitas describes her use of scripts pulled from memoirs, novels, and sociological research in her college classrooms to present a diverse assemblage of stories that facilitate conversations about consent without forcing students to discuss topics that are personal (151). Along with these literary narratives, Freitas argues for the need to add to students' own "inherited" stories regarding sex and consent (153). While these can initially be done privately, students practice writing these scripts and tales about sex they have heard, seen, or experienced "to get a sense of the wider stories that influence student realities and experiences," creating a canon of these various scripts about social, cultural, and societal expectations regarding sexuality and relationships (Freitas 153). Using Freitas's approach and creating a classroom canon centered around consent allows students to see the Salem witch trial documents and *Fear Street: 1666* as narratives that at once reify heteronormative, patriarchal scripts around consent, while also opening an avenue to discuss how early American views of consent have contributed to the cultural climate of sexual violence and assault seen in places such as the college campus.

We reread the key passages from the trials of Sarah Good to posit how we are to make sense of key conflicts and testimonials, and how to better understand the implications of the accusations made against Good in her own place and time. Thus, what emerges from our closer examination of Sarah Good's documents are *new* questions often driven more by empathy, rather than disassociation, unfamiliarity, or even uncomfortable humor. Instead of thinking it was strange for a woman to smoke a pipe in early

---

[10] When discussing resources, one can consider topics such as housing insecurity and women, as well as how the cows Good is said to have cursed stand in for the ways that women do not have access to capital and other resources for self-sufficiency or commerce.

America, students begin to posit that she may have done so to stave off the cold since she was often without the protection of shelter. New questions develop: Why aren't there more documents that detail why she never inherited her father's wealth? Is there a record of that denial of property rights? Who documented these events, and what was their bias or interest in the outcome of Good's trial? Even with the number of documents available from her trials, Sarah Good remains shrouded in a great deal of obscurity. Even as we interrogate these documents and sift through the details about Good embedded within them, the complete picture of who she is often remains relatively ambiguous for students. The goal is for students to see how this control over what picture we have of Sarah Good also speaks to the lack of her consent over her own narrative, and, thus, how her life can be viewed. We are kept from knowing her full story due to the silences in the record.

To further build on this methodology of analysis, we repeat the same approach and lines of inquiry with the other accused women. We develop case studies of each of them collectively in order to build the canon of our own scripts of the Salem witch crisis documents. We resist coming to firm conclusions, but rather do an initial read-through of what is odd, intriguing, and perplexing in the same manner as we undertake our examination of Sarah Good. Notably, we also focus on Tituba with this same approach to further diversify and complicate the construction of our canon. Tituba stands apart from the other accused witches for critically important reasons. Her racial identity, and the uncertainty surrounding her race category, requires a different set of questions and interrogations. Tituba's difference can be framed and observed through her positionality as "court records consistently refer to Tituba, and her husband, John, as ethnically Indian" and as a servant brought from Barbados to Salem by Samuel Parris (Ray 197, 33). Moreover, the development of the American cultural imaginary regarding the Salem witch crisis has further obfuscated Tituba's origins, with later writers changing her racial identity from "Indian to half-Indian, half African American, to, in Arthur Miller's play *The Crucible*, fully African American" (Ray 33).

I invite students to make general observations about what they find to be most compelling about Tituba's documents. Once this is done, they are then asked to consider the ways Tituba depicts different aspects of embodiment, especially regarding her subject position and how it is similar to and different from Sarah Good. In the questioning in her first examination, Jonathan Corwin records that Tituba is asked if she ever "see[s] something appear in some shape," to which she replies that she has "never see[n] anything" (Godbeer 83). After more intense scrutiny, though, Corwin again asks for Tituba to deliver up a description of the physical form that the Devil takes. Tituba relents after again being asked, "What appearance, or how doth he appear when he hurts them? With what shape or what is he like that hurts them?", to which Tituba delivers, "Like a man, I think" (Godbeer 83). Students are struck by Tituba's initial resistance to describe seeing anything whatsoever, and her eventual statement which is followed by "I think," which indicates to many that Tituba would be considered what we would now call a coerced witness. Her answers reflect forced consent to a narrative that she believes will sate Corwin's interrogation. Her answer followed by this qualifier of believing but not necessarily making a declarative proclamation resonates with the ways that consent is sometimes forced or coerced, given only to evade an uncomfortable conversation or worse repercussions that come with denial.

I ask students to apply pressure to the fact that Tituba eventually identifies a man as the embodied form that is in charge of the bewitching. While she does describe other women who work on behalf of this man, why is it significant to consider that Tituba makes it clear that the agent in control is a man? As such, we consider what Tituba's documents reveal to us about hierarchies and how they relate to gender and power in early America. She goes on to describe other physical likenesses of this man such as "like a hog, sometimes like a great black dog" (Godbeer 84). Furthermore, Tituba's interrogation includes descriptions of other animals such as a yellow bird and cats, but repeatedly she affirms that "the man" is the agent in control who commands her and others to commit actions: "The man sends the cats to me and bids me pinch them" (Godbeer 85). As scholars note, Tituba's testimonies are often described as the most inventive with fanciful and creative descriptions, twists, and narrative turns.[11] I ask students to take stock of the moments where Tituba's storytelling is most compelling. Another moment that stands out to students typically is the moment when Tituba describes going to Mr. Putnam's. Corwin asks her, "Where did you go?", to which she replies, "Up to Mr. Putnam's" (Godbeer 85). When he follows up with the question, "Who made you go?" Tituba replies, "A man that is

---

[11] See Elaine Breslaw, *Tituba, Reluctant Witch of Salem: Devilish Indians and Puritan Fantasies*, which argues that Tituba used Puritan fears in her confession to weave a tale that allowed her life to be spared (154). Mary Beth Norton shows how Tituba's creative description of the devil and book influenced the confessions and accusations of others involved in the trials (52). Maryse Condé's novel *I, Tituba, Black Witch of Salem* (1994) is an example of a writer being inspired by Tituba's inventive testimony.

very strong and these two women, Good and Osborne, but I am sorry" (Godbeer 85). Later in her testimony Corwin asks, "Who tells you so?" She replies, "The man, Good, and Osborne's wife" (Godbeer 85–6). Again, this strikes students as particularly memorable because it reifies a hierarchy where a "strong" man who remains unidentified is in charge, but it can also indicate Tituba's understanding that she must name someone. Attributing her actions to her submission to a patriarchal figure serves to elide her from being seen as the one consenting to the charges she is facing. This avoidance of claiming personal agency acts as a mitigating factor that she has no control over, which is especially critical given her racial identity, which makes her more vulnerable. Thus, she divulges the names of Good and Osborne, albeit reluctantly and even apologetically, when she determines that accusing an ambiguous, unnamed powerful man will not suffice.

In her second examination by Jonathan Corwin, Tituba clarifies that the man who came to her told her that he was God and that she must "serve him for six years and he would give [her] many fine things" (Godbeer 87). There are breakthrough moments of resistance, though, too, which I invite students to wrestle with. For example, when Tituba says, "I told him I could not believe him God. I told him I [would] ask my master and would have gone up, but he stopped me and would not let me" (Godbeer 88). Through this retort, I invite students to connect Tituba's moment of resistance in her interrogation process with the powerful acknowledgment of her own intellectual ability and discernment ("I told him I could not believe him God"). Furthermore, this resistance is tempered by her compliance ("I told him I [would] ask my master"), showing Tituba's relegating of consent to her master, playing into racial hierarchies so that she is not one who is in control of her body, where consenting would ostracize her and lead her to a violent end. We consider to what extent we believe Tituba's compliance is performative or sincere based on the rest of the text, but it opens up an intriguing dialogue about agency. Corwin asks, "What did he say to you when you made your mark?" (Godbeer 90). Tituba replies, "serve me, and always serve me" (Godbeer 90). Thus, I ask the question, what does Tituba's testimony tell us about her attitude toward servitude? How is she aligning her "master" in many ways with the devil? How does Tituba elide clear consent as a protective mechanism, and what does this say about women's control over their bodies, especially women of color? I also invite broader, further conclusions about Tituba's description of "the man with the two women." As such, examination of Tituba's testimony allows students to understand the concept of consent more broadly. Consent does not just apply to questions and concerns regarding the body, as is demonstrated in our examination of the Sarah Good documents. Consent can and should also be interrogated when we see individuals being coerced into consenting to a pre-scripted narrative.

Assignment #2: The Viewing

As a follow-up to the close reading of the Salem witch crisis documents, students watch Netflix's *Fear Street: 1666* independently. I let them know that it is the third installment of the series and, while they are encouraged to watch the other two films, they are only responsible for the material in the third installment. For students who do not watch all three, I provide a brief context of the entire series to situate the third installment; this way they are not alienated by being thrust into the final chapter with no grounding in the overall arc of the narrative.

The *Fear Street* film trilogy starts with Part 1, which is set in 1994. A group of teenagers begin to uncover the history of terrifying events that have haunted their town, Shadyside, for generations. As each installment unfolds, the teenagers begin to understand that all of the events plaguing their community are connected. In order to avoid becoming targets themselves and to prevent future generations from suffering, they must jump back into history to address the conflict and remove the curse. In a sense, the film series presents teenagers with the opportunity to rescript their own past to pave the way for a more fair and benevolent future. *Fear Street* moves the action to 1978 in Part 2 and concludes with Part 3 in 1666, indicating that there is a direct connection that can be traced between our current moment and the conflict rooted in the construction of early America in the 1600s.

The main framework I want students to focus on when we look at *Fear Street: 1666* is the shift from a twentieth-century setting (1994) to an early American setting (1666). We also briefly discuss that director Leigh Janiak along with screenplay writer Kate Trefry has made some interesting departures from the narrative expectations set forth in R.L. Stine's original *Fear Street* book series, which the film trilogy is loosely based on. Janiak presents the audience with complex characters, platonic as well as queer relationships, and characters who build social networks in order to resolve conflict by working together. The film version stands in contrast to some of the problematic dynamics in Stine's book series, which frequently pitted girls against one another—often for the sake of garnering validation from boys. Janiak's depiction of relationships, particularly relationships between girls that would not be expected or sanctioned in a Puritan society, is arguably one of the greatest strengths of the film adaptation.

In *Fear Street: 1666*, Deena (played by Kiana Madeira), the protagonist from the previous installments of the series, finds herself teleported from 1994 back in time to 1666 and now occupying the body of Sarah Fier, the witch who is believed to be responsible for the curse haunting the town of Shadyside. The branding of Sarah Fier as a witch is the result of her budding romance with another girl in seventeenth-century Shadyside, Hannah Miller (Olivia Welch). The two girls meet with a widow in the forest to gather hallucinogenic berries for a party that the youth of the town are having that evening. They also find that this old woman has a book of black magic, implying that she may be a witch. Once the party begins, a group of the town's youth drink and consume the berries. Under the influence of these substances, Caleb (Jeremy Ford) tries to force himself onto Hannah, ripping at her clothes. Sarah intervenes, and the two girls leave together to a secluded area of the woods where they have a sexual encounter. During their encounter the leaves rustle, indicating that they were being watched by a third party. Following this instance, the town pastor begins to act strange, the town's water and food supplies are seemingly poisoned, and ultimately the pastor kills twelve children. The cause of these calamities is instantly said to be witchcraft, and Caleb then accuses Hannah and Sarah of being witches and thus the ones responsible for the horrors that have plagued the community. The two girls are eventually caught, tried, and sentenced to death. Sarah is able to convince her persecutors to spare Hannah's life by falsely confessing to being the one witch responsible (Figure 5.1). Sarah is then hanged.

Figure 5.1 Shot from *Fear Street Part 3: 1666*. (Credit: NETFLIX.)

The romantic relationship that develops between Sarah Fier and Hannah Miller exemplifies a resistance to a Puritanical expectation for compulsory heteronormativity, which was projected onto women in 1666. Any consent to a queer relationship, or exercise of a woman's power to be the one consenting to and initiating sexual acts, was often attributed to witchcraft and the occult. This entrapment, as Janiak's work establishes, transcends the Puritan period and still impacts women in the twenty-first century. In interviews, Janiak has articulated the importance of portraying a queer as well as racially diverse cast in her narrative. According to Janiak, it was essential that "*Fear Street* was led by people who society has ... traditionally called an 'other,' and that's kind of where this idea of having our main characters be queer came from." While Janiak's vision is a departure in many ways from Stine's original text, the Netflix film series does carry over one critically important theme present in Stine's original book series, as Janiak describes it: "infinite repeatability" (Netflix Staff).

I clarify the importance of mapping out connections between the Salem witch crisis documents and this film in particular. Understanding the concept of thematic repetition necessitates that students take Stine's central argument that society can find itself doomed to repeat the sins of its past on a continual time loop seriously, and as such, students have the task of tracing any references to the documents we have read with the film to build a classroom awareness of these similarities. They are also expected to examine key differences between the texts, such as the ways environments are presented physically as well as socially. I ask them to consider what similar stories are being told in both texts, and I invite them to comment on whatever piques their interest more broadly in terms of a comparative analysis. I tell them ahead of time that we are going to re-watch some of the most terrifying scenes present in the film in class together so that they are prepared. Framed in this way, many students assume we will re-watch scenes depicting gory, bloody violence. There is an uncertainty about which particular scenes we will revisit, which stimulates their engagement further. Drawing on the importance of the multiple forms of fear operating in *Fear Street: 1666*—the fear of false accusations, the fear of being outed, the fear of sexual violence, the fear of violence and death in general—I also ask them to consider which scene they would define as the scariest scene in the film and for what specific reasons.

Marginalization is a critical fear the film grapples with as well. Oftentimes students will positively comment on the casting choices made that represent diversity in the film. With the casting of actors of color, including Kiana Madeira, Benjamin Flores Jr., and Julia Rehwald, it is important to consider the way two discussion points, fear and representation, also factor into the way we consider the early American cultural critique a film such as *Fear Street* has to offer. Students are more accustomed to discussing diverse representation in contemporary media, but coupling that topic with a discussion of a fear many college students currently grapple with in the twenty-first century—the threat of sexual violence—produces new provocative lines of inquiry. In an article for the *Los Angeles Times*, Danielle Broadway asserts that "*Fear Street: 1666* reflects how patriarchal power often gaslights women from their experiences and the way racial profiling can be covered up under false personas of justice" ("Here's Everything"). Therefore, we cannot disentangle discussions about bodily autonomy, consent, and security from discussions about the many forms of marginalization, including racial exclusion, that the film sets to redress through the diverse casting decisions. Furthermore, Broadway insists that the film "reflects the way in which marginalized communities are often blamed for their circumstances, even when it is a corrupt—and in this case, cursed—system that designs things to be the way they are" ("Here's Everything"). To further complicate the "system" Broadway references, I argue that there are multiple systems of oppression operating in tandem and in competing ways throughout the film, which sets students up to see how these systems were established in early America. We can recognize those systems at play in the film through the ways in which Janiak troubles them with her casting decisions, and then use that knowledge as a base to return to another closer examination of the Salem witch trial documents after discussing the film in class.

Upon Closer Inspection

In our next class session, we examine scenes from the film which depict moments of explicit consent as well as scenes that depict the terrifying threat of bodily violation. We delve into the key scene of accusation, wherein questions of consent play a critical role in the witch hunt that follows. Caleb divulges to a heated mob that he has proof that the town is being cursed by witches, relaying the fabricated scenario that Hannah Miller seduced him and that he witnessed Miller and Sarah Fier lying with the devil in the forest (*Fear Street* 36:38–37:16). At this point in the film, the viewing audience is already aware that Hannah Miller has spurned Caleb. In an earlier scene, Caleb is depicted grabbing Hannah in the middle of a raucous party in the woods under the full moon, tearing at her clothing. In trying to seduce her, Caleb beckons Miller, "Come to the woods with me," to which Miller retorts, "Entertain yourself with someone else." She eventually states, "Get off of me" before clearly articulating to Caleb that she does not consent by saying "Stop" (*Fear Street* 14:20–14:24). When Miller clearly tells Caleb to stop, he is tearing at Miller's clothing. Caleb further says, "Quit teasing me," when Sarah Fier steps in and fights off Caleb, preventing any further escalation of Caleb's assault on Hannah (*Fear Street* 14:26–14:28). The fellow townspeople mock Caleb after Fier makes a witty quip insinuating Caleb is better suited to mate with a mule. This previous scene indicates that Caleb's later testimony of witnessing the two lying with the devil is a retaliatory invention, one made up to punish both Fier and Miller for insisting upon Miller's right to maintain bodily autonomy, not giving in and not consenting to his attempt at asserting a toxic masculinity through sexual violence. Hannah's clear refusal and clear message that she is not affirming Caleb's aggressive handling of her body become the catalyst for Caleb's attempt to frame the women, since they controlled the situation, not him.

Hannah's clear refusal to consent, and the support she receives from Sarah in asserting a fightback in response to Caleb's sexual advances, is then contrasted with a scene of affirmative, clear consent. As Hannah and Sarah go to the woods together, they begin kissing, whereat Sarah pulls back from Hannah, stating that she "can't" continue because it is "wrong"; recalling Caleb's violent grasping at Hannah's blouse, Hannah gently starts to remove Sarah's blouse, but pauses before continuing, stating, "Tell me to stop and I shall" (*Fear Street* 15:39–15:46). The tenderness and Hannah's explicit request for consent models how to engage sexually with care. It presents a *right* way to have a mutual exchange of intimacy.

Re-watching these scenes in the classroom sets up a clear connection between understanding the ways that the film is connecting fear and safety to bodily violation, controlled consent, and expression of sexual desire and intimacy, even when it is not socially sanctioned. Caleb's toxic masculinity that does not ask for consent is juxtaposed against the queer coupling of Sarah and Hannah, depicting a healthy sexual encounter with declarative consent. Therefore, when the mob, incited by Caleb's false testimony, pursues Hannah Miller and Sarah Fier, it becomes all the more alarming and an indicator that they are both being persecuted for their non-heteronormative desire, one that is not coerced by some sort of evil or witchcraft, but one both girls agree to pursue. What I contextualize as "the most terrifying" scene in the film is the moment where the mob encircles Hannah Miller. Elijah Goode yells at Miller, "Silence!" and then exclaims to Caleb in reference to Miller's body, "Check her for marks" (*Fear Street* 38:15–38:17).

The terror for the audience in that moment is that Hannah Miller's bodily autonomy is about to be violated, and we see her struggle and fight against Caleb who eventually rips her clothing. Caleb's actions recall the earlier party scene where Hannah refuses to consent to his advances, but there is no bystander coming to her aid here. Instead, Hannah is then dragged off by several men in the mob. We initially see Miller's hair up when Caleb begins his attack, and as she is carried away, she is still clothed but her ability to consent is ignored, and she has no control over her own bodily movement. As the scene progresses, Miller's hair is down and completely disheveled, and Elijah Goode's voice proclaims with great authority: "We will search every house, every inch of wood, we will not rest, and we will not have mercy" (*Fear Street* 38:47–38:55). I pause after this scene, and the collective weight in the room feels quite heavy. I again ask, "What if we framed our entire discussion based on the premise that this is the most terrifying scene in the film? If the main force of terror in the film is the threat of social as well as physical vulnerability, as well as the violation of consent, how does our understanding shift the way we receive the larger narrative?"

Presenting students with an opportunity to map out other moments in the film that depict specific and welcomed consent between characters helps alleviate some of the heaviness in the discussion and acts as a means to see the ways the film also models appropriate consent and tender moments of intimacy. Scenes like the romantic encounter between Sarah and Hannah stand as a welcome contrast to some of the other moments in the film that students note as being particularly fearful. As a class, we can then make connections between some of the broader fears present in the film to identify more clearly specific fears plaguing women: bodily autonomy, safety, and the fear of not having control over one's own ability to consent. Shifting between analyzing moments of terror and tenderness does not shut down discussion but rather creates a space where a more nuanced and prolonged discussion about such a difficult topic is possible. We also work to contextualize the brute action of violation that takes place in specific scenes with dialogue that promises a continual threat of repeat violations. It also encourages, albeit anachronistically, students to imagine that women in the 1600s could have had supportive, encouraging friendships and relationships filled with tenderness and consensual intimacy. Such imagined past scripts promote a sense that early America is not a monolith and that the social interactions between women should not be strictly characterized as adversarial and accusatory just because our record of such is scant. For example, when Sarah and Hannah fall into the hands of the angry mob, Sarah confesses to the crowd that she was the one in league with Satan, that she "clouded" the mind of Hannah, boldly proclaiming, "It was me. It was only me. It was always me" (*Fear Street* 1:01:18–38:55). In a moment of touching sacrifice, Sarah's statements serve to indict her, saving Hannah, but also carry with them the subtext of romance and support. Sarah recognizes that the way she "clouded" Hannah's mind was not with the occult but with romantic feelings, which again challenges Puritan heteronormativity. Rather than trying to save her own life through a coerced confession, as some of the women accused in Salem did, Sarah confesses to save Hannah, also allowing Hannah the opportunity to publicly hear Sarah's deepest feelings for her, even if it means Sarah must hang as a result. Thus, we add to our collective canon of scripts seen in *Fear Street: 1666* and the Salem witch trial documents that speak to how women in early America were persecuted, but also now we add the possibility that they could experience autonomy and pleasure in relationships built on consent and cooperation—like that of Sarah Fier and Hannah Miller—even within such rigid gendered roles.

Assignment #3

After viewing *Fear Street: 1666* and having a difficult yet pivotal conversation about the specific scenes that present bodily violation, autonomy, and explicit moments of consent, we revisit the Sarah Good and Tituba documents. This time, I have students get into groups, and they are directed to re-examine the accusations. I remind them of the context we began with—an understanding of the ways women's bodies were believed to have been weaker than men's and more susceptible to possession during the Puritan era (Reis 38). They are also directed to focus more closely on descriptions of women's bodies, and I have them circle any time the word "bare" appears. Through this annotation practice, students closely read for the physical descriptions of the accused women, and in doing so, they consider the ways these bodies are depicted as vulnerable and weak, but also powerful, menacing, and therefore in need of containment.

I direct students to apply this sharper close-reading approach to documents they read in Assignment #1. They revisit texts such as Samuel Sibley's testimony against Sarah Good which describes her in parts with "naked breast and bare footed and bare legged" (Godbeer 80). Sibley also refers to her as a "nasty slut," ultimately stating that she should be killed. This re-examination helps to crystallize the hostility of the Salem environment toward vulnerable women, particularly those who exposed their own bodies but also those who were forcibly exposed (Godbeer 80). During the trials, much like in *Fear Street: 1666*, women's bodies were examined to look for marks or signs of possession or dalliance with the devil. I also direct students to enrich their analysis through a comparison of Sarah Good's and Tituba's experiences, with a focus on the differing ways embodiment is depicted in each set of documents to deepen their understanding of embodiment and consent. They can see, then, how racialization factored into the trials and tribulations these women were subjected to in early America. Our goal, here, is to further nuance the ways social identities interact with how bodies are violated or encroached upon without consent.

We ask larger questions, such as: How are each of these figures different from one another in terms of class, race, and, more generally, social status? How can we understand the complexity of the varying degrees of danger that each of these women faced in their own time and place within an understanding of a race, class, and gender schema? What new insights can this understanding about these women help us to make more generally about Puritan society and the Salem witch crisis at the time? Why do we tell these stories about the Salem witch trials in the ways that we do now? What do we include in our contemporary depictions, what do we omit, and how does this inform American culture more broadly? I also use these larger questions to extend beyond the immediacy of this comparative lesson, which is focused strictly on Salem witch crisis documents and *Fear Street: 1666*. As such, I use a comparative framework as well as the recursive practice of tracing connections between early American texts alongside and against contemporary depictions in other units throughout the course for continuity. Hence, this practice becomes a major theme throughout the course, and students are continually expected to nuance their close-reading observations about early American texts within an understanding of issues with consent in our current moment. Students, then, can look for how the cultural milieu of Protestants surrounding bodily autonomy, gender roles, control of sexuality, and consent still govern the ignoring, silencing, or minimizing of sexual assault and abuse in other texts, but also in U.S. culture at large.

Conclusion: Back Thenness to Nowness

Tackling issues of sexual assault and consent in the classroom can be difficult work, but broaching this sensitive topic is critically important because an examination of issues of violence and violation of consent builds a level of connection and community, which makes future conversations around difficult topics such as gender discrimination, racism, and misogyny more productive within the walls of the classroom. By encouraging discussion rather than silence, students learn to exchange a diverse range of perspectives on the subject of sexual assault and consent in a safe environment and in a productive manner. Furthermore, by delving into the abyss of some of our deepest, darkest fears from having one's consent disregarded, as well as the threat of bodily violation, we can create classroom spaces that foster growth, encourage sensitivity, and spark students to engage in advocacy. Supplementing discussion of the primary Salem witch crisis documents with *Fear Street: 1666* creates an opportunity for a comparison which reveals that early issues regarding consent and gendered sexual violence are not new phenomena. This approach also substantiates that there is still much more work to be done in addressing the social and cultural roots that allow the perpetuation of these heinous acts. I offer just one approach for bridging together popular media and early American texts to get students to see how the past continues to influence the present. Depending on the various student learning outcomes that are established for different types of courses, educators can use this as a model and reflect on the ways that they can adapt this text pairing to fit the differing needs of various types of classes.[12] A number of pedagogical adaptations can be made to include a comparative approach to the Salem documents and *Fear Street: 1666*, just as there are a seemingly never-ending list of fears rooted in early America that persist in our current moment. Exploring such subject matter can feel daunting, and addressing these in an early American literature course initially seems confusing; yet, bridging the time gap, moving past the back thenness to a nowness, can help students engage with the topic of sexual violence and violation with enough distance to create comfort, but also guide them to bring the discussion from the past into the present. When we face it together, it is my hope that we can all feel buoyed and strengthened to have the courage individually as well as collectively to face our fears. Through close reading and dialogue we can change the culture of sexual violence through advocating for proper consent and help to heal the wounds that have plagued the nation since its inception.

---

[12] For example, *Fear Street: 1666* can be taught alongside Godbeer's introduction with only the Tituba documents assigned. Other selected documents could be read alongside an analysis of brief clips from the film, with an accompanying lecture discussing how racialization and gender factor into the texts. One could also start an American literature survey course with the film as an open invitation to think about what stories we more broadly tell about early American society, and that course could routinely connect back and map on additional persistent American fears not identified in the film.

Works Cited

Breslaw, Elaine G. *Tituba, Reluctant Witch of Salem: Devilish Indians and Puritan Fantasies*. New York UP, 1996.

———. *Witches of the Atlantic World: A Historical Reader & Primary Sourcebook*. New York UP, 2000.

Broadway, Danielle. "Here's Everything Explained in 'Fear Street Part 3: 1666'—The Epic Netflix Finale." *The Los Angeles Times*, July 16, 2021, https://www.latimes.com/entertainment-arts/movies/story/2021-07-16/fear-street-part-3-1666-ending-explained-netflix-spoilers (last accessed November 11, 2014).

Chilling Adventures of Sabrina. Created by Roberto Aguirre-Sacasa. Netflix, 2018–20.

Condé, Maryse. *I, Tituba, Black Witch of Salem*. Translated by Richard Philcox. Ballantine Books, 1994.

Fear Street Part Three: 1666. Directed by Leigh Janiak. Netflix, 2021.

Freitas, Donna. *Consent on Campus: A Manifesto*. Oxford UP, 2018.

Games, Alison. *Witchcraft in Early North America*. Rowman & Littlefield, 2010.

Godbeer, Richard. *The Salem Witch Hunt: A Brief History with Documents*. Bedford/St. Martin, 2018.

Gulley, Alison, editor. *Teaching Rape in the Medieval Literature Classroom: Approaches to Difficult Texts*. Arc Humanities Press, 2018.

Hall, David D. *Worlds of Wonder, Days of Judgment: Popular Religious Belief in Early New England*. Alfred A. Knopf, 1989.

Hirsch, Jennifer S., and Shamus Khan. *Sexual Citizens: A Landmark Study of Sex, Power, and Assault on Campus*. W.W. Norton, 2020.

Karlsen, Carol. *The Devil in the Shape of a Woman: Witchcraft in Colonial New England*. W.W. Norton, 1998.

Netflix Staff, "'Fear Street': How R.L. Stine's Book Series Became Our Ambitious New Film Trilogy." Netflix, June 30, 2021, https://about.netflix.com/en/news/fear-street-how-rl-stines-book-series-became-our-ambitious-new-film-trilogy (last accessed November 11, 2014).

Norton, Mary Beth. *In the Devil's Snare: The Salem Witchcraft Crisis of 1692*. Alfred A. Knopf, 2002.

Ray, Benjamin C. *Satan and Salem: The Witch-Hunt Crisis of 1692*. University of Virginia Press, 2015.

Reis, Elizabeth. *Damned Women Sinners and Witches in Puritan New England*. Cornell UP, 1997.

Reising, Russell. "The Early American Literature Survey." *Teaching the Literatures of Early America*, edited by Carla J. Mulford. Modern Language Association, 1999, pp. 259–71.

6

Sex Education: Teaching Revolutionary Constructs of Womanhood through AMC's *Turn*

Patrick M. Erben and Cryslin Ledbetter

In season 3 of the British TV show *Sex Education* (Netflix), Otis Milford, a high schooler whose mother is a sex therapist, discusses with his principal the explicit film his peers produced and publicly screened to express their need for open conversations about sexuality and gender. When chided by his principal, Hope Hadden, for drawing negative attention to the school and jeopardizing its funding (which leads to her firing), Otis replies: "The issues we talked about have always been there. People just haven't felt safe enough to raise them. That's what's changing" (38:00). Otis asks Hadden what her plans are now, to which she responds:

> I've been trying to get pregnant for three years. I'm currently trying to start another round of IVF . . . You have no idea what it's like to wake up to the feeling of failure every morning . . . I'm clearly having some kind of breakdown. [Otis: How are you a failure?] Because my . . . my body won't . . . won't . . . It doesn't do . . . the . . . The one thing it's supposed to do. The one thing I want it to do. (38:14–43; pauses in the original)

Hadden's presumed failure to properly educate the youth of the fictional Moordale Secondary School is thus overshadowed by her inability to comply with powerful constructs of womanhood—especially the expectation of becoming a mother. Ironically, Otis and Hadden have this conversation in the waiting room of the clinic where Otis's middle-aged mother just gave birth to an unplanned baby, while Hadden has come to fill out the paperwork for another round of IVF treatments. Through this conversation, the show intertwines the students' rebellion with Hadden's desperate quest for motherhood as responding to the same restrictive heteronormative and patriarchal sex/gender scripts. Education and the figure of the educator here function as enforcers of these limitations while also presenting the potential for their abrogation.

Whereas *Sex Education* features a range of characters and plots driving toward a more fluid sex/gender construction, American viewers of the show's third season (released September 2021) witnessed the U.S. Supreme Court (SCOTUS) argue and decide *Dobbs v. Jackson Women's Health Organization* between 1 December 2021 and 24 June 2022, overturning its 1973 landmark ruling in *Roe v. Wade* and significantly limiting women's reproductive rights. Reading *Sex Education* vis-à-vis the overturning of *Roe v. Wade* thus suggests the difficult question of how contemporary education—at the secondary and collegiate level—can respond. More specifically, Justice Samuel Alito's repeated insistence in writing the opinion of the court in *Dobbs* that the kind of liberty protecting a woman's right to abortion would have to be "deeply rooted in the history or tradition of our people" demands our attention to the ways in which early American cultural and political precedents inform contemporary debates about sexuality and gender (25).[1] How can teachers at different educational levels connect newly ignited conflicts over reproductive rights and, more broadly speaking, sex/gender roles to precedents in the colonial and revolutionary period?

---

[1] Alito evokes the term "rooted" in various combinations with "history" and "traditions" twenty-five times in the *Dobbs* case, both in citing previous SCOTUS cases and in his own interpretation. As Amanda Taub demonstrates in her May 19, 2022 *New York Times* article, Alito specifically pointed to the writings of seventeenth-century English jurist Matthew Hale as constitutive of the "history and tradition of our people" (*Dobbs*). Taub expands on the elements of Hale's jurisprudence on English common law—which was transposed to the American colonies and then the United States; according to Taub, Hale worked to restrict women's rights within marriage and over their bodies and, infamously, set in motion "centuries of jurisprudence and jury instructions that treated the moral character of rape victims as the paramount concern in rape cases, and often presumed that they were lying if they could not produce corroborating witnesses or other outside evidence for their claims. Hale also wrote in his influential common-law treatise that marital rape could not be a crime because marriage itself constituted irrevocable consent to sex—but only for the wife." Taub reflects on the irony that Hale's English common law concepts such as the doctrine of coverture (which subsumed all of a woman's rights and property as covered by her father, husband, or closest male relative) were eventually eliminated in American law, while his limitations to women's rights over their own bodies are now reclaimed by Alito and others as constitutive of the country's "history and tradition."

In the past few years, moreover, many states have enacted so-called divisive concept laws that limit how and whether allegedly controversial topics, especially those relating to race and sex/gender identity, may be taught and discussed in class. In Georgia, a "trio of censorship laws passed in 2022" has recently infused educators with fear and apprehension over their ability to touch any subject potentially deemed controversial, even if it is not explicitly mentioned in these laws.[2] Banking on these laws and their vague definition of "divisive concepts," the school district of Cobb County (a northwest Atlanta suburb) fired a fifth grade teacher, Katie Rinderle, for reading the best-selling children's book by Australian author Scott Stuart—*My Shadow Is Purple*—to her class and talking to students about accepting differences among their peers (Sonnenberg). The earlier "Resolution of the State Board of Education of the State of Georgia, June 3, 2021," moreover, sought to eliminate any instruction allegedly based on the concept that "fault, blame, or bias should be assigned to a race or sex, or to members of a race or sex because of their race or sex" (3). Importantly, the indicator of such "bias" would rest solely with the audience—that is students and, by extension, their parents—who may "feel discomfort, guilt, anguish, or any other form of psychological distress on account of his or her race or sex" (3). Divisive concepts laws implemented across the United States—along with widespread political efforts to eliminate diversity, equity, and inclusion programs as well as legislation hostile to LGBTQ+ rights—place educators in general in a stark predicament. More specifically, how should college instructors train future teachers who in their jobs will face restrictive laws, parental ire, and a potentially career-threatening backlash for teaching unvarnished versions of American history, literature, and culture?[3]

This chapter, a collaboration between university professor Patrick M. Erben and English Education undergraduate student Cryslin Ledbetter, presents a layered approach to the pedagogical dilemmas produced by this

---

[2] In Georgia, these laws include "the Protect Students' Rights Act, commonly known as the 'divisive concepts' law; a 'Parents' Bill of Rights;' and one known as the 'harmful to minors law,' which allows for the removal of restriction of materials parents deem 'pornographic' or otherwise harmful. Together, the laws censor class discussion, give parents the right to refuse instruction they disagree with and ban 'offensive' reading materials from school libraries" (Sonnenberg).

[3] It is worth noting that earlier versions of the "divisive concepts" law in Georgia extended restrictions to higher education, thus severely limiting academic freedom. As originally introduced, Senate Bill 377 (LC 49 0750) required the "units of the University System of Georgia [i.e. all public colleges and universities] [...] to prevent the use of curricula or training programs which act upon, promote, or encourage certain concepts" (1).

upswell in restrictive reproductive rights laws and equally constricting educational legislation, especially on issues of sexuality and gender. First, Erben briefly introduces a triangulated assignment from his upper-level early American literature course, which asks students to analyze the interconnections among (a) an early American primary text, (b) a contemporary text (including film, TV, video games, etc.) picking up similar issues, and (c) a present-day political, cultural, or social issue undergirding this transhistorical artifact pairing. Specifically, Erben highlights the reason for teaching the AMC show *Turn: Washington's Spies* to highlight debates about gender roles in early America and today. Second, Ledbetter presents her course project, a reflection on teaching Judith Sargent Murray's famous 1790 essay "On the Equality of the Sexes" alongside *Turn* in secondary school environs. She follows up with a detailed lesson plan for using the early American essay and the contemporary TV show to help pre-collegiate students think through past and present constructions and contestations of women's roles in a way that does not overtly place teachers on the radar of hyper-vigilant culture warriors but endows students with the critical skills to examine sex/gender discourses in their own everyday experiences and communal contexts. This essay therefore discusses how college instructors and student teachers can debate important issues surrounding sexuality and gender in early America and today.

Early American Rhapsody: Class Contexts

In subtitling my upper-level early American literature course "Early American Rhapsody," I pun not only on Queen's most famous song, "Bohemian Rhapsody," but showcase my course's play with its generic elements—its episodic nature, contrasting elements, and improvisations. Similarly, my course presents a mash-up of early American topics with popular culture, contemporary literary texts, and hot-button topics ripped from the headlines of the day. One topic is what Diana Taylor calls "the scenario of conquest" in early American literature and the ways in which contemporary storytelling—such as the graphic novel *Ghost River* (see Chapter 1) and Louise Erdrich's Pulitzer Prize-winning novel *The Night Watchman*—resists transhistorical colonialist language and politics.[4] As an example of settler

---

[4] Erdrich's novel notably celebrates the Turtle Mountain Chippewa's successful resistance to the 1950s Indian Termination policies, while *Ghost River*, as Fenton and Lucas demonstrate so evocatively in the opening chapter of this collection, seeks to find regenerative ways of storytelling to try to remediate the erasures of history.

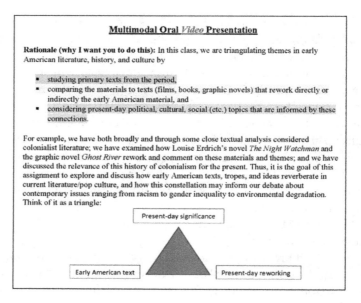

Figure 6.1 Assignment sheet from ENGL 4003: Early American Literature, Summer 2021. (Credit: Patrick M. Erben.)

colonial politics in the present, the course discussed the violent suppression of protests against the construction of the Dakota Access Pipeline through ancestral lands and water supplies of the Standing Rock Reservation of the Lakota people in the 2010s (Crane-Murdoch). I adapt the triangulation principle to a variety of topics, including gender and sexuality, while also applying it to different assignments such as multimodal projects, research papers, and oral presentations (see Figure 6.1). The unit on gender and sexuality includes a range of early American texts, including "The Examination of Mrs. Ann Hutchinson at the Court at Newtown" and *The Coquette*, both of which usually elicit powerful responses from students. The first time I taught *Turn: Washington's Spies* (AMC, 2014–17), I primarily intended it as a reflection of contemporary portrayals of the Revolutionary War in popular culture. It was through student responses—among them Cryslin's triangulation of the show with Judith Sargent Murray's essay and current debates about "divisive concepts"—that my focus *turned* (pun intended) to its intelligent portrayal of women characters.

Turn is based on Alexander Rose's 2006 book *Washington's Spies: The Story of America's First Spy Ring*. The show focuses on a group of men and women in the (predominantly) loyalist Long Island town of Setauket, who are, through various circumstances, recruited into covert activity obtaining and relaying information to George Washington and the Continental Army. Characters in *Turn* fictionalize historical figures such as Abraham Woodhull (the central figure of the Culper Spy Ring), while taking the liberty of ascertaining the identity of "Agent 355" appearing in extant communications definitively as Anna Strong, the wife of Setauket tavern keeper Selah Strong. Anna Strong and several of the show's other female characters can be analyzed as representative of gender types prevalent during the colonial and revolutionary period, while turning such types on their head and thus allowing students to analyze their constructedness and critically examine their sociocultural valences.

The show's central female character, Anna Strong, turns from *feme covert*—contained by her husband's legal status and property—into *feme sole* when he is arrested by British soldiers. Yet this apparent weakening of her social position allows Strong to subvert political and gendered expectations by freeing her to engage in espionage activity with Abe Woodhull (her ex-fiancé) and illicitly rekindle their former relationship. Simultaneously, Strong rebuts sexual advances from the villainous British officer Simcoe. In contrast, the show's (initially) most cliché Republican mother figure, Abe's wife Mary, eventually turns out to have only dissembled her loyalist affinities and supports Abe's spying activity for the patriot cause. That the show does not romanticize Strong and Woodhull as one-dimensional heroic figures becomes apparent in its focus on Strong's former enslaved woman Abigail, who is, along with her son, freed by the British officer Hewlitt as a result of Lord Dunmore's proclamation (against the will of Anna Strong) but must cope with the tenuous position of a freed woman of color in revolutionary America. Abigail engages in spying activity not out of patriotic principle but to gain advantages for herself and her son. Her "turn" thus reveals the protracted liminality of formerly enslaved women, and her spying skills are derived from the observational skills she had to cultivate as an enslaved and thus largely invisible person. Moreover, sexuality as a stereotypically seductive female power appears in the (aptly named) actress Philomena Cheer and the historically grounded Peggy Shippen. On the surface, both use their sexual power for social advancement, especially in the mutable political conditions of the British occupations of New York City and Philadelphia. Both, in turn, become romantically involved with British spy master Major André, but it is his seductiveness and duplicity which allows him to manipulate both women for his covert activities, leading to their eventual downfall.

The portrayal of women in *Turn* opens up multiple avenues for both synchronic and diachronic intertextual analysis. Laterally, connecting *Turn*'s revolutionary period women to Judith Sargent Murray's "On the Equality of the Sexes" allows students to complicate their pre-existing notions of early American concepts of gender as immutable or uncontested. Students today often assume that feminist ideas have emerged only recently and, by and large, imagine revolutionary women as mono-dimensional types neither possessing nor seeking an advanced education. An in-depth analysis of Murray's essay, therefore, reveals a self-possessed woman's voice not only calling for educational equality but, more stridently, exposing women's alleged intellectual inferiority as a product of concerted social circumscriptions that are far from natural or God-given. Close analysis of the women in *Turn* then allows students to compare these characters to elements of Murray's argument—especially that women's innate and equal abilities were purposely stunted but would, in a revolutionary atmosphere, no longer yield to male domination. In spite of allegedly inferior intellectual attainments, the female characters of *Turn* play indispensable parts in the drama of Washington's earliest intelligence service. Across time, early American constructions of womanhood and their inversions in *Turn* resonate with students who— acutely aware of recent political debates about gender roles and reproductive rights—can find multiple access points for examining the ways in which gendered power and disenfranchisement operate transhistorically.

For students who may still tend toward essentialist assumptions about feminist strides that make early American gender debates irrelevant today, an introduction to the bizarre backlash against Heather Lind, the actress who portrayed Anna Strong in *Turn*, will help bridge the temporal divide and link issues such as sexual assault in the show to their counterparts in the present. Lind revealed in a 2017 Instagram post that former president George H.W. Bush had groped her and made sexual jokes during a photo shoot promoting *Turn*. Spokespeople for Bush did not deny Lind's allegations but dismissed their significance by referencing his age and disability (Phillips and Rosenberg). Public opinion almost universally turned against Lind, and social media posts portrayed her as an out-of-control feminist, wielding her fame to defame a beloved elder statesman.[5] Just

---

[5] Tweets lashing out at Lind directly responded to her Twitter handle: @heatherglind. Some representative Tweets include: "You're a terrible actress (and person) so I doubt you'll get another role, but on the off chance you do, I'll be boycotting" (Kyle @KS, October 25, 2017); "You are despicable. Using a 94 year old man to further your career. A curse on your house" (@KevinHe09012015, October 25, 2017); "You are ridiculous calling out The former President for sexual assault. You ugly feminist have taken humor and turned it into a dirty word" (@marniehutchinso, October 25, 2017).

as her character Anna Strong could not afford to vent grievances against powerful men publicly, Lind suffered the wrath of a public construing her accusations as an unforgivable transgression against a sacrosanct patriarchal order.

In my early American literature course, discussions of the interweaving of past and present flowed freely; we connected the continued silencing of strong and outspoken women (such as the social media backlash against Lind) to Murray's learned refutation of women's alleged intellectual inferiority, and to the women of *Turn*, who skillfully navigated the slippages between loyalist and patriot allegiances, allowing them to become expert spies and collectors of intelligence. As an English education student preparing to teach high school, however, Cryslin Ledbetter recognized that the far greater challenge lies outside the higher education classroom, specifically in the conveyance of these issues in an educational environment overshadowed by high-stakes political restrictions to critical inquiry and difficult conversations. Instead of a traditional paper, Ledbetter decided to research, reflect, and plan a lesson combining a focus on early American texts identifying women's roles (education, social standing, legal standing, etc.) as a key issue in revolutionary and early national discourse with an analysis of AMC's *Turn*, as well as contemporary debates about women's rights. Ledbetter studied English and History high school curricula, textbooks, and standards, while interviewing a local high school teacher on her experiences teaching sexuality and gender issues in American literature in the current political environment. Following her introductory reflections on her research below, Ledbetter presents a lesson plan for a high school American literature course that combines Judith Sargent Murray's "On the Equality of the Sexes" with *Turn*, as well as a metacognitive student reflection on their assumptions about early American and contemporary womanhood.

Anna Strong and "Divisive Concepts" of American Womanhood: Textual/Pedagogical Contexts[6]

The *Oxford English Dictionary* defines the word "strong" as "physically vigorous or robust; not readily affected by disease or adverse conditions; healthy." While male Americans sought to portray themselves as strong and powerful counterparts to their British adversaries during the American

---

[6] This section was written by Cryslin Ledbetter, a student in ENGL 4003: Early American Literature, Summer of 2021, and serves as a contextualization of her lesson plan.

Revolution, they did not consider women their physical and intellectual equals. Nevertheless, revolutionary and early national women wielded literary platforms as the means for conveying covert and overt messages demanding the same rights and recognition as men. Judith Sargent Murray's essay "On the Equality of the Sexes" presents an argument for the need to educate "strong" women, not to become superior to men but to be intellectual—if not quite yet political—equals. According to Murray, men enforce this distinction in order to remain in control of women through unequal education. Murray questions this sociocultural construct: "Are we deficient in reason? We can only reason from what we know, and if an opportunity of acquiring knowledge hath been denied us, the inferiority of our sex cannot fairly be deduced from thence" (404). She argues that women must not be judged from this lack of knowledge but receive an education that, based on their equal God-given mental faculties, allows them to rise to the same intellectual status as men. Murray frequently plays with meanings of the words "strength" or "strong," especially the way they differed when applied to the mental and physical attributes of women and men. In arguing for equal intellectual and educational attainment for women, Murray satirizes men's "animal power" by comparing it to the superior physical strength of many creatures of "the field" (406); similarly, she asks her readers to admit that "there are many robust masculine ladies, and effeminate gentlemen" (406). Assigning physical and mental strength solely based on a person's sex, for Murray, is as arbitrary as claiming that women have inferior intellect based on an unequal education—in other words, a socially constructed inequality. For men or women, "strength" of body or mind is a quality attained through cultivation and training rather than presumably innate differences.

With an apt (though unintended) pun on Murray's definitions of "strength," AMC's series *Turn: Washington's Spies* centrally features Anna Strong, who refuses the predisposed notion of what a woman should be, creating a contemporary popular culture representation of Murray's ideal woman by commanding her own education and sociopolitical roles. Strong rises above her assigned tasks as tavern keeper's wife and, in her central role in the Culper Spy Ring, often becomes a voice of reason for the men in her life. By the same token, Strong also displays strength in her autonomous control over her body—both in choosing a sexual relationship with Abraham Woodhull and in rebuffing sexual assaults from Captain Simcoe. In short, while Strong's husband resides in prison, she is able to take control of her sexuality. On the surface, both Judith Sargent Murray's essay "On the Equality of the Sexes" and AMC's *Turn* simply cover the familiar subject matter of the American Revolution. Read for more covert messaging, however, both the essay and the show allow students to untangle inversions of conventional constructions of womanhood in both the revolutionary period and today.

Unfortunately for today's students, divisive concept legislation and restrictive policy language—such as the "Resolution" of the State Board of Education of the State of Georgia—limit exploring the subversive implications of Murray's "On the Equality of the Sexes" because of negative connotations as a "feminist" text. Feminist pedagogy, however, disrupts such misconceptions. Laura R. Micciche, in her book chapter "Feminist Pedagogies," describes the teaching of such texts as "shar[ing] a common goal of actualizing social justice through teaching and learning methods" (128). Micciche's ideal feminist pedagogy, instead of delving into the political aspects that drive current government reforms and resolutions, connects students' personal experiences in the context of "world-making," leaning on the maxim adopted during second-wave feminism: "The personal *is* political" (129). With a focus on connecting students' personal experience to larger political debates, I present specific approaches and supporting materials for teaching "On the Equality of the Sexes" and *Turn* in secondary school classrooms. "On the Equality of the Sexes" allows students to examine early national debates about womanhood through Murray's trenchant critique of an educational system that conditions women for inferiority and then casts the resulting inequality as indicative of an inherent intellectual difference between men and women. *Turn: Washington's Spies* presents a set of female characters who, on the surface, embody conventional revolutionary period concepts of womanhood to undermine and complicate such simplistic constructions. The show's central trope of changeable political and personal allegiances during the American Revolution serves as a powerful conduit for allowing students to question seemingly stable assumptions about womanhood, gender, and sexuality in contemporary discourse.

Navigating Learning Outcomes and State Requirements

Georgia's standards for teaching American literature in high school separate into three sections: Reading Literary, Reading Informational, and Writing Conventions. These standards explicitly determine what educators can teach in the classroom. For example, standard ELAGSE11-12RL1 asks students to "[c]ite strong and thorough textual evidence to support analysis of what the text says explicitly as well as inferences drawn from the text, including determining where the text leaves matters uncertain," and standard ELAGSE11-12RI6 asks students to "[d]etermine an author's point of view or purpose in a text in which the rhetoric is particularly effective, analyzing how style and content contribute to the power, persuasiveness, or beauty of the text" ("11th–12th Grade English Language Arts Georgia Standards of Excellence [ELA GSE]"). These standards, however, do not define what educators cannot teach in the classroom, and they certainly do not prepare teachers for conflicts arising from the ways in which students are predisposed by home life or political affiliation to accept or dismiss specific concepts. Georgia's "Resolution," however, explicitly states that educators cannot "approve for use, make use of, or carry out ... instructional practices that serve to inculcate in students the [...] concepts" of race and gender inequalities. The discrepancy between Georgia's standards (which specifically encourage teachers and students to probe textual uncertainties) and the "Resolution" thus tasks educators with navigating a vaguely defined middle ground where they adhere to both, making sure to refrain from offending specific students, while developing lesson plans to educate students according to state standards.

My goal was to develop a lesson plan based on Murray's "On the Equality of the Sexes" and AMC's *Turn* which adheres to Georgia's standards while also deferring to the limitations presented in the "Resolution" and incorporating specific feminist pedagogies. In order to compare my new lesson plan to existing practices, I researched the American literature materials used at Bremen High School.[7] After borrowing the primary textbook used in American literature teacher Jessica Allen's classroom, *Prentice Hall Literature: Timeless Voices, Timeless Themes* (Duer et al.), I searched the text specifically for feminist writings which align with my specific inquiry. While the textbook does not mention Murray's essay, the only writings by women in the section "A Nation is Born" (1750–1800) are Phillis Wheatley's "To His Excellency, General Washington" and "An Hymn to the Evening," as well as Abigail Adams's "Letter to her Daughter from the New White House." Focused solely on the Adams section, the textbook asks questions suggesting her purpose for writing as primarily aesthetic rather than also political: "Adams lived in an age when writing an entertaining, informative letter was highly prized. Would you describe

---

[7] A suburban city of approximately 6,500 residents, Bremen is located forty-six miles west of Atlanta ("City-Data").

Adams as a good letter writer?" (Duer et al. 196). Praising Adams as "one of the most influential American women of her time," the textbook unfortunately does not allow students to imagine the role that non-elite women, such as Anna Strong, played in the Revolution; in focusing on Adams's advanced letter-writing skills, the book neglects to acknowledge Murray's critique of an unequal educational environment for men and women (192).

In moving from this research to developing my own didactic strategies, I thus needed to find a way to deconstruct the false binary between women's private intellectual achievement and their public voicelessness engrained in the *Prentice Hall Literature* textbook's casting of Abigail Adams as emblematic for all women in the period. My lesson plan therefore incorporates various methods of feminist pedagogy derived from Laura R. Micciche and balks against limiting students' ability to develop their own conceptions regarding America's cultural and literary history. Specifically, I base my lessons upon the maxim "The personal *is* the political," which allows students to recognize a variety of personal actions among revolutionary women as powerful political statements. In *Turn*, for example, Anna Strong hanging specific petticoats out to dry as covert messages to her spy ring paradigmatically reveals this intertwining. In the classroom, leaning heavily upon students' experiences and the sociocultural opinions each student brings similarly encourages them to recognize their personal concepts as shaped by political assumptions. Micciche comments:

> Pamela Annas [...] advocates a pedagogy that values personal experience to "ground [students'] writing in their lives rather than to surmount their lives before they write" [862]. Her goal is to help students discover their voices while paying attention to how women's voices have been historically muted by inequitable cultural conditions. (130)

Anna Strong presents an unequivocal example of a muted woman as historians ignore her role in the American Revolution. In my project, I created two options from which educators can choose: one which accompanies a one-day, 1.5 hour class period, and one which allows educators to spend an entire week on my chosen texts. My lessons include various means of reflection for students, allowing them to "discover their own voices while paying attention to the ways in which women's voices have been historically muted" (Micciche 130). In the limited space of this chapter, I am only able to include the one-day, 1.5 hour lesson plan.

Critical Approach to Feminism: The Relation Between AMC's *Turn: Washington's Spies* and Murray's "On the Equality of the Sexes"[8]—A Lesson Plan

Central Focus: In this lesson, students will develop critical thinking skills by viewing scenes from the series *Turn*, reading Murray's essay, and applying the author's purpose along with background historical context to establish long-lasting connections between feminist literature and popular culture. As they do so, they will consider whether the same views of women's education and political autonomy are still present today.

State Content Standards:

- ELAGSE11-12RL1: Cite strong and thorough textual evidence to support analysis of what the text says explicitly as well as inferences drawn from the text, including determining where the text leaves matters uncertain.
- ELAGSE11-12RL9: Demonstrate knowledge of eighteenth, nineteenth, and early twentieth century foundational works (of American Literature, British Literature, World Literature, or Multicultural Literature), including how two or more texts from the same period treat similar themes or topics.
- ELAGSE11-12RI2: Determine two or more central ideas of a text and analyze their development over the course of the text, including how they interact and build on one another to provide a complex analysis; provide an objective summary of the text.
- ELAGSE11-12RI6: Determine an author's point of view or purpose in a text in which the rhetoric is particularly effective, analyzing how style and content contribute to the power, persuasiveness, or beauty of the text.
- ELAGSE11-12W1: Write arguments to support claims in an analysis of substantive topics or texts, using valid reasoning and relevant and sufficient evidence. a. Introduce precise, knowledgeable claim(s), establish the significance of the claim(s), distinguish the claim(s)

---

[8] The components listed in this lesson plan are standard requirements that teachers must list for their units, including time signatures of activities. I have omitted certain elements, such as differentiation for space.

from alternate or opposing claims, and create an organization that logically sequences claim(s), counterclaims, reasons, and evidence. b. Develop claim(s) and counterclaims fairly and thoroughly, supplying the most relevant evidence for each while pointing out the strengths and limitations of both in a manner that anticipates the audience's knowledge level, concerns, values, and possible biases. c. Use words, phrases, and clauses as well as varied syntax to link the major sections of the text, create cohesion, and clarify the relationships between claim(s) and reasons, between reasons and evidence, and between claim(s) and counterclaims. d. Establish and maintain a formal style and objective tone while attending to the norms and convention.

Student Learning Goals and Objectives: Students will analyze the effect that pre-existing gender roles have on women's education and political autonomy and develop their own opinions as to whether these roles produce a productive or nonproductive lasting effect on society. Students will annotate the text as they read, tracking the author's purpose and tone throughout the essay. Students will use critical thinking skills after the reading as they view and strategically analyze clips from the series to explore the differences between the view of women during the American Revolution and the view of women today. Ultimately, students will combine these strategies to reach a conceptual understanding of the ways in which contemporary discourse still too often casts concepts of womanhood, gender, and sexuality as seemingly stable and unchangeable—rather than mutable and socially constructed.

Prior Academic Knowledge: Students already have competency in analyzing an author's tone and purpose as well as a character's desires and motives. They should be able to utilize textual evidence to unpack these literary elements and develop and defend argumentative positions. Students already have a working knowledge of the historical period and context of the American Revolution.

Instructional Strategies and Learning Tasks

Launch/Activator (10 minutes): I start the lesson to engage and motivate students with a pre-reading assessment chart in which students will explore their preconceptions regarding women in the 18th century and how gender roles can affect political inequality. Students rate statements on a scale of 1–5 with 1 being "completely disagree" and 5 being "completely agree" (see Figure 6.2).

Instruction (20 minutes): I construct a short, student-based discussion in which I ask the students to defend their arguments from the pre-reading activity. Students stand in the middle of the classroom if they have 3 or more statements that rate 5 on their activity. As the ratings decrease, students stand closer to the walls of the room to create a center–periphery visualization of students' responses that allows them to understand themselves as part of a spectrum of ideas and opinions. After being thus arranged in the room, each student should be prepared to defend their argument. I then ask students how societal norms have changed throughout the years and whether they believe that women's rights have changed since the 18th century based only on previous experiences among themselves, younger siblings, friends, etc. In this way, the following discussion of Murray's essay and *Turn* is prepared by and contrasted with their personal and cultural experiences. I briefly mention AMC's series *Turn: Washington's Spies* and ask students who are familiar with it to discuss whether they believe the show's representation of revolutionary period women is or is not an accurate representation of historical conditions. This connection to popular culture will then serve as a segue to discussing the multivalent quality of gender roles and the plasticity of their representation in early American writing and contemporary media.

Structured Practice and Application (50 minutes): During this time period, students read "On the Equality of the Sexes" by Judith Sargent Murray either independently or in groups. Before reading, I ask the students to pay special attention to the speaker's tone and identify her purpose throughout the essay. I ask the students to annotate as they read, underlining important lines or writing in the margins of the papers and then compare Murray's calls for educational equality to their preconceived notions of 18th-century womanhood. After a robust discussion of the text, my students next view a scene from *Turn* that showcases Anna Strong and her autonomous actions as part of the Culper Spy Ring. They dialogue about this scene and then put it in conversation with Murray. I next ask students to write a brief fictional letter by Anna to a personal female friend not featured in the show. In the letter (which students turn in), students should imagine Anna's perception and vindication of her actions in light of critiques pointed at her implicit or explicit transgressions against conventional womanhood. Students will thus have to reflect on the ways in which Strong's character embraces or embodies Murray's precepts, and, by extension, consider whether their earlier understanding of 18th-century women needs to be revised based on the essay and scene from the show.

Closure (10 minutes): I end class by asking some of the students to read their letters out loud for peer feedback. In contrast to letters inhabiting Strong's perspective, I ask whether students believe women's roles have either changed or not changed since the revolutionary period as portrayed in Murray's essay and *Turn*.

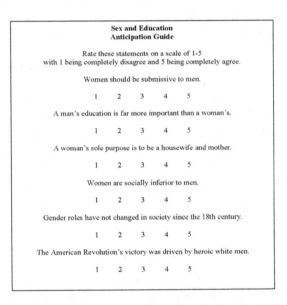

Figure 6.2 Pre-reading activity chart. (Credit: Cryslin Ledbetter.)

In this lesson, students thus compare their preconceived notions of women's roles during the American Revolution to both an original early American document (Murray's essay) and a contemporary pop culture rendering (*Turn*). Certainly, this approach merely forms the beginning of what should become a longer reflective process for students who are often preconditioned to hold specific concepts of womanhood and may also be reticent to share their views—especially if they are at all aware of political debates about gender and sexuality. The inclusion of the TV show is designed, at least in part, to break down this reluctance and make connections to historical perspectives on gender through a medium that appeals to them in visual and narrative terms. Rather than rejecting such lines of inquiry as part of a "divisive concept" they should avoid, the personal grounding of the lesson's activities hopefully encourages them to test their experiences in comparison to original early American texts and contemporary pop culture portrayals. Following Micciche's feminist pedagogy, such differentiated activities encourage "student writers to try out a personal voice [...], reveal estrangement from dominant texts, and write from an interrogatory rather than argumentative stance" (132). To put it differently, pursuing inquiry and gaining knowledge independently should help students pre-empt falling into default political positions, instead questioning their assumptions and learning to frame their positions more deliberately. While this entire process may be cause for discomfort for some students, this is the point of the lesson. It is from this position of discomfort or uncertainty that students can begin to reflect on the very process through which they form conceptions of abstract subjects such as American history, womanhood, gender, and gender roles. Perhaps, they may come away from this lesson wondering: Why did I think heroic, white men drove the American Revolution? My challenge for educators is to ask themselves how we can get students to delve into their own metacognitions. Ultimately, to return once more to Otis's words in *Sex Education*, will students be able to discuss "[t]he issues [that] have always been there," though they "just haven't felt safe enough to raise them"? (38:00).

Works Cited

"11th–12th Grade English Language Arts Georgia Standards of Excellence (ELA GSE)." Internal Support, https://www.georgiastandards.org/Georgia-Standards/Pages/ELA.aspx

"City-Data." Bremen, Georgia (GA) Profile: Population, Maps, Real Estate, Averages, Homes, Statistics, Relocation, Travel, Jobs, Hospitals, Schools, Crime, Moving, Houses, News, Sex Offenders, http://www.city-data.com/city/Bremen-Georgia.html (last accessed November 12, 2024).

Crane-Murdoch, Sierra. "Standing Rock: A New Moment for Native-American Rights." *The New Yorker*, October 12, 2016, https://www.newyorker.com/news/news-desk/standing-rock-a-new-moment-for-native-american-rights (last accessed November 12, 2024).

Dobbs v. Jackson Women's Health Organization. 597 U.S. Supreme Court, https://www.supremecourt.gov/opinions/21pdf/19-1392_6j37.pdf (last accessed November 12, 2024).

Duer, Amy, et al. *Prentice Hall Literature: Timeless Voices, Timeless Themes*. Prentice Hall, 1999.

Kyle [@KS]. "You're a terrible actress (and person) so I doubt you'll get another role, but on the off chance you do, I'll be boycotting." Twitter, October 25, 2017, twitter.com/heatherglind/status/896556916192817152/photo/1.

@marniehutchinso. "You are ridiculous calling out The former President for sexual assault. You ugly feminist have taken humor and turned it into a dirty word." Twitter, October 25, 2017, twitter.com/heatherglind/status/896556916192817152/photo/1.

Micciche, Laura. "Feminist Pedagogies." *A Guide to Composition Pedagogies*, 2nd ed., edited by Gary Tate et al. Oxford UP, 2013, pp. 128–45.

Murray, Judith Sargent. "On the Equality of the Sexes." *The Bedford Anthology of American Literature*, Shorter Second Edition, edited by Susan Belasco and Linck Johnson. Bedford/St. Martin's, 2014, pp. 401–6.

Phillips, Kristine, and Eli Rosenberg. "George H.W. Bush 'has patted women's rears' but Never Meant to Offend, Spokesman Says: Two Actresses Said the Former President Grabbed Them from Behind as They Posed for Pictures at Past Events." *The Washington Post*, October 26, 2017, https://www.washingtonpost.com/news/arts-and-entertainment/wp/2017/10/25/george-h-w-bush-apologizes-for-attempt-at-humor-after-actress-accused-him-of-groping/ (last accessed November 12, 2024).

"A Resolution." *State Board of Education of the State of Georgia*, June 3, 2021, https://simbli.eboardsolutions.com/Meetings/Attachment.aspx?S=1262&AID=1274907&MID=93474 (last accessed November 12, 2024).

Rose, Alexander. *Washington's Spies: The Story of America's First Spy Ring*. Bantam Books, 2006.

"Season 3, episode 8 [no title]." *Sex Education*, September 17, 2021, Netflix, https://www.netflix.com/watch/81191733?trackId=14170286.

"Senate Bill 377-LC 49 0750. 2021-2022 Regular Session." Georgia General Assembly, https://www.legis.ga.gov/legislation/61345 (last accessed November 12, 2024).

Silverstein, Craig, creator. *Turn: Washington's Spies*. AMC Studios, 2014–17.

Smith, Bubba [@KevinHe09012015]. "You are despicable. Using a 94 year old man to further your career. A curse on your house." Twitter, October 25, 2017, twitter.com/heatherglind/status/896556916192817152/photo/1.

Sonnenberg, Rhonda. "Georgia Teacher Fired for Reading Children's Book about Acceptance in Class." Southern Poverty Law Center, June 22, 2023, https://www.splcenter.org/news/2023/06/22/georgia-teacher-fired-reading-childrens-book-about-acceptance-class (last accessed November 12, 2024).

"Strong, adj." *OED Online*, Oxford UP, June 2021, www.oed.com/view/Entry/191802 (last accessed November 12, 2024).

Taub, Amanda. "A 17th-Century Judge Still Exerts Influence on Women's Rights." *The New York Times*, May 19, 2022, A.6, Proquest, https://www.proquest.com/newspapers/17th-century-judge-still-exerts-influence-on/docview/2666761786/se-2?accountid=15017 (last accessed February 3, 2024).

Taylor, Diana. *The Archive and the Repertoire: Performing Cultural Memory in the Americas.* Duke UP, 2003.

PART III

STAGING THE NATION: FROM THEATER TO TELEVISION

Section Overview

Nationhood takes center stage in Part III as contributors postulate how contemporary concerns drive and shape representations of early America in staged musicals and dramas as well as in comedic genres. Chapter 7, **"Performing, Remembering, and Reiterating: Early America on Stage"** by **Shira Lurie** launches the section in her examination of popular musicals depicting early American history often overlooked due to *Hamilton*'s popularity: *1776, Bloody, Bloody Andrew Jackson,* and *The Civil War* (also known as *Freedom's Song*). Lurie's piece pushes beyond simple questions of accuracy in its consideration of issues surrounding adaptation and public memory. It demonstrates how each show uses a different era of early American history to tell a version of the American story that, "[d]espite these changing circumstances [of each], ... reveal Americans' commitment to triumphalist and white-centric historical narratives." Taken together, the four musicals, she argues, facilitate an investigation of how contemporary concerns have shaped representations of early American history and their popular reception, reminding us that historical memory is influenced much more by the demands of the present than the facts of the past. They force us to consider what is gained and what is lost when history is adapted to the stage, and we come to see, Lurie contends, "a shocking lack of evolution in the American musical theater canon's treatment of early American history" wherein "[r]emembering the past should push us beyond our current concerns and structures, and toward a better, more just future."

"Aaron Posner's *JQA* as Layered History: Promoting Aesthetic-Historical Reflection in a Texas Theatre's Production" by **Sarah Ruffing Robbins** shifts readers to dramatic representations of history in her examinations of Posner's play on John Quincy Adams (sixth president of the United States) by a regional theatre company in Chapter 8. Her chapter proposes a theorization that shifts from retrospective emphases toward analyzing how historical drama can create a forward-looking call to audiences' sociopolitical conscience via aesthetic-historical reflection. "Strategically, if indirectly," Ruffing Robbins writes, "Posner's text nods to a heritage of drama revisiting America's past to offer correctives and inspiration for later times ... In asserting 'evocation' and 'provocation' over 'accuracy,' Posner calls for historical drama to press audiences into a critique of 'where we are now,' a reflective enterprise even more vital than immersing in history itself for its own sake." Using interviews, noted scripts, and details from two performances, Ruffing Robbins argues that *JQA* engages with audience awareness of current, large-scale political dangers and harnesses historical resources that could aid navigation through a history-of-now shaped by political turmoil, a pandemic's threats, and philosophical anxieties around democracy's future.

Anne Roth-Reinhardt's "*Ted Lasso* and Early American Identity" then takes on the award-winning Apple TV+ show *Ted Lasso* in Chapter 9, especially its eponymous protagonist, by positioning him alongside early American homespun characters such as Yankee Doodle, Jonathan from Tyler's *The Contrast*, and Melville's *Israel Potter* as a fulcrum for addressing the contestation of American identity and its representation in the early Republic and today. Roth-Reinhardt's chapter asks: Can the bumpkin have the answers and, if so, is the America-positive plot and its message somehow regressive in the twenty-first century? In other words, can viewers feel good about an unprepared American succeeding after four years of the Trump administration? Ultimately, Roth-Reinhardt contemplates whether and how we can accept ignorant characters in both the early American texts and in the contemporary TV hit as representatives of American moral authority when the nation bears the stain of generations of systemic and often legal racial discrimination and oppression. She writes, "The glittering brand trafficked as 'America' has long depended on the willful forgetting of a sordid domestic and geopolitical history and, in today's political climate where symbols of America have been weaponized, both metaphorically and literally, characterization of America as a force for good can be tough to swallow." Yet, *Ted Lasso*'s popularity in the aftermath of the 2016 Trump election, she considers, could also very well be the embracement of a counternarrative: "an alternative to the American values advertised by the Republican president." "Democracy, as seen through the show," she writes, "empowers communities through collective agency rather than greedy individualism" where "'belief'" itself "can upset oppressive systems and change the world," as long as, like Lasso, we stay "true to [our] values rather than trying to dominate another."

7

Performing, Remembering, and Reiterating: Early America on Stage

Shira Lurie

On March 14, 2016, the cast of the smash-hit musical *Hamilton* (2015) performed at the White House—a special event hosted by the Obamas that spotlighted *Hamilton*'s interplays between theater, history, and contemporary politics. In his opening remarks, the president told the crowd that in the figure of Alexander Hamilton, Lin-Manuel Miranda "identified a quintessentially American story." He said that, "In each brilliantly crafted song, we hear the debates that shaped our nation, and we hear the debates that are still shaping our nation" ("Remarks by the President"). Indeed, the links between past and present were palpable even to those not in attendance; a video from the event of Christopher Jackson as George Washington singing "One Last Time" to the outgoing President Obama has nearly eleven million views on YouTube.[1]

Nearly fifty years prior, a similar event took place. On February 22, 1970, the cast of *1776* (1969), a popular musical about the Second Continental Congress's decision to declare independence, performed at the White House at the invitation of President Richard Nixon. "We believe this is the right play for the right time and place," Nixon announced in his introduction that applauded the musical's focus on "patriotism" and the founding story (qtd. in Harbert 251–2). Both Obama and Nixon knew that how and what Americans remember about their past is strongly linked to the issues of the present. As a result, it is no surprise that both presidents feted shows that encouraged pride and loyalty to the nation and its leaders.

---

[1] As of February 9, 2022. https://www.youtube.com/watch?v=uV4UpCq2azs.

Hamilton and *1776* are, of course, pillars of the genre, but they are not the only musicals about early American history. Other shows have attempted to set the eighteenth and nineteenth centuries to song, including *The Civil War* (1999), also known as *Freedom's Song*, which depicts the American Civil War, and *Bloody Bloody Andrew Jackson* (2009), which offers a satirical look at its titular figure. Each of these four productions uses a different era of early American history to tell its own version of the national story. As a result, these shows provide insight into how Americans represent and draw meaning from their past.

Scholars who have explored theatrical treatments of early American history have rightly pointed to these shows' power to disseminate and bolster particular historical narratives. "With its widespread appeal, [*Hamilton*] has the potential to shape how Americans understand the nation's early history for some time to come," observe scholars Renee C. Romano and Claire Bond Potter (6). Despite academics' discomfort with the notion, most Americans receive their historical educations from media, museums, and politics, and not from professional historians—a reality, according to historian Andrew M. Schocket, that is unlikely to change. "[We] would like moviemakers, politicians, activists, and judges to have a better sense of history and how it works," but "we should not expect historical discussion on the American Revolution or, for that matter, any complex historical process to take the form of factually accurate, deeply nuanced, properly sourced, logically sound, civil debate across the spectrum of mass culture" (211).

Yet, these shows are products of specific moments in time, and, so, are works of historical memory, not history. While the latter is a discipline that forms arguments based on interpretations of historical evidence, the former is a cultural construction of stories about the past that speak to the issues of the present. Historical memory is, as Edward Said has put it, a way of forming "a coherent identity, a national narrative, a place in the world, though ... the processes of memory are frequently, if not always, manipulated and intervened in for sometimes urgent purposes in the present" (179). These musicals, each in their own way, represent a mode of remembering America's shared past that is tied up in the contexts of their creation.

In 1969, when *1776* premiered on Broadway, the United States was mired in the Vietnam War and experiencing tectonic social and cultural shifts domestically. During this time of anxiety and uncertainty, *1776* comforted audiences with a celebratory story of the nation's founding dripping with patriotic assurances of the American spirit's resolve and righteousness. Likewise, *The Civil War*'s implication that Americans are ultimately united and committed to justice probably soothed audiences when it premiered in the late 1990s, just after the Clinton–Lewinsky scandal. Amid increased partisan suspicion, the show's embrace of Lost Cause and whiggish tropes asserted that Americans are less divided than they seem and that moments of conflict have historically driven the nation toward progress.

Bloody Bloody Andrew Jackson advanced a more critical tone. It emerged in 2009 and took aim at the cult of celebrity that had dominated the 2008 presidential election. However, Indigenous communities denounced the show's satirical treatment of genocide, indicating that perhaps the production misjudged the "post-racial" moment that the Obama era supposedly initiated. Similarly, *Hamilton*, for all its success, also faced its fair share of disapproval. While many critics first praised the show's race-conscious casting and pro-immigrant message during the Trump campaign and early presidency, some have since condemned its erasure of race and slavery. Further backlash followed the show's controversy-laden turn in Puerto Rico and its premiere on Disney+ just a few months after the murder of George Floyd by police. Still, *Hamilton*'s widespread appeal is undeniable, and its continued resonance reveals the complexities of and struggles over American historical memory in our current moment.

Despite these changing circumstances, all four of these shows' creations and receptions reveal Americans' commitment to triumphalist and white-centric historical narratives. Even the seemingly progressive examples of *Bloody Bloody Andrew Jackson* and *Hamilton*, when dissected, reveal conservative and comfortable stories that either paper over the injustices of white supremacy or confine them to the past. All told, the last five decades of American musical theater have shown a remarkable consistency when depicting the nation's early history—a phenomenon that points to the stranglehold that exceptionalism has on American historical memory.

1776 debuted on Broadway in 1969 as Americans worried over the increasingly bloody war in Vietnam and growing cultural rifts at home. The previous year had brought the Tet Offensive, My Lai Massacre, and assassinations of Martin Luther King, Jr. and Robert Kennedy. Amid the tumult, Richard Nixon won the presidency and promised a slow withdrawal of American troops from Vietnam (Isserman and Kazin 221–40). But the following year, 9,500 American soldiers died in the continued fighting (266). Meanwhile, civil rights, feminist, and anti-war activists maintained their vocal criticisms of American society and government, and the developing counterculture pushed back against all kinds of conservative social norms (Brick; Gitlin). The period's uncertainty fed disillusionment, anxiety, and frustration with government among those on the Left, and intolerance, anger, and disgust with activists among those on the Right.

But *1776*, a musical dramatizing the proceedings of the Second Continental Congress and the eventual signing of the Declaration of Independence, is awash in American exceptionalism. The musical focuses on the character of John Adams and his effort to convince his reticent colleagues to vote for independence from the British Empire. In Adams's quest to secure a declaration of American independence, the show offers audiences a reassuring story about the indisputable righteousness of the American experiment and its odds-defying origins—undoubtedly, a soothing antidote to the difficulties of the time. Indeed, audiences responded to the patriotic messaging; *1776* ran on Broadway for almost three years, and in 1972, Warner Brothers adapted it into a film (Greenfield 262).

While the musical depicts the tense debates over independence, it never actually questions the wisdom of separating from the British Empire. Those who promote independence, like John Adams and Benjamin Franklin, are the story's heroes (even if the former is "obnoxious and disliked") ("But, Mr. Adams").[2] These men are charged with overcoming the stubborn, backward thinking of those who oppose them, like John Dickinson of Pennsylvania. Adams opens the show with a soliloquy lamenting the Congress's obstinacy to the obvious course of action: "For ten years King George and his Parliament have gulled, cullied, and diddled these Colonies with their illegal taxes ... and still this Congress won't grant any of my proposals on Independence even so much as the courtesy of open debate!" (Edwards and Stone 1). Adams always provides a concrete list of grievances in his arguments for independence, but his opponents offer only vague assertions of loyalty to "the greatest empire on earth" or cowardly rationalizations (39). "If I thought we could win this war, I'd be at the front of your ranks," declares Samuel Chase of Maryland; "But you must know it's impossible!" (87). By presenting independence as the only logical and just option, the show implies that the American national project is unassailable, a message that *Hamilton* will echo nearly fifty years later.

As independence draws nearer, the show doubles down on its patriotic messaging. "Through all the gloom, I see the rays of ravishing light and glory!" sings Adams. "I see Americans – all Americans, free forever more!" ("Is Anybody There?"). His optimistic prophecy, of course, omits the struggles of those who are not elite, white, English-speaking, able-bodied men.

---

[2] All songs referenced from *1776* are from Edwards, *1776* (Original Broadway Cast Recording).

American freedom, in this telling, holds no room for nuance. Instead, the audience is treated to a vision of America that is unabashedly hopeful and empowering: one that celebrates the indomitable American spirit. As Benjamin Franklin insists near the close of the show: "And just as Tom here has written, though the shell may belong to Great Britain, the eagle inside belongs to us!" ("The Egg"). The message landed. In the *New York Times*, critic Lewis Funke affirmed that the show delivered not only "laughter" and "poignancy," but "above all, a kindling of pride and inspiration."

It also promises success even against long odds, a reassuring message to those wondering how (and if) the Vietnam War would end. "Even though the outcome is never in any very serious doubt, *1776* is consistently exciting," observed one review (Barnes). Indeed, despite an obvious ending, the show captures the tensions of the debates and the unlikely triumph of the independence advocates. Early on, independence is rendered nearly impossible by the passage of a resolution that Congress could only endorse the measure by unanimous vote, not a simple majority (Edwards and Stone 51). Pennsylvania's crucial vote is only secured at the last moment when Franklin intervenes, demanding that the delegation be polled so that Dickinson's colleagues can outnumber him (137–8). In the script, even the announcement that the resolution on independence has passed comes with the stage direction of "surprise" (140). The miraculous victory, snatched at the last moment from the jaws of defeat, depicts the American founding as an underdog story—one whose improbable outcome seems the product of divine intervention, a comforting message for a country mired in a bloody, seemingly endless jungle war.

Audiences at both ends of the American political spectrum found something to love in *1776*. Those on the Right described the show as a respectful homage to the nation's founding principles and a timely testament to the American spirit. One high-ranking naval official wrote to director Stuart Ostrow praising the show's "refreshing and reassuring demonstration that very fundamental things about our Nation and what it stands for are still respected." He also highlighted the show's popular and critical success, noting that "good old-fashioned patriotism" can still thrive in the modern climate "in spite of cynics" (qtd. in Harbert 247). Critic Glenna Syse suggested that "America's most bellicose cynics—the disillusioned and contemptuous, the scoffers, the grumblers, the protesters and the disenchanted" would be well served by a set of tickets to the show. "Then maybe we could get this country moving again," Syse observed. To conservatives, the show represented an important celebration of American history at a time when national pride was under attack both at home and abroad—a message further strengthened by the show's depiction of those who questioned independence as weak and cowardly. The Assistant Commandant of the Marine Corps even wanted to bring the show to Vietnam to inspire the troops (Harbert 246–7).

Those on the Left, however, saw in *1776* an implied irreverence for elites and a ringing endorsement of revolution. "We are taught too much respect for our sacred forefathers these days," observed a Berkeley journalist who praised the show for humanizing the Founding Fathers. Moreover, *1776* explains to the "old . . . why young people are rioting in the streets" and inspires "compassion for great men giving birth to great schemes" (qtd. in Harbart 248). For those engaged in political activism and cultural critique, the show affirmed that revolution was an American tradition.

Despite the Right's praise, the Leftist interpretation is what the show's creative team had in mind. Although never made explicit in the content of the show, they hoped audiences would draw connections between past and present and understand revolution as a legitimate political solution that aligned with American principles. In a piece that compared the Kent State shooting with the Boston massacre, *1776*'s book writer Peter Stone drew a line between "those troubled times and these" and argued that "the lessons of the past [should be] applied to the problems of the future" (qtd. in Harbert 245). Indeed, the show affirms that rebelling against status quo power structures constituted a patriotic act. Notably, the creators embodied these critiques of current American society in a conservative celebration of the founding era—and one, in particular, that celebrates rich, white men as the heroes of the American story. *1776* also has an implicit anti-war message. Ostrow confessed in his memoir that, to his mind, the show aligned with "the protest to end the war in Vietnam. America was thwarting Vietnam's revolution in much the same way England sought to defeat us in 1776" (Harbert 246).

But *1776* still spoke to conservatives, so much so that the Nixon White House invited the cast to perform in commemoration of George Washington's birthday. However, some maneuvering occurred behind the scenes. Prior to the performance, a member of Nixon's staff informed Ostrow that the president wanted three numbers omitted: "Cool, Cool, Conservative Men," a song criticizing conservatives, "Momma, Look Sharp," a song about the costs of war, and "Molasses to Rum," a song about slavery and northeastern hypocrisy. Clearly, some of the production's left-leaning messaging did not escape Nixon's notice. But the cast and crew refused to acquiesce, and the president backed down, allowing the performance to go ahead unedited (Harbert 252).

The widespread success of *1776* within such a divided political climate speaks to the triumphalism embedded in popular memory of the American founding shared across the ideological spectrum. As Schocket argues, those on the Right favor an "essentialist" lens to advance a conservative interpretation that encourages strict patriotism to the founders' legacy. It celebrates government institutions and traditions "from which straying would be treason and result in the nation's ruin" (4), whereas those on the Left have an "organicist" framework that interprets the American Revolution as ongoing and incomplete, creating a nation in constant need of perfecting (5). Both *1776*'s creation and its reception demonstrate how personal political ideas encouraged Americans to understand the founding story in the way they found most comforting and appropriate given modern challenges. It was, as Nixon said, "the right play for the right time and place" (qtd. in Harbert 252). Or, in other words, the show provided a historical memory comforting and pliable enough for the divisions and challenges of the late 1960s and early 1970s. *1776* provided both the Left and Right with a celebratory version of the American founding that spoke to their particular angsts. Yet, despite their differences, both interpretations drew from the same reassuring assumptions about American exceptionalism embedded within the musical.

Like *1776*, *The Civil War* premiered at a time of deep division. When it debuted on Broadway in April 1999, the American political climate was growing increasingly hostile amid rising partisan animosity and mistrust. During the course of Bill Clinton's presidency, his administration suffered multiple scandals, including "Travelgate," in which several White House travel office staff were fired for misuse of funds and replaced by friends of the Clintons, and "Whitewater," in which investigations into a failed real estate investment resulted in criminal convictions for the Clintons' business associates, but cleared them of any wrongdoing (Serrianne 236–40). In January 1998, news broke of an affair between the president and a White House intern named Monica Lewinsky. Initially, Clinton denied the allegations, even while under oath. But after Lewinsky turned over DNA evidence to the FBI, the president reversed course and admitted to having an inappropriate relationship. The House of Representatives impeached Clinton for perjury and obstruction of justice, but the Senate acquitted him (Serrianne 240–6). The incident, as well as the other various controversies that plagued the Clinton administration, stoked partisan division, with each side growing increasingly suspicious of the other.[3]

---

[3] For more on the scandals of the Clinton era, see also Haynes Johnson, *The Best of Times: America in the Clinton Years*.

The Civil War, like its earlier counterpart, offers a version of American history that soothed these national anxieties. Despite the contentiousness of the topic, the song cycle avoids delving into the controversial issues of slavery, secession, sectionalism, reconstruction, and reparations. The show simply follows the experiences of Union and Confederate soldiers, those on the homefront, and the enslaved through the course of the conflict, emphasizing the hardships endured by all. In doing so, it presents the Civil War as, paradoxically, a nationally unifying story—an event where every American struggled and suffered, side by side. "The show aspires to provide an uplifting, unifying tribute to the resilience and sacrifices of the people," explained writer Gregory Boyd (qtd. in Greenfield 76). Troublingly, this approach echoes the late stages of Reconstruction when white northerners abandoned Black civil rights and the punishment of the former Confederacy in favor of peace and reconciliation grounded in white supremacy. In the years that followed, veterans from both sections embraced a culture of remembrance that emphasized their shared sacrifices and valor in the war. White Americans largely chose a romanticized version of the conflict that focused on common experiences, rather than the divisive issues that had caused and fueled the war.[4] The musical borrows heavily from this memory tradition, spinning a comforting narrative that the depth of unity among Americans will always overcome superficial differences.

Even in its characters, *The Civil War* emphasizes the theme of universalism by presenting generic representatives of the Union, Confederacy, and enslaved. One critic noted: "Although the program offers a traditional list of actors and their roles, hardly anyone onstage is ever identified by name, indicating that the audience is meant to view these characters as Everymen and Everywomen" (Leydon). Ben Brantley of the *New York Times* concurred, suggesting that "the absence of character-defining specificity was [presumably] deliberate, an attempt to extend the show's universal resonance" ("History Soldiering On"). This trope also helps bridge the gap between past and present, encouraging audience members to see themselves in those foolishly fighting their fellow countrymen.

From opening number to finale, *The Civil War* avoids the multitude of differences between the Union and Confederacy in favor of vague assertions of both sides' similarities. The beginning of the show, sung by

---

[4] For works on postwar memory traditions, see David Blight, *Race and Reunion*, and Nina Silber, *The Romance of Reunion*.

Union Captain Emmett Lochran, introduces the audience to this conceit: "Brother, my brother, one blue and one gray, will meet upon a quiet field the morn of Judgment Day" ("A House Divided").[5] As both sides go off to war, the lyrics and staging grow more overt. In "By the Sword/Sons of Dixie," Union and Confederate soldiers sing in call and response to each other and conclude the song by singing the same lyrics about victory in battle. As scholar Thomas A. Greenfield notes, "At the song's conclusion, the two armies appear to meld into a single entity, united in all but the color of their respective uniforms" (76). As the war takes its toll, all soldiers lament the futures they have "stolen" from their "brothers, be they blue or gray" ("Judgment Day"). By the end of the show, the lyrics have lost any remaining shred of subtlety. "When all is said and done, I guess we're all the same," sings Lochran; "The words we speak, our hopes, and the God we claim. It's you and me, just a different name" ("Northbound Train"). One is left to wonder why they went to war in the first place.

The answer, of course, is slavery—a part of the show that exists in ahistorical isolation from the trials of the battlefield and homefront. Rather than the motivator for secession and founding principle of the Confederacy, the show depicts slavery as a distinct story, one in which the suffering of a separated married couple, Clayton and Bessie Toler, mirrors that of the white soldiers and their wives. The musical leaves the details of slavery, even its geographic location, unspecified. While the script features quotations from historical figures like Abraham Lincoln, Confederate Vice President Alexander Stephens's famous statement that the "cornerstone" of the Confederate Constitution was "that the negro is not equal to the white man; that slavery – subordination to the superior race – is his natural and normal condition" is conspicuously absent (Cleveland 717–29).

Likewise, the show does not depict the horrors of slavery and instead diminishes them into abstract calls for freedom. "So throw my brother's chains away, no more to be exiled. And get down on your knees and pray we'll all be freedom's child," sings a fictionalized Frederick Douglass ("Freedom's Child"). *The Civil War* also limits enslaved resistance to moments of fervent prayer. "Freedom ain't coming soon enough for me. And sure enough ain't coming for free," sing the Tolers. "If prayin' were horses all of us would ride. And I'd be by your side" ("If Prayin' Were Horses"). In reality, enslaved resistance during the Civil War intensified

---

[5] All songs referenced from *The Civil War* are from Jack Murphy and Frank Wildhorn, *The Civil War: The Complete Work*.

existing pre-war patterns and included theft, escape, aid of Union soldiers, and violent rebellion.[6]

Just as it does not depict the realities of slavery, the show also avoids emancipation. Instead, it opts for a vague declaration that "the chains are gone" from an unnamed Black soldier in the show's closing number ("The Glory"). Rather than a passage from the Emancipation Proclamation, the song quotes the unifying message of Lincoln's Second Inaugural Address: "With malice toward none. With charity for all ... Let us strive on to finish the work we are in, to bind up the nation's wounds" ("The Glory"). This simplistic treatment of a complex issue avoids the difficulties and divisiveness of Reconstruction and the lack of reparations for slavery that followed the 13th Amendment. Instead, the show favors an optimistic narrative of inevitable progress grounded in the assumed innate justice of the American experience. Just like *1776*, *The Civil War* takes a triumphant and exceptionalist framework as a given when presenting the early American story.

The musical's treatment of slavery aligns with the Lost Cause interpretation—a memory tradition long denounced by historians and embraced by neo-Confederates. In this version of events, the Confederacy formed to protect states' rights, not slavery, and fought a defensive, honorable war to defend their homes from a Yankee invasion. They lost only because they were outgunned and outmanned by the Union—an inevitability that does not call into question the bravery of Confederate soldiers or the righteousness of their cause (Gallagher and Nolan 1–2). The Lost Cause narrative took hold in the postwar period, even among white northerners, because it made reconciliation achievable (Blight 255–99). Once again, many white Americans found it comforting to put aside political, social, and moral questions in favor of a nostalgic narrative that emphasized shared struggles in an honorable, if regrettable, war. The show embraces other elements of the Lost Cause tradition, as well. For instance, in a song called "Virginia," Confederate Captain Billy Pierce laments the disappearance of the idyllic antebellum south: "There was a time, a time of splendor and grace. When the world moved by at a kinder pace. There was a land, a land to pleasure the eyes, where the old was new and the foolish wise." The Lost Cause's sentimental and wistful portrait of the antebellum south depoliticized the Confederacy and instead encouraged

---

[6] For more on enslaved resistance, see Stephanie M.H. Camp, *Closer to Freedom: Enslaved Women and Everyday Resistance in the Plantation South*; Thavolia Glymph, *Out of the House of Bondage: The Transformation of the Plantation Household*; William A. Link, *Roots of Secession: Slavery and Politics in Antebellum Virginia*.

an empathetic connection with Confederate soldiers fighting to defend hearth and home.[7]

During the late 1990s, a time of deepening partisan fracture and suspicion, the show's embrace of Lost Cause and whiggish narratives likely assured audiences that current discord was superficial. Americans have always had more in common than they have realized. What is more, the show also implied that divisions have historically driven the nation toward progress. After all, although it does not specify how or why, the show makes clear that the war brought about the end of slavery. Yet, despite this comforting messaging, critics panned *The Civil War*. They took issue not with the show's problematic historical portrayal, but rather its repetitive and bland plot. Rather than remarking on the Lost Cause mythology or trappings of exceptionalism, the reviews simply complained that *The Civil War* was unentertaining. "The show arranges its archetypal elements into confoundedly static patterns, laying out all its cards in its opening minutes and then failing to combine them in ways that would build to revelation or strong emotional response," wrote Brantley ("History Soldiering On"). "Every number offers one simple idea and then reiterates it," commented another reviewer (Harris, "The Civil War"). The show closed on Broadway after only seven weeks and lost millions of dollars (Greenfield 78).

But while *1776* and *The Civil War* met different fates at the box office, audiences and reviewers accepted uncritically the historical memories both musicals advanced. *1776* succeeded and *The Civil War* stumbled due to each show's artistic attributes; no one quibbled with or critiqued their triumphalist interpretations of history. *Bloody Bloody Andrew Jackson* and *Hamilton*, however, did not enjoy the same receptions. Their presentations of American founding history sparked controversy, causing some to reject as problematic the historical memories these shows presented.

Bloody Bloody Andrew Jackson appeared at the start of the Obama era, opening off-Broadway at The Public Theater in 2009 and moving to Broadway the following year. The show's debut followed closely after the 2008 presidential campaign, which initiated a new style of mass politics emphasizing the Internet, celebrity endorsement, and the cult of personality (Dong et al. 75–88). This period also marked the heyday of comedic political commentary, with shows like *The Daily Show*, *The Colbert Report*, and *Saturday Night Live* offering political observations and often skewering

---

[7] See Silber, *The Romance of Reunion*, for more on how sentimentalism encouraged reconciliation and reunion between white Americans from both sections.

Republican vice presidential candidate Sarah Palin. Barack Obama's election to the presidency seemed to be a watershed moment in American history—almost 150 years after the end of slavery, a Black man had ascended to the highest office in the land. But while some heralded a "postracial era," Obama's campaign and presidency brought to the fore all kinds of white anxieties about race and power. The culture wars drove a "conservative resurgence," in which wedge issues and the theatrics of the newly formed Tea Party movement formed a powerful backlash to the Obama Democrats (Dombrink 11).

In contrast to the more implicit messages of *1776* and *The Civil War*, the creators of *Bloody Bloody Andrew Jackson* presented their opinions about modern America explicitly in almost every aspect of the show. The musical's sound and style immediately tip audiences off to the show's enmeshing of past and present. *Bloody Bloody Andrew Jackson* depicts the seventh president as an emo rockstar, complete with leather pants and introductions like "Ladies and Gentlemen, Governor Andrew Jackson! Yeah! That's right, motherfuckers, Jackson's back!" ("Rockstar").[8] This artistic choice is meant to evoke the angst and bluster of the young nation. "Emo rock is a kind of post punk [characterized by] deeply emotional boys with guitars who are very upset about girls who did not go out with them in high school," explained composer and lyricist Michael Friedman. "This is a show about a deeply emotional boy, the adolescence of a country, and the growing pains of both" ("Behind the Music"). The musical introduces this conceit in its opening song in which Jackson begins by complaining about being snubbed by a girl and transitions immediately into entitled bravado: "But it's the early nineteenth century and we're gonna take this country back for people like us" ("Populism, Yea, Yea"). It is clear from the outset that this is not the hagiographic tale of *1776*. Rather, the show follows Jackson from his youth to his presidency, emphasizing his populist appeal and violent tendencies. It is a much more stylized, sarcastic, and critical version of American history. The goal, according to Friedman, was for audiences to reflect on the national story and ask themselves "[w]hat it means to be American" ("Behind the Music").

The genre is also a commentary on the state of contemporary American politics. Rather than a condemnation of the Left or Right, the show criticizes the entire political culture for its emphasis on celebrity and

---

[8] All songs referenced from *Bloody Bloody Andrew Jackson* are from Michael Friedman, *Bloody Bloody Andrew Jackson* (Original Cast Recording).

outrage, instead of public service and policy. "This Andrew Jackson is the public figure as American idol and empty vessel for popular dissatisfaction," remarked reviewer Charles Isherwood, "and, as such, is a clear emissary from the current moment" ("Theatrical Stumbles"). Scholar Julie A. Noonan observed, "Jackson's campaign language and rock star comparisons are reminiscent both of Obama's sudden rise to popularity and of McCain's attempt to appear as a rebel or maverick despite his longevity in governmental service" (21). Other commenters drew additional connections to Bill Clinton, John Edwards, and Sarah Palin.[9] Friedman even endorsed these interpretations, explaining that Jackson encapsulated all of modern America's best-known figures: "Jackson sometimes feels like he's directly out of the Tea Party and then sometimes he feels like he's Obama" ("Behind the Music").

But the show does not solely reserve its mockery for politicians; it also admonishes those credulous citizens taken in by charisma and populist rhetoric. "Everything he says is right!" cheer Jackson voters ("Crisis Averted"). In the show's publicity materials, the production states that *Bloody Bloody Andrew Jackson* begs the question: "is wanting to have a beer with someone reason enough to elect him? What if he's really, really hot?" (Musical Theater International). Clearly, Jackson-as-Rockstar is meant to encourage viewer self-reflection on the political theater that dominated the early Obama era. "There's not a show in town that more astutely reflects the state of this nation than *Bloody Bloody Andrew Jackson*," averred Brantley ("Ideal President").

The musical even uses modern vernacular and phrases. The number "Crisis Averted" presents Jackson's 1828 presidential campaign as if it were a twenty-first-century TV ad: "My name is Andrew Jackson, and I'm here to speak with you about the future of this incredible country. These are complicated times. And today, we're going to need to make some complicated decisions. But we're going to make those decisions together" ("Crisis Averted"). The song goes on to announce that "it's morning again in America," a reference to Ronald Reagan's famous campaign spot from 1984. These references encourage audience members to draw links between the past and present and question whether the disdain they feel for the stage version of Jackson and his supporters may be a projection of their distaste for their own political climate.

---

[9] See Joe Meacham, "Rocking the Vote," and Ben Brantley, "Old Hickory, Rock Star President," for examples.

In a stylistic choice even riskier than those described thus far, the musical uses satire to critique Jacksonian America's white supremacy. Evocative of the then-popular *Colbert Report*'s satirical critique of conservatives, the musical attempts to "punch up" by having racists unabashedly display their racism, thus making them the butt of the joke (Richards 167). For instance, Rachel Jackson's lament in "The Great Compromise" begins, "I always thought I'd live in a house with a dog, and some kids, and some slaves." But the center of the show is Jackson's violence against Indigenous peoples and his removal policies. The show comments on dispossession with a white couple newly arrived in Florida rationalizing that "it's a real tragedy that Jackson moved all the Indians," but "it *is* nice it doesn't snow ... So, it's like, really great that he did that. But we *definitely* don't condone it" ("Crisis Averted"). The show takes a darker tone in "Ten Little Indians," a parody of the racist children's rhyme. The song charts the "disappearance" of Indigenous peoples, although, confusingly and problematically, the white supremacists are no longer the punchline. "Four little Indians hiding in a tree. One passed out drunk and then there were three," sings the chorus ("Ten Little Indians"). In addition to this racist stereotype, the song upholds the inaccurate and dangerous trope of the "vanishing Indian"—a myth that erases the present existence of hundreds of thousands of Indigenous peoples.

Even before the show arrived on Broadway, Indigenous leaders denounced it, arguing that the satirical treatment of genocide minimized the tragedy and played generations of suffering for laughs. While in development at The Public, producers belatedly invited Indigenous collaborators and friends to attend performances. Many expressed discomfort and outrage at the musical's comedic take on history. "Seeing the show made me ashamed to be in that theater," reported Steve Elm, the Artistic Director of Amerinda, an Indigenous production company. "I felt like there was a joke that I wasn't in on, and actually that I wasn't welcome in that theater ... because this play seemed to be expressly written without any idea that there are native people still alive" (Levine). Similarly, Betsy Theobald Richards observed that in falsely portraying Jackson's removal policies as personal revenge for the deaths of his parents by Indigenous warriors (a complete fabrication), the show "implied that the dominant culture's imagined historic 'savages' are complicit in their own suffering" (168). Richards decided to leave her role as the Native Theater Initiative Fellow at The Public in response (165).

Above all, Indigenous commenters and their allies pointed out that the satirical critique did not land. "The play is an exercise in racial slurs against Native Americans justified with a thin coating of white shaming," observed Rhiana Yazzie. In the wake of the backlash, The Public Theater's associate artistic director, Oskar Eustis, admitted that while he believes "the point that this production is making . . . is ultimately pro-native, there are an awful lot of ways in which it may not be perceived that way" (Yazzie). Still, the creative team made only minimal adjustments before moving the show to Broadway and decided to leave untouched Jackson's parents' murder as the catalyst for the story (Richards 170). The controversy has haunted subsequent productions, even leading some companies to cancel their runs (Purcell).[10]

In this way, *Bloody Bloody Andrew Jackson* unintentionally encapsulated another element of the Obama era; instead of signaling a post-racial America, the Obama administration only sharpened anxieties about race, power, and belonging. "When Obama's tenure began, rather than being perceived as a healing balm for the nation," observed scholar Heather Harris, "his presence in the White House served to peel the bandage off of the country's infected and festering racial wound" (xiv). So, while white critics largely celebrated *Bloody Bloody Andrew Jackson*'s irreverent take on American politics, Indigenous commentators pushed back on the idea that every part of the nation's history was ripe for satire and that white supremacy was a thing of the past. The disconnect reveals the deep roots of conservative historical memory traditions, even within those who aim to criticize them. *Bloody Bloody Andrew Jackson* tried to present a comedically critical historical memory that unified audiences in laughing at Jackson, condemning white supremacy, and reflecting on the problems within their own political culture. But, in the end, the creators propped up a white-centric narrative that perpetuated the racist stereotypes, myths, and "othering" embedded in the historical memories they claimed to mock. Indigenous consultants and critics noted how poorly the show's historical messaging aligned with the creative team's professed intentions, a critique some observers have also made of another of The Public's projects.

Hamilton: An American Musical debuted at The Public Theater before transitioning to Broadway in 2016. That year, of course, marked the end of Obama's second term and the contentious presidential election between Hillary Clinton and Donald Trump. *Hamilton*'s stratospheric rise and nagging controversies certainly aligned with the mood of the Obama era's

---

[10] For more on depictions of Indigenous peoples in popular culture, see Philip Deloria, *Indians in Unexpected Places*.

close—progressive promise mixed with disappointment and a conservative retrenchment. As the Trump era dawned, questions about Obama's legacy swirled. Like with *Hamilton*, some challenged Obama's widespread popularity by criticizing him as a centrist hiding beneath Leftist trappings.

The links between *Hamilton* and the Obama administration are both real and symbolic. In the first year of its popularity, *Hamilton* was so strongly connected to the Obama White House that one scholar suggested, "Miranda was set up as a court composer for the administration" (Christopher 59). Miranda debuted an early version of the opening number at the White House early in Obama's first term. After *Hamilton* opened, both the president and first lady saw the show. They then hosted a special *Hamilton* event at the White House in early 2017. But the links are also present in the musical's content. "[Miranda's] Hamilton is a symbol for the age of Obama," writes historian Nancy Isenberg. "His Hamilton is given Obama-like qualities: He is superior (a genius), pragmatic (concerned with finance, credit, and banks), stubborn (unrelenting and contentious); his most far-fetched attribute is that of a hip, multicultural pop star" (298). Writer Lonely Christopher concurs that *Hamilton* "is specifically an Obama-era phenomenon" for its uncritical veneration of "watery neoliberal principles" that "ignore the unresolved legacy of slavery in favor of identifying with our national myths by venerating the Founding Fathers as 'young, scrappy, and hungry' self-starters fighting against subjugation" (59). Others are more positive. "*Hamilton* is about the mutability of identity in American history," argues Adam Gopnik in the *New Yorker*; "It is President Obama's point about America's open-ended and universally available narrative brought to life on stage."

Indeed, the show's race-conscious casting aligns with ideas about race and power highlighted by the Obama presidency. In *Hamilton*, George Washington, the first president, is played by a Black man. Likewise, performers of color portray all of the major characters besides King George III. President Obama himself endorsed the choice: "With a cast as diverse as America itself, the show reminds us that this nation was built by more than just a few great men" (Kornhaber). Race-conscious casting challenges the long-standing relationship in American politics between whiteness and power, as well as critiquing contemporary systemic racism. Historian Benjamin L. Carp notes that *Hamilton*'s creative team developed the show amid the fallout of Eric Garner's and Michael Brown's murders by police officers: "the fact that the cast members are people of color allows Miranda to connect the eighteenth-century Revolution to contemporary activism against police brutality" (292).

Hamilton also takes aim at rising xenophobia with an explicitly pro-immigrant narrative, a resonant rebuttal to the Trump campaign's intentional stoking of white fears of immigration. For instance, during his candidacy announcement in June 2015, in what would be one of countless racist statements, Trump erroneously claimed, "When Mexico sends its people, they're not sending their best ... They're bringing drugs. They're bringing crime. They're rapists" (Ye Hee Lee). Amid this climate, *Hamilton* advanced an inclusive, optimistic message. The show describes Hamilton as a destitute immigrant who worked hard to make it in America, "coming up from the bottom" ("Alexander Hamilton").[11] Hamilton's journey from friendless newcomer to cabinet secretary testifies to the value immigrants bring to the nation and implies the justness of American capitalism. It has even become a tradition for the line "Immigrants! We get the job done!" to draw enthusiastic audience applause ("Yorktown").

The production's progressive credentials expanded beyond the book and lyrics. When Vice President Elect Mike Pence saw the show in November 2016, the cast delivered a message to him at the curtain call. "We, sir, are the diverse America who are alarmed and anxious that your new administration will not protect us, our planet, our children, our parents – or defend us and uphold our inalienable rights, sir," read Brandon Victor Dixon from a prepared statement. "But we truly hope that this show has inspired you to uphold our American values and work on behalf of *all* of us" (Framke). The video of the incident went viral. In 2018, in the wake of the Parkland school shooting, Miranda and Alex Lacamoire, *Hamilton*'s music director, performed at the March for Our Lives protest in Washington, D.C. (Kreps). That same year, Miranda performed "Dear Theodosia" at a Families Belong Together March protesting the Trump administration's family separation policy for migrants at the southern border. Miranda described the song as a "lullaby" in honor of the "parents right now who can't sing lullabies to their kids." "And we're not going to stop until they can sing them to their kids again," he vowed (Kiefer). The links between *Hamilton* and resistance to the Trump administration spread to the fandom, as well. At the Women's March and other protests, participants carried signs with lyrics from the show (Davis).

However, much of *Hamilton*'s would-be progressivism has drawn criticism from the Left. Several scholars have pointed out that race-conscious

---

[11] All songs referenced from *Hamilton* are from Lin-Manuel Miranda, *Hamilton: An American Musical* (Original Broadway Cast Recording).

casting erases issues of race and slavery from early American history. There are no actual characters of color in the show, just performers of color embodying white people. Furthermore, slavery is rarely mentioned and never seen, except for a passing Sally Hemings reference. And the show does not grapple with settler colonialism at all. "With a cast dominated by actors of color, the play is nonetheless yet another rendition of the 'exclusive past' with its focus on the deeds of 'great white men' and its silencing of the presence and contributions of people of color in the Revolutionary era," observes scholar Lyra D. Monteiro (59). Even more troubling, almost all of the main characters were enslavers—Washington, Hamilton, Jefferson, Madison, Mulligan, and the Schuyler family. Writer Ishmael Reed has been among the most vocal critics of the show for this reason. "Can you imagine Jewish actors in Berlin's theaters taking roles of Goering? Goebbels? Eichmann? Hitler?" he famously demanded ("Black Actors Dress Up"). Reed has also taken issue with the show's use of African American music and culture to tell a white story: "Now the masters, the producers of this profit hungry production, which has already made 30 million dollars, are using the slave's language: Rock and Roll, Rap and Hip Hop to romanticize the careers of kidnappers, and murderers" ("Black Actors Dress Up"). Reed even wrote his own play, *The Haunting of Lin-Manuel Miranda* (2020), to dramatize his critique.

Scholars have also taken issue with the musical's description of Hamilton as an immigrant. In reality, Hamilton was a migrant, moving from one British colony to another. He was also no underdog. Hamilton enjoyed tremendous privileges due to his race, religion, gender, and language. And, most importantly, unlike ninety percent of other migrants arriving in America during this period, Hamilton was a free person (Harris, "Greatest City" 71–93). In addition, depicting Hamilton as a Latino man erases the many barriers to upward mobility for non-white immigrants, both in the eighteenth century and the twenty-first (Lurie 139).

In keeping with its Obama-era roots, *Hamilton* offers audiences a conservative narrative in progressive clothing. Indeed, the show reinforces traditional messaging about the United States and its history. It glorifies the Founding Fathers, treating them as the prime movers of the early national story. It ignores the foundational roles that slavery and settler colonialism played in the formation and development of the early United States. It promises a meritocratic economic and political system in which those who work "non-stop" are rewarded. Most importantly, it grants an unquestioning endorsement of the righteousness of the United States. Unsurprisingly, *Hamilton*, like *1776*, enjoyed the support of many on the Right, despite the creative team's Left leanings. "This show brings unlikely folks together," Obama once joked. "In fact, *Hamilton* I'm pretty sure is the only thing that Dick Cheney and I agree on" ("Remarks by the President").

Though still widely beloved, controversies continued to plague *Hamilton* in early 2019 when producers mounted a three-week run in Puerto Rico with Miranda returning to the titular role. Although partially a fundraiser, the production drew criticism due to Miranda's prior support of the Puerto Rico Oversight, Management, and Economic Stability Act (PROMESA), which created an unelected oversight board that forced austerity measures on the island. Initially, the show was scheduled to play at the University of Puerto Rico's theater. But an outcry focused on PROMESA's tuition hikes and slashing of worker benefits forced a relocation. The university community also spoke out against the show's message. Student leader Maria Celeste Sánchez stated that it was "insulting" for the show to play in Puerto Rico "knowing full well that the United States has been [its] oppressor for more than 100 years" (Jackson). Still, despite the protests, *Hamilton* sold out for its limited run, and Miranda received a lengthy standing ovation upon his first entrance (Pollack-Pelzner).

The release of the *Hamilton* movie (a recording of the Broadway production) on Disney+ stoked further controversy. It premiered in July 2020, just weeks after the murder of George Floyd by police and a wave of Black Lives Matter demonstrations. The context provoked another round of criticism that accused *Hamilton* of erasing the centrality of white supremacy and racial injustice in American history. "In light of such political discord and the expression of so much pain, it starts to feel as if *Hamilton* relies on a sense of national reconciliation and healing that simply never happened," observes Christopher (76). To many, the distance between the imagined America of *Hamilton* and the real one of the twenty-first century had simply grown too great.

Despite these controversies, *Hamilton* remains, of course, a global phenomenon with unprecedented popularity and cultural resonance. Both its sustained success and backlash speak to the struggles over American historical memory in recent years. Like *1776*, it is popular among both the Right and Left, essentialists and organicists. Yet *Hamilton* has also unleashed a firestorm of criticism. Clearly, the Trump era's challenges have caused some Americans to embrace a celebratory founding story and others to reject it. Nevertheless, *Hamilton* represents another example along the through line of Broadway's triumphalist and conservative treatment of early American history.

Though separated by decades and different circumstances, *1776*, *The Civil War*, *Bloody Bloody Andrew Jackson*, and *Hamilton* all share the same rigid assumptions at the heart of their stories. Even *Bloody Bloody Andrew Jackson*, a show ostensibly designed to mock the dominant memory traditions that uncritically venerate "great" men, ultimately reinforced a white supremacist historical narrative. In the end, all four of these shows reveal a shocking lack of evolution in the American musical theater canon's treatment of early American history.

But one thing *has* changed: the response to the more recent productions has included dissenting voices. While *1776* enjoyed virtually universal praise and *The Civil War*'s problematic depiction of history went unremarked upon, both *Bloody Bloody Andrew Jackson* and *Hamilton* experienced pushback from those critical of the historical narratives they advanced. This is an encouraging development that will hopefully move creatives beyond the tired triumphalist and white-centric tropes that have thus far dominated the genre. Historical memory should be more than a balm for the wounds of the present moment or a comforting, triumphant tale for those with power. Remembering the past should push us beyond our current concerns and structures, and toward a better, more just future. Theater, a place of collective perception, imagining, and reckoning, could be the place where that transformation begins.

Works Cited

1776. By Sherman Edwards and Peter Stone, directed by Peter Hunt. 46th Street Theatre, New York, 1969.

Barnes, Clive. "Theater: Spirited *1776*." *The New York Times*, March 17, 1969, p. 46.

Blight, David. *Race and Reunion: The Civil War in American Memory*. Harvard UP, 2001.

Bloody, Bloody Andrew Jackson. By Michael Friedman and Alex Timbers, directed by Alex Timbers. Bernard B. Jacobs Theatre, New York, 2010.

Brantley, Ben. "Ideal President: A Rock Star Just Like Me." *The New York Times*, October 14, 2010, p. C1.

———. "Old Hickory, Rock Star President." *The New York Times*, April 7, 2010, p. C1.

———. "Theater Review: History Soldiering On." *The New York Times*, April 23, 1999, p. E1.

Brick, Howard. *The Age of Contradictions: American Thought and Culture in the 1960s*. Cornell UP, 2000.

Camp, Stephanie M.H. *Closer to Freedom: Enslaved Women and Everyday Resistance in the Plantation South*. U of North Carolina P, 2004.

Carp, Benjamin L. "World Wide Enough: Historiography, Imagination, and Stagecraft." *Journal of the Early Republic*, vol. 37, no. 2 (2017), pp. 289–94.
Christopher, Lonely. "Great Moments with Mr. Hamilton." *Bigotry on Broadway*, edited by Ishmael Reed and Carla Blank. Baraka Books, 2021, pp. 44–78.
The Civil War. By Gregory Boyd, Frank Wildhorn, and Jack Murphy, directed by Jerry Zaks. St. James Theatre, New York, 1999.
Cleveland, Henry. *Alexander H. Stephens, in Public and Private: With Letters and Speeches, Before, During, and Since the War*. National Publishing Company, 1886.
Davis, Shanice. "Lin-Manuel Miranda Reacts to Outpour of 'Hamilton' Signs at Nationwide Protests." *Vibe*, February 3, 2017.
Deloria, Philip. *Indians in Unexpected Places*. UP of Kansas, 2004.
Dombrink, John. *The Twilight of Social Conservatism: American Culture Wars in the Obama Era*. New York UP, 2017.
Dong, Qingwen, Kenneth D. Day, and Raman Deol. "The Resonant Message and the Powerful New Media: An Analysis of the Obama Presidential Campaign." *The Obama Effect: Multidisciplinary Renderings of the 2008 Campaign*, edited by Heather E. Harris, Kimberly R. Moffitt, and Cahterine R. Squires. SUNY Press, 2010, pp. 75–88.
Edwards, Sherman. *1776* (Original Broadway Cast Recording). Sony, 1969.
Edwards, Sherman and Peter Stone. *1776: A Musical Play (based on a conception of Sherman Edwards)*. Viking, 1970.
Framke, Caroline. "Mike Pence Went to See *Hamilton*. The Audience Booed – But the Cast Delivered a Personal Plea." *Vox*, November 19, 2016.
Friedman, Michael. "Behind the Music: BBAJ." *Broadway.com*, March 20, 2011.
———. *Bloody Bloody Andrew Jackson* (Original Cast Recording). Ghostlight Records, 2010.
Funke, Lewis. "1776, 'Like It Was.'" *The New York Times*, September 8, 1968, D1.
Gallagher Gary W., and Alan T. Nolan. *The Myth of the Lost Cause and Civil War History*. Indiana UP, 2000.
Gitlin, Todd. *The Sixties: Years of Hope, Days of Rage*. Bantam Books, 1987.
Glymph, Thavolia. *Out of the House of Bondage: The Transformation of the Plantation Household*. Cambridge UP, 2008.
Gopnik, Adam. "*Hamilton* and the Hip-Hop Case for Progressive Heroism." *The New Yorker*, February 5, 2016.
Greenfield, Thomas A. *American Musicals in Context*. ABC-CLIO, 2021.
Hamilton: An American Musical. By Lin-Manuel Miranda, directed by Thomas Kail, Richard Rogers Theatre, New York, 2016.
Harbert, Elissa. "'Ever to the Right'? The Political Life of *1776* in the Nixon Era." *American Music*, vol. 35, no. 2 (2017), pp. 237–70.
Harris, Heather E. *Neo-Race Realities in the Obama Era*. SUNY Press, 2019.
Harris, Leslie M. "The Greatest City in the World?: Slavery in New York in the Age of Hamilton." *Historians on* Hamilton: *How a Blockbuster Musical is*

Restaging America's Past, edited by Renee C. Romano and Claire Bond Potter. Rutgers UP, 2018, pp. 71–93.

Harris, Mark. "The Civil War." *Entertainment Weekly*, May 7, 1999.

Isenberg, Nancy. "'Make 'Em Laugh': Why History Cannot be Reduced to Song and Dance." *Journal of the Early Republic*, vol. 37, no. 2 (2017), pp. 295–303.

Isherwood, Charles. "Theatrical Stumbles of Historic Proportions." *The New York Times*, December 12, 2021, AR1.

Isserman, Maurice, and Michael Kazin. *America Divided: The Civil War of the 1960s*. Oxford UP, 1999.

Jackson, Jhoni. "A Breakdown of the Controversy Surrounding Lin-Manuel Miranda & 'Hamilton' in Puerto Rico." *REMEZCLA*, January 10, 2019.

Johnson, Haynes. *The Best of Times: America in the Clinton Years*. Harcourt, 2001.

Kiefer, Halle. "Lin-Manuel Miranda Sings a *Hamilton* Lullaby at Saturday's Families Belong Together Protest." *Vulture*, June 30, 2018.

Kornhaber, Spencer. "*Hamilton*: Casting After Colorblindness." *The Atlantic*, March 31, 2016.

Kreps, Daniel. "Lin-Manuel Miranda, Ben Platt Release New Song for March for Our Lives." *Rolling Stone*, March 19, 2018.

Levine, D.M. "Native Americans protest 'Bloody Bloody Andrew Jackson.'" *Politico*, June 24, 2010.

Leydon, Joe. "The Civil War." *Variety*, September 28, 1998.

Link, William A. *Roots of Secession: Slavery and Politics in Antebellum Virginia*. U of North Carolina P, 2003.

Lurie, Shira. "Who Tells Which Story? Teaching *Hamilton*, History, and Memory." *The Hamilton Phenomenon*, edited by Chloe Northop. Vernon Press, 2022, pp. 129–50.

Meacham, Joe. "Rocking the Vote in the 1820s and Now." *The New York Times*, October 24, 2010, AR6.

Miranda, Lin-Manuel. *Hamilton: An American Musical* (Original Broadway Cast Recording). Atlantic Records, 2015.

Monteiro, Lyra D. "Race-Conscious Casting and the Erasure of the Black Past in *Hamilton*." *Historians on* Hamilton*: How a Blockbuster Musical is Restaging America's Past*, edited by Renee C. Romano and Claire Bond Potter. Rutgers UP, 2018, pp. 58–70.

Murphy, Jack, and Frank Wildhorn. *The Civil War: The Complete Work*. Atlantic Records, 1999.

Musical Theater International, *Bloody Bloody Andrew Jackson*, http://www.mtishows.com/bloody-bloody-andrew-jackson (last accessed November 12, 2024).

Noonan, Julie A. "The Rock Star Figure: Authenticity, Satire and Legacy in *Bloody Bloody Andrew Jackson* (2006)." *Studies in Musical Theatre*, vol. 10, no. 1 (2016), pp. 19–36.

Obama, Barack. "Remarks by the President at '*Hamilton* at the White House.'" March 14, 2016, Washington, D.C., https://obamawhitehouse.archives.gov/the-press-office/2016/03/14/remarks-president-hamilton-white-house (last accessed November 12, 2024).

"'One Last Time'—*Hamilton* at The White House," YouTube, uploaded by *Hamilton*, January 10, 2017, https://www.youtube.com/watch?v=uV4UpCq2azs (last accessed November 12, 2024).

Pollack-Pelzner, Daniel. "The Mixed Reception of the *Hamilton* Premiere in Puerto Rico." *The Atlantic*, January 18, 2019.

Purcell, Carey. "Controversial Musical *Bloody Bloody Andrew Jackson* Canceled in Raleigh." *Playbill*, January 14, 2015.

Reed, Ishmael. "'Hamilton: the Musical:' Black Actors Dress Up Like Slave Traders . . . and It's Not Halloween." *CounterPunch*, August 21, 2015.

———. *The Haunting of Lin-Manuel Miranda*. Archway Editions, 2020.

Richards, Betsy Theobald. "Responding to *Bloody Bloody Andrew Jackson* & Claiming the Power of Native Voice." *Bigotry on Broadway*, edited by Ishmael Reed and Carla Blank. Baraka Books, 2021, pp. 163–72.

Romano, Renee C., and Claire Bond Potter. "Introduction: History Is Happening in Manhattan." *Historians on* Hamilton: *How a Blockbuster Musical is Restaging America's Past*, edited by Renee C. Romano and Claire Bond Potter. Rutgers UP, 2018, pp. 1–14.

Said, Edward. "Invention, Memory, and Place." *Critical Inquiry*, vol. 26, no. 2 (2000), pp. 175–92.

Schocket, Andrew M. *Fighting Over the Founders: How We Remember the American Revolution*. New York UP, 2015.

Serrianne, Nina Esperanza. *America in the Nineties*. Syracuse UP, 2015.

Silber, Nina. *The Romance of Reunion: Northerners and the South, 1865–1900*. U of North Carolina P, 1993.

Syse, Glenna. "'Timing' Is Right for the Message." *The Des Moines Register*, May 18, 1969.

Yazzie, Rhiana. "New Native Theatre Protests 'Bloody Bloody Andrew Jackson.'" *Star Tribune*, June 4, 2014.

Ye Hee Lee, Michelle. "Donald Trump's False Comments Connecting Mexican Immigrants and Crime." *The Washington Post*, July 8, 2015.

8

Aaron Posner's *JQA* as Layered History: Promoting Aesthetic-Historical Reflection in a Texas Theatre's Production

Sarah Ruffing Robbins

When Stage West of Fort Worth, Texas, presented *JQA*, a historical drama about President John Quincy Adams, in October 2021, their production was not the first for Aaron Posner's play. But this staging took advantage of its own local context, on the one hand, and long-standing knowledge of Posner's larger oeuvre, on the other, to create a memorable portrayal of the nation's past that, in review now, offers illuminating ideas about historical drama as a genre for today. The Texas production drew on Posner's ongoing approaches for crafting scripts reflecting an awareness of theatre history and the place of history in theatre. At the same time, the Fort Worth version of *JQA* also enacted a specific local vision. The play became the first COVID-era in-person production for the local theatre company, then eager to draw local audiences back to live performances. The play might have seemed a risky choice for a "red state" company, given Posner's shift in this text from his more familiar genre of adapting material by forerunners like Chekhov, plus the play's focus on the lesser-known of the two Adams presidents, and its progressive political stance. But Stage West's leaders know their audience. They also had a strong prior relationship with the playwright and his work to draw upon in envisioning their production. Thus, retrospectively, the Fort Worth *JQA* offers a striking example of one play's successfully claiming a moment and venue for addressing a receptive audience, while calibrating that local context with textual features affirming the power of historical drama itself to examine contemporary issues proactively. Accordingly, this essay interprets a particular 2021 production of *JQA* as strategic engagement with the historical drama genre to capitalize on a generative context in time, place, and cultural exigence (Figure 8.1). This *JQA* staging met local needs by aligning with its playwright's political and aesthetic

Figure 8.1 In-the-round staging drawing Fort Worth audiences into *JQA*'s conversations. (Credit: Evan Michael Wood.)

vision for historical drama to offer up an admittedly imagined past in service of the present.

Wherever it might be performed, Aaron Posner's play invites directors, actors—and audiences—into generative engagement with history through the drama's dialogic structure. In constructing a series of personal-as-political conversations from JQA's long life,[1] playwright Posner embraces an approach to historical drama promoting critical consideration of the present. Posner's play thereby positions John Quincy Adams as a vital cultural resource for twenty-first-century life. That is, Posner envisions the lesser-known President Adams's life as providing fertile reimagined historical exchanges to foster layered-time connections through art. Stage West's production of *JQA* embodied this goal for scripting the past by capitalizing on features in the text that could speak to a particular staging moment and locale while reiterating the recurring efficacy of historical drama as genre.

JQA presents a series of two-person conversations between Adams and other historical figures, several of them likely more familiar to audiences

---

[1] Given the play's title, the essay will often refer to John Quincy Adams as JQA.

than he is. Starting in 1776 with his youth, initial dialogues involve a young John Quincy, his parent-president, and his oft-cited mother Abigail. Subsequent scenes in the ninety-minute drama include a conversation between JQA and George Washington (who presses the young man into public service) and one wherein his wife Louisa initially resists, but then accepts, moving to Russia for the young Adams's ambassadorship. With later dialogues bringing in a crafty Henry Clay, a blustering Andrew Jackson, a visionary Frederick Douglass, and a humble young Abraham Lincoln, the play overlays a decades-long national history onto the life of its main character. Through the sequence of one-on-one conversations, JQA embodies both a leader empowered by a privileged family and a figure constrained by temperament and shifting national priorities. Tensions between those forces of change and the founders' most idealistic ideas form one theme, as audience members move through pivotal moments in Adams's eighty-year life, ending in the late 1840s with the Civil War looming.

Strategically, if indirectly, Posner's text nods to a heritage of drama revisiting America's past to offer correctives and inspiration for later times. *JQA*, admittedly, lacks the recognizable currency of better-known U.S. historical dramas—whether a longtime staple like Arthur Miller's *The Crucible* or the newer phenomenon of Lin-Manuel Miranda's *Hamilton*. Nonetheless, Posner's play—like those forebears—revisits important events and figures from earlier periods in American history to encourage audiences to resist elements in their own time that run counter to an idealized national compact. For *The Crucible*, Miller explicitly declared, the witch hunts of Salem during the colonial era served as a warning against the parallel abuses of McCarthy-era Communist hunts and scapegoating (Crucible *in History* 8–13, 28–29, 45). For the more recent *Hamilton* blockbuster, aspects of the title character and his associates that Miranda highlighted presented an aspirational vision of a multicultural United States—one welcoming immigrants, resisting despotism, and embracing progressive possibilities in governance. Blending the warning mode of Miller with the optimism of Miranda, Posner offers a series of dialogues between his title character and various contemporaries, who illuminate both JQA himself and varying potential versions of American values. On the warning side, for example, scenes with Andrew Jackson and Henry Clay forecast national events embodying a less-than-ideal American ethos, one embracing raw populism (Jackson) or sell-out compromises that enable the continuation of slavery (Clay). Posner balances such unsettling exchanges with more upbeat conversations early in the play, such as John Quincy Adams's writer-mother Abigail confidently asserting that "[t]o be good, and to do good, is the whole duty of man."[2] Similarly, the title character's nation-affirming words in an imagined conversation with a youthful Abraham Lincoln in the final scene reassure the audience of America's sustained potential while proleptically girding young Lincoln for future challenges. Seemingly coaching Lincoln as a just-emerging leader, JQA dubs the U.S. "an amazing country," "A Miraculous country," "aspirational . . . and inspirational . . . and just plain extraordinary" (Posner, *JQA 2020 Performance Draft*).

In a YouTube interview, Posner himself asserted that his historical drama was really about the "today" of his own original writing moment. Describing his process and goals to casting director Kim Heil of the San Diego Repertory Theatre, which mounted a production ahead of Stage West's, Posner declared: "I think this is pretty clear: I'm really writing about today. I'm writing about what I'm observing and what I'm feeling about . . . our relationship to government now . . . How can I engage with these people [his characters] that will help me move towards something to talk about what's going on right now?" (Posner, YouTube interview). Taking the playwright's cue, to analyze the specific Fort Worth production of his play about political history in the early days of U.S. nationhood, this essay's upcoming sections will underscore *JQA*'s efforts to address the challenging American history of today through a reimagined chronicle of a past president's lived experiences. On a complementary front also aligned with the playwright's vision, this analysis will spotlight directorial choices made in the Texas production that illustrate an applied theory of historical drama as a rhetorically purposeful public aesthetic action.

In genre terms, this interpretation proposes a cultural utility abiding in deep reflection on the layered histories enacted in the Texas *JQA*'s particular production choices. Informed by conversations with director Emily Banks and long-standing interactions with Stage West's self-aware culture as a regular audience member,[3] this analysis also draws on comparative

---

[2] Posner's script for the San Diego production—which served as the draft script in Fort Worth—printed this line from Abigail as one of two headnotes on its cover page; one actor states this line and attributes it to Abigail in the prologue opening the play. The second headnote on the script (which Stage West generously shared with me) comes from Frederick Douglass; in the same prologue where Abigail's "be good, and to do good" line occurs, a different actor delivers the Douglass statement and names him as source. In-text citations in this chapter will reference this unpublished version of the script as follows: Posner, *JQA 2020 Performance Draft*.

[3] I thank Emily Scott Banks, director of the Fort Worth *JQA* production, for encouraging me to see the play as having "layers" in conception and performances. For Banks, considering not only the version she directed, but future productions as well, *JQA* has "got such weight to it now, and so many layers."

study of previous productions of the play. Similarities and differences across those distinct stagings both affirm core rhetorical goals evident within the text itself and reaffirm that any printed version of a play remains open to the collaborative forces of theatrical production. More broadly, the *JQA* example of historical drama as public action asserts a role for the arts as cultural pedagogy for American democracy, neither pedantically didactic nor shirking the responsibility linked to aesthetic-historical layered reflection. In the specific case of Fort Worth's 2021 *JQA*, a full appreciation of the production's approach to historical drama requires recognition of the playwright himself as a writerly historian of drama as culture-maker (one analytical layer). Equally important, an assessment of the Texas production entails tapping into past stagings of the play at other venues (another layer of interpretation). Further, the design, application of stage directions, and portrayal of dialogue within the text itself convey stages of personal experience and growth for Adams himself across time. Accordingly, this production used depiction of Adams's maturation to purposefully spotlight stages in the nation's ongoing evolution, through choices made by the Texas creative team that wove all these multidimensional layers of themes and stagecraft together in performance. If this mandate seems a tall order for a single production in one local theatre, consider this: such cultural stewardship reminds us, as audiences but additionally as scholars who are also teachers, to listen, learn, and then seek ways to enact our own agency as citizens along with other multiple publics.

Layering Scholarship on Historical Drama as Genre

Though examination of any historical drama can benefit from connecting with prior scholarship, for this play and its author, spotlighting the context of genre history, method, and theory is especially salient. Aaron Posner, who for the drama's original production served as both playwright and director, has deep appreciation of theatre and literary history, as illustrated in his multiple adaptations of playwrights such as Chekhov and Shakespeare. Posner also signals the purposeful and scholarly dimensions of his decision making in his production notes for *JQA*. There, he identifies the "godparents" of this drama as "Shaw and Brecht" and advocates for directorial decision making to allow the play's ideas to "be discovered, and then activated. *Intentionality is essential*" (*JQA 2020 Performance Draft*; original emphasis). Through this notation, the playwright both guides and empowers directors and other creative team members to dig deep into the layers of historical portrayal in his text, then use their own intentional choices to reinforce artistic engagement with history as a purposeful task.

Studies of American historical drama as genre often emphasize that it re-envisions events and individuals audiences already "know" about, or, in some cases, think they know. In that vein, scholars like Jeffrey Richards have traced ways that the earliest stagings of plays in the youthful U.S. Republic incorporated "local American factors," even when the texts themselves were imported "from London or Dublin" (2), and even as the first American playwrights were just beginning to "pen their own plays" with a careful eye on British models (3). Thus, Richards, as well as Jacqueline O'Connor, Elizabeth Maddox Dillon, and Laura Mielke, have demonstrated that, from the beginning of the new U.S. Republic, theatre and history have been intertwined, with the genre both producing records of the past and using that process to shape the present and future of the nation.[4]

While Posner's prior work adapting dramas by other playwrights certainly involved doing a brand of historical work, creating his own historical drama from scratch for *JQA* presented new opportunities for navigating a continuum between accuracy, on the one hand, and advocacy, on the other. Recent research on techniques of the historical drama genre and their cultural implications have blended critique of some representational practices with questions about authenticity. For instance, Heidi L. Nees's analysis of outdoor historical dramas depicting Native American history builds on work by Native historian Philip Deloria to argue that such texts too often generate "problematic representations that tend to cater to audience expectations built on generalizations and stereotypes rather than accurate depictions" (79). In contrast, while lauding *Under the Cherokee Moon* (a production of the Cherokee Heritage Center in Oklahoma), Nees identifies multiple techniques forging what her essay title designates as "new paths to representation," such as presenting accurate artifacts in printed programs, involving audience members as participants, using Cherokee language, and incorporating authentic period clothing, humor, and affirmations that Cherokee people are not "trapped in the past" (88–9). Nees finds the technique of "[a]ssigning roles to audience members in this historical drama" (often "displacing different identities") especially effective, since it "encourages empathy without resorting to catharsis" (96). While bemoaning the play's inability to become a regular offering for audiences, Nees nonetheless claims that its

---

[4] See Jacqueline O'Connor's study of "documentary drama," *Documentary Trial Plays*, Elizabeth Maddox Dillon, *New World Drama*, and Laura Mielke, *Provocative Eloquence*.

approach "offers innovative possibilities through which others may navigate some of the representational politics at play in staging Native American histories, figures, and cultures" (99). Taking a different position on questions about authenticity, Stephanie Russo argues in favor of anachronism as a viable technique for historical dramas self-consciously eschewing accuracy in favor of addressing rhetorical goals ("'You are'"). Russo's case study focuses on efforts to update audiences' perceptions of Emily Dickinson in dramatizations that reject authenticity as a goal.

Posner's affinity for adaptation might suggest he would self-position more on Russo's side than Nees's in terms of a commitment to authenticity and accuracy versus crafting a vision of history to appeal to today's audiences.[5] In fact, his production notes indicate a more nuanced perspective incorporating both fidelity to core historical facts and crafting past/present reverberations toward proactive audience response to social issues of today:

> Simply put, while the play is not historically *accurate*, . . . it is largely historically *feasible*. The personalities of the characters are consistent, I believe, with history as I understand it. The meetings imagined her[e] *could have* taken place, though many of them never did . . . and if they did, I can only imagine that they were quite different than anything depicted here. The goal has never been accuracy, but rather evocation, provocation, and prompting discussion about where we are *now*. (Posner, *JQA 2020 Performance Draft*; original ellipses and italics)

In asserting "evocation" and "provocation" over "accuracy," Posner calls for historical drama to press audiences into a critique of "where we are now," a reflective enterprise even more vital than immersion in history itself for its own sake. That is, dramatically depicting the past serves the present, so much so that a consideration of current relevance should be accessibly layered onto any historical drama's representations of the past.

Relatedly, Posner's play interrogates cultural memory. In scene after scene, dialogues between the play's namesake and other characters address national (and personal) issues: who should become public leaders in a particular moment, what to do about slavery's stain on the *polis*, how to

---

[5] *New York Times* writer Elisabeth Vincentelli's review of the California-based production of *JQA* senses that Posner's affinity for Chekhov adaptations has carried over into his *JQA* script, which she reads as his doing "something similar with a real figure" ("*JQA* Review").

navigate regional tensions. But these same conversations also look ahead, with Adams and each of his conversation partners speculating—sometimes implicitly, sometimes quite directly—on the future accounts of those same issues and the roles that various historical narratives will claim in those rememberings. The dialogues show that our choices about what to foreground in history-telling processes illuminate both the past and the present, thereby fostering varying value systems that undergird institutional structures, social practices, and even everyday life.[6] In the introduction to his monograph *Dramas of the Past on the Twentieth-Century Stage* (2013), Alexander Feldman similarly observes that "performances of official culture place certain historical phenomena centre stage, while consigning other experiences, and other lives, to the wings of history" (2). Through a study of what he terms "historiographic metatheatre," Feldman singles out a cluster of dramatic texts that pay purposeful attention to this culture-defining work, sometimes, in the process, seeking to move previously marginalized perspectives to more prominent positions in the social landscape constructed by, and sustained in, historical narratives. Because the concept he defines anticipates Aaron Posner's approach, Feldman's framework merits attention for analysis of *JQA* here:

> Historiographic metatheatre is a term that can be applied to all of those works, and parts of works, in which self-reflexive engagements with the traditions and forms of dramatic art illuminate historical themes and aid in the representation of historical events. The description of these works as historiographic rather than simply historical is indicative of the playwrights' interest in not only the events of the past but also the way in which they are constituted in the discourse of history; how history is written and how one conceives of history, in philosophical and ideological terms, prior to and during the process of writing it. The description of these works as metatheatrical rather than simply theatrical indicates the same kind of perspectival displacement. Metatheatre

---

[6] Alison Landsberg, for instance, in *Prosthetic Memory*, locates the construction of cultural memory "at the interface between a person and a historical narrative about the past, at an experiential site such as a movie theater or museum." For Landsberg, such engagements with the past can have personal as well as social impact, as "the person [in an audience] does not simply apprehend a historical narrative but takes on a more personal, deeply felt memory of a past event through which he or she did not live. The resulting prosthetic memory has the ability to shape that person's subjectivity and politics" (2).

is the self-conscious counterpart to dramatic art—theatre's acknowledgement of its own artifice—and these plays, by exposing the theatricality within theatre, provoke questions as to the artifice, the spectacle, and the dramatic constructs of the world beyond. (Feldman, 2–3)

Neither the written directions in Posner's draft performance script nor commentary in the YouTube video interview he gave to the casting director of the San Diego *JQA* production directly references Feldman or invokes the term "metatheatre." Yet, lines in the script convey *JQA*'s commitment to historiographic metatheatre, in Feldman's terms, as well as to asking questions about representation, authenticity versus accuracy, and ways to position audience members themselves as historical actors/agents.

The opening sequence of the "Prologue," with the play's four actors designated (as in the script) as A, B, C, and D, seems well aligned with Feldman's points:

A: What you will witness here today . . . *never happened.*
C: As far as we know . . .
D: Though, of course, none of us were there.
B: We're not pretending to be *historically accurate* . . .
A: We're just *pretending.*
D: This is not *historical fiction* . . . but *fictional history.*
C: So, if you didn't know . . . now you know. (Posner, *JQA 2020 Performance Draft*)

Here, Posner announces directly to the audience, at the very beginning of the play, that the historical drama they are about to witness is not a chronicle seeking accuracy but instead an aesthetic exercise in rhetorical imagining. Toward what end? In grounding my analysis of Posner's reimagined history of an early republic's president in the particular production at Stage West, this essay argues that historical drama can promote a forward-looking call to audiences' sociopolitical agency through aesthetic-historical layered reflection.

In applying Posner's script language and her own experience-based affiliation with his larger oeuvre to this production's staging approaches, director Emily Banks developed a forward-looking historical drama. Along the way, this *JQA* production addressed audience awareness of then-current, large-scale political dangers. Meanwhile, staging choices also highlighted historical resources that could aid attendees' navigation through their own associated lived experiences, which were being shaped by national political turmoil, a pandemic's lingering threats, and philosophical anxieties around democracy's future. In particular, the Fort Worth production cultivated its audience's critical engagement with past, present, and future via a modeling of proactive listening.

Weaving Together Posner's Vision, Script Detail, and a Director's Choices

Part of the pragmatic appeal of this play for local and regional theatres like Stage West may lie in its requiring only a four-person cast (despite its chronological sweep). If the number of players required is small, however, the casting vision for the dialogues is ambitious. Posner's vision, as articulated in his notes for the *Performance Draft* provided to me by Stage West, emphasizes the diversity he calls for in casting, with cross-race and cross-gender role assignments shifting across the dialogues. Taking on different character assignments in different scenes, each actor plays both Adams and others. Posner's script thereby forces audiences to "see" an Adams presidency (as well as other life stages) embodied in a young person of color and a grey-haired woman rather than only in the image of a staid white man like those dominating Founders' portraiture. Thus, actor A, designated only as a woman in an approximate age range of 20s to 30s, embodies both the youngest iteration of JQA and, in the final dialogue, the youthful Congressman Abraham Lincoln; in between, she speaks as JQA's wife Louisa in the early years of their marriage. Actor B, specifically identified in the script directions as "African-American," takes on the role of the title character in the early to mid stages of his political career, but also becomes Frederick Douglass in a later dialogue with JQA and, disconcertingly, speaks as Andrew Jackson in a different scene.[7] Actor C, described in the casting notes as a man in his 50s, plays the elder President Adams in an early conversation between a boy-JQA and his father. This same cast member also embodies a mid-career JQA as President and a somewhat cynical, if also pragmatic, Henry Clay. Finally, Actor D, described in the

---

[7] Posner's script depicts JQA as having a core moral vision for the nation, including a wish for equality for all, even in the early stages of his political career. Thus, for the audience, seeing an African American actor embodying Adams is consistent with the playwright's overall characterization of the title figure. Having the same actor soon shift to a brash, unpolished, and racist Andrew Jackson, on the other hand, is jolting, especially since the playwright clearly assumes his audience will associate Jackson with such racist acts as Indian removal which he enforced despite a Supreme Court decision opposing that plan.

notes as a woman ranging between her 60s and 80s, carries the multiple parts of an elderly JQA and, earlier in the play, George Washington and Abigail Adams, as well as, toward the close, Louisa, JQA's wife, in old age.

Since the play presents a series of dialogues, with most scenes taking place in small interior spaces, one attraction of this text for regional theatre groups (besides its cast of only four) may be its potential for compact staging. Indeed, Posner's notes describe the play's setting as a "simple, flexible space that can easily be transformed for the various scenes" (*JQA 2020 Performance Draft* 2). In fact, one production mounted prior to Fort Worth's was a summer 2021 staging by the Colorado-based Butterfly Effect Theater (BETC), which used a small traveling trailer, open to audience view on one side, to take *JQA* into outdoor community settings. Another (a San Diego production during the confining days of early COVID) presented only a filmed version with a one-room set.

If low production costs offer one attraction for local theatres like Stage West, other aspects of *JQA* assert large-scale themes, including the national and global resonances that small-scale exchanges like the play's intimate dialogues can actually have. Individuals and their choices matter to history, this play insists. Such moments shape lives far beyond one's own personal experiences, domestic settings, and chronological lifetimes. Posner's script underscores this theme in part by countering the play's focus on the august white New England Adams family with the cross-gender, cross-race, and cross-generational four-actor cohort, as noted above.

Stage West's Embrace of Posner and *JQA*

Founded in 1979, Stage West espouses a vision for theatre's cultural work seemingly at odds with its "red state" location, yet well aligned with both its loyal clientele and its goals for the local community. Besides a commitment to "excellent acting, directing" and "[m]eticulous attention to creative detail," the organization carefully selects plays demonstrating "a willingness to step outside of the box with new, thought-provoking material" presented in "a safe environment" eager to take on "meaty material" ("About," Stage West website). Accordingly, each season blends comedic plays with more serious fare, and the 2021–22 line-up was no exception. Besides *JQA*, Stage West adopted several other provocative scripts engaging challenging social issues. Both *Church and State* and *On the Exhale*, for instance, tackled school gun violence and raised questions about how government and other social institutions can best support victims and their families. While these plays, like *JQA*, took on national-level political debates with strong local resonance (gun control; voting rights; gender, class, and race relations), the team guiding text selection leavened such fare with genres like broad farce (*Scrooge in Rouge*) and satire (*Witch*).

If *JQA*'s finding a home at Stage West signaled a strong progressive commitment to the arts as a social force, Posner's play also fit the theatre's prior positive experiences with the playwright. As executive producer Dana Schultes observed, "[t]he staff has long loved Aaron Posner's work. It is fresh, relevant, and bridges the past with today." Though previous offerings drew on his Chekhov adaptations, *JQA* appealed to Schultes in part due to her "own affinity for American history, paired with the excellent storytelling and writing" (Schultes).

Email and Zoom conversations with Stage West's executive producer Dana Schultes and director Emily Scott Banks, both during the rehearsal period and after the play's closing, affirmed that this particular staging aimed to capitalize on a new production context, on multiple levels.[8] Nationally, by October 2021, Joe Biden had been in office for months, so the Trump-oriented anxiety that was such a striking subtext for earlier productions of the play (including the first staging directed by Posner himself in D.C.) had faded somewhat. Although many lines still resonated with concerns about flawed leadership models that were even more central to previous shows,[9] the production led by Banks's direction could maintain such implicit calls for stability versus demagoguery while also celebrating signs of more stable national leadership. For instance, a scene where George Washington persuades JQA to accept an ambassadorship as the younger Adams's first political position signaled a number of traits in this "Washington" portrayal that drew parallels to Biden—including dark glasses on Nancy Sherrard (visibly grey, eldest of the four actors) and a pair of Secret Service types who looked far more like today's protective guardians (with prominent ear plugs, for example) than any the first U.S. president would have had.

---

[8] Toward the end of a Zoom interview we had after the Fort Worth run, Banks mused about distinctions between the previous major productions in Washington D.C. and California: "[s]o everybody received it in a way that's like totally different than the way that we received it here"; and she predicted that "the next time it's done, you know it will be in a different moment" (Banks, interview).

[9] Peter Marks's review of the original D.C. production, referenced above, predicted audiences would easily recognize the "slew of lines in 'JQA' that encourage you to think of what's going on today," and the "deficits of this political moment." Thus, for Marks, a line where Henry Clay urges Adams to put in the long work required to build compromises rather than "'playing more golf than governing'" is, for Marks, a direct hit on Trump (Marks, "John Quincy Adams").

Other changes in this production's details both reflected shifts in the national political context between the initial April 2019 staging for the Arena Stage in D.C. and the Texas one in fall 2021. Significantly, Schultes and Banks were empowered to carry out such refinements in part because of Stage West's long-standing ties with the playwright due to having produced several of his other plays and, more directly, through consultations with Posner as they prepared their staging. If this collaborative approach is unusual, it is consistent, nonetheless, with Posner's stated vision for historical drama, outlined above, as needing to be more about the present than the past. Such a philosophy, after all, should be open to organic scripting and staging choices.

As just one example of this flexibility, the Fort Worth production eliminated a conversation with James Madison that had been added for a previous staging in San Diego. As Banks explained, the California staging had been mounted "in an election year," calling for additional "timely" connections with questions about Trump.[10] By fall 2021, this dialogue could be cut, Banks felt, in line with a direction "from Aaron to us" to identify and delete "anything that read too on the nose or dated." For Banks, the change affirmed Posner's "stated goal . . . not to preach or proselytize," something the Madison scene "was verging on," in her view. In other words, the *JQA* staging in Fort Worth not only depicted dialogues from the past between Adams and other figures, it also benefited from ongoing dialogue between the playwright (who had directed the play's maiden production) and the 2021 Texas director, mounting an updated version of Posner's script in ways that would ensure that his big-picture mandate of current relevance should take precedence over any words on the page of the original script.

Also significantly, the Stage West production was being prepared around the time of another transition for the play itself. As Banks explained, besides the factor of prior collaborations, Posner chose "to work with us, because this was one of the final versions of his script before it [went] into publication." Part of that process involved recognizing potential refinements that would maintain the text's ability to "be so relevant," while still being "a history piece" whose elevated language made conscious space for an "idiomatic vernacular of now" (Banks, interview). In that context, one set of rewrites involved the scene with Frederick Douglass and JQA. Through

---

[10] The Madison scene, eliminated in Fort Worth, was set to have Adams, soon after the end of his presidency, visit the elder statesman and Founding Father. Bemoaning the obvious flaws of his successor Jackson, Adams's lines suggest a direct critique of Trump's election as a "horrible dream" that had seemed "practically unimaginable" but came to envision "the end of the country as we know it!" (Posner, *JQA 2020 Performance Draft* 33).

collaborative (re)composing, Banks indicated, the production's Douglass, his castmates, and, ultimately, the audience could arrive at a version of the venerable abolitionist who, despite his recognition of the nation's failings, does not seek "to burn it down"; instead, Banks seemed to have her Douglass stress that the ideals of "the beautiful words and poetry that create the mythology of our country" could become "actually true" (Banks, interview). Overall, in other words, shifts in the play's content ranging from deletion (like the prior Madison scene) to additions and refinements generated a rhetorical embodiment of the ongoing layering process that Posner and his Stage West partners embrace as a method for creating and sustaining historical drama as a genre of social relevance as well as aesthetic craft.

Closely related to this organic, collaborative script refinement, another aspect of this production—its specific casting choices—reaffirmed a core element of the playwright's original vision, in this case with even fuller intersectional range than in earlier shows. Like prior stagings, Stage West used four actors with a mix of genders and racial identities (Figure 8.2). More than in previous versions, however, Banks's team presented the complete range of age differences Posner's written script calls for. In that regard, Nancy Sherrard's presence, besides the striking performative links

Figure 8.2 Stage West's multigenerational, multiracial cast for *JQA*. (Credit: Evan Michael Wood.)

to Biden mentioned above, would be particularly compelling in her portrayals of a sage Abigail Adams and an elder-stateswoman version of JQA. Particularly poignant was Sherrard's late-in-life JQA repeating to Lincoln the "be good" and "do good" advice which Sherrard-as-Abigail had earlier given her son—as well as the nation, given the play's matching trajectory of a gradually maturing JQA mirroring the progression of the nation from youthful Republic forward. As Banks herself explained, showing audiences the full range of ages requested in Posner's script highlighted the play's embodiment of "the aging of the characters reflecting against the aging of America," with the "aging through periods" of Adams's life mirroring a progression from a national youth through "America's adolescence" and into a hoped-for maturity of vision. That is, while previous productions doubtless also devoted careful thought to casting, the Stage West foursome was especially well chosen to embody key themes from the play.

For example, Banks's casting made powerfully visible the playwright's vision of the American presidency as open to formerly excluded intersectional identities, since Stage West's second female actor, Shyama Nithiananda, was a young woman of color. Nithiananda performed the boy Adams in an early scene alongside the senior Adams (JQA's father), then later portrayed JQA's wife Louisa in a middle dialogue, and finally spoke as a young Abe Lincoln near the close of the play. Therefore, audiences could not avoid seeing Posner's envisioning the American nation as welcoming young people of color—including women—into the most prominent leadership roles. Spotlighting this optimistic stance, in fact, Banks characterized her own view of the JQA–Lincoln scene as "he's passing the hat to the next generation, and we know that the hat that's been passed" to this Lincoln will help her-him become, in our national imagination, "another great founder" (Banks, interview). And having the play's embodiment of Lincoln reside in the presence of the production's youngest actor—a women of color—this staging affirmed the vision of Posner's original script to embrace a multicultural America and push ahead for even fuller enactment of that idea in the future.

Balancing this affirming read on Nithiananda's presence in several scenes, the Fort Worth production also offered a reiteration of a familiar feminist critique of gendered tensions around domestic versus social roles. The United States did, in its earliest stages, and it often continues to, depend on women's willingness to shoulder inequitable burdens in domestic life. The mere presence of the Abigail Adams character in this play of course recalls her well-known call to the male founders to remember the ladies—and their failure to do so in the nation's original articulation of democracy in action. For the nation's "fathers," only all men are created equal. Thus, as director Emily Scott Banks reflected, Posner does ask audiences to see "the family aspect" of American national history, "of what you sacrifice and give up for those who are great," and to grasp that, while "supporting them," we should also attend to "a question that we always kind of wrestle with on a personal level in society, with women and children." Accordingly, if Nithiananda's embodiment of Lincoln in the play's final dialogue staked a claim for women's national-level leadership, her Louisa character's reluctance, earlier in the play, to relocate to Russia for her husband's ambassadorship offered a poignant critique of perennial constraints on women's place in civic society. As Banks noted, *JQA* does remind its audience of the price that is frequently exacted on domestic life—"women and children" in particular—so that men like John Quincy Adams can thrive politically.

But the Fort Worth production, overall, cast a spotlight on optimistic elements in Posner's text. The production's space, like its script adjustments and casting, also contributed to a more optimistic overall tone in the play than most previous reviewers had seen in earlier versions.[11] One aspect of the space's positive ambiance emerged from a match between the venue and a then-emerging hope that the COVID pandemic was fading in strength and divisive impact. True, audience members had to show vaccine cards to enter the Sunday matinees that imposed extra safeguards, even beyond those for other performances.[12] Still, watching the show live, in a large arena staging versus on the small set of the traveling trailer in Colorado or via Zoom as for the San Diego, California, production, fostered a mix of intimacy and wide-open possibility. Each audience member could see others throughout the performance via the in-the-round configuration. For Stage West veteran attendees, being in the new Evelyn Wheeler Swenson Theatre, with its larger seating capacity, promoted a feeling of expansive growth in the play's themes as well as for the theatre organization itself.[13] Furthermore, during the matinees with their ramped-up safeguards,

---

[11] See my fall 2021 blog review of *JQA*, published shortly after I attended two shows, under this title: "How to Enact Democracy?"

[12] Stage West established a "Safe Sundays" plan for the 2021–22 season for audience members who wished to attend productions but preferred for everyone to be masked.

[13] As executive producer Dana Schultes explained, in fall 2021 this new performance space was a logical choice for *JQA*, in part because its size allowed for maximum social distancing in "the first in-person show after the 18-month COVID shut-down," but also because it offered the first of many chances to try out a "different seating map"— a strength of the flexible new space that would also benefit future shows. In addition, Stage West management welcomed the chance to "show off" the exciting new space.

seeing all of the others masked fostered a sense of shared community care in a liminal space-time exhibiting a commitment to protecting each other. For north Texans who had been hearing angry anti-mask discourse from state-level leaders all through the pandemic, a counter-commitment of accepting collaborative care was palpable. Further, for all the Fort Worth performances, the 360-degree expanse of activity on stage helped open up the action beyond the tighter focus of the play's one-on-one conversations, as if to remind audience members of the historical drama's repeated connections between experiences as intimate as two-person conversations and the larger social networks in which we live and shape national culture.

Banks made specific directing choices that capitalized on the space thematically. During each dialogue, Banks assigned the two actors not taking part in that exchange to locations around the edges of the set, where they positioned themselves as listening intently to what was being said by the two speakers. As she observed later, having the other actors stay on the edge of the stage "helps the audience lean in": because the actors are "modeling that behavior in a real way, it gives you [the audience] a guide" into the vital citizenship work of listening (Figure 8.3). Relatedly, she noted, having directed other Posner plays at Stage West before, his plays, in

Figure 8.3 Adams's portrait next to an actor modeling engaged listening to a mid-career Adams. (Credit: Evan Michael Wood.)

general, are "scripted" to remind audience members that they are watching a drama, making the experience of live theatre "very meta" indeed (Banks, interview). Through Banks's repeated emphasis, in her staging choices for the actors, on active listening and reflection as an ingredient supporting democratic praxis, the Stage West production tapped into recurring approaches from Posner's larger oeuvre. In collaboration with the playwright, the team making specific decisions for this production situated his historical drama in a tradition of art as an aesthetic teaching force.

Leaning into Layered Reflection to Envision the Future

Posner's focus on historical drama as more of a map for shaping the nation's future than a straightforward recovery of the past is hardly unique for the genre, of course. As a 2021 treatment of Arthur Miller's familiar staple *The Crucible* argues, for instance, the genre of historical drama, in both its scriptmaking and its particular production strategies, can actually align with the cultural work of moral philosophy. In an interpretation of Miller's work, accordingly, Aziz and Korsten posit "Theatre as Intervention" (1143). That is, they declare, Miller's play is similar to work by "democratic theorists such as Martha Nussbaum or Richard Rorty," who aim to "promote liberal democratic values and edify people by making them morally good" (1144). This characterization of historical drama is equally consistent with both Posner's evolving scripts for *JQA* and Banks's responsive direction of his work. Like the cultivation of sympathy and empathy Aziz and Korsten ascribe to *The Crucible*, which they see as calling up "a utopian future" (1142) in a "democracy to come" (1148), the Texas production of *JQA* purposefully presented past and present in layered action actually aimed, primarily, at envisioning a better future for the nation.

Numerous elements in Posner's *JQA* script and the Banks-led Fort Worth production clearly affiliate with that vision. For instance, although Posner has described his original conception of this drama as anticipating an electoral battle between two political family dynasties—the Clintons and the Bushes—by the time of the first production in Washington, D.C., Donald Trump had taken office and was already well on his way to stoking fears among progressives. The Trump context for viewing *JQA* would be noted repeatedly in reviews of early productions (Vincentelli, Wittman). They foregrounded Trump-related areas of critique, as in Peter Marks's review of the D.C.-based premiere pointing to the play's emphasis on "how the behavior of a leader raises and lowers the moral temperature of the nation." They also stressed the significance of some *JQA* dialogue partners, such as Andrew Jackson, a Trump favorite then enshrined in the Oval Office with a portrait, and Frederick Douglass, whom Trump joltingly described in 2017 as if still alive, and "being recognized more and more" (Merica). Interestingly, meanwhile, one recurring theme in anti-Trump activism leading up to and during the time of *JQA*'s first productions involved comparisons between the 45th President and Joseph McCarthy, based in a rhetorical demagoguery some found eerily reminiscent of the infamous senator.[14] On a broader level beyond the issues embodied in Trump's problematic actions while in the White House, the play script and the Fort Worth staging aimed to look beyond the 45th President. That is, "be good and do good" emerges as a mantra for the audience and America, beyond the particular concerns of any one deficient leader—be it Andrew Jackson or Donald Trump. By explicitly and implicitly urging audience members to adopt the advice Abigail Adams offers to her son in an early scene and, then, near the play's close, having JQA invoke the same phrase to a young Lincoln, Posner clearly announces his text's moral agenda—one consistent with Aziz and Korsten's foregrounding of historical drama as enacting a social intervention.

Posner himself has confirmed that such a vision for historical drama's power has guided work on *JQA*—in script craft, in his directing for the first production in D.C., and in mentoring subsequent ones: "We're all grappling with what it means to be an American right now, and what a real American is, what patriotic means, and how to, how we identify as American or don't identify, or what that word means to us when we choose or don't choose to wear it" (Posner, YouTube interview). For the fall 2021 Texas production, director Emily Scott Banks also affirmed this blend of reflective listening, questioning, and hope in describing her setup of the final moment onstage. The four actors having stepped off, a spotlight hit the red coat they had traded back and forth throughout, whenever one of them became Adams. If this red coat of leadership could

---

[14] In a worried essay for the *New Yorker* in 2020, David Remnick invoked Trumpian statements beginning as early as 2017 and extending into Trump's re-election campaign as consistent with a study by historian Richard Hofstadter of "right-wing leaders" like Joseph McCarthy, as exhibiting "angry minds" in their discourse and "a genius for creating confusion, creating turmoil in the hearts and minds of the country" (Remnick, "What Donald Trump"). Even earlier, Albert Eisele called out Trump's "refusal to denounce" Joseph McCarthy and noted that candidate Trump could be critiqued as "shar[ing] Joseph McCarthy's ability to 'brilliantly manipulate the media,' 'preach phony populism' and 'tap into real anxieties but offer no solutions'" ("Trump Rhetoric").

be donned in different times by different individuals across time, as seen throughout the play, this lighting choice indicated that the mantle now awaited other wearers and democratic doers. Having the final moment of the production focus on this image of implicit opportunity, as if the stage awaited audience members' own donning of their various versions of the role, Banks sought to convey "that sense of we've done something here tonight; it's not perfect; it's not finished." Meanwhile, around the outer edges of the in-the-round stage, messy remnants of earlier dialogues lay about discarded but not entirely forgotten, awaiting re-set, since "the next [actor] to come in and pick it up" would have more nation-making work to do (Banks, interview). Agency for democracy's future, this closing image suggested, would lie not with the play text or its presentation, but with the audience. To "be good" and "do good" for the nation, this Texas production of the Posner script conveyed, would ultimately depend not on previous inhabitants of the stage and their actions, but on new social agents and their choices yet to come.

Works Cited

"About Stage West." *Stage West Theatre*, https://stagewest.org/about.

Aziz, Aamir, and Frans Willem Korsten. "Theatre as Intervention: Responsibility/Irresponsibility or Literature's Classical Role in Democracy and Miller's *The Crucible*." *English Studies*, vol. 102, no. 8 (2021), pp. 1142–50.

Banks, Emily Scott. Personal interview. February 11, 2022.

Butterfly Effect Theatre of Colorado. "'JQA' by Aaron Posner." BETC, https://betc.org/event/jqa-by-aaron-posner/ (last accessed November 13, 2024).

Dillon, Elizabeth Maddox. *New World Drama: The Performative Commons in the Atlantic World, 1649–1849*. Duke UP, 2014.

Eisele, Albert. "Trump Rhetoric Overshadows Eugene McCarthy's 100th birthday." *The Hill*, March 29, 2016, www.thehill.com/blogs/pundits-blog/presidential-campaign/274559-trump-rhetoric-overshadows-eugene-mccarthys-100th (last accessed November 13, 2024).

Feldman, Alexander. "Introduction." *Dramas of the Past on the Twentieth-Century Stage: In History's Wings*. Routledge, 2013, pp. 1–28.

Landsberg, Alison. "Introduction: Memory, Modernity, Mass Culture." *Prosthetic Memory: The Transformation of American Remembrance in the Age of Mass Culture*. Columbia UP, 2004, pp. 1–24.

Marks, Peter. "John Quincy Adams Is the Anti-Trump in the New Play 'JQA.'" *The Washington Post*, March 18, 2019, www.washingtonpost.com/entertainment/theater_dance/john-quincy-adams-is-the-anti-trump-in-the-new-play-jqa/2019/03/18/8eb2ac4a-48da-11e9-93d0-64dbcf38ba41_story.html (last accessed November 13, 2024).

Merica, Dan. "Trump: Frederick Douglass 'is being recognized more and more.'" *CNN*, February 2, 2017, www.cnn.com/2017/02/02/politics/donald-trump-frederick-douglass/index.html (last accessed November 13, 2024).

Mielke, Laura L. *Provocative Eloquence: Theater, Violence, and Antislavery Speech in the Antebellum United States*. U of Michigan P, 2019.

Miller, Arthur. The Crucible *in History and Other Essays*. Methuen, 2000.

———. *The Crucible: A Play in Four Acts*. Penguin, 2003.

Nees, Heidi L. "New Paths to Representation; or, How *Under the Cherokee Moon* Broke the Outdoor Historical Drama Mold." *Theatre History Studies*, vol. 34 (2015), pp. 79–102.

O'Connor, Jacqueline. "Introduction: Legal Representation." *Documentary Trial Plays in Contemporary American Theater*. Southern Illinois UP, 2013, pp. 1–21.

Posner, Aaron. *JQA*. 2020 Performance Draft provided to essay author.

———. *JQA*. Directed by Emily Scott Banks, Stage West, October 10, 2021 and October 17, 2021, Fort Worth, Texas.

Posner, Aaron, and San Diego Repertory Theatre. "REP Associate Producer and Casting Director [Kim Heil] Chats with JQA Playwright, Aaron Posner over Zoom." YouTube, uploaded by San Diego Repertory Theatre. August 24, 2020, https://www.youtube.com/watch?v=K17Jxz5f51E (last accessed November 13, 2024).

Remnick, David. "What Donald Trump Shares with Joseph McCarthy." *The New Yorker*, May 17, 2020, www.newyorker.com/magazine/2020/05/25/what-donald-trump-shares-with-joseph-mccarthy (last accessed November 13, 2024).

Richards, Jeffrey H. "Introduction." *Drama, Theatre, and Identity in the American New Republic*. Cambridge UP, 2005, pp. 1–16.

Robbins, Sarah Ruffing. "How to Enact Democracy? *JQA* at Stage West Deftly Asks This Question about the Past and Today." October 11, 2022, www.sarahruffingrobbins.com/2021/10/11/how-to-enact-democracy/ (last accessed November 13, 2024).

Russo, Stephanie. "'You are, like, so woke': *Dickinson* and the Anachronistic Turn in Historical Drama." *Rethinking History*, vol. 25, no. 4 (2021), pp. 534–54.

Schultes, Dana. Personal interview. March 17, 2022.

Vincentelli, Elisabeth. "'JQA' Review: Fictional History That Resonates Today." *The New York Times*, October 31, 2020, www.nytimes.com/2020/10/25/theater/jqa-review-fictional-history.html (last accessed November 13, 2024).

Wittman, Juliet. "BETC Takes Flight With New Name, the Butterfly Effect, and *JQA*." *Westword*, July 4, 2021, https://www.westword.com/arts/betc-takes-flight-with-new-direction-and-name-the-butterfly-effect-12021585 (last accessed November 13, 2024).

9

Ted Lasso and Early American Identity

Anne Roth-Reinhardt

The fumbling, out-of-place American has long been a familiar type, especially in fiction written in the first half century of America's independence. Often unschooled but always proficient in a type of homespun morality, these characters, usually male and always white, provided comic relief but also offered a way to navigate the developing ideological landscape of the United States. Writers of the nascent United States knew they were green, and they recognized that the American cultural scene and its participants were certainly less sophisticated than those of England and Europe. The lack of polish did not mean that Americans were not somehow winning, however, and the characterization of the ideological high ground as clearly American provided a useful substitute for European cultural sophistication. True to form, writers speaking as Americans suggested—even insisted—that their inexperience freed them from all that was wrong with the rest of the world.

While the formation of the American nation and the construction of the so-called American "self" riffed on European standards, its fashion, both cultural and material, provided a way to set the American character apart and even elevate it from that of the Old World. "Homespun," in many ways, becomes the byword for a local simplicity preferred to European polish and, as with material homespun, is defined through both its construction and contrast.[1]

---

[1] A longer analysis of the cultural work of homespun can be found in my dissertation: "Frayed Homespun: Colonial Clothing and Literary Revision in Melville, Sedgwick, and Hawthorne."

Royall Tyler's *The Contrast* (1787), the first American play performed in the United States, for example, mocks the shallowness of foreign fashion and those who follow it to elevate the cultural priorities of newly minted Americans and the country they embody; however, the play depends on and therefore reinforces popular culture by echoing the conflicts of Sheridan's *The School for Scandal*. Likewise, Silas Lapham's unrefined and rugged industrialism in *The Rise of Silas Lapham*, William Dean Howells's 1885 novel, snags on the sharp Brahmin society of Boston and sets Lapham apart, often cringingly so, from the Eurocentric, old-moneyed community that depends on and values inheritance rather than innovation; Daisy Miller, the title character of Henry James's 1878 novel, shows up as her authentic American self and refuses to abandon the manners appropriate to her life back home in Schenectady while on European tour, but the refusal to adopt European customs while leading her best life leads her to lose hers after being struck with Roman fever. While certainly meeting different ends (Lapham loses his wealth but not his life), both these characters suggest the American spirit to be green, energized, and innovative, but impossible to sustain within European or European-centric societies.[2]

Ted Lasso, both the series streaming on Apple TV+ and the show's title character, seems to repeat the disconnect between European and American values embodied in characters like Silas and Daisy.[3] Theodore "Ted" Lasso, a Division II American football coach who led his team, the Wichita State Shockers, to an NCAA championship, accepts a job in the British Premier League from Rebecca Welton, the new owner of A.F.C. Richmond, who recently assumed leadership of the club in the divorce settlement with her former husband, Rupert Mannion. Like past American characters sojourning across the Atlantic, Ted stands out as an outsider: his puckish enthusiasm and regional adages, not to mention his Kansas twang, differ from the sophistication and poise of Welton and the rest of the community and position him as a laughingstock among the media and fans of A.F.C. Richmond. And, like his literary compatriots from the pages of Tyler, Howells, and James, Lasso neither claims a false expertise nor pretends

---

[2] While the continuous repetition and, as a result, reinforcement of European mores in *The Contast* makes Tyler's criticism of Sheridan difficult to separate from his admiration, the conflicts plaguing Silas and Daisy in Howells's text and James's novella more clearly expose European manners and expectations as shallow and damaging constructions.

[3] All references to *Ted Lasso* are to season 1, and specific episodes are referred to by their titles.

to know his way around the English landscape. He knows he does not know soccer and that his version of football does not translate to the language or strategies of "the beautiful game," as soccer/football is often called. To be clear, Lasso accepts the job to coach in the British Premier League without any European football experience and, as he openly admits, very little knowledge of the game. It is this inexperience that makes Lasso's résumé so attractive to Welton as she looks to hire a new coach. While viewers almost immediately realize that Welton has brought in Ted to "destroy" the team—"the only thing my ex-husband ever loved"—the rest of the characters, including Lasso, assume the hire bizarre but legitimate. "Are we crazy for doing this," Lasso asks his assistant coach as they travel to England to begin their work. The answer from Coach Beard and seemingly the rest of the community, at least for the first few weeks of Lasso's tenure, is a raucous and sometimes angry "yes" ("Pilot").

Even though the first season of *Ted Lasso* ends with Lasso's Richmond Greyhounds relegated from the Premier League after a heart-breaking loss to Manchester United, Lasso appears to have saved the team rather than destroyed it as Welton intended. The team, formerly a disconnected, often-antagonistic diverse group whose star resembled more middle-school bully than athletic icon, transforms itself under Lasso's coaching into a club that works together for the common good while recognizing and supporting individual strengths. Players and staff feel seen and supported, and the team members—even in their losses—believe in each other. It is this movement to believe, an idea that is overtly communicated by Lasso through the all-caps directive "BELIEVE" crookedly posted above the locker room door, that prompts the metamorphosis of the club, leads Welton to work in the interest of the team rather than against it, and encourages everyone to be better people. Without any knowledge of soccer or the Premier League, the inexperienced white American equipped with nothing more than a good attitude and democratic values has shown up and made everything better without following the rules or the expectations of his position or the league.

The show seems to celebrate that "the best export of America is America itself," as critic Megan Garber suggests in *The Atlantic*, but the currency created through American philosophy and idealism has a more complicated exchange in the twenty-first century. The glittering brand trafficked as "America" has long depended on the willful forgetting of a sordid domestic and geopolitical history and, in today's political climate where symbols of America have been weaponized, both metaphorically and literally, characterization of America as a force for good can be tough to swallow.

While the popular and critical success of Ted Lasso, recognized as both himself and the nation within the show,[4] demonstrates that the public is ready for a feel-good story about America and Americans, celebrating the unprepared white leader, however, perpetuates a type of dangerous amnesia after four years of the proudly unprepared first Trump administration (2016–20). An American-centric optimism like Lasso's might endear America to itself; however, it willingly forgets the responsibility and the veritable firepower of the United States and, like the characters from Tyler's *The Contrast*, claims a moral authority without owning the stain of generations of systemic and often legal racial discrimination and oppression. The homespun, out-of-place Lasso replicates a familiar character type but, given its placement within modern times, the reprisal of the "American bumpkin" misrepresents the understanding of America as it has developed throughout the nation's relatively short history. To offer up the American as an uncultured rube before the last half of the twentieth century was to admit (and perhaps to justify) that the United States was a fledgling nation, at least in comparison to those established in other continents, and, as a result, it could be excused from making a mistake now and again. As the United States established itself as an economic and military superpower in the twentieth century, however, claiming inexperience or even innocence seemed (and still seems) conveniently short-sighted and dangerously ironic. This chapter reckons with the complications of the Lasso phenomenon against other white inexperienced fictional outsiders from the eighteenth and nineteenth centuries, such as Jonathan from *The Contrast* and Israel Potter from Melville's 1855 *Israel Potter: His Fifty Years of Exile*. Can constructing the bumpkin *as* America produce a force for good, or does it effectively ignore the responsibility of a nation that is now clearly mature enough to take responsibility for its actions and prepare itself in ways expected of a mature nation? Can we responsibly celebrate America for its democratic values given the historic means of their delivery? Can the power of democratic ideology burn off the detritus it has picked up over the years?

---

[4] The insults hurled against Lasso by the community call out his Americanness to communicate his "otherness" and inexperience and, as a result, increase the weight of the insult. In the first episode alone, fans scream things like "Fucking Yank" coupled with "wanker" during his press conference, and soccer captain Roy Kent, in the first exchange with his new coach, compares Lasso to "Ronald fucking McDonald" ("Pilot").

The Contrast and *Israel Potter*

Placing Ted Lasso alongside "homespun" characters from Tyler's *The Contrast* and Melville's *Israel Potter* provides context for the analysis of Ted Lasso as an underprepared yet positive representation of America. The bumpkins of *The Contrast* and *Israel Potter* share a rustic, unsophisticated characterization of nation, but Tyler and Melville use the representation for different ends. Tyler's Jonathan of *The Contrast* shines when positioned against the shallow Jessamy and Billy Dimple, two power-grabbing Eurocentric cads. Dimple's sophistication only camouflages his despicable intentions, and Jessamy's imitation of his employer reminds the reader that Dimple's actions are meant as a cautionary tale—Eurocentrism is a poisonous contagion. The bumpkin Jonathan may laugh when he should hiss at the theater; he may misunderstand the prostitute as the "deacon's daughter" (Tyler 459); and he may speak in American vernacular rather than quote Chesterfield; however, these social missteps celebrate America as innocent and unstained by the attractive temptations of the Old World. Jonathan and his employer, Colonel Manly, remind the audience that "probity, virtue, [and] honour, though they should not have received the polish of Europe, will secure to an honest American the good graces of his fair countrywomen, and, I hope, the applause of the Public" (Tyler 491).

Melville creates the American character as a rustic exemplar in *Israel Potter* through his elevation of homespun Israel Potter over more celebrated American homespun types. In this way, he criticizes popular American mythology of the nineteenth century and praises innocence and even unpreparedness as valuable American traits. *Israel Potter* (1855), Melville's only work of historical fiction, bases its plot on *The Remarkable Adventures of Israel R. Potter* written in 1824. While the two texts are alike in their narrative arcs and cast of characters, they differ in authorial intention. The purpose of the original, as evidenced by its ending, is to argue for the compensation Private Israel R. Potter never received for his service in the Revolutionary War. Melville, rather than complain about unfair treatment of his protagonist, uses his characterization of Israel to illuminate the value of those under-represented by history against more famous figures like Israel Putnam and Benjamin Franklin. For example, Melville plays with the similarities in the names of Israel Potter and General Israel Putnam to elevate the story of the unprepared Private Potter over the established General Israel Putnam. Putnam, characterized by Melville as "broadcloth," famously never hesitated when called to military service, "fly[ing] to battle at a moment's notice." But Israel Potter, seen here through the homespun-like fabric of "linsey-woolsey," while anxious to serve his country like Putnam, "whipped up his team and finished [plowing his field]." Potter, Melville writes, "before hastening to one duty ... would not leave a prior one undone" (Melville 14). Israel Potter has neither a commission nor military training, and so appears completely unprepared for battle. Yet Melville seems to suggest that preparedness pales alongside the work ethic demonstrated by Potter. Unpreparedness grows as a positive trait through Melville's juxtaposition of established ambassador Benjamin Franklin, who wrote under the moniker "Homespun," with the homespun character of Israel Potter. Potter stands out as an unprepared American through his disorientation with French expectations in Melville's novel while Ambassador Franklin not only savvily navigates Paris but uses his knowledge of French culture to take advantage of the naive Israel (57–61). Through references to and depictions of Putnam and Franklin, *Israel Potter* complicates the historical understanding of Americanness by comparing and contrasting characterizations of broadcloth, linsey-woolsey, and homespun, and then uses the ideological complications to subtly criticize popular mythology of America in the nineteenth century. *Ted Lasso*, through its reliance on American types like Melville's Potter and Tyler's Jonathan, furthers a tradition that establishes the authenticity of the unprepared "American" against the backdrop of the Old World.

"The Eyes of All People Are Upon Us"

Claiming a character like Lasso as the emblem of nation has long been the practice of those telling the story of the United States. Those writing the nation into being in the late eighteenth and nineteenth centuries recognized that great nations had long histories, and the recent colonial past carried by the new Republic seemed ill suited to tell the story of revolutionaries and their heirs. Instead, as theorists such as Sacvan Bercovitch, David Levin, Perry Miller, Jean O'Brien, Henry Nash Smith, Robert Tilton, and Laurel Thatcher Ulrich remind us, authors created national heroes out of remnants of the recent past and fashioned a myth of origin that passed—and still passes—as truth. A colonial character like John Endicott, the longest-serving governor of the Massachusetts Bay Company, when imagined in fiction, transforms from stalwart Puritan to fiery revolutionary at the hands of Nathaniel Hawthorne in "Endicott and the Red Cross." Likewise, nineteenth-century historians like George Bancroft joined Hawthorne and his Romantic coterie in fashioning the American hero, as David Levin argues in his seminal *History as Romantic Art* (1963), as a "prophetic exemplar of the country" (qtd. in Bercovitch

148–9). The understanding of America as created through the American exemplar, what John McWilliams identified as "mirror images of one another," was exacted in such a way that "no one was quite sure whether the individual should be defined through the nation, or the nation through the individual" (6). Bolstered if not dependent on the Puritan understanding of their place in the world as a "beacon" and a "city upon the hill," as professed by John Winthrop aboard the *Arbella* back in 1630, authors and historians creating the ideal American and, by extension, a mythologized America, understood that export was always the project and that the stakes were high. As Winthrop reminded those who joined his project back in the seventeenth century, "We shall find that the God of Israel is among us, when ten of us shall be able to resist a thousand of our enemies." But if they should fail, then what they understood of themselves as exceptional would instead "open the mouths of enemies to speak evil of the ways of God." Not only would their mission be seen as a cautionary tale, but their intentional community would encourage the world to shun God rather than trust him (Winthrop 47).

American values materialized and then exported through characters created out of what Levin calls the "idealization of American motives" (qtd. in Bercovitch 48) seem even more precious when Americans find themselves in a new environment. Puritans like Winthrop came to more fully understand their covenanted relationship with God as a chosen people when placed against and tested by the unfamiliar North American landscape and its Indigenous people. Writing centuries before but proving central to the American myth making of the late-eighteenth and nineteenth centuries, Mary Rowlandson in *A Narrative of the Captivity and Restoration of Mrs. Mary Rowlandson* (1682), for example, recognized her captivity as a gift and proof that she was a chosen child of God: "Before I knew what affliction meant, I was ready sometimes to wish for it ... 'For whom the Lord loveth he chasteneth, and scourgeth every Son whom he receiveth' (Hebrews 12.6). But now I see the Lord had His time to scourge and chasten me" (Twentieth Remove). Calvinists like Rowlandson were certainly strangers in a strange land, but their unfamiliarity and eventual survival reinforced the strength and worth of their purpose as a result of their chosen ideology.

The trajectory from the religious exceptionalism of the Puritans and the secular manifestation of America and Americans as "chosen" materializes through Benjamin Franklin's *Autobiography* (1791). Franklin, through his exceptional and perhaps unlikely rise to respectability despite his humble beginnings, exemplifies not only the American value of self-reliance but his uncanny good fortune as an outsider. The story told of Benjamin Franklin, especially his arrival in Philadelphia, echoes the teleology furthered by Rowlandson's account even if it does not share its existential weight. Published some fifty years after Franklin left Boston for a freer existence in unfamiliar Philadelphia, the *Autobiography of Benjamin Franklin* popularizes the "exported" Franklin as a national type. The young Franklin, long frustrated by the limits placed on him by his employer and, because his employer was also his brother, the limits of his family, secures passage out of town and then arrives on foreign shores with only a few coins—not to mention wet socks—in his pocket. Bedraggled and laughably curious to the women he passes, what Franklin does not know about the new land works in his favor as the coins in his pocket buy more than enough bread, and the local house of worship allows him to sleep through service. The obstacles faced by Franklin prove no match for his can-do, optimistic spirit and, as a result, suggest his type as an exemplar to be imitated. Additionally, the practical advice offered in chapter nine of *The Autobiography* outlines a "Plan for Attaining Moral Perfection" (and perhaps the first of many American-published self-help checklists) for its readers. Franklin's moral directives and the character he constructs in print offer a mode of living that does not depend on Old World values. Franklin, in fact, celebrates America and Americans as decidedly "other," but always white, by famously dressing for the mythic frontier rather than the court by donning a coonskin cap while in Paris. The trajectory from Franklin to Lasso is hardly straightforward; in fact, Ted Lasso more closely resembles characters that riff on the type of character embodied by Franklin, the man who signed his name as "Homespun" and quipped in *Poor Richard's Almanack*.

Yankee Doodle

The character of Ted Lasso first appeared in an NBC Sports Premier League promo back in 2013. Titled "An American Coach in London," the four-and-a-half-minute short begins with Lasso dialing Buckingham Palace to speak with the Queen, and then goes on to explain to the camera that he was "brought over [to Tottenham Hotspur] to, ya know, implement [his] coaching style," seemingly unaware of the differences between European football and American football as he claims, "football is football no matter where you play it: you've got grass, you've got cleats, you've got helmets with masks on." When his misunderstanding of the game's measurement is corrected during a press conference (he is told that British football is divided by halves rather than quarters, for starters), he retorts that with ties and without playoffs his job "just got a lot easier," and then asks rhetorically, "No ties and no playoffs? Why do you even do this?"

In contrast to the version of Ted Lasso introduced by NBC Sports, the character of Ted Lasso on Apple TV+ owns all the ignorance of the American coach without the arrogance. His retort "my job just got a lot easier," when delivered in the first episode, lands without the swagger of the NBC Sports version of the character but, at least at the beginning of season 1, depends on Lasso's ignorance for its message as well as comic relief. Underestimating the white American continues a familiar plot device, and it leads to a predictable conclusion where the rube wins in the end. What "Yankee Doodle" began in the eighteenth century, *Ted Lasso* continues into the twenty-first.

"Yankee Doodle," the American folk song scholars date from the late 1740s, is said to have been transformed by the British from a song sung by Americans to a satiric dig bent on ridiculing and exposing the inexperience of colonial Americans. The song, as Leo Lemay discusses in "The American Origins of 'Yankee Doodle,'" among various comic elements mocks the "ignorance and cowardice" of the young rustic Brother Ephraim who "sold his Cow / and bought him a Commission," and later "wouldn't fight the Frenchmen there / for fear of being devoured" (443). While class mockery seems to fit the relationship between the military force of the British and the ragtag militia assembled by the colonials, the pre-Revolutionary dating of the song reminds the reader, both in the eighteenth century and today, that a lighthearted underselling, even a willing self-deprecation, is a "dominant tradition of American humor," according to Lemay (444). He writes: "Colonial Americans learned to reply to English snobbery by deliberately posturing as unbelievable ignorant yokels. Thus, if the English believed the stereotype, they would be taken in by the Americans. And, if they were taken in, the Americans had reversed the snobbery and proven that the English were credulous and foolish" (444–5).

Unlike the premise of "Yankee Doodle," Coach Lasso's ignorance is no posture, however. As he puts it, "You could fill two internets with what I don't know about football" ("Pilot"). He concedes without apology that he has never coached football, never coached a professional team, and struggles to make sense of practice routines, the language of the sport, and the rules of the game. While he looks for ways to remember new information ("let me use it in a sentence so it sticks," he says when trying to absorb vocabulary like "gaffer" and "pitch") ("Pilot"), Ted is more interested in the health of the team and the growth of his players than becoming an expert of the game. For example, in the first episode as he travels to his new job, he reads a dogeared copy of Kerouac's *On the Road* on the plane while his assistant coach responsibly studies soccer tactics. Ted Lasso, at least on paper, looks to be a clear picture of white American arrogance (or, at best, ignorance) and, because of his unfamiliarity with everything British, seems like the perfect means for Rebecca Welton, the club's new owner, to enact her revenge against her philandering ex-husband. As reporter Trent Crimm sums up during the initial press conference with Lasso, Lasso is "an American who's [sic] never set foot in England, with no football experience whatsoever, whose athletic success has only come at the amateur level—a second tier one at that—and has now been charged with the leadership of a Premier League football club, despite clearly possessing very little knowledge of the game or its basic strategy" ("Pilot").

The hiring of Ted Lasso banks on the disconnect between his folksy persona and the seriousness it takes to compete in the British Premier League. One would think, based on the response of the media and the fan base, that the "seriousness" expected from a head Premier League coach would be the composite of everything Coach Lasso is not. While an expert-level understanding of the game and previous experience would be expected, characteristics of arrogance and privilege seem to be assumed or at least tolerated in a Premier League coach, at least based on the behavioral norms established by the former coach. The entire scene with soon-to-be fired A.F.C. Richmond coach George Cartick gives the viewer a sense of the behavior normalized in this sort of position. Cartick, a middle-aged man dressed in short soccer shorts, behaves in ways often attributed to adolescent males rather than professional men. Entering the room, Cartick pretends to flick another man's testicles and uses a homophobic slur to characterize the decoration of the office. He calls Welton "love" and "a cheeky one" and tells her to "get whatever [she] needs to say off her impressive chest" so that he can get to practice. It comes as no surprise after this exchange that Welton cites "casual misogyny" as partial grounds for dismissal ("Pilot"). What then-presidential candidate Donald Trump dangerously characterized as "locker room talk" in the infamous 2005 "Access Hollywood" video (Bullock) seems to be the norm of the outgoing British leadership rather than the American direction it will assume. "Serious," at least in *Ted Lasso*, does not mean thoughtful or prepared or even better: in this case, while it may mean more experience in the game, it does not carry the gravitas one might expect.

Familiar constructions of the American persona, at least in the eighteenth and nineteenth centuries, depend on the relationship between American inexperience and European seriousness. The new republic of the United States had fought a revolution to define what it was not, but in the late-eighteenth and nineteenth centuries, it had not yet settled on what it would be. Contrast became the means of definition in the absence of a settled identity in the early days of the nation and, more than two centuries later, contrast still provides a convenient yet imperfect means to define the nation. Low expectations like those sung in "Yankee Doodle" and the ones surrounding Ted Lasso make victories achieved all the sweeter, but the work of *Lasso*, much like the representations of Americans from Howell and James, comes from what it distances rather than what it determines. While the comedic effect of characters like Ted Lasso may draw on the low expectations of Americans by the British, what the white bumpkin does not know and therefore cannot imitate, in many ways, is what saves him and ends up elevating him over the fashioned sophistication of the British or the Eurocentric American. The Boston aristocracy mocking Silas Lapham, the earnest, unsophisticated entrepreneur in Howell's *The Rise of Silas Lapham* (1885), falls in the reader's estimation because while the Bostonians certainly know more than Lapham, they use their position to widen the gap that divides the community rather than bridge it. Daisy Miller, James's 1878 title character, has no interest in learning the rules of European society and, as a result, suffers the social exclusion of the established ex-pat community in Europe. While Daisy dies because of her willing naivety, she appears the most logical when placed against the shallowness of the community and the bewildered reception she suffers while on a European tour.[5]

Daisy, like Lapham, suffers for being unprepared and unfamiliar, but James's text and Howells's work roundly criticize the values held by the communities who fail to receive the Americans, even if the status quo is preserved at the end of both novels: Daisy dies for her missteps, Lapham retreats to country life after his business failings, and the cultural norms they challenged through their presence continue. It would seem, then, that *Ted Lasso* more resembles the morality tale articulated through Tyler's *The Contrast*. For although the play depends on European sources, the victory achieved by those outside fashionable circles celebrates virtue, characterized here as "homespun," and exposes Eurocentrism as false. The emperor,

---

[5] Lapham's Silas and James's Daisy establish the American-as-outsider as a familiar type. While there are certainly other texts one might gesture toward—Mark Twain's *A Connecticut Yankee in King Arthur's Court* (1889), for example—the narratives of Silas and Daisy depend on their construction as outsider and subsequent failure because of their ineffective or outright refusal to adopt European manners.

it would seem, wears no clothes. Consider Tyler's character of Jonathan in *The Contrast* alongside that of Billy Dimple and Jessamy, Dimple's servant. Jonathan, a self-described "waiter" of Colonel Manly from Massachusetts, fully misunderstands the social geography of New York and, as a result, provides a type of mean-spirited amusement for Dimple, Jessamy, and the play's audience. Unlike the famous entry of Benjamin Franklin into Philadelphia, who, at least according to his *Autobiography*, seems to benefit from his initial lack of cultural familiarity, Jonathan trusts the wrong people and stumbles repeatedly. In *The Autobiography*, though, rather than being mocked for his ignorance upon arrival, Franklin's failure to translate both currency and the regional word for "biskit" and "three penny loaf" gains him a windfall of bread and change in his pocket, and falling asleep in church, for Franklin, yields no rebuke (chapter 3). Additionally, Franklin's 1791 account presents the women of Philadelphia, his future wife, even, as amused rather than disgusted by his "most awkward, ridiculous appearance" (chapter 3). In *The Contrast*, however, Jonathan's failure to translate the culture of the big city hinders his ability to navigate eighteenth-century New York. It is interesting, especially when placed alongside the representation of Americanness in *Ted Lasso*, that Jonathan does not seem to care to know what he does not know; he is unimpressed by the French phrases, what he calls the "outlandish lingo" used by Jessamy, and he doesn't consider that what he hears as "girl hungry" is actually "a little gallantry" (Tyler 460).

All that Jonathan does not know is leveraged as a type of comic opportunity by Jessamy and Billy Dimple, the play's fashionable cads, in order to take advantage of Jonathan for their amusement. The reader or viewer of the play understands Jessamy and Dimple to be villains disguised as gentlemen, but the other characters do not realize the ruse until it is almost too late. The end of the drama reinforces the play's message, and what is referred to as "the polish of Europe" loses out to what the play refers to as the "honest American" (491). What Jonathan does not know, as it turns out, places him above the Chesterfield-quoting "polished" pseudo-Europeans whose manners may fit them to good society but fall short of virtue and honor. Like Jonathan of *The Contrast,* Lasso never claims to know much and, even as the character slowly develops across the first season, viewers can tell that Lasso's humility, selflessness, and even his lack of preparation are in stark contrast with the bullies of the show. We know very little about Lasso as the series begins, but his character appears commendable because Lasso falls outside a culture that seems to be choking on its own poison. "In a business that celebrates ego," writes reporter Trent Crimm in his feature article on the new coach, "Ted reins his in" ("Trent Crimm:

The Independent"). And, as a result, Lasso has no interest in needing to make others low to go high. In fact, he will not even wield a type of moral authority or hierarchy appropriate to his position—his style of coaching encourages his players to lead because he steps away to make space for them. It is as if Lasso has watched plays like *The Contrast* and realizes the surest way to fail is to play the role he does not know—in his case, that of Premier League Coach—as Jonathan first falls flat while following the script of New Yorker handed to him by the dastardly Dimple and Jessamy.

What is most interesting, however, is that although Jonathan fails to understand his position in New York City in *The Contrast*, both literally and culturally, he has a clearer understanding of positionality in the nascent Republic than his French-speaking, Chesterfield-quoting compatriot. Jessamy actively tries to position himself as higher than Jonathan in the way he mocks and manipulates his ignorance of city life. The men may share the same social class as they both serve other men as servants or, as Jonathan puts it, "waiters," but Jessamy successfully leverages his "appearance" and "lingo," as Jonathan calls it, to set himself apart and even position himself as equal or even greater, as he suggests later in the play, than his employer. Jessamy, in other words, performs the social position he aspires to and, as a result, reinforces the divide that separates him from his employer Billy Dimple. Jonathan, a "true blue son of liberty," as he calls himself, delegitimizes class hierarchy by failing to distinguish it and, as a result, announces that "no man shall master me" (Tyler 457). Jonathan's purposeful ignorance forwards the essence of American Democracy: no man must bow to another and, as Walt Whitman, often called the poet of American Democracy, will remind the nation some fifty years later, we "are not contain'd between ... hat and boots" (34) and the elevated among us, as Whitman writes in the Preface to *Leaves of Grass*, "tak[es] off his hat to [the people] not they to him" ("Preface"). Clothing, for Whitman as well as Tyler, materially communicates and reinforces the ideology professed through the text. That Jonathan is out of step with New York fashion clearly saves him from the social schema that masters Jessamy if not the city. What is clear to him, however, is that the landholding of his family and the whiteness of his skin are what permit him to ignore class hierarchy. Almost immediately upon his entrance, Jonathan points to his family's landholdings—"my father has as good a farm as the Colonel"—and bristles at the suggestion that he is a servant which, based on his response, he translates as a racial epithet (Tyler 457). Calling himself a "waiter" distances himself from servitude-as-enslavement even as it acknowledges that idealized class blindness only works for landed white men in the new Republic.

The characterization of Ted Lasso echoes that of Jonathan in *The Contrast* and, like the eighteenth-century play, demonstrates the power of a willful ignorance within a stratified or even toxic community. The ignorance Lasso maintains disrupts the binary that positions one entity against another: his passive refusal of cultural rules challenges the system rather than reinforces it. Lasso's ignorance as resistance, at least at the onset of the series, is not seen as revolutionary. Welton hires him because of his ignorance, and his behavior reaffirms the low expectations of Americans held by the British. The revolution, however, comes through the space Lasso opens in his refusal to imitate and "play the game" expected of a Premier League coach. Rather than direct behavior, Lasso normalizes and then reinforces community values; rather than prescriptive, authoritative leadership, Lasso gifts the team with fictional narratives that match the player to encourage their thinking rather than insist on compliance.

Fostering independent rather than dependent learning as Lasso does strengthens the team's internal leadership, and the community spirit of the team raises those individuals who were previously struck down or undervalued. The plot development of the series realizes that every character—including Lasso—is more than they seem at the onset. The kit manager Nate, as Garber reminds us in her article, emerges from his insecurity into a football strategy wonk; captain Roy Kent directs his rage into productive leadership; the backstory of arrogant and cruel Jamie Tartt, the team's rising star, provides some explanation for his bad behavior; and Welton and other female characters of the show, initially stereotyped as shallow and vindictive, develop as interesting, dynamic individuals rather than the stock positions they seem to fill early in the show. The success of the team and the positive development of individual characters does not arrive because they are merely unprepared or early in their development; the success of Lasso and his coterie happens because while each character is interested or at least affected by human behavior, no one—especially Ted Lasso—pretends to know more than they do.

Using his position as a national and cultural outsider to somehow assume a position of power is not what Lasso does, however. Placing the NBC Sports promo that first introduced Lasso to audiences alongside the show that developed from it differentiates the humble ignorance of Lasso-the-character from the arrogant unawareness articulated by Lasso-the-promo. Where the latter dismisses that which is unfamiliar through his tone and posture, the former appreciates unfamiliarity as an opportunity to learn rather than leverage his position to convince A.F.C. Richmond that he, in fact, has all the answers. The new world of Premier League football, at least for Lasso-the-character, becomes a place to learn through rather than a landscape to dominate. In the Apple TV+ series, Lasso sees his newfound situation as something to wonder *about* rather than wonder *at*; he exercises curiosity rather than assume all that he does not understand is wrong. There are limits to Lasso's curiosity, but these instances are limited to offside rulings on the soccer pitch and crossing the street when cars drive on the left rather than right side of the road.

Of course, leveraging curiosity to "win" by somehow elevating yourself over others seems like a very "American" thing to do. Winning by way of "curiosity" stinks of posture rather than an authentic wondering about the people around you; it seems more like a contemporary pose that banks on the recognized value that vulnerability and humility have in the present-day United States. Additionally, "curiosity" within the history of the United States and the development of the American persona depends on a binary that placed "curiosities" against white, Christian settlers, who would later proudly appropriate what they deemed the "nativeness," as Turner's "The Significance of the Frontier in American History" posits, to create an identity that was "a steady movement away from the influence of Europe, a steady growth of independence along American lines" (4).

True curiosity as an American characteristic, therefore, seems like new territory for the unassuming Kansan Ted Lasso. While Lasso satisfies the bumpkin stereotype in many ways, the creators of the show, as Garber puts it in the *The Atlantic*, have "complicated the caricature"; it is the curiosity of Lasso that best defines him and, as a result, redeems the white male outsider from the United States through their version of contemporary, post-Trump "Americanness." Defining and even elevating yourself through "othering"—what many of us remember as a parental caution or rebuke during our formative years—was popularized by both candidate and later president Donald Trump on too many occasions to name and is the opposite of genuine curiosity about the world and the people within it. Lasso instead seems to follow the advice of then-First Lady Michelle Obama offered during the 2016 Democratic National Convention as she directed her audience to "go high" when others "go low" rather than "stoop" to the level of the bully.

In fact, in one of the most popular moments of the first season, Lasso recounts the "othering" he had experienced: how he had been a type of curiosity rather than someone to be truly curious about. "Guys have underestimated me my entire life," Lasso recounts during a game of darts with the dastardly Rupert, Welton's ex-husband, "and for years I never understood why" ("Diamond Dogs"). Driving his son to school one day, as Lasso tells the story, he sees a quote attributed to Walt Whitman painted on a wall: "Be curious, not judgmental." The sentence sparks a type of epiphany in Lasso who, as he explains, began to realize that "all them fellas that used to belittle me, not a single one of them was curious" ("Diamond Dogs"). To "judge" depends on both elevation and separation between one person and another. Lasso, like any of us who have been made to feel apart or "outside," unwillingly offered the means for those doing the "judging" to determine their position through constructed contrast. This lack of curiosity falsely reinforced that these "fellas" had "everything figured out so they judged everything, and they judged everyone" ("Diamond Dogs"). Their judgment, Ted shares, had nothing to do with him but everything to do with others' lack of curiosity. Lasso's experiences as a social outsider led to the curiosity he practices while a national outsider in England and within the British Premier League.

Curiosity is not a common attribute shared by American protagonists and heroes, however. Not only literary characters but players on the geopolitical stage of the United States historically advance through domination rather than admitting that there is much to learn. The texts I cite in this essay—*The Contrast, Israel Potter, Daisy Miller,* and *The Rise of Silas Lapham*—may not reinforce an alpha-protagonist in the vein of classic heroes like Odysseus or even classic frontiersman Natty Bumppo from Cooper's *Leatherstocking* series,[6] but their narratives depend on the recognized might one culture holds over another and end with moral or social certainty rather than encourage curiosity. The reference to Whitman recognizes "curiosity" as an American trait through contrast since Lasso references the quote in response to Rupert's dismissal: America gets to claim "curiosity" because the Brit does not. Yet the "Americanness" of the exchange comes more from its parallel with "Yankee Doodle" than Lasso's "curiosity" monologue. While the audience already recognizes Rupert as British by episode 8 in season 1, Lasso, much like the turn of events associated with "Yankee Doodle," leverages Rupert's low expectation of him by reinforcing himself as the national and cultural outsider. Ted initiates the darts exchange with Rupert by acknowledging that "y'all take your darts over here pretty seriously, huh?" and suggesting that snooker, the other game he believes the British take seriously, sounds more "like a brand of cookies" that he'd love to "devour" while "curl[ed] up on a couch under a weighted blanket,

---

[6] Natty Bumppo, the main character in several of James Fenimore Cooper's novels, offers a literary manifestation of the American self articulated and idealized in Turner's "The Significance of the Frontier in American History" (1893).

watch[ing] *You've Got Mail*" ("Diamond Dogs"). Cornhole, Ted remarks, is more his game and, through this, Lasso reinforces himself as a national and cultural outsider by identifying a bar game universally recognized as less sophisticated than those played by the British.

Truly curious, however, is that the quote attributed to Whitman was not written by Whitman, as an Internet search will quickly reveal. Encouraging curiosity does seem like something Whitman *would* do through his writing, but the closest we get to what Lasso quotes comes from a stanza in book 48 of "Song of Myself" in *Leaves of Grass*: "And I say to mankind, Be not curious about God, / For I who am curious about each am not curious about God, / (No array of terms can say how much I am at peace about God / and about death)" (76). The Whitman-inspired story shared in the episode provides the viewer with some useful background on Lasso since, at this point in the series, we know very little about the title character other than we should cheer for him because we hiss at Rupert. The importance of the quote, however, comes through not in its lack of authenticity but in the way it leverages "curiosity" as an American trait because of the absence of it among the English men and women at the bar. No one, not even Rebecca, suspects Ted of doing the hustling rather than being hustled even though he is the one who initiates and determines the stakes of the contest. The collective gasp when Ted hits the bullseye after he exclaims, "Oh, wait a second. I forgot I'm left-handed" shows the effectiveness of Ted's ruse because of the English willingness to believe what Ted suggested through his "snooker" and "cornhole" remarks, not to mention his professed ignorance of the game: "Whatever you say, Rupe-a-dupes. Yeah. Just let me know if I'm winning or losing, all right?" ("Diamond Dogs"). Ted wins here because no one challenges the legitimacy of the Whitman quote or the performance of American as ignorant cultural outsider, and the bully gets bested by the Yankee Doodle yokel who can hardly cross the street in England let alone strategize on the soccer pitch.

Success and failure, as Lasso mentioned to Crimm during his interview, have little to do with the playing of any game. For Lasso, it is not about winning or losing, but rather about "helping these young fellas be the best versions of themselves both on and off the field" ("Trent Crimm: The Independent"). Ted's unbelievable ignorance seems to reinforce what the players and the fan base believe about the "fucking Yank" ("Pilot"). And understandably, fans feel mocked and angry that someone with so little knowledge about the game, and from America, no less, has been recruited and is now being paid to coach a game and a team about which they feel very strongly. Believing the stereotype embodied by Lasso, however, has the same effect as it did in "Yankee Doodle," as the team and a large percentage of the fan base, while first underestimating the American, grow to somewhat accept him, although not embrace him, as a part of the community. "If the Lasso way is wrong," writes the skeptical Trent Crimm, "it's hard to imagine being right" ("Trent Crimm: The Independent").

Homespun

Claiming curiosity as an American attribute ignores past representations of national character against foreign landscapes. While the United States has demonstrated a strategic interest in other countries, describing American foreign policy as "curious" discounts the complicated relationship between the U.S. and the rest of the world. And American types characterized in literature, while not always representative of nation, often carry their enthusiasm for American values and are surprised by the lukewarm reception upon arrival. Melville, however, offers a longer consideration of Americans and their values against foreign landscape and culture in *Israel Potter*. Potter, like Lasso, finds himself out of place and seemingly ill equipped to navigate the situation in front of him. As an outsider, Potter, like Lasso, illuminates the value of his position by succeeding in places he should fail, and while both characters eventually fall short of their goals, the Americanness they share affects positive change in the community.

Melville's novel *Israel Potter* resurrects the autobiography of Israel R. Potter, originally advertised as the narrative of an unlucky private who survives the Battle of Bunker Hill only to become a prisoner of war and spend the next fifty years trying to get home. In the novel's preface, Melville shares how he happened upon the narrative and, in doing so, reinforces the story's authenticity and suggests the American values of simplicity, self-reliance, and thrift to be both practical and actionable. The novel appears, at first glance, to be a bad-luck story of an American rustic who, for the most part, lives a "plain old homespun" life, but often finds himself at the wrong place at the wrong time (Melville 149). Forbidden to marry the girl he loves, young Israel leaves his father's home in search of financial and personal independence. He gains employment in various locales and eventually tries his hand at a seafaring life. The War for Independence draws his interest and employs his service, including heroic duty at Bunker Hill, but his assigned ship is quickly captured by the British, binding him to England. What follows is an adventure, not quite as tragic as the biographical fodder for the novel which narrates Israel as a forgotten, unlucky exile, longing for home, but always found retreating when he wishes to be advancing across the Atlantic. The fictional Israel may liberate himself from imprisonment, but his freedom is tenuous and short-lived. Recruited as a courier, Israel traffics state secrets to Benjamin Franklin in Paris, where he endures the wisdom of the envoy and makes the acquaintance of John Paul Jones. Neither Franklin nor Jones, unfortunately, returns Israel to the homeland he seeks. Israel's quiet homecoming fifty years after his capture ironically collides—quite literally—with jubilant processions honoring the "heroes that fought" in the Battle of Bunker Hill. After the adventure of exile comes to a close, Melville quickly cuts to the end, allowing a chance reunion between Israel and the ruins of his home before he dies, "fading . . . out of being—his name out of memory" (192).

Melville's resurrection of the "rustic" and "linsey-woolsey" Potter in fiction promotes "homespun" as an actionable and practical American value, and *Ted Lasso*, nearly two centuries later, does the same. Potter, although lacking the recognized national credentials of other characters like Franklin or John Paul Jones, continues to support the tenets of American democracy without hesitation and demonstrates to the reader that an unflappable consistency furthers American values more than cultural sophistication.

Like Lasso, Potter does not pretend to understand the social and political fashions across the Atlantic and, like Lasso, this lack of understanding and honesty about both saves him and offers straightforward American values as the answer to social and political quandaries. For example, Potter, an escaped prisoner of war, wanders the English countryside looking for shelter and a way home. During this time, village laborers direct him toward the estate of Sir John Millet, a benevolent landholder who, according to a local carpenter, is often known to hire additional workers. The initial exchange and eventual relationship between Potter and Millet, based on the original encounter documented by the *real* Israel Potter and fictionalized by Melville, emphasizes the rejection of class hierarchy and, as a result, suggests that the American character is stronger if not superior to that of the British. The novel takes gentle jabs at the English work ethic by leading Israel, eager and ready to work at four o'clock in the morning, to the still-darkened estate and empty fields of Millet. Here, across the Atlantic, the workday begins at seven rather than at summer sun-up (Melville 27). While different understandings of the workday may first perplex and then reassure Israel of American grit and dedication, what distinguishes the American as formidable is Israel's refusal to recognize Millet's title. Repeatedly through the scene, Israel responds to Millet's queries by calling him "Mister" rather than the title of "Sir," as appropriate to his station, and even when Millet questions Israel's behavior, the American demonstrates an almost visceral response to the conferring of titles:

> "Mr. Millet," exclaimed Israel aghast, the untasted wine trembling in his hand, "Mr. Millet, I—"
> "Mr. Millet—there it is again. Why don't you say Sir John like the rest?"
> "Why, sir—pardon me—but somehow, I can't. I've tried; but I can't. You won't betray me for that?"
> "Betray—poor fellow! Hark ye, your history is doubtless a secret which you would not wish to divulge to a stranger; but whatever happens to you, I pledge you my honor I will never betray you."
> "God bless you for that, Mr. Millet."
> "Come, come; call me by my right name. I am not Mr. Millet. You have said Sir to me; and no doubt you have a thousand times said John to other people. Now can't you couple the two? Try once. Come. Only Sir and then John—Sir John—that's all."
> "John—I can't—Sir, sir!—your pardon. I didn't mean that." (Melville 29)

That Millet not only insists on being called "Sir," but that he employs a type of paternal, rudimentary strategy to break Israel of what he deems a bad habit or a type of involuntary tic recognizes the knight's benevolence but also what appears to be a foolish insistence. The wealth of Sir John Millet places Israel and the other laborers under his rule and employment. Must obeisance be paid through one's titles as well as one's service? The answer, according to the narrative treatment of events, seems to be "no." Melville's text leads Millet to the same conclusion as the reader: insisting on titles lowers good men into petty postures, and the physical revulsion of Israel recognizes the strength of American resistance and the impossibility of British victory. "[If] all your countrymen [are] like you," states Millet, "there's no use fighting them" (Melville 28).

While Tyler's Jonathan gives context and historical background to the character of Ted Lasso, Melville's Israel bears a stronger resemblance to the earnest football coach. The exchange between Millet and Potter in *Israel Potter* complicates the character of American as "bumpkin" or as national and therefore cultural "outsider" since Potter's resolve amidst cultural pressure proves admirable rather than laughable. While Jonathan, Israel, and Ted, in their respective stories, stumble through unfamiliar social landscapes, Jonathan is made to seem foolish and only rises to nobleness at the play's conclusion. The national and therefore cultural unfamiliarity of Potter and Lasso, in contrast, elevates their characters by setting them apart from the failings (or at least the shortcomings) in two different centuries of British life. Israel Potter, quite literally through his inability to say "Sir John" cannot reinforce the broken system insisted upon by his employer; Ted Lasso, through his ignorance of the Premier League as it exists both on and off the field, stands above those who have succumbed to its baseness. The coach preceding Lasso encourages if not creates a hostile environment through sexist jokes and, in his wearing of short shorts, a lack of concern for inadvertent genital exposure. Lasso covers up naked pictures posted in the locker room rather than contribute to the toxic work environment cultivated by his predecessor and, on the first full day on the job, brings Welton cookies ("or, as y'all call 'em here, 'biscuits'") and suggests a daily "breakfast with the boss" because "we can't really be good partners unless we get to know each other" ("Biscuits"). What Israel Potter refuses to say by insisting on "mister" rather than "sir" and Lasso refuses to repeat interrupts the status quo of British society.

The uncomplicated consistency demonstrated by Potter and Lasso challenges cultural norms in England and, in the case of Lasso, changes behavior. Melville's characterization of French ambassador Franklin as morally tainted further reinforces the importance of cultural consistency against the lure of European fashion. The reader of *Israel Potter* is introduced to Franklin after sympathizers of the Revolution tap Potter to traffic sensitive information to Franklin in Paris. Franklin, the original, self-declared "homespun," mocks Potter's unfamiliarity with Parisian customs and relentlessly benefits from Potter's ignorance. By first insisting that the corked bottle of brandy contains poison, and then claiming the bottle for himself, Franklin resembles the despicable Billy Dimple and Jessamy of *The Contrast* rather than the "homespun" Manly from Tyler's play (Melville 59–60). Additionally, the pithy commandments quoted by Melville's Franklin exhaust Israel and, quite honestly, his reader. Here Franklin sounds more like a broken record than a revolutionary icon as he lectures Potter on thrift and sobriety, and the independence he encourages isolates Potter rather than empowers him (48–50). Statements like "Always get a new word right in the first place ... and you will never get it wrong afterwards," "Plain water is a very good drink for plain men," and "To have to spare, is to have to give away" fall flat with both Israel and the reader and fashion Franklin as more stuffed shirt than font of wisdom (Melville 49–50).

Most disappointing of all, however, is that Franklin fails to recognize his younger self in Israel Potter. The young Potter's arrival in Paris begins with several miscues as he fails to read the cultural landscape. Muddy and bespattered, Israel cannot understand the remonstrations of the boot-black man and, in response, kicks over his box and flees without apology (39). Even though Israel, like Franklin in Philadelphia, subsided on the equivalent of penny loaves and a generous exchange rate while in exile, Franklin encourages thrift and uses cheaply bought bread to discourage Potter from exploring Paris instead of encouraging him to see obstacles as opportunity as Franklin was able to realize in his youth.

There are no established ex-pats in *Ted Lasso*, at least in season 1, to demonstrate the effects of British manners on even the most "homespun" among us. Instead, the viewer measures the moral nobility of Lasso alongside the brokenness of the British. Lasso sounds a lot like both Jonathan of *The Contrast* and Franklin's comic persona in *Poor Richard* in the adages he shares while navigating the strange world that is A.F.C. Richmond. When feeling uncomfortable in new situations, Lasso reminds others that there is no such thing as "last-day-of-school jitters" ("Biscuits"), and that "taking on a challenge is a lot like riding a horse ... If you're comfortable while you're doing it, you're probably doing it wrong" ("Pilot"). Preparing to practice is essential, Lasso quips, because "your body is like day-old rice. If it ain't warmed up properly, something real bad could happen" ("All Apologies"), and players need to function as a team or, as Lasso puts it, "a group of people who care ... not unlike folks at a hip-hop concert whose hands are not in the air" ("Diamond Dogs"). While Lasso's statements are met with bemusement and often confusion, they eventually land with their recipient, except for the "kissing your sister" remark Lasso uses to describe games that end in a draw to his horrified locker room ("The Hope That Kills You"). The truisms of Lasso and characters like Jonathan of *The Contrast*, at least at first glance, reveal the measure of disconnect between British sophistication and the American rustic. Compared to the moral shortcomings of Eurocentric characters like Jessamy and Billy Dimple in Tyler's play, however, we applaud Jonathan for his moral consistency and recognize his unfamiliarity as an asset rather than a detriment. Jonathan, Ted Lasso, and even Israel Potter should fail: they are unprepared to succeed in unfamiliar environments and discouraged by the low expectations of their communities. Yet what they accept as truth protects them from the lure of power promised through the cultural hierarchy modeled by others. Somehow these characters succeed when, by all accounts, they should not. It is Potter rather than John Paul Jones who lights the fires at Whitehaven to successfully take the British fort (Melville 116), and it is Potter who witnesses John Paul Jones's famous rejoinder, "I have not yet begun to fight," in the battle against the *Serapis* (145). And even though Welton underestimates Lasso, gives him the job because of her low opinion of his abilities, and repeatedly sets him up to fail, the consistency Lasso brings as an American "bumpkin" improves the community rather than sinks it. Tyler's drama and Melville's reworked biography unapologetically promote the rube, the rustic, and the American over the toxic culture of the British; *Ted Lasso*, rather than celebrating the unprepared stranger, reminds its viewer of the power of consistency and the strength of true democratic values.

At the end of season 1, Coach Lasso rallies his team by alluding to perhaps the most famous overmatched American team in sports history—the 1980 U.S. men's hockey team ("The Hope That Kills You"). In his book *Miracle on Ice: How a Stunning Upset United a Country*, Michael Burgan reminds us that the U.S. team, made up of amateur players, seemed no match for the more experienced Soviets who came into the contest with four gold medals and a roster of soldiers rather than the young players and college students of the U.S. team (4). The game, viewed by an over-capacity crowd in Lake Placid, New York, offered an opportunity to measure American energy against Soviet strength and, while the contest was athletic rather than political, the dominance of one team over the other would symbolically reinforce the rhetoric of the victor. The U.S. took the lead in third period and was able to hold off the Soviets for the last ten minutes of the game and, as the clock sealed the American victory, commentator Al Michaels announced the U.S. win by asking the TV audience, "Do you believe in miracles?" The question may appear rhetorical in print but celebrates an ideology rather than questions its veracity. Ted Lasso, by quoting Michaels to inspire his clearly outmatched Greyhounds, not only reminds the team that the unlikely can happen, but he indicates that American values can be a powerful export, and that underestimating the underprepared or outmatched "bumpkin" is unwise.

The release of *Ted Lasso* in the final months of the first Trump administration gave the show's audience an alternative to the American values advertised by the Republican president. Democracy, as seen through the show, empowers communities through collective agency rather than greedy individualism; the "America" driving Lasso sounds more like the "Yes We Can" of former president Obama than the "Make America Great Again" of his successor. Like Obama, Lasso directs us to "believe" without offering the object for our belief; Obama illuminates the potential of the collective in his directive "yes we can" without indicating and therefore limiting what we can do. "Believe" is the byword that propels Lasso and his philosophy, and the directive asks us to "believe" without specifying the "what," therefore rejecting dependency on a singular objective. To believe asks that we move forward without knowing where we are going; to believe understands that our success depends on forces beyond our control. Whether it be the collective efficacy created by merely "believing," as in the streaming series *Ted Lasso*, or Israel Potter's unshakable belief in a Revolution that professed equality, "belief" can upset oppressive systems and change the world. Just as Israel Potter won a victory for American values by refusing to capitulate to British culture in his exchange with John Millet (and later King George), Ted Lasso succeeds because the "Lasso way," as Trent Crimm calls it, depends on staying true to *his* values rather than trying to dominate another.

Works Cited

Bercovitch, Sacvan. *The Puritan Origins of the American Self: With a New Preface.* Yale UP, 2011.

Bullock, Penn. "Transcript: Donald Trump's Taped Comments About Women." *The New York Times*, October 8, 2016.

Burgan, Michael. *Miracle on Ice: How a Stunning Upset United a Country.* Compass Point Books, 2016.

Franklin, Benjamin. *The Autobiography of Benjamin Franklin.* 1791. E-book, Project Gutenberg, 2009, https://www.gutenberg.org/files/20203/20203-h/20203-h.htm (last accessed November 13, 2024).

Garber, Megan. "The New Comedy of American Decline." *The Atlantic.* December 3, 2020. www.theatlantic.com/culture/archive/2020/12/ted-lasso-emily-paris-unquiet-americans/617275/.

Hawthorne, Nathaniel. "Endicott and the Red Cross." *Twice-Told Tales.* 1837. Modern Library, 2001, pp. 339–45.

Howells, William Dean. *The Rise of Silas Lapham.* Penguin Classics, 1983.

Hunt, Brendan, Joe Kelly, and Bill Lawrence, creators. *Ted Lasso*, Season 1. Apple TV+, 2020–21.

James, Henry. *Daisy Miller and Other Tales.* Edited and with an introduction by Stephen Fender. Oxford UP, 2017.

Lemay, Leo. "The American Origins of 'Yankee Doodle.'" *The William and Mary Quarterly*, vol. 33, no. 3 (1976), pp. 435–64.

Levin, David. *History as Romantic Art.* Stanford UP, 1959.

McWilliams, John. *Hawthorne, Melville, and the American Character: A Looking-Glass Business.* Cambridge UP, 1984.

Melville, Herman. *Israel Potter: His Fifty Years of Exile.* 1855. Penguin, 1982.

Miller, Perry. *The New England Mind.* Harvard UP, 1982.

NBC Sports Premier League Film featuring Jason Sudeikis. NBC, August 3, 2013.

Obama, Michelle. "Remarks by the First Lady at the Democratic National Convention." Democratic National Convention, July 25, 2016, Wells Fargo

Center, Philadelphia, PA, https://obamawhitehouse.archives.gov/the-press-office/2016/07/25/remarks-first-lady-democratic-national-convention (last accessed November 13, 2024).

O'Brien, Jean M. *Firsting and Lasting: Writing Indians out of Existence in New England*. U of Minnesota P, 2010.

Potter, Israel R. *The Life and Remarkable Adventures of Israel R. Potter*. Project Gutenberg, 2021, https://www.gutenberg.org/files/66684/66684-h/66684-h.htm. htm (last accessed November 13, 2024).

Roth-Reinhardt, Anne. *Frayed Homespun: Colonial Clothing and Literary Revision in Melville, Sedgwick, and Hawthorne*. 2012. University of Minnesota, PhD dissertation, https://conservancy.umn.edu/server/api/core/bitstreams/10db66d4-30b9-4dfa-acf9-645ac5610a6b/content (last accessed November 13, 2024).

Rowlandson, Mary. *Narrative of the Captivity and Restoration of Mrs. Mary Rowlandson*. 1682. E-book, Project Gutenberg, 2009, https://www.gutenberg.org/files/851/851-h/851-h.htm (last accessed November 13, 2024).

Sheridan, Richard Brinsley. *The School for Scandal and Other Plays*. Edited and with an introduction by Eric S. Rump. Penguin Classics, 1989.

Smith, Henry Nash. *Virgin Land: The American West as Symbol and Myth*. Harvard UP, 2009.

Tilton, Robert. *Pocahontas: The Evolution of an American Narrative*. Cambridge UP, 1994.

Turner, Frederick Jackson. "The Significance of the Frontier in American History." 1893. E-book, Project Gutenberg, 2007, https://www.gutenberg.org/files/22994/22994-h/22994-h.htm (last accessed November 13, 2024).

Twain, Mark. *A Connecticut Yankee in King Arthur's Court*. Edited by Allison R. Ensor. Norton Critical Edition. W.W. Norton, 2018.

Tyler, Royall. *The Contrast*. 1787. E-book, Project Gutenberg, 2009, www.gutenberg.org/files/29228/29228-h/29228-h.htm (last accessed November 13, 2024).

Ulrich, Laurel Thatcher. *The Age of Homespun: Objects and Stories in the Creation of an American Myth*. Alfred A. Knopf, 2001.

Whitman, Walt. "Preface to *Leaves of Grass*." 1855. *Famous Prefaces: The Harvard Classics* (1909–14). E-book, Bartleby.com, https://www.bartleby.com/39/45.html (last accessed November 13, 2024).

———. "Song of Myself." *Leaves of Grass*. 1891–2. *The Walt Whitman Archive*. Edited by Matt Cohen, Ed Folsom, and Kenneth M. Price. University of Nebraska, Lincoln, Whitmanarchive.org/published/LG/1891/poems/27.

Winthrop, John. "A Model of Christian Charity." 1630. E-book, Hanover Historical Texts Collection, 1996. https://history.hanover.edu/texts/winthmod.html.

PART IV
GRAMMARS OF COLONIAL VIOLENCE

Section Overview

The final and, in many respects, most expansive section of the collection, "Grammars of Colonial Violence," connects memory and history via a layered look at historical "girl bosses," American slavery in African film, and race and the epistolary tradition. **Kirsten Iden's "'The Truth is Much Different': Eliza Lucas Pinckney's Literary Lives and the (Re)Production of Colonial Violence"** begins this work in Chapter 10 in her investigation of the literary life of Eliza Lucas Pinckney, the eighteenth-century South Carolina planter who allegedly introduced indigo to the colony. In a challenge to "static notions of early Southern womanhood," recent and current biographers, Iden notes, have "elevated [Pinckney] to the status of an early American 'Girl Boss' who defies the odds and the patriarchy ... all while retaining her (white) femininity." These recovery efforts, she claims, consistently deploy contemporary gender politics to insulate the figure of Eliza from the realities of colonial slave society from which she profited. By seizing upon Eliza's negotiation of gender expectations as the central conflict, Iden's chapter tracks how these biographies valorize Eliza's accomplishments as a female, while ignoring the ways in which she weaponized white womanhood to achieve autonomy at the expense of enslaved people. "[M]odern authors," she states, have thus "attempted to walk a precarious historical tightrope by presenting Eliza Lucas Pinckney as both a victor and victim of circumstance, failing (or perhaps refusing) to critically interrogate the intersectionality of her race, gender, and class identities." Though "it is tempting to dismiss these fictional accounts of Eliza's life as outmoded relics or overblown romances," Iden contends that scholars must "engage with these misleading narratives," given their popularity, and recognize their role in shaping the public imaginary of early American history in ways that perpetuate "a dangerous sentimentalization of the past." Iden's piece thus forges a much-needed model for critically reappraising present-day recovery projects to help mitigate the perpetuation of colonial violence of the past in the present.

Steven W. Thomas moves the collection outside of America in Chapter 11 in order to squarely examine American history and its cultural representation from broader geopolitical perspectives. **"African Cinema on American Slavery"** brings to the fore an archive of African films historically marginalized in scholarly conversations about slavery: *Ceddo* (1977), *Black Goddess* (1978), *West Indies: The Fugitive Slaves of Liberty* (1979), and *Sankofa* (1993). Thomas's analysis of these texts situates them in their political and cultural contexts—in particular the explicitly Pan-African vision and theory of "Third Cinema" so different from that of its Hollywood and European studio counterparts—and appraises their work with the colonial archive to excavate the experiences, cultures, and lives of enslaved Africans. He states that such work "challenge[s] the Eurocentric metanarrative of history, recuperate[s] an African public memory," and "affirm[s] a transnational Black political movement." Finally, he argues that "these films ... juxtapose multiple moments in time and multiple locations in geographic space ... to politically provoke audiences to question where they came from and where they are going." As these films question frameworks of the European-American nation state and Western narratives of progress, they contribute much-needed critical threads to current U.S.-American conversations about the representation of slavery on screen.

In the last essay of the collection, **"Epistolary Writing and the Afterlife of Letters from a Woman of Color,"** Lisa Vandenbossche looks at the American actress turned British royal Meghan Markle and the widely publicized controversy over her 2019 letter to her father, Thomas Markle, as a window into reseeing the anonymously published 1808 novel *The Woman of Colour: A Tale*. Vandenbossche, thus, explores "transhistorical connections in language, publication, and reception that draw these disparate examples into a single, epistolary tradition." Like Markle, Vandenbossche argues, the novel's central character, Olivia Fairchild, uses the epistolary genre as a powerful tool to express her own vocality and reframe her narrative; yet, she transforms into the public spectacle of the tragic mulatta when her private correspondence crosses into the public space making her an object for the readers' voyeuristic gaze. "Linking the Markle court case with the anonymous 1808 novel *The Woman of Colour*," Vandenbossche contends, "calls attention to the ways in which these seemingly disparate geographic and temporal examples echo earlier questions of privacy, control, and even racialized difference that is inherent in the epistolary form."

Ultimately, Vandenbossche's analysis makes visible the stunning ways in which contemporary discourse around celebrity, authorship, and privacy overlap with issues of race and gender rooted in eighteenth- and early nineteenth-century transatlantic epistolarity and publication networks. "In exploring the ways in which these texts and their reception move from domestic to public space—at times against the wishes of those who author them," Vandenbossche shows "the often unseen and uncompensated labor that Olivia Fairchild, Meghan Markle, and countless women of color have been asked to do throughout time and continue to be asked to do to this day."

10

"The Truth is Much Different": Eliza Lucas Pinckney's Literary Lives and the (Re)Production of Colonial Violence

Kirsten Iden

In the opening lines of the children's picture book *Eliza Pinckney* (1977), author Susan Lee addresses the specter of the stereotypical "Southern Belle": "The southern lady is a well-known type. You may have read about her in storybooks. In these stories she was pictured as shy, sweet, and unselfish. Dressed in fine clothes, she sat on her front porch sipping lemonade all day. She was much too helpless for hard work. When there was trouble, she fainted" (3). "The truth," she tells us, "is much different" (3). From Harriott Horry Ravenel's *Eliza Pinckney* (1896) to Natasha Boyd's historical romance *The Indigo Girl* (2017), efforts to convey the "truth" of Eliza Lucas Pinckney's story have produced a popular, but ultimately misleading, body of work on this historical figure.[1] In an effort to challenge static notions of early southern womanhood, Eliza Lucas Pinckney has been elevated to the status of an early American "Girl Boss" who defies the odds and the patriarchy by bringing indigo to South Carolina, all while retaining her (white) femininity. What many of these recovery projects fail to acknowledge, however, is that Eliza Lucas Pinckney's success and status were (and are) a product of violent colonialism, not an exception to it.

Eliza Lucas Pinckney's own letters help drive this narrative. Much of what we know about the historical Eliza Lucas Pinckney comes from her surviving letterbook, which is housed at the South Carolina Historical

---

[1] For reasons of clarity, I will use the full name "Eliza Lucas Pinckney" when discussing her as a historical figure, and the name "Eliza" when I discuss her as a literary character. This essay covers Eliza Lucas Pinckney's life both before her 1745 marriage (when she was "Eliza Lucas") and after; however, to keep the naming conventions consistent, I will use "Eliza Lucas Pinckney" regardless of the time period.

Society. The letters within the book span approximately thirty-five years, from 1739 to 1762, and collectively they form one of the largest archives of pre-Revolutionary women's writing known to exist. Eliza was sixteen years old when she copied her first letter in the letterbook and had just moved with her family from the island of Antigua to South Carolina. Eliza Lucas Pinckney's father was unexpectedly called back to Antigua for military duty, and with her brothers at school in England, Col. Lucas had little choice but to entrust his oldest daughter with the day-to-day duties of managing the family's three plantations. During this time, she experimented with the cultivation and manufacture of indigo into saleable dye. Eventually, indigo became Carolina's second largest export prior to the Revolutionary War, further enriching Lowcountry planters and entrenching their reliance on enslaved people's knowledge and labor. In 1744, she married a prominent Carolina attorney and planter, and her two sons (Charles Cotesworth Pinckney and Thomas Pinckney) were prominent early national figures.[2] Eliza Lucas Pinckney, then, became the woman behind history's "Great Men."

Eliza Lucas Pinckney never published during her lifetime, and her presence in traditional print archives is relegated to a few brief mentions in legal documents. The preservation of Eliza Lucas Pinckney's letters and story is directly attributable to her female descendants, who have collected, protected, and disseminated her work for the past 250 years.[3] For much of this time, knowledge of Eliza Lucas Pinckney was contained within South Carolina folklore. This began to change following the 1997 publication of

---

[2] Thomas Pinckney was a major in the Continental Army and a major general in the United States Army, serving during the Revolutionary War and War of 1812. He was also the Governor of South Carolina (1787–89), Minister to Great Britain (1792–96), Federalist candidate for Vice President in 1796, and member of the United States House of Representatives from 1797 to 1801. Charles Cotesworth Pinckney is considered a lesser known "Founding Father." He served in the Continental Army, achieving the rank of colonel and a general in the United States Army. He was a delegate representing South Carolina at the Constitutional Convention and one of the signers of the Constitution. In 1796 he was named Minister to France and played a key role in the XYZ Affair. He was the Federalist nominee for President of the United States in 1804 and 1808. Antebellum author William Gilmore Simms published an elegy titled "Monody, on the Death of Gen. Charles Cotesworth" in 1825.

[3] Eliza Lucas Pinckney's letterbook was first passed down to her daughter, Harriott Pinckney Horry. In her essay "Eliza Lucas Pinckney: Evolution of an Icon," historian Barbara Bellows laudably pieces together the letterbook's intergenerational journey throughout the nineteenth century (148–9) and discusses how "every generation [of Eliza's descendants] has felt free to shape her image to reflect itself" (147).

The Letterbook of Eliza Lucas Pinckney (edited by Elise Pinckney) and the definitive *The Papers of Eliza Lucas Pinckney and Harriott Pinckney Horry Digital Edition* in 2012.[4] With this increased access to her work, writers, literary scholars, and historians have utilized the archive as an opportunity to highlight the significant, yet often obscured, contributions women—in particular southern women—made to colonial American society. In this sense, there is a kind of poetic justice to the recovery of Eliza Lucas Pinckney as a historical figure, a woman whose name recognition now certainly eclipses that of her male relatives. Yet this recovery has also forced scholars to acknowledge the sources of her power and the ways in which she weaponized white womanhood to achieve autonomy at the expense of enslaved people.[5]

Popular writers have seized upon Eliza Lucas Pinckney's negotiation of gender expectations as a young woman and proxy planter within the original letterbook as the central conflict for their biographies and stories. Making this conflict the center of the narrative allows authors and readers to valorize Eliza Lucas Pinckney's accomplishments as a female planter while conveniently subjugating or repackaging the issue of slavery.[6] Both Eliza Lucas Pinckney the historical figure and Eliza the fictional character serve as compelling foils to the endlessly problematic Southern Belle, exemplified by the impetuous and indulgent protagonist of Margaret Mitchell's *Gone With the Wind*, Scarlett O'Hara. Scarlett is a master of artifice, an embodiment

---

[4] All references to Eliza Lucas Pinckney's letters are taken from *The Papers of Eliza Lucas Pinckney and Harriott Pinckney Horry Digital Edition*, hereby abbreviated as *Digital Edition*. Each letter is identified in the database by Eliza Lucas Pinckney's initials followed by a four-digit number (for example, ELP0888). The *Digital Edition* contains all known writings attributed to Eliza Lucas Pinckney, including her letterbook, recipe book, recipients' copies of Pinckney's letters, and letters written post-1762. The *Digital Edition* also includes documents related to Pinckney, but not written by her, such as the wills of George Lucas, Ann Mildrum Lucas, and Charles Pinckney, marriage settlements, loan/mortgage agreements, and letters between other members of her immediate family. Documents in *Digital Edition* are formatted as close to the original manuscript source as possible. I have preserved that formatting here.

[5] Lorri Glover's 2020 biography *Eliza Lucas Pinckney: An Independent Woman in the Age of Revolution* offers a sustained discussion of Eliza Lucas Pinckney as a "planter-patriarch," highlighting her role "atop a hierarchy replicated on plantations throughout the colonial Southeast and Caribbean" (44).

[6] In Cokie Roberts's *Founding Mothers: The Women Who Raised Our Nation*, she opens the book by surmising that if Eliza Lucas Pinckney were alive today, she would be "the subject of talk-show gabfests and made-for-tv movies, a child prodigy turned into a celebrity" (1).

of neo-Confederate fantasies of white power.[7] Eliza Lucas Pinckney's story, in contrast, serves an alternative, "real life" vision of southern womanhood that is predicated on values often defined as quintessentially American—hard work, ingenuity, and progress. Eliza as character, though, cannot be the heroine of the story if her successes are a product of the coercion, exploitation, and abuse of others. Within fictional accounts, these less-than-savory realities of enslavement are instead often displaced onto already disagreeable male characters. The focus of these retellings thus becomes Eliza's ability to overcome the misogynistic views of men, as opposed to an enslaver's ability to appropriate Black knowledge and labor.

This essay examines three popular retellings, from 1896 to 2017, of Eliza Lucas Pinckney's life to demonstrate the power and longevity mythologized historical narratives have for contemporary audiences. Though the motivations of these writers are unique, the stories are remarkably similar in how they deploy gender politics to insulate the figure of Eliza from the realities of an eighteenth-century slave society. Enamored with the task of bringing this woman back into the historical record (an admittedly laudable goal), popular writers have created and fostered a narrative for Eliza Lucas Pinckney that is not only inaccurate but that replicates white supremacist fantasies of racial difference. The earliest accounts of Eliza highlight her maternalistic nature, portraying her as the mother of great men, a paragon of virtue, and a teacher to "a race of savages" (Ravenel 323). Twentieth- and twenty-first-century imaginings of Eliza have thankfully moved beyond the overt racism of Ravenel's text. The depictions of plantation life are more nuanced, and Eliza herself has transitioned from a behind-the-scenes character (maker of great men) to a player in her own right. In order for readers to laud Eliza Lucas Pinckney as a smart, capable, and powerful woman, however, we must grapple with the source of that power. We must admit that she was, as Stephanie Jones-Rogers terms them, a "Mistress of the Market": white women who "created freedom for themselves by actively engaging and investing in the economy of slavery and keeping African Americans in captivity" (xvii).[8] Instead, modern authors

---

[7] The literary construction of the "South" as a mythical space is a common lens for modern Southern Studies. For more on the role of Margaret Mitchell's *Gone with the Wind* and the creation of white cultural fantasy, see chapter 1 of Scott Romine, *The Real South: Southern Narrative in the Age of Cultural Reproduction* (27–59).

[8] While Jones-Rogers's book focuses on nineteenth-century, non-elite white women, her thesis regarding white women's participation in the slave economy—and historians' reluctance to acknowledge that—is broadly applicable here.

have attempted to walk a precarious historical tightrope by presenting Eliza Lucas Pinckney as both a victor and victim of circumstance, failing (or perhaps refusing) to critically interrogate the intersectionality of her race, gender, and class identities.

It is tempting to dismiss these fictional accounts of Eliza Lucas Pinckney's life as outmoded relics or overblown romances. The fact of the matter is, however, that they are engaging, accessible, and much more popular than the original texts they are based on. Scholars need to engage with these misleading narratives because popular novels shape early American literary and historical figures in the public imagination. Within these historical fictions the line between real and imaginary is often blurred beyond recognition, enabling a dangerous sentimentalization of the past. The purpose of this chapter is not to point out historical inaccuracies in works of fiction; identifying these "gotcha" moments, while cathartic for the scholar, does little to establish a broader understanding of myth making (both explicit and unintentional) in historical narratives. Instead, the focus of this chapter is to consider how authors have chosen to depict Eliza and for what ends. Examining Eliza Lucas Pinckney's literary lives reveals the residual impact uninterrogated recovery work has in perpetuating colonial violence.

Early Accounts of Eliza Lucas Pinckney

Harriott Horry Ravenel's 1896 book *Eliza Pinckney* is the most detailed account of Eliza Lucas Pinckney's life prior to Elise Pinckney's edited collection of letters in 1972. Ravenel's text recounts the story of Eliza Lucas Pinckney and her family, and it is punctuated with reprinted letters from Pinckney herself. Ravenel then uses the topics Pinckney addresses in her letters as jumping-off points for extended dialogue regarding life in colonial Carolina. Though Ravenel presents her work on Pinckney as non-fiction, it is clear she sees herself as both a recorder of the past and as the latest in a line of Pinckney-descended women designated to protect and disseminate the esteemed family's legacy. Historian Barbara Bellows describes the relationship between Eliza Lucas Pinckney and her female descendants in terms of genealogical co-dependence: "In their role as family archivists, the Pinckney women have not only been keepers of records but also the winnowers, interpreters, and subtle shapers of family history. Eliza Pinckney's influence, the belief in the persuasive power of the written word, burned brightly through her female descendants, and they, in turn, have kept her memory alive" (148). As Ravenel describes the various sources she consulted to produce her book, she situates herself within that tradition. Not only did she read the "Family Legend,"[9] she also listened to the accounts of Pinckney's grandchildren, in addition to consulting "our native historians, Ramsay, Moultrie, Drayton, etc." (vii).[10] The appearance of the word "legend" is notable here, as this narrative genre presents a story that exists somewhere between reality and myth. Ravenel's statement of research confirms the ease with which history, genealogy, and lore are intertwined.

In the introduction to *Eliza Pinckney*, Ravenel asserts that her text is a history of the title subject; yet Ravenel's designs are beyond a mere recreation of her life and times. Instead, Ravenel contends that Eliza Lucas Pinckney's life story might be read as a metonym for the rise of the nation:

> She might be presented as a typical southern matron, a representative of her class; but to the general reader her life is, perhaps, most interesting when viewed as an instance of that force of environment which did so much for the making of America. We hardly recognize now, how much the country moulded the people, and formed, not perhaps character ... but the feeling and opinion,—the opinion which makes action. (2)

Ravenel's characterization of Eliza as a multifaceted figure invites her late nineteenth-century readers to reconceive of women as historical actors.

---

[9] Ravenel explains that the "Family Legend" is an unpublished manuscript written by Maria Henrietta Pinckney, the daughter of Charles Cotesworth Pinckney and granddaughter of Eliza Lucas Pinckney. While the "Family Legend" was, according to Ravenel, "too diffuse and intimate for publication" (viii), Maria Henrietta Pinckney did publish a defense of nullification titled *The Quintessence of Long Speeches, Arranged as a Political Catechism* in Charleston in 1830.

[10] Much like the Pinckney, Horry, and Ravenel families, Harriott Horry Ravenel's list of historians are all members of a small circle of elite, white Carolinians who amassed power and fortune in the colonial and antebellum periods. David Ramsay was a physician, historian, member of the South Carolina legislature, and a delegate to the Continental Congress. His most well known work is the two-volume *The History of South Carolina: From Its First Settlement in 1670 to the Year 1808*. William Moultrie was a governor of South Carolina and general. He is best known for his defense of a small fort on Sullivan's Island, South Carolina, during the Revolutionary War, which was named Fort Moultrie in his honor. In 1802, Moultrie published *Memoirs of the American Revolution, so far as it Related to the States of North and South Carolina, and Georgia*. John Drayton II was a federal judge and governor of South Carolina. Drayton published several books, including a natural history of South Carolina, though it is likely that Ravenel is referring to his 1821 publication *Memoirs of the American Revolution, from Its Commencement to the Year 1776, Inclusive; As Relating to the State of South Carolina and Occasionally Referring to the States of North Carolina and Georgia*.

Eliza Pinckney challenges the idea of separate spheres by suggesting that Eliza's indigo work was a gift to the not-yet-formed United States, thereby casting her as an important actor of the early Republic in her own right. Interestingly, it is not an ideological connection that Eliza has to "the making of America," but the physical connection wrought from her relationship with the land. In the pages that follow, Ravenel's Eliza becomes a shining example of American possibility, a woman who embraces region and cultivates a life of significance. Ravenel's argument reflects Cathy Davidson's analysis of the early American novel as a genre that "extend[ed] the discussion of political and social problems to those who were not 'at the table' as laws and policies were being formalized ... Novels challenged the very distinction between 'private' and 'public' life" (35). Invoking the common American literary trope of an individual embodying the values of the nation, Ravenel likens Eliza to those illustrious Founding Fathers like Benjamin Franklin, but with one key difference: she was a Founding Mother.

Of course, Eliza could not make America by herself. Ravenel does not discuss what life was like on the Lucas Pinckney plantations for people other than Eliza and her immediate family, though this may stem from the fact that the real Eliza Lucas Pinckney seldom addressed enslaved men, women, and children in any detail.[11] Within the letters, enslaved people are ever present, yet ancillary figures, whose actions are mediated through the eye of the enslaver.[12] The void left by Eliza Lucas Pinckney in the historical archive presents an opportunity for Ravenel to fill in her own narrative.

---

[11] One notable exception within the letterbook is an enslaved man named "Quash," who was later baptized and went by the name John Williams. While Eliza Lucas Pinckney does not write about him in personal terms, he is named in multiple private and public documents between 1743 and 1763. Williams was a skilled carpenter whose knowledge and expertise were instrumental in building indigo vats on the Wappoo plantation in the early 1740s. He was included as part of Eliza Lucas Pinckney's "dowry" in her marriage settlement to Charles Pinckney. Charles Pinckney then used Williams to build Pinckney Mansion on Meeting Street in Charles Town. Shortly after its completion in 1750, Williams was manumitted and worked as a free person of color in Charles Town. For more on John Williams, see chapter 7 of Andrea Feeser, *Red, White & Black Make Blue: Indigo in the Fabric of South Carolina Life* (99–108), and Tiffany Momon, "John 'Quash' Williams, Charleston Builder."

[12] For example, a 1741 letter from Eliza Lucas Pinckney's future husband Charles Pinckney reveals how enslaved people were vital components of local communication systems: "The inclosed designd to go by Mary-Ann was by accident left behind by wch. you will perceive how much out of order I was when you expected me I might indeed have sent a verbal message afterwards had I imagind you would have given your self the trouble to go to Mr. Hunts [...] to meet me" (ELP0968).

At the end of *Eliza Pinckney*, however, a frustrated Ravenel laments the critiques some have leveled at Eliza's "bygone civilization" for being "indolent, ignorant, self-indulgent, cruel, overbearing" (322). These criticisms are unfair, she argues, because "those of the southern states had more to do":

> They had to train and teach a race of savages,—a race which had never known even the rudiments of decency, civilization, or religion; a race which, despite the labors of colonists and missionaries, remains in Africa today as it was a thousand years ago; but a race, which, influenced by these lives, taught by these southern people for six generations, proved in the day of trial the most faithful, the most devoted of servants, and was declared in 1863 by the northern people worthy to be its equal in civil and political rights. (323)

That Ravenel chose to end her book on Eliza Lucas Pinckney with this statement as opposed to a comment on her title subject confirms to readers that her agenda reached beyond mere documentation. In her revisionist history, slavery is a cooperative endeavor in which white intellectual labor is magnanimously bestowed upon lesser beings. Ravenel's painfully racist diatribe is representative of many nineteenth- and early twentieth-century texts that endeavored to rationalize the early American plantation as a benevolent space. Ravenel also follows in the tradition of what George Boulukos terms the "grateful slave trope." Emerging in eighteenth-century fictions, the grateful slave trope envisions a "sentimental planter or overseer" who attempts to reform the brutality of plantation slavery. This reformer is depicted as "actively earning the slaves' gratitude through benevolence, with an increasing tendency to present the debt of gratitude in pseudo-contractual terms, and a decreasing tendency to show him as intentionally imposing, or mystifying his authority" (Boulukos 21–2). One goal of this trope, Boulukos argues, is "using emotional response to oppression and torture as a way of distancing oneself from responsibility for such aspects of the colonial enterprise" (14). By ending her story of Eliza Lucas Pinckney with the grateful slave trope, Ravenel posits Eliza as a model, or legend, for those magnanimous planters who educated the enslaved in the generations that followed.

In many ways, Ravenel's text is a relic rightfully left in the past, a voice best forgotten. At the same time, Ravenel's work is relevant to modern scholars because it elucidates the enduring connection between the plantation myth and contemporary work on figures such as Eliza Lucas Pinckney. In the Ravenel passage, for example, she focuses on teaching as an ameliorative force in the lives of enslaved peoples. Though Ravenel's comments refer to the southern states broadly, at least two of Eliza Lucas Pinckney's letters mention her intention to teach enslaved children how to read.[13] This fact is reiterated by both popular writers and scholars as evidence of Eliza Lucas Pinckney's exceptional behavior as an enslaver and implicitly a kinder and gentler "master."[14] Read within the context of Boulukos, however, we see the inherent danger of engaging in this line of thinking. Perhaps even more so than her male counterparts, Eliza Lucas Pinckney and her literary iterations easily assume the role of sentimental reformer, which in turn insulates them from critique. While it is easy to identify these issues within Ravenel's *Eliza Pinckney*, more contemporary accounts of Eliza Lucas Pinckney's story, those that are not invested in Lost Cause ideology, obscure the connections between Eliza as a powerful woman and as an enslaver.

The first fully fictionalized account of Eliza Lucas Pinckney's life is Frances Leigh Williams's *Plantation Patriot: A Biography of Eliza Lucas Pinckney*, published in 1967.[15] Williams's primary focus is the five-year period beginning in 1739, when the Lucases arrive in South Carolina, and it concludes with the 1744 marriage of Eliza to Charles Pinckney. Like Ravenel, Williams makes the "indigo affair" the centerpiece of her story by fashioning it as a micro-narrative of America's national story. In doing this, Emily Smith argues that "Williams alters Pinckney so that Pinckney adheres to

---

[13] In a 1741 letter to Charles Pinckney, Eliza Lucas Pinckney notes that she has "a Sister to instruct, and a parcel of little Negroes whom I have undertaken to teach to read" (ELP0747). By 1742, she expanded her plan to include what seems to be a sustainable educational design for the plantations' enslaved population. She explains to Miss Bartlett: "I devote the rest of the time till I dress for dinner to our little polly and two black girls who I teach to read, and if I have my papa's approbation (my Mamas I have got) I intend for school mistress's for the rest of the Negroe children another scheme you see" (ELP0115).

[14] This was not a radical move on Eliza Lucas Pinckney's part. While teaching enslaved peoples to write in South Carolina was prohibited in their 1740 Slave Codes, reading was not banned until the early nineteenth century. Unlike writing, which empowered its practitioners to explore the possibilities and limitations of identity, reading "was taught purely to inculcate Christianity [and] Christianity was believed to inculcate docility" (Monaghan 321).

[15] Unlike most Eliza Lucas Pinckney biographers, Frances Leigh Williams (1909–78) was not a direct descendant of her novel's subject. Williams was, however, deeply invested in southern literature and history. A cousin of novelist Ellen Glasgow, Williams wrote several books on Confederate naval commander and pioneering oceanographer Matthew Fontaine Maury, as well as *A Founding Family: The Pinckneys of South Carolina*.

developing tropes of female and American identities; thus Pinckney becomes written with the bold strokes of cultural shorthand" (43). Whereas Ravenel's concern is rehabilitating the southern woman, Williams's iteration of Eliza emphasizes her quintessentially "American" character—hardworking, tenacious, optimistic, ambitious—while simultaneously highlighting the unique experiences of Eliza in Carolina.

Eliza's trials with indigo serve as the engine that drives Williams's story, but most of the conflict in *Plantation Patriot* arises when Eliza must negotiate the expectations of being both female and a planter. The demands of the plantation necessitated a quick transition of power from George Lucas to Eliza, and immediately following his departure for Antigua, Eliza is faced with her first major obstacle: rice planting. Throughout the early part of the novel, Williams establishes Eliza's credentials as a planter: her instinctive draw to the natural world, intellectual curiosity, self-discipline, and a desire for innovation. After "consult[ing] carefully with her neighbors to be sure that she was having it [rice planting] done just the way they did," Eliza is finally able to perform the role she seemed destined to play.

Despite her skills and knowledge, Eliza's authority is subverted by her physical appearance. To highlight this tension, Williams introduces a fictional enslaved man named Solomon into the narrative: "She promptly ran into a difficulty she had feared. Solomon, who had served as a foreman of the field hands under Mr. Millington and been continued in that capacity by Major Lucas, obviously found it hard to accept orders from a sixteen-year-old girl. The stalwart slave did not actually defy her, but he was extremely slow in carrying out her instructions" (71). Within Williams's narrative, Solomon's support is crucial to Eliza's success for several reasons. As the foreman, Solomon occupies a position of authority over other enslaved people. If Solomon is reluctant to work for Eliza, it seems unlikely that he would force the other field hands to follow Eliza's timeline. Without their labor, the rice would not be planted (or planted incorrectly), and without a successful crop, the Lucas plantations would fall further into debt. Troubled, yet resolute, Eliza's recourse is to double down on her planter persona with the hope that the situation "would eventually change if she proved able in her management" (71). By positioning Solomon as an impediment to Eliza's self-actualization, Williams attempts to neutralize the uncomfortable reality of Eliza's position as an enslaver. Citing her gender and age, Williams suggests that Solomon's contempt for Eliza is not based on what she does, but rather who she is. As readers, our sympathies are directed entirely toward Eliza despite the fact that her primary concern is "maximum production from the Wappoo acres" (71). The focus of the scene thus becomes Eliza's ability to overcome the misogynistic views of men, as opposed to an enslaver's ability to suppress the resistance of a slave.

Williams does not offer any alternative explanation as to why Solomon is unwilling or unable to work at the pace Eliza demands, though similar acts of resistance are documented throughout the archives and secondary historical sources. As a skilled slave with experience of working for several masters, Solomon could have been attempting to take advantage of Eliza's naivety, or perhaps his "slowness" was a function of her unrealistic expectations for rice planting. Within the narrative Williams has created, however, Solomon's thoughts and motivations do not matter. His character is a hollow vessel whose body is only animated through Eliza's narrative rendering. Regardless of the origin of Solomon's slowness, it is evident that Eliza believes she has the right, and the ability, to read his body's movements as duplicitous. This detail implicitly acknowledges the systematic violence that undergirded the plantation structure, a violence that is otherwise silenced in *Plantation Patriot*. Williams contains the conflict between Eliza and Solomon by noting that his behavior was not outright insubordination, but a test of boundaries. Had Solomon committed an act of open resistance, Eliza would have had to use physical violence as well, whether directly (or more likely) through the use of a male overseer. Luckily, the conflict never accelerates to that point because Eliza quickly earns the respect of the enslaved laborers through her own display of labor.

Williams cites Eliza's extraordinary work ethic as a point of mutual respect between enslaver and enslaved, though the work that she performs is quite different from that of the slaves. Seeking to put the conflict with Solomon behind her, Eliza approaches plantation management with a hands-on approach that surprises even the hardiest laborers: "Perhaps the most astonished of her field hands were the men assigned to 'slash and box' the pine trees to catch the turpentine that dropped from the cut. The men had little thought that Eliza would show up in the pine woods to watch their work, but she did" (72). Eliza's presence in the pine woods was unusual considering it was undoubtedly located a significant distance away from the main dwelling house and traversing the woods in her dress would have made the trek all the more arduous. Williams's decision to locate Eliza in the pine woods signals to readers that she is willing and able to immerse herself in all aspects of plantation management.

The "slash and box" technique that Williams mentions was used for the production of turpentine, which was a particularly labor-intensive task. Performing such physically demanding work required both strength and stamina, and it seems as though Williams chose this space for Eliza to visit because it reflects the qualities Eliza tries to display as a new master. As with Solomon, the enslaved laborers in the pine woods are not given a voice to express their thoughts on Eliza's presence, though Williams's description of their astonishment implies that they are impressed by her initiative. The irony of Williams's scene is that what Eliza's "labor" ultimately amounts to is the surveillance of others' labor. In all likelihood, those laboring in the pine woods dreaded Eliza's presence because it restricted their actions to those prescribed by their labor. It is in this moment of suggested commonality that the relief between master and slave is most stark.

With the respect of her slaves obtained, an increasingly confident and ambitious Eliza meets the villain of the story: indigo-maker Nicholas Cromwell. Williams's Cromwell is based on the historical figure of the same name who was sent to Carolina by George Lucas to help his daughter produce saleable indigo.[16] With Cromwell's arrival, it seems as though Eliza must prove herself to be an able planter all over again. The task is far more difficult with Cromwell because, as a white man, his very presence on the plantation carries a certain amount of authority, despite the fact that he is technically an employee of Eliza. The inherent violence of the plantation system tacitly supported Eliza when she dealt with slave resistance; with Cromwell, however, no such safety net exists. Cromwell's knowledge of the indigo-making process further compromises Eliza's position because it creates a relationship of dependency—one that she worries may undermine the master–slave power dynamic that she recently cultivated (122).

On the surface, Cromwell seems to possess the necessary credentials to be a planter, especially when compared with young Eliza. Williams demonstrates the superficiality of these qualifications, however, by depicting him as an abuser of male power. As she observes Cromwell's work, Eliza is struck by the "harsh rudeness" he visits on the Lucas slaves. Eliza excuses the behavior until Cromwell kicks one of the slaves for misunderstanding an order. It is this inappropriate outburst of anger that finally compels Eliza to admonish Cromwell for his behavior. Cromwell's impassioned response signals to readers that he cannot be an effective planter: "'I gotta drive them,' he declared belligerently, [']to get a lick o'work out of them. They are lazy savages from the jungles of Africa and won't work'" (117). Cromwell's speech and actions are characterized by excess and impulsivity.

---

[16] In a 1785 letter written to one of her children, Eliza Lucas Pinckney accuses Cromwell of sabotaging the Lucas dye by adding too much lime to it (ELP0671). Cromwell's alleged motivation was to protect the indigo industry in his native Montserrat, but the notoriously finicky nature of the dye-making process could be the real reason.

His reliance on the overt exercise of violence stands in contrast to Eliza, who despite feeling "a cold fury seize her" at Cromwell's abuse, provides a measured response: "'They have worked extremely well for us,' she said with as much control as she could muster. 'I shall tolerate no abusive treatment of them'" (117). Cromwell is visibly angered by the response, but ultimately acquiesces to Eliza for the time being. Williams amplifies the contrast between Eliza and Cromwell to demonstrate that not only is Eliza a more moral person, but she is also a better master. Eliza's skillful reading of both the slaves' bodies and her own body allows her to situate herself (quite literally) in an authoritative position. In contrast, Cromwell's inability to read these bodies produces an inappropriate response of physical force.[17]

Eliza's successful cultivation of indigo fulfills the promise she made to her father and earns her the respect of nearly everyone she encounters (Cromwell excepted). Yet *Plantation Patriot* does not end on this triumphant moment. Instead, a new conflict arises as the Lucas family prepares to reunite in Antigua: Eliza's affinity for her adopted home. By likening her to the indigo plant, Williams manufactures a connection between Eliza and Carolina: "[S]he had quite lost her heart to this new country. She felt that, like her indigo plants, she too, had become accustomed to the soil of Carolina" (143).[18] Williams's emphasis on Eliza as a South Carolinian is pivotal to her iteration of the Eliza Lucas Pinckney legacy because it reimagines the plantation as a source of patriotic production. Having only produced a few small cubes of dye, Eliza's initial success is not so much about impacting colonial trade as it is about proving her efficacy as a planter, a daughter, and as a woman. Eliza's physical reaction to holding the dye demonstrates how personal the process was. Andrew Deveaux, Eliza's elderly neighbor who aided her in the cultivation process, describes Eliza's face as "a mixture of rapture and amazed humility," while Eliza herself "felt as if she could hardly breathe" (124).[19] Her reaction is contrasted with

---

[17] For more on the interactions between overseers and enslavers, see Tristan Stubbs, *Masters of Violence: The Plantation Overseers of Eighteenth-Century Virginia, South Carolina and Georgia* (77–102).

[18] The historical Eliza Lucas Pinckney did not share this romantic attachment to Carolina. In several letters, she makes clear her preference for the refined culture of London, which she contrasted with her "remote corner of the globe" (ELP 0761 and ELP0888).

[19] The historical Andrew Deveaux was a French Huguenot with indigo cultivation expertise. He settled in South Carolina prior to 1714 and was a neighbor of the Lucases and Pinckneys. Eliza Lucas Pinckney mentions Deveaux in several letters, noting that he was "very kind in Instructing me in planting affairs" (ELP0739).

that of the unscrupulous Cromwell, whose first and only comment about the dye is that it is "An inferior grade. On Montserrat, I'd be ashamed of such dye" (125). Of course, this is exactly the point: South Carolina is not Montserrat, just as Eliza is not like Cromwell. Lacking the ruthless drive of the typical slave owner, Eliza, and by extension the plantation she runs, reflects the ideals of the emerging republic.

The novel ends with Eliza, now nearly seventy years old, receiving the designation of "plantation patriot" from none other than President George Washington himself.[20] Eliza and her daughter Harriott meet Washington at Hampton Plantation during his tour of the southern states in 1791. It is here that Washington gives the following speech:

> Madam, this is a meeting to which I have long looked forward. As a planter, I pay my respects to you for your early work with indigo and later with silk culture. You are both a planter and a patriot. Your sons truly reflect your love of principle and their country will soon call them to even greater service. Mothers like you light fires that are never extinguished. As long as that happens, we have nothing to fear for our Republic. (169)

Crowned by Washington as a model republican mother, Williams's Eliza reaps the rewards of a life well cultivated: two sons who faithfully serve their country. This compliment from Washington seems to be of secondary importance, however. His primary connection to Eliza is through their shared identity as planters. Unlike the traditional Republican Mother, whose identity as a political being is dependent on her ability to care for others, Eliza is recognized as an actor in her own right.[21] Washington's approbation of *all* Eliza's roles—planter, patriot, and mother—likely resonated with

---

[20] President George Washington did visit Hampton Plantation, the home of Eliza Lucas Pinckney and her daughter Harriott Pinckney Horry, in 1791. When she died in 1793, Washington served as a pallbearer at her funeral, likely due to his relationship with her son, Charles Cotesworth Pinckney. This connection between Eliza Lucas Pinckney and Washington is often highlighted in biographical sketches to emphasize her historical importance. There is no historical evidence that Washington made such a speech to Eliza Lucas Pinckney.

[21] Linda Kerber's 1976 article "The Republican Mother: Women and the Enlightenment—An American Perspective" defines women's political position in the early Republic through the ideology of "republican motherhood." A Republican Mother was one whose "life was dedicated to the service of civic virtue; she educated her sons for it; she condemned and corrected her husband's lapses from it" (202).

Williams's contemporary audience in the late 1960s as they dealt with issues of women's equality. At the same time, Williams is deafeningly silent when it comes to addressing the ways in which Eliza's Founding Mother narrative depends on the erasure of Black voices.

Discovering *The Indigo Girl*

Natasha Boyd's 2017 novel *The Indigo Girl* covers the most researched period of Eliza Lucas Pinckney's life, from 1739—when her father left her in charge of the family's three Carolina plantations—to her 1744 marriage to Charles Pinckney. This was Eliza Lucas Pinckney's most active writing period and the time during which she participated in bringing the indigo crop to fruition. While the average reader is often shocked to learn that a 16-year-old girl was given such a heavy responsibility, historians have noted that, because of high mortality rates in Carolina and unstable sociopolitical structures both locally and abroad, such arrangements, though not the norm, were common enough.

Some of Eliza Lucas Pinckney's letters suggest that her activities were viewed with a degree of skepticism by those around her, though it does not seem that such critiques were taken seriously. In a letter to her friend Mary Bartlett, she notes that "[a]n old lady in our Neighbourhood is often querrelous with me for riseing so early as 5 o'Clock in the morning, and is in great pain for me least it should spoil my marriage, for she says it will make me look old long before I am so." Eliza Lucas Pinckney is largely unbothered by this meddlesome neighbor, noting that,

> I believe she is mistaking for what ever contributes to health and pleasure of mind must also contribute to good looks but admiting what she says I reason with her thus, If I should, look older by this practise I really am so; for the longer time we are awake the longer we live ... thus then I have the advantage of the sleepers in point of long life so I beg you will not be frighted by such of apprehensions as those suggested above and for fear of yr. pretty face give up yr. late pious resolution of early rising. (ELP0126)

The tone of this letter suggests that Eliza Lucas Pinckney was not seriously concerned about her neighbor's criticism. If Eliza Lucas Pinckney were acting in a way outside the bounds of propriety, it is unlikely that she would engage this woman with such an irreverent reply. It is even more unlikely that she would reproduce the encounter in a letter and then subsequently record that letter in her letterbook for posterity. Rather, the letter reads as a teaching moment, in which the slightly older Eliza is attempting to advise her friend in the ways of self-improvement.

Fictional accounts like *The Indigo Girl* tend to amplify this tension between Eliza's values and eighteenth-century gender mores as a means to set her apart both from other women and from the social expectations of the day. Early in *The Indigo Girl*, Eliza sees this moment as an opportunity to bring about a new world order. In this moment of possibility, Eliza imagines her "fantasy": "A wish to be someone of import. To not be owned as chattel by a father or one day by a husband. But this [Carolina] was not England. And something about this place where we'd made our home, where people around us were trying to create a new world from the ground up, made everything seem possible" (Boyd 10). What Boyd skillfully does in this moment is underscore the intersectionality of Eliza's identities; she wants to be someone of importance, but how that manifests is dependent on her age, her gender, her location, and her race. Whereas these identities exist as part of an ever-shifting and irrepressible undercurrent within the historical letters, Boyd's Eliza can name and thus control how she appears. Eliza's fantasy operates on these binaries: England represents stasis, Carolina represents possibility. Men are enslavers, and women are the enslaved. Her power does not come from breaking down these binaries, but from having the ability to choose how she participates within them.

Throughout *The Indigo Girl*, Eliza equates her position as a white woman to that of an enslaved person, even as her experiences highlight the distance between the two. In the above passage, Eliza refers to herself—and all women—as "chattel" who are owned by their husbands and fathers. This refrain is repeated throughout the novel, as Eliza faces significant pressure from her mother and a cadre of suitors to marry and thus relinquish control of plantation operations. The suitor subplot of *The Indigo Girl* has some precedent in one of Eliza Lucas Pinckney's real letters. In a 1739 letter to her father, Eliza Lucas Pinckney rebuffs two potential marriage candidates suggested by her father, noting that she does not know one of the men well enough, and as for the other, "the riches of Peru and Chili if he had them put together could not purchase a sufficient Esteem to make him my husband ... a single life is my only Choice and if it were not as am yet by Eighteen hope you will aside the thought of my marrying yet these 2 or 3 years at least" (ELP0736). Unlike *The Indigo Girl*, where marriage is a constant point of tension, this letter is the only explicit mention of potential suitors in the letterbook prior to her marriage to Charles Pinckney in

1744. While it is unclear exactly how much pressure Eliza Lucas Pinckney was under to marry, it seems that she had some amount of autonomy in choosing whom and when to wed.

In *The Indigo Girl*, Boyd's Eliza must continually fight off men who appear more eager to curtail her ambitions than anything else. When Henry and John Laurens come to court Eliza, she is obliged to take them on a tour of the Wappoo plantation, a task that she finds both exasperating and dehumanizing: "I felt like I'd spent a morning at the market, only this time the prime auction items were me and the land upon which I was paraded about" (154). It is easy to see why the average reader would feel sympathy for Eliza, who is forced to entertain the overtures of men she is not interested in romantically or otherwise. Nearly all the white men in *The Indigo Girl* form some kind of impediment in Eliza's journey to self-actualization and independence.

This passage is a frustrating example of whitewashed history. Eliza's dismay at feeling like an item at the market seems almost laughable given that she is actively participating in a system where human beings are literally bought and sold. Her credulity is all the more shocking when we consider Eliza's physical proximity to Charles Town, the largest hub for the transatlantic slave trade in North America. Situated within a society that actively endeavors to strip away personhood through the brutal commodification of Black bodies, Eliza's conception of "enslavement"—and Boyd's as well—is seemingly disconnected from reality. While Eliza may lack the independence to do as she pleases, her unpleasurable walk with the Laurenses is worlds away from the slave auctions occurring mere miles down the road. Eliza's (mis)use of enslavement as a metaphor in the novel brings to mind the famous letter from Phillis Wheatley Peters to Reverend Samson Occom, in which she notes the obvious dissonance in white slave-holding colonists decrying British tyranny: "How well the Cry for Liberty, and the reverse Disposition for the exercise of oppressive Power over others agree,—I humbly think it does not require the Penetration of a Philosopher to determine" (153).[22] Wheatley Peters's observation is a challenge both for the character of Eliza and perhaps Boyd herself. Either Eliza is not intelligent enough to comprehend the irony of her auction metaphor, which would stand in direct contrast to her character, or she is refusing to acknowledge the socioeconomic realities

---

[22] Carretta's *Complete Writings* uses the name "Phillis Wheatley." I have chosen to also include her married name "Peters," which aligns with recent scholarship by Zachary McLeod Hutchins and Honorée Fanonne Jeffers.

of her position as an elite white person, which would render her complicit in the slave-holding enterprise.

Boyd seems to anticipate this critique of Eliza and chooses to resolve it by doubling down on the gender argument. During a quaint domestic sewing scene, Eliza chats with her friend Mary Bartlett about the newly passed "Act for the better ordering and governing of Negroes and other Slaves in this Province" and expresses sympathy for those enslaved people who rebel.[23] Mary is aghast when Eliza posits that slavery is morally wrong, which prompts her to deliver an incisive observation to her friend, one that challenges the high ground that Eliza has claimed: "Mary sucked at the end of a red thread and held a needle up to see the eye. 'Yet, you own slaves and so do I'" (155). Just as it appears that Mary has destabilized Eliza's narrative, our protagonist responds by reaffirming traditional gender norms as a means to abdicate any responsibility. "'Actually, you don't and I don't. Our fathers do,' Eliza corrects; 'What I can do is be fair and just while they are in my care'" (155). It is fitting that this scene between Mary and Eliza takes place in a drawing room while both women busy themselves with sewing. Employing herself in woman's work (the only time she does so in the novel), Eliza posits herself as an innocent bystander in a man's world, a victim of their coercive power.

Boyd's mental gymnastics are not new in this sense. Writers as far back as the nineteenth century have operated using similar tropes. Wealthy and elite whites have long depicted the ills of slavery as a product of morally deficient white men, whose greed and appetites—monetary, social, and carnal—were the true reason for slavery's evils. More often than not, these men were not the plantation owners themselves, but poorer whites employed as overseers or traders, such as Simon Legree from Stowe's *Uncle Tom's Cabin*. By absolving elite white enslavers of explicit displays of violence, this logic created a rhetorical opening for those same people to put forth a paternalistic narrative of enslavement. Similar to Williams's *Plantation Patriot*, Boyd deploys this trope of the evil overseer via Starrat, one of the

---

[23] The Act for the better ordering and governing of Negroes and other Slaves in this Province (often abbreviated as the 1740 Slave Codes or Negro Act of 1740) was a series of fifty-eight statutes passed by the South Carolina General Assembly that constricted nearly every aspect of an enslaved person's life, from the buying and selling of commodities to traveling in groups larger than seven. The statutes also addressed citizens' behavior toward enslaved persons, with a particular emphasis on communal surveillance. The statutes were a direct response to the Stono Rebellion in 1739. These statutes served as a model for other southern colonies' slave laws.

overseers who worked on the Lucas's Waccamaw plantation in the 1740s.[24] When young Eliza visits the Waccamaw plantation, it is as though she has stepped into another world. The whipping post (which Eliza's father, Col. Lucas, instructed to be removed) stands as the most prominent feature of the space. And Starrat's body most notably carries all the hallmarks of the degenerate institution:

> Starrat was a portly sort with a brusque manner and the vague odor of something stronger than ale sweating from his pores. His face was a few days past a clean shave, which smacked of laziness rather than the cultivation of a beard. It was still too hot for beards late in summer. Frankly, there were a few too many small mulatto children running around the slave dwellings for my liking. (22)

Though Eliza will not say the quiet part out loud (another subtle nod to her genteel status), Boyd's readers immediately understand Eliza's observation of Starrat's excesses includes unchecked sexual predation. It comes as little surprise to the reader when, in chapter fifteen, we discover that Starrat has raped an enslaved woman named Sarah, prompting Eliza to come in and save the woman from his clutches by uprooting her and her children to the Wappoo plantation.

In chapter forty-three, Starrat receives the punishment readers have likely anticipated—he is killed on Waccamaw plantation—though the exact circumstance of his demise is somewhat shocking, as he is shot in the head while sleeping. Despite the violent end of her overseer, presumably at the hands of a man or woman her family enslaves, Eliza is unfazed. She does not make inquiries into who has fatally shot Starrat; she does not consider how this act might affect her family's holdings, nor is she worried about the potential for a larger uprising or rebellion. Instead, Eliza feels relief. Reasoning that "his sins must have finally caught up with him," Eliza insists that she will "breathe easier knowing that Starrat was no longer inflicting himself upon this earth" (307). With the demons of slavery exorcized from the text, the novel can move forward unencumbered with Eliza's story.

Similar to the scene in *Plantation Patriot* in which Eliza "earns" the respect of the enslaved by working alongside them, *The Indigo Girl*, in these moments of labor, manifests an imagined fellowship between Eliza and the

---

[24] Not much is known about Starrat, not even his first name. According to the *Digital Edition*, Starrat may have been one of three men living in the area at that time.

men and women she enslaves, though again, this fantasy is belied by her physical presence. Chapter thirty opens on the day the indigo plants are to be harvested. Eliza wakes to the "low rhythmic melodies of field songs," a signal that the labor of the harvest has already begun. Boyd's scene invokes an image of the plantation as a georgic fantasy space, in which enslaved laborers are invested in the cultivation of indigo for the same reasons that Eliza is. Once she arrives at the fields, Eliza notes that "All our workers, young and old, played a part. Hours passed. The atmosphere was one of camaraderie and excitement. *We* were united in a common cause" (217; emphasis added). Despite Boyd's attempt to rescript history through inclusive language, the romantic patina of the scene is easily worn away upon analysis. While Eliza is impressed by the bucolic singing of the field slaves that awakens her from slumber, this highlights the fact that they do not have the luxury of sleeping as she has. Likewise, the blatant euphemism of "workers" for enslaved people obscures the violence of forced labor and ignores the compulsory nature of this "camaraderie."

The Indigo Girl parallels earlier retellings of Eliza Lucas Pinckney's life in several substantive ways. Its most significant departure comes in the character of Benoit Fortune, a young man formerly enslaved by the Lucas family in Antigua, who appears again in Carolina alongside Nicholas Cromwell, the indigo specialist. Benoit, familiarly called "Ben" by Eliza, is not based on any historical figure, though the novel's characters have a storied past growing up together on the plantation. Eliza's reaction upon seeing Ben immediately signals to readers that he will be a pivotal part of the narrative, though it is unclear exactly what role he will play:

> I couldn't get Ben out of my head. He'd grown taller. Stronger. His head was shaved close. His fair skin was burnished and smooth, though I imagined he shaved whiskers upon his jaw now that he was a man and not a boy. Not that I'd ever touched his face. The thought of it now sent ribbons of curiosity looping through my insides. My fingers tingled as if I could feel the rough texture of skin. Sucking in a breath, I was shocked at myself. I was marveling, that was all. Marveling at the miracle of seeing a person I'd thought never to see again. (146–7)

Despite Eliza's insistence that her "marveling" is the result of her surprise, the charged language of this passage apprises readers to a sexual desire in Eliza that had heretofore been dormant. It seems clear that Boyd, who has previously written romance novels, intends for this moment to be an awakening for Eliza, an entrance into womanhood. As she goes to sleep that night, Eliza, fighting against her "racing heart," surmises that "My life felt on the very cusp of some great change. Some movement toward destiny" (147). But to view this as some kind of coming-of-age love story, readers must ignore the power dynamics of the eighteenth-century slave society in which these characters live. Boyd facilitates the reader's ignorance through the use of first-person perspective; time collapses as we view Ben through Eliza's eyes.

When the characters are firmly placed within that historical framework—Eliza the character is based on a real person, after all—this meeting becomes something far more sinister. Through the eyes of the white protagonist, Ben is reduced to corporeal components. Furthermore, Eliza's appraisal of Ben's Black body renders him open and accessible to her gaze. Willingly or not, he is the object of her desire, though he cannot reciprocate. In this way, the encounter between Eliza and Ben echoes the experience of early American slave markets where white (male) slave holders inspected and evaluated the bodies of enslaved men, women, and children for sale. As historian Walter Johnson argues, the process of purchasing chattel served an important symbolic function for enslavers: "As they narrated their upward progress through the slave market, slaveholders small and large were constructing themselves out of slaves. Whether slave buyers figured their independence as coming of age or coming into their own, as investment, necessity, or benevolence, it was embodied in slaves (88). To be clear, Eliza does not purchase Ben in the novel, nor does she visit any slave markets. That being said, Eliza's consumption of Ben's body becomes a catalyst for her self-actualization as a woman, and eventually, as a planter.

Eliza and Ben do not consummate any kind of relationship in the novel. The few physical interactions between the characters are fleeting, but impactful: Ben's arm wraps around her waist as Eliza steps off a ladder, and their fingers graze under the water of an indigo vat. The most intimate contact between the two occurs when they briefly hold hands one evening, which makes her palms burn with excitement (194). Despite this longing, Eliza realizes that she cannot enter into a romantic relationship with Ben because their attachment is inextricably bound by slavery. Instead, they are star-crossed (non) lovers, or as Eliza puts it, "Our friendship was the friendship of two connected souls who'd met in the shade of trees on a sugar plantation when our hearts were pure" (247). Here the purity of Eliza stands in marked contrast to the lascivious Starrat. White men may sexually abuse enslaved women, but the white female enslaver does not abuse her power in that way. Serving as an object of unrequited desire, Ben facilitates Eliza's sexual awakening, which is then fully realized at the end of the novel when she marries Charles Pinckney.[25]

Ben also plays an important role in the novel because he possesses knowledge that Eliza needs to be a successful planter. Though he is originally introduced as a kind of apprentice to Cromwell, Ben is the one who in fact has the requisite expertise in growing and processing indigo. For his part, Cromwell has little desire to see Carolina indigo succeed, as he believes it could lessen British reliance on the indigo produced in Montserrat where he is from. This conflict places Ben in a difficult situation. On the one hand, he feels loyalty to his friend, Eliza. On the other hand, he is owned by Cromwell, who has asked him to sabotage the Carolina indigo in exchange for his eventual freedom. Shortly following his arrival in Carolina, Eliza confronts Ben about his aloof behavior, hoping to bridge the distance between "slave" and "master" (178). Boyd does not give the reader insight into Ben's interior thoughts, but he counters by asking Eliza why she has not taught any of the enslaved people on the plantation how to read, as Eliza had taught him years earlier. Eliza recognizes Ben's negotiation tactic and agrees to teach the enslaved how to read in exchange for his cooperation: "'Someone else may control your future.' My hand squeezed his sinewy forearm. 'But you control *mine*. You just said you are here to help me. So help me. Please. I'll do what I can for Quash and the children here. But please'" (181). Ben seemingly agrees to this arrangement. On its surface, the scene appears to subvert the master–slave relationship with Eliza rhetorically positioning herself subordinate to Ben.

Within the logic of the novel, Eliza's form of enslavement is depicted as cooperative, opposed to coercive. As readers, we are supposed to believe that Eliza and Ben are working together because they share a mutual respect as well as a common enemy. The alliance should be viewed positively because it compels the protagonist closer to her goal while improving the lives of enslaved people living on the plantation. The fruits of this alliance between Eliza and Ben serve as further support that Eliza is, and will be, a "good" master. The good master narrative, in turn, is supported

---

[25] Saidiya Hartman's *Scenes of Subjection: Terror, Slavery, and Self-Making in Nineteenth-Century America* theorizes rhetoric of seduction between master and slave, noting that "The presumed mutuality of feelings enchanted the brutal and direct violence of master–slave relations . . . the term 'seduction' is employed here to designate this displacement and euphemization of violence, for seduction epitomizes the discursive alchemy that shrouds direct forms of violence under the 'veil of enchanted relations'—the reciprocal and mutual relations of master and slave" (88).

by key biographic details from the real-life Eliza Lucas Pinckney, such as how she taught enslaved children how to read.

At the climax of the novel, Eliza discovers that Ben has gone back on his word and tries to sabotage the dye by pouring lye in it. This betrayal threatens to undermine Eliza's fantasy of a new world in which a woman can be independent. As Eliza confronts Ben about his duplicity, the novel's convoluted racial and gender politics are thrown into relief: "'I *need* to be free,' he said. 'Me too,' I choked out and saw my anguish reflected back to me in his eyes. 'You were closer to freedom than I ever was. I want to be free too. And you . . .' My tears were hot knives against my icy wet cheeks. 'You, Benoit Fortune, just took *my* chance of freedom away from me'" (248–9). As with the scene where Eliza likens her courtship to a slave auction, Eliza's lamentation that Ben was "closer to freedom than I ever was" is willfully ignorant at best. Ben tries to elicit sympathy from his supposed best friend, but Eliza refuses to acknowledge his needs and desires; all she can see is her own anguish "reflected back" in his eyes. Once again, Ben's personhood is effectively rendered from his body through the white gaze. With Ben's commodified body thoroughly used up (Eliza has had her sexual awakening and learned how to be a "good" enslaver), his continued presence in the text creates a point of tension for both Eliza and the reader. The taboo attraction between Eliza and Ben is tolerated within the world of the novel because Ben has knowledge that Eliza needs to become a fully actualized character. With the indigo situation resolved, Eliza must reckon with Ben's purpose in her life. Readers must likewise consider the consequences of indulging in this interracial fantasy. In a world where people are chattel, how can there be any kind of consensual relationship between enslaved persons and free? How can Eliza hold the moral high ground over someone like Starrat? How can readers find pleasure in the historic brutality of slavery? To prevent the novel from collapsing under the weight of these questions, Boyd must reroute readers' attentions. The next day, Ben runs away and is never seen again.[26]

In "A Note from the Author," Boyd earnestly acknowledges that parts of her novel may not be entirely accurate, though her intentions are pure: "Forgive me, dear reader, for any anachronistic mistakes, either accidental of willful, or for any besmirching of the character of ancestors long dead. My intent was purely to revive the memory of a remarkable young girl, who perhaps due to her youth or her gender, or being eclipsed by the

---

[26] It is unclear whether Ben drowned in a nearby river or continued his escape.

accomplishments of her sons, was largely forgotten by history" (337). This *mea culpa* is part of the literary tradition for Pinckney writers, who valorize recovery and position their authorial interventions as the means to an (imperfect) historical end. Bringing the *character* of Eliza Lucas Pinckney to life serves as a strategy to revise what was (and sometimes still is) the notoriously white, male-dominated narrative of early American history. In this sense, there is a certain poetic justice to Pinckney's story and the long line of women who have ushered it forth.[27] Much like Pinckney herself found creative ways to produce and disseminate her knowledge in the eighteenth century, writers like Boyd have utilized fiction to render the obscure visible. "It may not have been 100 percent accurate," Boyd admits, "but she [Pinckney] was heard loud and clear. Almost three hundred years later, I guess that's all she can ask for" (388).

The problem with such approaches to early American figures is that our hearing is often selective, and while the work of recovery can be a radical, and even a transgressive act, the figures themselves may not be. This dissonance can be profoundly unsettling. Eliza Lucas Pinckney led a remarkable life that has historical significance. She was also an enslaver. Pinckney was an indefatigable entrepreneur who was also born into generational wealth reaped from Caribbean plantations.[28] Throughout her letters, she advocated for a wider understanding and recognition of women's abilities, yet she also saw education as a mechanism for control. If we credit Pinckney with possessing the skills and knowledge to develop indigo as a commodity crop in South Carolina, then we must necessarily concede that she knew about the grueling conditions that she subjected enslaved people to as they skillfully grew, harvested, and processed plants into dye. The survival of her story depended on the system of chattel slavery in America; it did not exist despite it.

Pinckney's story teaches us that recovery work is not a singular act but a recurring, and often messy, process of historical and cultural contextualization. Just as any historical figure is impacted by the time and place in

---

[27] Writing about Eliza Lucas Pinckney (both scholarly and popular) is dominated by women. One important exception is David Ramsay, *The History of South Carolina: From Its First Settlement in 1670 to the Year 1808*, which is a point of origin for some of the lore about Eliza Lucas Pinckney.

[28] For more information on Eliza Lucas Pinckney's family prior to the events of the letterbook, see Carol Walter Ramagosa, "Eliza Lucas Pinckney's Family in Antigua, 1668–1747," and Harriet Simons Williams, "Eliza Lucas and Her Family: Before the Letterbook."

which they lived, so too are those who read and analyze their work. Each time past and present converge, the narrative is altered again. This instability can be challenging, as it allows for the reproduction of incomplete, misleading, and at times dangerous, stories. Yet the process of recovery also creates space for challenging problematic narratives and producing more nuanced interpretations of the past.

Works Cited

Bellows, Barbara. "Eliza Lucas Pinckney: The Evolution of an Icon." *South Carolina Historical Magazine*, vol. 106, nos. 2 & 3 (April/July 2005), pp. 147–65.

Boulukos, George. *The Grateful Slave: The Emergence of Race in Eighteenth-Century British and American Culture*. Cambridge UP, 2012.

Boyd, Natasha. *The Indigo Girl*. Blackstone Publishing, 2017.

Davidson, Cathy. *Revolution and the Word: The Rise of the Novel in America*, 2nd ed. Oxford UP, 2004.

Feeser, Andrea. *Red, White & Black Make Blue: Indigo in the Fabric of Colonial South Carolina Life*. U of Georgia P, 2013.

Glover, Lorri. *Eliza Lucas Pinckney: An Independent Woman in the Age of Revolution*. Yale UP, 2020.

Hartman, Saidiya. *Scenes of Subjection: Terror, Slavery, and Self-Making in Nineteenth-Century America*. Oxford UP, 1997.

Hutchins, Zachary McLeod. "Provocation: 'Add New Glory to Her Name': Phillis Wheatley Peters." *Early American Literature*, vol. 56, no. 3 (2021), pp. 663–7.

Jeffers, Honorée Fanonne. *The Age of Phillis*. Wesleyan UP, 2022.

Johnson, Walter. *Soul By Soul: Life Inside the Antebellum Slave Market*. Harvard UP, 1999.

Jones-Rogers, Stephanie. *They Were Her Property: White Women as Slave Owners in the American South*. Yale UP, 2019.

Kerber, Linda. "The Republican Mother: Women and the Enlightenment—An American Perspective." *American Quarterly*, vol. 28, no. 2 (Summer 1976), pp. 187–205.

Lee, Susan. *Eliza Pinckney*. Children's Press, 1977.

Momon, Tiffany. "John 'Quash' Williams, Charleston Builder." *Journal of Early Southern Decorative Arts*, vol. 41 (2020), https://www.mesdajournal.org/2020/john-quash-williams-charleston-builder/ (last accessed November 14, 2024).

Monaghan, E. Jennifer. *Learning to Read and Write in Colonial America*. U of Massachusetts P, 2007.

The Papers of Eliza Lucas Pinckney and Harriott Pinckney Horry Digital Edition. Edited by Constance Schulz. U of Virginia P, Rotunda, 2012.

Pinckney, Elise. "Eliza Lucas Pinckney: Biographical Sketch." *The Letterbook of Eliza Lucas Pinckney*, edited by Elise Pinckney and Marvin R. Zahniser. U of South Carolina P, 1997.

Ramagosa, Carol Walter. "Eliza Lucas Pinckney's Family in Antigua, 1668–1747." *South Carolina Historical Magazine*, vol. 99, no. 3 (July 1998), pp. 238–58.
Ramsay, David. *The History of South Carolina: From Its First Settlement in 1670 to the Year 1808*. W.J. Duffie, 1858.
Ravenel, Harriott Horry. *Eliza Pinckney*. Charles Scribner's Sons, 1896.
Roberts, Cokie. *Founding Mothers: The Women Who Raised Our Nation*. HarperCollins, 2004.
Romine, Scott. *The Real South: Southern Narrative in the Age of Cultural Reproduction*. Louisiana State UP, 2014.
Smith, Emily. "'I Acquit the Author': Domestic Fictions of Eliza Lucas Pinckney in Frances Leigh Williams's *Plantation Patriot*." *Southern Studies*, vol. 12, no. 3 & 4 (Fall/Winter 2005), pp. 41–53.
Stubbs, Tristan. *Masters of Violence: The Plantation Overseers of Eighteenth-Century Virginia, South Carolina, and Georgia*. U of South Carolina P, 2018.
Wheatley, Phillis. *Complete Writings*. Edited by Vincent Carretta. Penguin, 2001.
Williams, Frances Leigh. *Plantation Patriot: A Biography of Eliza Lucas Pinckney*. Harcourt, Brace, and World, 1967.
Williams, Harriet Simons. "Eliza Lucas and Her Family: Before the Letterbook." *South Carolina Historical Magazine*, vol. 99, no. 3 (1998), pp. 259–79.

11

African Cinema on American Slavery

Steven W. Thomas

Starting in the 1970s, a pioneering generation of African filmmakers from Nigeria, Ghana, Ethiopia, Senegal, and Mauritania made several important and influential films about transatlantic slavery. Those dramatic fictional films are, in chronological order, *Ceddo* (dir. Ousmane Sembene, Senegal, 1977), *A Deusa Negra/Black Goddess* (dir. Ola Balogun, Nigeria, 1978), *West Indies: The Fugitive Slaves of Liberty* (dir. Med Hondo, Mauritania, 1979), and *Sankofa* (dir. Haile Gerima, Ethiopia, 1993). These films belonged to a self-consciously Pan-African film movement that participated in conversations about anti-colonial politics, debated the challenges of nation building, and attempted to answer the question of transnational forms of Black solidarity. Moreover, reflecting the diversity of perspectives on Pan-Africanism and the question of slavery, the essay film *I Is a Long Memoried Woman* (dir. Frances-Anne Solomon, 1990), which creatively adapted the poetry by Guyanese writer Grace Nichols, can be read as a feminist counterpoint to the above list of male-directed films. In addition to the films about the transatlantic trade and the relationship between Africa and the Americas, there is also a film about the trans-Sahara slave trade: *Shaihu Umar* (dir. Adamu Halilu, Nigeria, 1976). Read in comparison to films about the transatlantic trade, it complicates the historical metanarrative about slavery. Produced a decade later by a younger generation of filmmakers, John Akomfrah's *Testament* (Ghana, 1988) not only explores the relationship between postcolonial Ghana and the legacy of slavery but also meditates retrospectively on the successes and failures of Pan-African political ideals that had held such promise in the 1960s and 1970s for African and African Diaspora filmmakers such as Ousmane Sembene, Med Hondo, Ola Balogun, Adamu Halilu, and Haile Gerima. All of these filmmakers participated in conversations at festivals and conferences on Pan-Africanism and the "Third Cinema" film movement. There, they discussed earlier movies about slavery, including Marxist films such as *Tamango* (dir. John Berry, 1958), *Burn!* (dir. Gillo Pontecorvo, 1969), and *The Last Supper* (dir. Tomás Gutiérrez Alea, 1976). In doing so, this cohort of Pan-African filmmakers took up some of the theoretical tools of Marxist cinema that they then critically examined and repurposed to invent a new approach to cinema that could challenge the Eurocentric metanarrative of history, recuperate an African public memory, affirm a transnational Black political movement, and ultimately provoke audiences to political action.

Taken together as a body of work, they present an alternative to Hollywood and Hollywood-style movies about the history of slavery. As I have demonstrated elsewhere in a historical survey of films about slavery from 1903 to 2020,[1] in contrast to the American film and TV industry that tended to represent slavery as something safely in the past, Marxist and Pan-African filmmakers in the 1950s–1990s were interested in the unfolding of a more complex historical dialectic. While American filmmakers saw their art as a drama of individuals overcoming adversity, Marxist filmmakers were interested in social structures and systemic oppression, and Pan-Africanist filmmakers were interested in a repressed historical memory and a revolutionary Black identity. While American films foregrounded individuals dreaming of freedom, the Marxist and Pan-African films foregrounded communities organizing to achieve it. Although Pan-Africanist filmmakers were certainly influenced by Marxism, they also found its somewhat clinical focus on the structure of oppression and revolt to be unsatisfying as it did not provide a culturally usable past for developing a Black identity and did not fully appreciate the deeper resources within Black culture for sustaining resistance. Some of them also questioned the Eurocentric historical metanarrative assumed in both Marxist and capitalist conceptions of human development, and so they invoked an alternative African time frame.

This chapter has three aims. First, most basically, it will value an archive of African films that has been somewhat marginalized both in the scholarly conversation about slavery on the screen and by the commercial mechanisms of distribution and exhibition. Second, it will analyze the films by situating them in their political and cultural contexts—in particular the

---

[1] See Steven W. Thomas, "Cinematic Slavery: A Genealogy of Film from 1903 to 2020." For analysis of why these older films are important for new Hollywood movies such as *The Woman King*, see Steven W. Thomas, "Where Is African Cinema in Hollywood?"

Pan-African conversations and debates within "Third Cinema" in which these filmmakers actively participated and that makes these films so different from the films produced by American and European studios. Motivating their artistic experimentation were the political circumstances of postcolonial nation building in Africa, Asia, and the Caribbean in the 1960s and 1970s as well as the racial politics in America and Europe. This chapter will also put the context of their Pan-African vision and Third Cinema project in dialogue with another intellectual context, the recent work in the field of Early American Studies whose literary and historical scholarship interrogates the colonial archive and excavates the experiences, cultures, and lives of enslaved Africans that have been silenced in that archive. In a sense, these films anticipate by three decades some of the academic conversations happening now, most notably Saidiya Hartman's influential *Lose Your Mother* (2007)—a book that blends scholarship and memoir and that not only interrogates the gaps in the archive but also reflects upon her own personal relationship as an African American to the African continent by investigating Africa's role in the transatlantic slave trade while questioning the relevance of Pan-African ideologies. In a way, somewhat similar to academic scholarship on the history of slavery in the twenty-first century, these filmmakers saw their films as interrogations of the archive (and in fact explicitly said so in interviews).[2] Third, finally, my argument is that these films, both in terms of content and artistic form, juxtapose multiple moments in time and multiple locations in geographic space in order to politically provoke audiences to question where they came from and where they are going. As such, they put in question the European-American frameworks of the nation state and the western metanarrative of progress. My essay concludes with analysis of theoretical statements by the filmmakers themselves along with their intellectual allies to show how, importantly, the filmmakers and philosophers of this era participated in an ongoing intellectual conversation about how art, literature, and film can creatively inspire a new sense of what it means to be human.

---

[2] I discuss how the filmmakers theorize their own work at the end of this chapter. See interviews by these filmmakers in Gabriel, *Third Cinema*, Jackson, "Decolonizing the Filmic Mind," and Ukadike, *Questioning African Cinema*. Conference presentations by filmmakers and their intellectual allies are in Pines and Willeman, *Questions of Third Cinema*, and Givanni, *Symbolic Narratives/African Cinema*. For an overview of these filmmakers including discussion of statements they have made, see Pfaff, *Twenty-five Black African Filmmakers*, and Bakari and Cham, *African Experiences of Cinema*.

Scholarly Frameworks and Conversations

These films are well-known classics of African cinema by some of the most prominent and influential directors from that continent, but unfortunately are relatively unknown to the American conversation about how slavery is represented on screen. For example, in his introduction to a collection of essays on films about slavery, *Celluloid Chains: Slavery in the Americas through Film* (2018), Rudyard Alcocer says that there are no African movies about American slavery (xv). The editors of *Celluloid Chains* present their book as a sequel to Natalie Zemon Davis's study *Slaves on Screen*, which also does not include any African cinema. Ironically, one of the African movies that I discuss here, Akomfrah's *Testament*, was made explicitly in response to one of the films analyzed in *Celluloid Chains*: Werner Herzog's somewhat offensive farce, *Cobra Verde* (1987). This gap in the scholarly conversation about how slavery is represented on screen is unfortunate because African films provide a culturally significant alternative to the Hollywood approach (for example, *12 Years a Slave, Harriet, Django Unchained*, and *Mandingo*).

Perhaps one problem is disciplinary silos, as a result of which scholars of American literature and history may not be aware of the field of African cinema, but certainly another problem is lack of access to these films, some of which are hard to get. Some of these films faced censorship or push-back (such as the case with *Ceddo, West Indies*, and *Sankofa*), which limited their distribution and exhibition. Others may have been produced in national industries where distribution was limited by a lackluster state apparatus, such as *Black Goddess* and *Shaihu Umar*. Fortunately, just as I began writing this chapter, one of them, Haile Gerima's *Sankofa*, was restored by the influential American director and producer Ava DuVerney and released on Netflix in September 2021. The Criterion Collection, with help from Martin Scorsese's World Cinema Project, has begun to digitize other films by Med Hondo. A print of Halilu's *Shaihu Umar* was rediscovered in the archives of the Nigerian Film Corporation in 2016 and a digitally restored version premiered in 2018 with support from Germany's Arsenal—Institute for Film and Video Art. Hopefully, the others will also be recuperated in more accessible formats.

I suggest there may be another reason why classic African cinema about slavery may not be accessible, and that is partly because its frame of reference, such as its sense of historical chronology, is different from the American and European films. Although all filmmakers may aim for their movies to provide a "usable past" for their audiences, the "usable past" in self-consciously Pan-African cinema has a more global frame of reference than the U.S. national framework that one typically finds in Hollywood films. For North American and British film audiences, slavery is part of a national past that was overcome by moral suasion, and the political purpose of such films is national healing—with explicit encouragement from both the U.S. government and civil society to "integrate" film and TV (Campbell 144; Cripps 379). In contrast, African cinema challenges the hegemonic and arguably neoliberal representations of the "white savior" in films such as Spielberg's *Amistad* (1997) and Apted's *Amazing Grace* (2006) by instead foregrounding African cultural resources and networks for resisting and surviving slavery. African cinema was also responding to a different set of concerns—their status as newly independent, postcolonial nations in a globalized (and arguably neocolonial) world order and the role traditional culture would play in the formation of new modern nation states. They also posited a different metanarrative of world history that centered a Black-centered chronology rather than a Eurocentric chronology. Therefore, in order to make these films more legible for students and audiences today, one must situate them in a different interpretative framework.

In addition to appreciating these films in their own intellectual context, we might also use them to reflect on our own scholarly moment. On the one hand, the artistic goals of the movies resemble the academic goals of histories of Black life, such as those by American scholars Jennifer Morgan, Marisa Fuentes, Saidiya Hartman, and others. This body of scholarship has foregrounded the problematic limits of the archive for understanding the thoughts and feelings of enslaved people—the thoughts and feelings that the films aim to imaginatively convey. Their work informs new scholarship on "public memory" that examines "the consolidation and circulation, and sometimes the revision, of perceptions of a shared past" (Rex and Watson 7). Similar to these scholars, the generation of African filmmakers whom I discuss here also saw their films as critical interrogations and challenges to the implicit racism of a hegemonic public memory. On the other hand, there may be a difference in what forms of African culture and which political issues these filmmakers aimed to foreground that remain absent from the America-oriented scholarship. For example, one of Hartman's points in *Lose Your Mother* about public memory and heritage tourism—a point that casts some "pessimistic" skepticism on a singularly "Black" identity politics and that reflects a "disenchantment" with what she considers "utopian" political movements (38–9)—is her first-hand observation of the ways in which West Africans have repressed their role in the transatlantic slave trade (72–3). I suggest that the issue that Hartman observes is precisely the political context that Pan-African filmmakers were self-consciously addressing in the 1970s–1980s in response to that repression. By uncovering the repressed history, their films had the power to force the African public to critically confront their political identities and recover an alternative legacy and Pan-African solidarity. The political context of the 1970s for African and other postcolonial political communities included intense debates about the configuration of the new nation states that were then being forged. Hence, the films about slavery were meant to provide a "usable past" for reimagining a revolutionary future for African states that could become more equitable and inclusive—the point being, films about slavery are never simply about the past they represent but also about the present of their audiences.[3] Unlike Hollywood cinema which tends to neutralize the political urgency of slavery by relegating its history as safely "past," the Pan-African cinema very deliberately uses montage film techniques to juxtapose past and present, mixing historical time registers, in order to raise questions about the persistence of slavery's legacy and global racism that is not only systemic but also transnational.

The Films in Context: Interrogating the Relationship between Past and Present

Considering that the topic of slavery was somewhat taboo in African polite society, why did Sembene, Balogun, Hondo, Gerima, and Akomfrah make some of their most important movies about it? Was slavery merely a metaphor for neocolonialism or a fear that Black people had been brainwashed by the American and European movie industries and needed to "emancipate themselves from mental slavery" (to paraphrase the famous line from Bob Marley's "Redemption Song")? Or was there a deeper interest in what it meant to be human and what an Afro-modernity could look like? The political context, as well as the debates among these filmmakers about how their art could best engage with that context, is a complex story.

---

[3] Scholars of cinema that make this point about the temporality of film include Roland Barthes, "The Romans on Film," in *Mythologies*; Robert A. Rosenstone, *History on Film / Film on History*; Marc Ferro, *Cinema and History*; Hayden White, "Historiography and Historiophoty"; and Andrew Higson, *English Heritage, English Cinema*, who are discussed in the introduction to Swaminathan and Thomas, *The Cinematic Eighteenth Century*, 2–3. Scholars of public memory make a similar point about the temporality of heritage sites, such as Rex and Watson, *Public Memory*, 156–7, Bodnar, *Remaking America*, 15, and Zelizer, *Remembering to Forget*, 3.

The context can be analyzed in three aspects. One aspect is the imminent political stakes for the newly constituted, postcolonial nations struggling to find a true sense of freedom. The second aspect is the cultural context in which African history and culture were derided and dismissed at worst and ignored and under-represented at best. For example, a multitude of scholars from W.E.B. Du Bois in the United States in the 1920 and 1930s to Edward Kamau Brathwaite in the Caribbean in the 1970s expressed frustration with "the systematic removal of any account of African contribution to the process and progress of world civilization" (Busia 741). The third aspect of this debate was what the term "Pan-African" could mean for a political and cultural revolution, and what "Third Cinema" could become as an alternative or oppositional form of art. In a conference attended by some of the African filmmakers discussed here, the film scholar Teshome Gabriel argued in his presentation titled "Third Cinema as Guardian of Popular Memory: Towards a Third Aesthetics" for the importance of cinema as a form of "popular memory" that could offer a counter-history to the hegemonic western history. He concludes, "Third Cinema, therefore, serves not only to rescue memories, but rather, and more significantly, to give history a push and popular memory a future" (Gabriel 64). Therefore, for the filmmakers of this Pan-African movement, cinematic counter-history was not simply about the past, but rather about layering temporalities: past, present, and future.[4]

Ousmane Sembene is often considered the father of African cinema following the decolonization of Senegal in the 1960s (Diawara, *African Film* 22). He wrote and directed many influential films, from *Borrom Sarret* (1963) to *Moolaadé* (2004). His film *Ceddo* (1977) offers an African perspective on the slave trade that illustrates a more African-centered transatlantic historiography. Historians might be reminded of work such as John Thornton's *Africa and Africans in the Making of the Atlantic World* (1992) about African economies, including slavery, at the time of the initial contact with Europe and what happened to these economies before and during the transatlantic trade. Thornton's study maps the different African empires and their role

---

[4] Teshome Gabriel's essay on cinema and public memory is echoed by scholars of public memory such as John Bodnar, who says, "Public memory is a body of beliefs and ideas about the past that help a public or society understand both its past, present, and by implication, its future" (15). Similarly, Rex and Watson's *Public Memory* shares the goals of Third Cinema when Watson asserts that "public memory is integral to uncovering, interrogating, and changing the implicit ways that racism, prejudice, and structural inequalities are maintained" (157).

in the developing Atlantic economy. But, unlike Thornton's history that is based largely on an archive of European accounts, Semebene's *Ceddo* presents a political point of view that centers African resistance to the globalizing religions of Christianity and Islam as well as to the economic practice of slavery. Set in a Wolof kingdom in Senegal roughly during the eighteenth century, the movie triangulates between three political forces: the Indigenous matrilineal African culture, patrilineal Islam, and European traders. The Imam has been gaining influence with the king, Demba War Thioub, forcing conversion to Islam and requiring that kingly succession follow patrilineal inheritance laws. The Ceddo, who maintain the matrilineal Indigenous practices, have rebelled by kidnapping the king's daughter, Princess Dior Yacine. The film provocatively condenses the European presence to two symbolic individuals, a Catholic priest and a slave trader, who never speak but have become a normalized everyday part of the economy of the kingdom. The trader sells alcohol and guns in exchange for enslaved people, and the priest silently accompanies him for most of the movie and is figured as a prolepsis for the future church that is to come to Africa.

The movie opens with a scene of ordinary life in the town, including women with goods to sell and the white man with a gun supervising enslaved Africans. The scene is interrupted by children shouting that someone has kidnapped the princess. Meanwhile, there is a public forum where the Imam demands that all unconverted individuals (that is the Ceddo) carry a bundle of sticks, to which the Ceddo leader responds by requesting a stop to the looting and enslaving of their people. In this scene, and throughout the movie, the Ceddo symbolically display a ceremonial staff (or *samp*) that signifies protected public speech, and its symbolism is important throughout the film. Later, the Imam tries to destroy it. However, distracting attention from the debate about slavery are the men competing for royal favor to gain the hand of Princess Dior in marriage. Several potential suitors attempt to rescue the princess. Behind the scenes, the Imam is secretly conspiring to consolidate his power by marrying the princess himself and by assassinating the king. What is noteworthy in the film is that instead of the competitive relationship between Christianity and Islam that one might expect, Sembene's movie shows a symbiotic relationship in which Islam is establishing a new political order that allows the Christian enslaver to prosper. While Europeans provide guns to the Imam, the Imam creates a new class of "outsiders" (the meaning of the word "Ceddo") or "state-less" people that are vulnerable to enslavement and trade to the Europeans. However, when the Imam later declares a jihad against the Ceddo and scapegoats them for doing all the things that in fact he was doing, the church is burned down during the battle. Soon after, the Ceddo seem to be defeated. In the climactic scene, the Ceddo begin a ritual of submission by shaving their heads and converting to Islam, but the public conversion ceremony is interrupted when Princess Dior returns to the village, having been informed by the Ceddo of the death of her father and the growing power of the Imam. Her movement is majestically slow and deliberate as she surveys the scene, while energetic jazz music plays to heighten the tension (Figure 11.1). In a sudden, surprising reversal of political alliances, the Princess snatches a gun from one of the Imam's guards and sides with the Ceddo, sparking a rebellion. Some Ceddo take guns and fight while others symbolically put their mouths on the barrels of the guns pointed at them. The movie concludes when the Princess approaches the Imam with the gun and shoots him—a scene perhaps inspired by Frantz Fanon's argument, in his seminal book *Wretched of the Earth* about anti-colonial revolution, that the African nations come into being through armed revolt. The movie's representation of this history is in some ways similar to what scholars were writing at the time Sembene was filming.[5] Reflecting on this history while condensing the complex

Figure 11.1 *Ceddo*, directed by Ousmane Sembene. (Credit: Janus Films.)

---

[5] One example is a seminal collection of essays from a conference on the "economic history of the Atlantic slave trade" that took place in 1975, two years before Sembene's movie was produced (Gemery and Hogendorn 201–5). Saidiya Hartman in *Lose Your Mother* relies on this scholarship for much of her contextualization of her travel to Salaga, the location of one of the largest inland slave markets in nineteenth-century Africa (189).

economic dynamic onto symbolic characters, the film communicates a Pan-African return to core Indigenous values against outside colonial forces.[6]

As one of the few African films about this time period and the African side of the transatlantic slave trade, it is significant that the temporal frame of the film is vague. As Mamadou Diouf and others have argued, the film not only conflates several historical events from the late seventeenth through the early nineteenth century, but it also inverts the way African historians usually narrate the dynamic between the Islamic marabouts, Wolof kings, and Ceddo armies (Diouf 243). For instance, the name of the Princess Yacine in the film could be an allusion to Yassin Buba, a *lingeer* (female ruler) of the Kajoor kingdom who aggressively maintained her power during the 1670s–1680s first by allying herself with a Muslim leader's jihad, but then changing her alliance to overthrow him. This complex story is told in detail by Douglas Thomas in his essay "The Lingeer's Jihad," which foregrounds (as does Sembene) the leadership roles of women, though traditionally these women would be the elders in the community, not the young, alluring figure in Sembene's film. But another possible allusion is her father's name, Demba War Thiub, in the film, which may reference Birma Fatma Cubb (Thiub being one way of writing Cubb in Wolof), a king (or *damel* in Wolof) of Kajoor in the 1810s–1820s. Or the story could allude to the attempted jihad of El Hadj Omar in 1852 to forcefully spread his puritanical vision of Islam from the western Sudan to the Wolof kingdoms of Senegal. Between the mid-seventeenth century and mid-nineteenth century, the Senegambia region underwent a complex political and economic shift, where the transatlantic trade of the European empires disrupted some of the traditional forms of political authority and shifted the locus of power from the trans-Sahara trade toward the Atlantic coast, requiring constant negotiation and renegotiation of alliances among Muslim marabouts, warrior-kings, Ceddo, and peasantry. One effect of this complex economic and political dynamic was several wars among marabout leaders and kings as well as jihads for purifying or reforming the kingdom (Colvin). Well before the Europeans arrived, the peasantry had already been converted to Islam partly as a form of protection from raids, but so too would the kings who engaged in the raids also create close alliances with the Islamic leadership. By the seventeenth century, the region had already become largely Muslim, so the question of religious "conversion" was not so much about

---

[6] See Robert Baum, "Tradition and Resistance," and Thomas Mpoyi-Buatu, "Sembene Ousmane's *Ceddo* & Med Hondo's *West Indies*."

whether to adopt Islam, but rather which version of Islam and which arrangement of political power.

However, somewhat different from Sembene's representation of the Ceddo as victims of European enslavers and the Imam's conspiring for power, historians tend to characterize the Ceddo as an army that served various kings by raiding their enemies. The constitution of the Ceddo is somewhat complicated. Although they were enslaved themselves, they also could occupy positions of power that served kings and enrich themselves by pillaging and enslaving others, including the peasantry (or *Ba-Dolo* in Wolof). Moreover, arguably, the dynamic social identity of the Ceddo was affected by the larger transformation of the Wolof kingdoms caused by the development of the Atlantic slave trade (Searing). The historical dynamic was complex, but it is clear that the film's presentation of the Ceddo as heroic figures of Indigenous culture resisting the corrupting foreign forces of Christianity and Islam is an idealization. One could criticize Sembene for this idealization as an avoidance of Africans' complicity with slavery by creating a binary between good Indigenous culture and bad foreign culture (Islam and Christianity). Nevertheless, the film does get at a kernel of truth within the mystical shell by identifying the complex socioeconomic forces unleashed by trading networks of Christian and Muslim empires that transformed the region.

Moreover, Sembene's movie had as much to do with contemporary politics of the 1970s as with the history (Gabriel, *Third Cinema* 89). In the late 1960s and early 1970s, one of the questions for Senegal was how the tacitly conservative Islamic brotherhoods (or marabouts), which by the mid-twentieth century had become such a pervasive social, economic, and political force, fit into President Leopold Sédar Senghor's vision for a progressive, socialist new state (Markovitz 89). Hence, we could read the movie's story of four figures—Islam, European Christianity, the Ceddo, and the Princess—as an allegorical fable that reflects upon that question by schematizing the process of a larger historical dialectic, rather than as a representation of a singular historical event. In this way, Sembene's contribution to the political conversation in West Africa in the 1970s is to privilege and center the Ceddo "outsiders" and the female *lingeer*, rather than male Islam and Christianity, in that historical dialectic.

One of the cinematic techniques for evoking a long view of historical time and juxtaposing different moments is through music. As Brenda Berrian has analyzed in rich detail, *Ceddo*'s soundtrack, by Cameroonian composer Manu Dibango, significantly mixes together Senegalese leitmotifs, Diola choral music, jazz, and American gospel, layering contemporary transatlantic Black culture over the historical narrative. The music functions cinematically as a sound-bridge connecting the historical temporal frame of the story (diegesis) with a surrealistic montage of images representing the present of contemporary postcolonial Africa. For example, as the enslaver brands the enslaved Africans with a hot iron, the extradiegetic American gospel presents a jarring commentary and signals a transatlantic solidarity between Africans in Africa and in the diaspora. The music and montage betoken the African American culture that is to come and invoke a spiritual Pan-African connection across space and time. Minutes later, the Catholic priest has a dream-vision of the future of African Christianity in which an African Catholic priest holds the Indigenous staff (or *samp*) in his hand while performing Christian funeral rites for what appears to be the same actor who plays the white colonial priest. At this moment, over a montage of documentary-like images representing modern postcolonial Africa, the soundtrack borrows from the Diola ethnic group's syncretic choral music that blends Indigenous African culture and Catholicism. The juxtaposition of different musical genres and temporalities raises questions about public historical memory and how we conceptualize the relationship between past and present, specifically, as scholars of public memory have argued, the ways in which the past persists in our present. Sembene was not the only director to utilize anachronistic music in this way; Med Hondo, Ola Balogun, and Haile Gerima also mix music from across Africa and the African Diaspora to communicate a transnational Pan-African solidarity and frequently deploy experimental jazz as a global Black musical artform to communicate a radical movement toward a progressive future, which is why jazz sometimes accompanies acts of revolutionary violence such as the Princess Dior's slaying of the Imam. The music and montage of documentary inserts invite the viewer of the film to speculate about parallels and correlations between the history depicted in the story and contemporary postcolonial politics of the late twentieth century.

Even more than Sembene's film, Med Hondo's *West Indies: Fugitive Slaves of Liberty* (1977) explicitly juxtaposed and layered multiple historical time frames. The English translation of the title misses some of the meaning of the bilingual original: *West Indies ou Les Negres marrons de la liberte*, which places the English phrase "West Indies" next to the French for "black maroons" rather than "slaves." The style of the film is musical theater, and the entire story takes place on a single theatrical stage designed as a slave ship. The different levels of the ship obviously are allegorical for political and class positions, and as the film continues, it becomes clear that the "slave ship" is also a metaphor for the "ship of state." The film moves back and forth through history. The setting for the main plot line is contemporary with the film's production (roughly the 1970s) and is about an election in the newly independent and unnamed Caribbean island. The election is obviously corrupted, as the four white representatives of Europe work together to get their Black comprador agent elected. As this modern-day plot unfolds, the film flashbacks to several stories to tell the history of the Caribbean from the beginnings of slavery through the Haitian Revolution to the present. By juxtaposing different temporal registers, all on the same physical set, it provides a visual metaphor for the argument that African, Caribbean, and African American intellectuals such as Kwame Nkrumah, Aimé Césaire, and W.E.B. Du Bois had been making, that the "neocolonial" new world order in the 1970s was just a new form of slavery.

The film's style, which communicates its meaning, is montage technique, cutting back and forth between different narrative time frames. The film opens on an elegant table on the stage, at which are seated the ruling elite—one representing capitalism, one religion, one philanthropy, one the Black comprador class, and over these, ultimately, the supervisor of empire. Behind them is a map of the world titled "Empire Colonial." They announce their plan to rid the world of "tiny people" whose overpopulation and demands interfere with a profitable new world order. From this highly theatrical opening, the film cuts to a montage of documentary-style imagery of a Caribbean island, men and women cutting sugar cane and harvesting bananas accompanied by musical drums. The film cuts back to the construction of the stage, the gigantic boat inside a hanger, with the French revolutionary slogan *"liberté, égalité, fraternité"* at the top, but also another sign, reminiscent of Orwellian newspeak, "independence = dictatorship." The film then cuts between scenes of political activists debating whether to vote when the election is obviously rigged, a priest singing clownishly to Black children about Jesus, and various scenes of interpretive African dance. The board member representing the philanthropic voice of the new world order encourages Black people to immigrate from the islands to France to satisfy a new demand for labor. Their propaganda for immigration is represented musically through a dance expressing the "happy and elegant" Black community in modern Paris, but this is juxtaposed with a scene, flashing back to history, of a slave auction. In this historical flashback, the actor who plays the African king selling his own people is the same actor who plays the comprador politician in the pocket of the white power structure. The analogy of "slavery" as a metaphor for neocolonialism is persistent throughout the film. After a comical pantomime of French historical dates

Figure 11.2 *West Indies ou les Nègres marrons de la liberté*, directed by Med Hondo. (Credit: Ciné-Archives.)

and figures and an interpretative dance of a slave revolt, a political speech proudly announces the end of slavery. The speech is ironically juxtaposed with a scene of contemporary times where the party of political elites are pledging their allegiance to France while below deck activists organize a protest rally against those elites. Police attack and murder one of the protestors (Figure 11.2).

The political context for the film is the question about the political status of newly independent (or not-so-independent) African and Caribbean states. The islands of Martinique and Guadaloupe had voted to become "departments" of France rather than independent. Related to this issue is that France requires cheap labor and is promoting immigration and assimilation. The film reflects conversations that were happening in France where the socialist labor movement debated whether foreign "blacks" from Africa and the Caribbean are included in their notion of "solidarity." The movie concludes with a Pan-African carnival, where they sing, "we are the Negroes kidnapped, we built the Americas from Africa ... Emigration is modern slavery, Negroes of Africa and America, we will fight on!"

In the political discourse among Black intellectuals in Europe, the Caribbean, and Africa in the twentieth century, the metaphor of "slavery" was often used to describe the political and cultural situation that they faced. Both Sembene and Hondo made movies about the Black immigrant experience—*La noire de* (1966) and *Soleil O* (1970), respectively—where that immigrant experience in France in the 1960s was compared to slavery. In her book *Worldmaking after Empire* (2019), Adom Getachew shows how communist and Pan-African political theorists and historians from the 1930s through the 1960s, such as W.E.B. Du Bois, Kwame Nkrumah, Eric Williams, George Padmore, and others, made the case for why capitalist empires were akin to slavery. Du Bois wrote, "[t]oday, instead of removing laborers from Africa to distant slavery, industry built on a new slavery approaches Africa to deprive the natives of their land, to force them to toil, and to reap all the profit for the white world" (qtd. in Getachew 82). What was at stake in the aftermath of World War II was the status of Black peoples in the UN charter and the new world order. Nkrumah and Padmore suggested that unless African peoples gained independence and equal recognition in the United Nations, they were essentially wage-slaves to the imperial power structure that had been built by enslaved people in the previous century. Getachew concludes, "In formulating empire as a problem of enslavement, anti-colonial nationalists framed their revolution as a movement from slavery to freedom" (83). Caribbean and African intellectuals such as Eric Williams and Kwame Nkrumah had been arguing that the ideals of political liberty encoded in the American 1776 Declaration of Independence were in fact precarious because of the economic dependence of the former colonies on the metropole. For the islands that were organized around cash crop monocultures, even basic necessities such as food had to be imported. Williams and Nkrumah criticized cultural nationalists who focused on a narrow sense of political independence. Against ethno-nationalisms, what they endorsed instead were Caribbean and African federations, economic cooperation across postcolonial nations, and cross-cultural forms of Black solidarity (Getachew 111–12). In this context, Pan-Africanism was not a simplistic "return" to some mystical motherland but a dialectical strategy for charting a real independence from colonial rule and the "neocolonial" world order that emerged in the 1960s. Also, in this context, a film about the history of slavery, including acknowledgment of the complicity of African empires with that history, was a provocative "push" (to use Teshome Gabriel's words for how Third Cinema is a counter-hegemonic form of public memory) away from backward-looking national pride and toward a more inclusive and equitable sense of cross-cultural solidarity across nation states.

This conversation about the politics of postcolonial nation building and Pan-African federation was directly relevant to the emergence of African cinema, specifically with regard to the economics of production and distribution. As narrated in the pioneering works of African Film Studies by Manthia Diawara and Nwachukwu Frank Ukadike, the movie business in the 1960s in sub-Saharan Africa was dominated by France and the United States. The French COMACICO (Compagnie Africaine Cinematographique Industrielle et Commerciele) and SECMA (Societe d'Exploitation Cinematographique Africaine) and the American AMPEC-Africa (American Motion Picture Export Company) controlled distribution in francophone and anglophone Africa. In response, many African countries strategized together ways to resist the domination of their cinema markets. Efforts by countries such as Nigeria, Burkina Faso, and Guinea to "nationalize" cinema were often met by fierce punitive tactics by the French and American companies (Ukadike, *Black African Cinema* 63). Individual nation states and individual filmmakers quickly realized they could not resist the Hollywood hegemony on their own terms but had to form strategic alliances. In this sense, the "Pan-African" approach to filmmaking was not only an ideological or cultural expression of "Blackness," but also a pragmatic political strategy that included some business savvy about how markets actually worked (Boughedir 240). African filmmakers realized that they needed to organize and unite in order to maintain an economically viable foundation for their artistic endeavors. The Fédération Panafricaine des Cinéastes (FEPACI, or, in English, the Pan-African Federation of Filmmakers) was the institutionalization of the political response to this economic problem. Moreover, in celebration of this Pan-African political spirit, in 1977, the same year that Sembene produced *Ceddo*, Nigeria hosted an enormous, month-long cultural festival—FESTAC—which featured music, art, literature, and film from across Africa and the globe, including appearances of star musicians Stevie Wonder from the United States and Gilberto Gil from Brazil. Gilberto Gil later made the soundtrack for the classic Brazilian film *Quilombo* (dir. Carlos Diegues, 1984) about maroon communities resisting enslavement. Hence, Pan-Africanism was not simply an ideological response to colonialism, but also a commercially practical one.

Perhaps inspired by the Pan-African connections between Nigeria and Brazil at FESTAC the year before, Ola Balogun's 1978 film *Black Goddess* also uses flashback techniques to juxtapose different historical moments and establish cultural continuity between Africa and the Americas. The film was an international co-production with his company, Afrocult Films, and a Brazilian company, Magnus Films. Balogun was one of the most important figures among Nigeria's first generation of filmmakers and helped establish film there both as an artist and as an administrator (Pfaff 23). He was a leader in the effort to "indigenize" film production and distribution and mentored the careers of other Nigerian filmmakers (Haynes 151). He produced one of the very first films in the Igbo language and in the Yoruba language, innovating what would become a hallmark of Nigerian cinema that adapts Yoruba theater to the screen (Balogun, *Cinema in Nigeria* 51–2). In collaboration with Ghana, he made the film *Cry Freedom!* (1981) about Nigeria's independence movement.

The opening scene of *Black Goddess* is a battle between two African states in the seventeenth or eighteenth century, resulting in some captives being sold into slavery, and then the movie immediately has a flash-forward to a scene of contemporary, urban Africa in the 1970s. It proceeds to tell the story of a man named Batatunde in Nigeria who is asked by his dying father to find his relatives in Brazil who had been enslaved centuries before. After arriving in Brazil, the man seeks out a Candomblé priestess in the hope that she can help him find his family. In Brazil, especially in Bahia, Candomblé is a cultural tradition that emerged in the late nineteenth century when elements from African cultures fused with elements from Catholicism. The documentary film *Bigger than Africa* (dir. Toyin Ibrahim Adekeye, 2018) focused on the Yoruba culture that persists across the Americas, but certainly other African cultures also contributed to this heritage.[7] As the plot of *Black Goddess* unfolds, Batatunde is happy to discover how his African cultural practices have been adapted to the American context as he learns one of the dances and falls in love with Elisa, the beautiful daughter of the priestess. She has a vision that they must travel to Bahia, and after they travel there together, he is thrown into a trance and has a dream about a conflict between enslaved Africans and their enslavers in Brazil in the eighteenth century. In this trance, he experiences the life of his ancestor Oluyole as an enslaved man while Elisa is revealed to be the reincarnation of Oluyole's love Amada, who is killed trying to escape the plantation. As in Med Hondo's *West Indies*, some of the same actors and actresses play the parts in both time periods to help establish continuity across time. And like Sembene's *Ceddo*, it juxtaposes jazz music with cinematic meditation on the relation between past and

---

[7] I have written about *Black Goddess* and *Bigger than Africa* in relation to Yaa Gyasi's novel *Homegoing* in my blog *Atlantic Literature*: http://atlanticliterature.blogspot.com/2019/06/homegoing-black-goddess-bigger-than.html.

present. While the story may take us back in time, the music takes us forward. Moreover, as Balogun remarked in an interview about the film, Batunde's dream vision where he becomes his enslaved ancestor reflects a Yoruba cultural perspective on the "cycle of life" and connection with one's ancestors (Pfaff 25). Before making *Black Goddess*, Balogun already had considerable experience filming Yoruba cultural traditions in several documentaries. Unfortunately, since *Black Goddess* only exists as a 35 mm print, it is not accessible in any VHS or digital format, so it has received no sustained scholarly analysis and has been completely ignored in surveys of films about slavery. Fortunately, it was exhibited at the New York African Film Festival in 2019.

Like *Ceddo*, *West Indies*, and *Black Goddess*, Haile Gerima's film *Sankofa* juxtaposes two moments in time. Its story begins in the present, when a white photographer is taking glamour shots of a black fashion model named Mona at Ghana's Cape Coast Castle that was built in 1674 as the headquarters of the Royal African Company. There, she encounters an African drummer who tells her, "Go back to your past. Return to your source." He is quoting from the writings of Amílcar Cabral, the famous Pan-African poet, philosopher, revolutionary, and diplomat born in what was then Portuguese Guinea. Similar to Frantz Fanon, Cabral theorized a complexly dialectical approach to tradition and progress in which returning to one's source was not a conservative return to an idealized, static past, but an engagement with one's history and traditions in order to move forward (Cabral 63). After Mona confronts this *griot*, she explores some of the castle where the enslaved people were captive, and then suddenly is transported back in time—a psychic Middle Passage—to a sugar plantation in Louisiana where she returns to a past incarnation of herself as the "house-slave" Shola in love with a "field-slave" named Shango, who is organizing a revolt. As the revolt unfolds, Mona/Shola learns from her elders the emotionally sustaining African cultural practices adapted for their communities. The metaphor of *sankofa*, which is an Akan symbol of the bird looking over its shoulder, symbolizes the relationship between historical memory and political future. This symbolic exploration of how we in the present remember the past is one reason why some critics praise it as one of the most important cinematic statements on slavery.[8]

The drama on the plantation weaves together the stories of several characters. Shola, we eventually learn, had been raped by her enslaver, and

---

[8] See Mark Reid, "Haile Gerima," and Christel N. Temple, "The Emergence of Sankofa Practice."

that painful memory repeatedly haunts both her and the film. Shango, whose name signifies the god of war, possesses traditional African knowledge of the healing power of plants and spirituality. So too does Nunu, who is presented as a mother figure, sustaining African culture by telling its history and its stories, in order to bind the community together in mutual support of each other. In one of the film's most striking and original scenes, the overseer is whipping several enslaved people, including a pregnant woman, who collapses, when, suddenly, the community of enslaved people surround the woman and brandish their machetes in a stand-off between them and the white overseers in order to create a space for Nunu to deliver the baby from the dying woman. But later in the film, Nunu's relationship to the community is complicated because her half-white child Joe, conceived when Nunu was raped, has been tutored by the white priest in Christian theology. The bi-racial Joe is violently conflicted about his identity, while Nunu laments that her son has abandoned his people and his culture for a Christian faith that is clearly hypocritical in that the priest allows the white enslavers to rape. In a fit of madness, he kills his mother. Later, out of intense guilt over his action, he kills the priest. At the end of the film, when the enslaved people begin their revolt, one of the most iconic shots is of Shola, as the camera angles up at her standing over the man who raped her, a machete in her hand (Figure 11.3). The film is remarkable for showing exactly what we never see in a Hollywood film—an organized Black community rooted in African traditions that is prepared to enact revolutionary violence against their enslavers.

All of these films use the cinematic techniques of flashback and montage to foreground the issue of continuity and discontinuity as a philosophical question.[9] For example, the drama of *Black Goddess* is not the discovery of that continuity, but the search for it. At the end of the movie, the hero Batatunde never finds his lost family, but he does find love. His psychic journey back in time through the mystical, cinematic dream does not recover his lost genealogy and does not compensate for the two-century-long gap in time, but it does give him wisdom and understanding. This technique was also used in a seminal film by one of Haile Gerima's colleagues from the Black filmmakers' movement known as the L.A. Rebellion that started at the UCLA film school: Julie Dash's cinematically gorgeous and emotionally complex *Daughters of the Dust* (1991), set among a Gullah/Geechee community in the late nineteenth century on one of the Sea Islands of

---

[9] For Gerima's own reflections on history and cinema, see his interview in Turner and Kamdibe (971–6).

Figure 11.3 *Sankofa*, directed by Haile Gerima. (Credit: Array.)

South Carolina.[10] In all of these movies, the interrogations of scenes of subjection and the afterlives of slavery raise many of the same philosophical questions that American scholars such as Saidiya Hartman would, years later, also raise. Although Hartman, in *Lose Your Mother*, is somewhat dismissive of the movie *Sankofa* for its naive assertion that African Americans can actually "return to the source" and their motherland (Hartman 90), I have aimed to demonstrate here that these movies offer a complex dialectic of past, present, and future. When Cabral theorizes the meaning of "return to the source," he foregrounds the very problem of identity, noting that Pan-Africanism was never simply an organic expression of African identity, but rather was invented outside of Africa by a Black, transnational petite bourgeoisie confronting the contradictions of their social identity, nervously in between dominant colonial (metropolitan) forms of culture and a variety of Indigenous forms of culture (Cabral 69).

---

[10] The best resource on Julie Dash's film is the one she published herself with bell hooks and Toni Cade Bambara, *Daughters of the Dust: The Making of an African American Woman's Film*. For a discussion of Gerima and Dash's influence on each other, see Allyson Nadia Field et al., *L.A. Rebellion: Creating a New Black Cinema*, especially Michael T. Martin's chapter "Struggles for the Sign in the Black Atlantic."

However, as powerful as these films were at challenging "Hollywood's white supremacist practices" and advocating for an African cultural sensibility, critics such as bell hooks have also observed that their narratives seem to revolve, problematically, around idealized female figures—sometimes as "positive mother figures" and other times as "sexual victims" (hooks 127). She points out moments in the movie *Sankofa* that seem to punish Mona/Shola, and other moments that preach at her in ways that repeat Hollywood's fetishistic interest in such representations of Black womanhood. Moreover, such historically problematic stereotypes of the Black mother and the tragically duplicitous mulatto in *Sankofa* posit a "sacralized" and ideologically innocent African precolonial past (Kandé 95). One might further argue that the contradictions inherent to social identity and the political conflicts that impede group solidarity (as recognized by theorists such as Cabral and Fanon) are displaced or resolved in the films by the figure of a woman who compensates for what is lacking in the political movement. For example, in *Ceddo* and other early films by Sembene, the women are represented as "agents of both group solidarity and social change" (Kindem and Steele 52).[11]

The issue of the image of "woman" in politically revolutionary cinema was an important part of the conversation among Black filmmakers and their allies at conferences and film festivals in the 1980s and 1990s. For example, at a conference on Third Cinema, Teshome Gabriel theorized the importance of women not only symbolically in African cinema but also actually in African society and progressive politics by pointing out the way in which women are the transmitters of popular memory (101).[12] However, in response to Gabriel, another conference participant, Mariama Hima, remarked that his idealization of the female figure obfuscated the complexity of the real lives of women; moreover, it ignored the more pressing issue, which is that most of the films were being made by men (Givanni 104). Ultimately, the conversation among Black filmmakers and intellectuals about a politically feminist and progressive representation of African identity led to an interest in films that portray a range of women's

---

[11] On the representation of women in these films, see also Nwachukwu Frank Ukadike, "Reclaiming Images of Women," and Karen Lindo, "Ousmane Sembene's Hall of Men."

[12] See also Teshome Gabriel, "Third Cinema as Guardian of Popular Memory." Gabriel's theorization of historical memory as transmitted via "invisible woman" and vernacular folk culture resembles not only Cabral's argument to "return to the source" of folk life but also American scholarship on public historical memory such as John Bodnar's argument in *Remaking America* that "public memory emerges from the intersection of official and vernacular cultural expressions" (14).

experience and that consider the relationship between race, gender, class, colonialism, and sexuality.

An example of the sort of film that bell hooks and others might be looking for—and that is productive to think about in comparison with *Ceddo, West Indies, Black Goddess,* and *Sankofa*—is the film adaptation of Grace Nichols's poem *I Is a Long Memoried Woman*, directed by Frances-Anne Solomon (1993). The film mixes together interpretative modern dance, dramatic reading of the poem, African music, images of archival materials, and conversation with the poet about what it all means. The film, like the poem, stages a polyvocal expression of different women's experiences and emotions. Some of the poems and scenes in the film are deeply painful, such as the recounting of a rape. Others are more playful, such as the satirical song mocking the "Massa" (enslaver) and the "Buckra woman" (white woman). Some characters aim to galvanize resistance and urge revolutionary violence, while others offer tender reflections on love, birth, and motherhood. As a whole, the film reflects not only the multiplicity of women's experiences but also different generations of women across history. In the way that it layers different temporalities and asserts transatlantic connections between Africa and the Americas, it is in some ways similar to the films by Sembene, Balogun, Hondo, and Gerima. However, the film differs in the way it concretizes their abstract sense of time and geography by emphasizing the gynecology of women's experience, the almost umbilical-cord-like connection linking women across the ages and across the ocean. The film opens with an interpretative dance of a woman giving birth, beautifully moving through white sheets to signify the tautness of the belly and the movement through the birth canal, as eventually a full-figured adult woman (not a child) is born, symbolizing the transfer of life and wisdom from one generation to another.[13] Adding to the text of the poem, the editing of the film expands on this theme by cutting to inserts, first of archival images of the Middle Passage, and then to scenes of contemporary London—a montage connecting past and present. But birth and intergenerational memory are not always idealized in this way. Later, the film laments having to give birth to the child of her enslaver who raped her and asks for the blessing of the spiritual mother and the African motherland to help her emotionally cope with her trauma. The poetry is vocally performed by two women who seem to speak to each other—sometimes as an echo, other times as a counterpoint. The poem concludes, "I have crossed an ocean, I have lost my tongue. From the root of an old one, a new

---

[13] Thanks to Nicole Aljoe for this insight and for recommending the movie.

one has sprung" (Nichols 94). As a whole, both the poem and its adaptation to film represent women's voices across time in order to historically recover Black enslaved women as intellectual subjects thinking about their situations, resisting their conditions, and putting into practice the cultural and social tactics of freedom rooted in West African traditions.

The ongoing debate about historical memory, gender representation, and African traditions were all part of the conversation in the 1970s and 1980s about the progress of the Pan-Africanist political movement. An important film that reflected retrospectively on this movement in relation to the history of slavery was John Akomfrah's film *Testament* (1988). Neither a fictional drama nor a film explicitly about slavery, it mixes genres (fiction, essay, and documentary) to critically reflect on the weight of history and the emotional connections across geography. It is a film about memory that juxtaposes personal memory of the *coup d'état* that overthrew Ghana's president, Kwame Nkrumah, and the historical memory of Elmina castle. The film begins with a statement about Nkrumah and the liberation movements he inspired throughout Africa. It suggests his overthrow by the military coup in 1966 "has haunted African politics since." By juxtaposing this haunting with scenes at Elmina castle, symbolizing the history of slavery, the film invites viewers to reflect on a long history. The main character, Abena, is a journalist who has been living in exile in England after the coup. She has returned to Ghana, presumably to interview the famous German filmmaker Werner Herzog and report on the making of his new film *Cobra Verde* (1987), which purports to be about the history of slavery in Africa. After Abena steps into the constructed set for Herzog's tribal scene, she remarks that her job feels like a "macabre joke" and criticizes Herzog's film as one of "simulated traumas, but no events." In fact, *Testament* was shot almost simultaneously with *Cobra Verde* and is partly a critical response to it and to the ways in which European and American cinema has imposed fake emotional content at the expense of "testaments" by Africans themselves about their real history (Sanches 104). But Abena also finds herself reflecting on Ghana's political past and future after she discovers that the government of Ghana has banned any public discussion of its former president Kwame Nkrumah and his political movement. Abena wanders the beach and the town in the shadow of Elmina castle looking for her former comrades whom she knew from her days as a member of Nkrumah's Convention Peoples' Party, but the people she meets avoid talking about that past. Her recollections are interspersed with archival footage of Nkrumah and his vision of an independent Africa as well as images of the sea, of trees, of the cemetery. The film has a rhythmic repetitive quality as if it is an invocation to bring back the dead. It concludes with Abena in a cemetery looking down a hole, as if it were a tomb still open.

In a way, Akomfrah's film is a meditation on the communal memory of the legacy of Nkrumah's Pan-Africanism and its repression in the politics of the emerging neoliberal post-colony. Akomfrah is deliberately commenting on the sort of films that are made about enslaved Africans by the western film industry instead of the sorts of films that were made by Pan-African filmmakers such as Sembene, Hondo, and Balogun. But there is a difference between Akomfrah and these older filmmakers. Akomfrah is the next generation of filmmaker inheriting the vision of Pan-Africanism and the filmic strategies of Third Cinema, but his filmmaking is more oblique and less confident in narrating a didactic political vision, instead reflecting on the disappointment that he and many Africans shared after so many of their leaders, such as Nkrumah, were overthrown when their political dreams of an African future were unrealized. His disillusionment is in some ways similar to Saidiya Hartman's "pessimistic" critique of the Pan-African dreams of Kwame Nkrumah in *Lose Your Mother*, but there is a significant difference. Hartman asserts a disidentification with Nkrumah's vision when she says, "the dreams that defined their horizon no longer defined mine" (Hartman 39). In contrast, Akomfrah's melancholy deconstruction of Ghana's recent political past aims to exorcize the dead and revive the core values of the anti-colonial political project. Those "dreams that defined their horizon" are still a part of his vision.

Toward a Theory of African Cinema

The filmmakers Ousmane Sembene, Med Hondo, Ola Balogun, Haile Gerima, Frances-Anne Solomon, and John Akomfrah, along with critics, scholars, and intellectuals, participated in film festivals and conferences about the social and political function of African film. As part of the conversation about subject matter, narrative structure, and cinematic style, they debated how to define the essence of an "African film language" or whether there even was such an essence or definable film language that unified the cinema across the continent.[14] They also brought theories of

---

[14] Diawara (*African Cinema*) and Ukadike (*Black African Cinema*) thoroughly analyze this debate. Ukadike's *Questioning African Cinema* collects interviews with filmmakers Sembene, Hondo, Gerima, and others, where they express their differing views on the topic. In 1986, some of the theorists and filmmakers discussed here debated these issues at a conference on Third Cinema, some of which was reproduced in *Questions of Third Cinema*, edited by Pines and Willemen.

Third Cinema as an alternative, anti-colonial film style into conversation with the question of African cinema's identity. As I have demonstrated above, some of the techniques of Third Cinema adapted Marxist cinema's use of montage to juxtapose moments in time and foreground social contradiction, but in addition also overlaid sound, documentary images, and cultural memories to forge a cinema responsive to the conditions of their audiences. Significantly, at the center of this debate were films about slavery, especially Sembene's *Ceddo* which was frequently cited by major scholars of Third Cinema and Black cinema, such as Teshome Gabriel and Clyde Taylor, as an exemplary test case in theoretical essays about how to define African cinema.[15] Debates could become quite heated over several key questions. One of these questions was the valuing of African traditions as, paradoxically, a source of strength and resilience against colonialism and slavery at the same time as they were in need of critique as an impediment to progress on social justice issues such as women's rights and equitable distribution of wealth. To this point about social conflicts, Sembene noted in an interview that "Africa has its own contradictions," distinct from Europe's, and pointed out in a somewhat Marxist dialectical fashion that if Africa had kings, then it also had serfs (Gabriel 111). In other words, African culture was certainly a source of resistance to enslavement, but at the same time, Africa participated in the slave trade. As the theorist of Third Cinema, Teshome Gabriel, observed, most filmmakers such as Sembene were inspired by Frantz Fanon who famously argued that the Black intellectual matured through three stages: first emulating European culture (which for the filmmaker meant European cinema styles); next, rejecting Europe in favor of recuperating African traditions and returning to an essentialist notion of Indigenous African cultures; and finally a third stage, coming to terms with the social contradictions in order to work progressively toward justice and a better society (Gabriel 7).[16] Hence, films about slavery were important for African cinema precisely because they raised two important questions: one being how to conceptualize this past and work through the contradictions toward a progressive future, and the second being how the art of cinema could do this.

One conference in particular, on "Africa and the History of Cinematic Ideas," held in London in 1995, is somewhat illuminating on these questions, especially since it highlighted the importance of films about

---

[15] Gabriel, *Third Cinema*; and Taylor, "Black Cinema."
[16] The Caribbean poet and scholar Edward Kamau Brathwaite argued something similar to Fanon in his influential 1974 essay "The African Presence in Caribbean Literature."

slavery for the larger conversations about Pan-Africanism and Black alternative cinema.[17] The keynote address, "Africa, the West, and the Analogy of Culture: The Cinematic Text after Man," by the influential Jamaican philosopher and novelist Sylvia Wynter, responded to the ongoing conversations mentioned above. There, she takes up V. Y. Mudimbe's argument in his well-known book *The Idea of Africa* that "Africa" is a construct in the western imagination that subordinates and subsumes African history to western history. In other words, in response to the question of whether there is such a thing as an essentially "African film language," one must wrestle with the fact that "Africa" as a totality is only understood in relation to western man's sense of history and self, and therefore insistence on "African-ness" and a static definition of an "African film language" are historically problematic.

Hence, considering that the films discussed above about slavery are all African films about a historical event prompted by a European-dominated Atlantic economy, one might ask whether a film such as *Shaihu Umar* (dir. Adamu Halilu, 1976) about an eastern (rather than western) oriented form of slavery might provide a useful comparative to the films about the trans-atlantic slave trade that I have analyzed above. This film was the first feature film in the Hausa language and one of the first major motion pictures produced by Nigeria's Film Unit, which later became the National Film Corporation (F. Balogun 23). It was not distributed commercially but was screened at the FESTAC Pan-African cultural festival hosted by Nigeria in 1977 (F. Balogun 70–1). It is a film about the trans-Sahara slave trade. The main character, Shaihu Umar, tells his story through a series of flashbacks. Raised by an impoverished single mother in western Africa after his father dies, he is forced into slavery and transported across the desert to Egypt. However, there, his enslaver notices his genius and tutors him in the Qur'an and Islamic philosophy. He becomes a prodigy in Egypt, but he longs to return to western Africa to reconnect with his mother. After a long journey and many adventures, he does so, and then eventually he opens a school in the country of his origin. His school becomes famous in western Africa as a center of Islamic learning, and indeed the movie opens with a shot of travelers making a pilgrimage to experience Shaihu Umar's wisdom. It is their visit that prompts Shaihu Umar to begin telling his story. Comparing this film to such films as *Sankofa* and *West Indies*, we might ask whether it

---

[17] The papers presented at the conference, including Sylvia Wynter's keynote address, are all included in *Symbolic Narratives/African Cinema*, edited by June Givanni.

offers an opportunity for a global or comparative view of the history of slavery, not one narrowly centered on the European trade.

A well-known work on the topic of comparative slavery is Orlando Patterson's magnum opus *Slavery and Social Death*. It analyzes data from sixty-six different "slave-holding societies," ranging from fifth-century Greece to the Saharan Tuareg in the 1960s, in order to assert the generalization that slavery is not essentially a property relation (as had been usually assumed), but is instead "the permanent, violent domination of natally alienated and generally dishonored persons" (Patterson 13). Patterson's general theory has been criticized both for not attending to the differences between different slave-holding societies and for not attending to the ways enslaved peoples maintained their sociality in spite of the condition thrust upon them. The film *Shaihu Umar* could be read in comparison with other films about slavery to test Patterson's hypothesis. The imaginative desire of the film is for Shaihu Umar to reconnect with his mother and his community from whom he was "natally alienated." Does the representation of this desire as a fantastic, improbable adventure agree with Patterson's hypothesis about natal alienation, or does Shaihu Umar's reconnection with his mother and achievement of social status in Egypt disagree with Patterson's concept of social death?

In addition to this theoretical conversation about whether Indigenous African slavery and trans-Saharan slavery functioned in the same way as transatlantic slavery, there were also practical political questions for African leaders and filmmakers at the time of the movie's production in the 1970s. One question concerns who is included in the Pan-African idea and its institutions such as the recently formed African Union, alongside the question of how the cultural relationship between northern Africa and sub-Saharan Africa should be conceptualized. For filmmakers, these questions might also implicitly raise the issue of whether the Pan-African film festivals were for all of Africa, or just for sub-Saharan Africa. Perhaps the film *Shaihu Umar*'s answer to that question was to explore connections across the Sahara and invoke a non-western metanarrative of history to potentially share across the continent.

However, it is not enough to simply observe that *Shaihu Umar* decenters the Eurocentric metanarrative of world history by replacing it with the Islamic one of the Sahel region of Africa. Certainly, many films could self-consciously represent an alternative metanarrative of a specific ethnic, regional, or religious view of history. But doing so assumes that cultures exist in isolation from each other, an assumption that Wynter, Fanon, and others all reject. Therefore, in answer to the question of African cinema's relation to the West, Sylvia Wynter takes her deconstruction of history further to argue that even the western ontology of the "human" is constructed by means of its *other*. She is critical of Hollywood movies about slavery and about the subjection of Black people as mere spectacles of an "otherness"—the "slave" and stateless Black person as a construct against which the "West" defines itself and through which it hypocritically claims its universal humanity. Just as Fanon critiques the false choice of European versus African traditions and instead proposes the project of creating a "new man," so too Wynter likewise critiques the notion of the "human" as a western notion constructed in relation to an African "other." Therefore, the role of African cinema is to culturally construct a new African ontology of the human that deconstructs and decenters the western sense of the "human." What this might actually look like in practice is not clear in Wynter's theoretical argument, but one of the films she focuses on as an exemplary case is Sembene's *Ceddo*, where she notes that the Ceddo are "defined in terms of alterity"—neither Christian, nor Muslim, but faithful to their African spirituality and a different sense of memory (Givanni 40). Here, Wynter echoes Clyde Taylor's argument that Sembene's *Ceddo* is an exemplary work of Third Cinema and "Afro-modernity" because it "rejects simple, dualistic dialectics" (that is, between West and African, or between Christian and Muslim), by instead presenting "social interaction as simultaneous struggle among many competing sources of domination" (Taylor 106). In other words, in contrast to the linear narrative temporality typical of Hollywood cinema where the otherness of the enslaved subject must be reincorporated into the nation state, Sembene's film is a dialogic encounter with the state-less to reconfigure our sense of human possibility.

Wynter's and Taylor's arguments about the "state-less" Ceddo and the importance of films about slavery for Pan-Africanism and the Third Cinema movement can be compared to the final chapter of Saidiya Hartman's *Lose Your Mother* where she similarly explores the historical memory of "state-less" communities such as the *nyemase* and *grunshi* in Ghana (arguably similar to the Ceddo in Senegal that we see in Sembene's movie). In the final pages, after working through the complexities of historical memory and the silences in the archive, and after reflecting on the ambiguities of the African American connection to Africa, Hartman posits that the unfinished project of her book—a project that she implies may be perhaps unfinishable—is the recounting of the history of these state-less communities in a way that adequately connects their history to her own (Hartman 189, 219). Hartman ends her book with an open question and with an unfinished project. In contrast, instead of hoping to make that historical connection, Wynter questions the metanarrative that undergirds that history. Wynter proposes that cinema may be the art form best suited to creating a new African ontology of what it means to be human and for fostering what Teshome Gabriel defined as an alternative "popular memory" of world history that informs that sense of our shared humanity.

Arguably, one thing that is significant here is that in conversations about what an African film language could contribute to a Pan-African understanding of world history and what it means to be human, the film chosen to think with is Sembene's *Ceddo*, a film not about the centers of African culture, but instead about its margins. For Sembene, as for Wynter, this was a film meant to provoke questions about what the future of a just and equitable African people could become and how a "popular memory" of the past might inform that future. The same could be said about the other films I have discussed here. It is perhaps also significant that the two most important films coming from Nigeria in the 1970s at the birth of its film industry—*Black Goddess* and *Shaihu Umar*—both aim to rethink African society and what it means to be human by investigating the long historical view of slavery. Along with *Sankofa*, *West Indies*, *I Is a Long Memoried Woman*, and *Testament*, these films eschew the American and Eurocentric conceptions of history and instead open up the possibility for an alternative cultural dynamic that (the filmmakers hoped) would inspire transnational solidarity in resistance to the neocolonial forces of global capitalism that (they feared) would re-enslave their communities.

Works Cited

Akomfrah, John, director. *Testament*. Black Audio Film Collective, 1988.
Alcocer, Rudyard J. et al, editors. *Celluloid Chains: Slavery in the Americas through Film*. U of Tennessee P, 2018.
Bakari, Imruh, and Mbye Cham, editors. *African Experiences of Cinema*. British Film Institute, 1996.
Balogun, Françoise. *The Cinema in Nigeria*. Delta Publications, 1987.
Balogun, Ola, director. *A Deusa Negra/Black Goddess*. Afrocult Foundation and Embrafilme, 1978.
Baum, Robert. "Tradition and Resistance in Ousmane Sembene's films *Emitai* and *Ceddo*." *Black and White in Colour: African History on Screen*, edited by Vivian Bickford-Smith et al. Ohio UP, 2007, pp. 41–58.
Berrian, Brenda F. "*Manu Dibango* and *Ceddo*'s Transatlantic Soundscape." *Focus on African Films*, edited by Françoise Pfaff. Indiana UP, 2004, pp. 143–55.
Bodnar, John. *Remaking America: Public Memory, Commemoration, and Patriotism in the Twentieth Century*. Princton UP, 1992.

Boughedir, Férid. "The Pan-African Cinema Movement: Achievements, Misfortunes, and Failures (1969–2020)." *Black Camera*, vol. 12, no. 2 (2021), pp. 236–56.

Brathwaite, Edward Kamau. "The African Presence in Caribbean Literature." *Slavery, Colonialism, and Racism*, edited by Sidney M. Mintz. W.W. Norton, 1974, pp. 73–109.

Busia, Abena P.A. "Long Memory and Survival: Dramatizing the Arrivants Trilogy." *World Literature Today*, vol. 68, no. 4 (1994), pp. 741–6.

Cabral, Amilcar. *Return to the Source: Selected Speeches of Amilcar Cabral*. African Information Service and Monthly Review Press, 1973.

Campbell, Edward D.C., Jr. *The Celluloid South: Hollywood and the Southern Myth*. Knoxville: U of Tennessee P, 1981.

Colvin, Lucie Gallistel. "Islam and the State of Kajoor: A Case of Successful Resistance to Jihad." *Journal of African History*, vol. 15, no. 4 (1974), pp. 587–606.

Cripps, Thomas. *Slow Fade to Black: The Negro in American Film, 1900–1942*. New York: Oxford UP, 1977.

Dash, Julie, bell hooks, and Toni Cade Bambara. *Daughters of the Dust: The Making of an African American Woman's Film*. The New Press, 1992.

Davis, Natalie Zemon. *Slaves on Screen: Film and Historical Vision*. Harvard UP, 2000.

Diawara, Manthia. *African Cinema: Politics and Culture*. Indiana UP, 1992.

———. *African Film: New Forms of Aesthetics and Politics*. Prestel, 2010.

Diouf, Mamadou. "History and Actuality in Ousmane Sembene's *Ceddo* and Djibril Diop Mambety's *Hyenas*." *African Experiences of Cinema*, edited by Imruh Bakari and Mbye Cham. British Film Institute, 1996, pp. 239–51.

Field, Allyson Nadia et al., editors. *L.A. Rebellion: Creating a New Black Cinema*. U of California P, 2015.

Gabriel, Teshome. *Third Cinema and the Third World: The Aesthetics of Liberation*. UMI Research Press, 1982.

———. "Third Cinema as Guardian of Popular Memory: Towards a Third Aesthetics." *Questions of Third Cinema*, edited by Jim Pines and Paul Willemen. British Film Institute, 1989, pp. 53–64.

Gemery, Henry A., and Jan S. Hogendorn, editors. *The Uncommon Market: Essays in the Economic History of the Atlantic Slave Trade*. Academic Press, 1979.

Gerima, Haile. "Master Class with Haile Gerima." New York African Film Festival, Lincoln Center, May 14, 2022.

Gerima, Haile, director. *Sankofa*. Mypheduh Films, 1993.

Getachew, Adom. *Worldmaking after Empire: The Rise and Fall of Self-Determination*. Princeton UP, 2019.

Givanni, June, editor. *Symbolic Narratives/African Cinema: Audiences, Theory and the Moving Image*. British Film Institute, 2001.

Halilu, Adamu, director. *Shaihu Umar*. Federal Ministry of Information, Nigeria, 1976.

Hartman, Saidiya. *Lose Your Mother: A Journey along the Atlantic Slave Route*. Farrar, Straus and Giroux, 2007.

Haynes, Jonathan. "Nigerian Cinema: Structural Adjustments." *African Cinema: Post-Colonial and Feminist Readings*, edited by Kenneth Harrow. Africa World Press, 1999, pp. 143–75.

Hondo, Med, director. *West Indies ou les Nègres marrons de la liberté/West Indies: The Fugitive Slaves of Liberty*. Les Films Soleil O, 1979.

hooks, bell. *Reel to Real*. Routledge, 1996.

Jackson, John Jr. "Decolonizing the Filmic Mind: An Interview with Haile Gerima." *Callaloo*, vol. 33, no. 1 (2010), pp. 25–36.

Kandé, Sylvie. "Look Homeward, Angel. Maroons and Mulattoes in Haile Gerima's *Sankofa*." *African Cinema: Post-Colonial and Feminist Readings*, edited by Kenneth Harrow. Africa World Press, 1999, pp. 89–114.

Kindem, Gorham, and Martha Steele. "*Emitai* and *Ceddo*: Women in Sembene's Films." *Jump Cut*, no. 36 (1991), pp. 52–60, https://www.ejumpcut.org/archive/onlinessays/JC36folder/Emitai-Ceddo.html (last accessed November 15, 2024).

Lindo, Karen. "Ousmane Sembene's Hall of Men: (En)Gendering Everyday Heroism." *Research in African Literatures*, vol. 41, no. 4 (2010), pp. 109–24.

Markovitz, Irving Leonard. "Traditional Social Structure, the Islamic Brotherhoods, and Political Development in Senegal." *The Journal of Modern African Studies*, 8, no. 1 (1970), pp. 73–96.

Mpoyi-Buatu, Thomas. "Sembene Ousmane's Ceddo & Med Hondo's West Indies." *Film and Politics in the Third World*, edited by John D.H. Downing. Atonomedia, 1987, pp. 55–67.

Mudimbe, V.Y. *The Idea of Africa*. Indiana UP, 1994.

Nichols, Grace. *I Is a Long Memoried Woman*. Karnak House, 1983.

Patterson, Orlando. *Slavery and Social Death: A Comparative Study*. Harvard UP, 1982.

Pfaff, Françoise. *Twenty-five Black African Filmmakers: A Critical Study, with Filmography and Bio-Bibliography*. Greenwood Press, 1988.

Pines, Jim, and Paul Willemen, editors. *Questions of Third Cinema*. British Film Institute, 1989.

Reid, Mark. "Haile Gerima: 'Sacred Shield of Culture.'" *Contemporary American Independent Film: From the Margins to the Mainstream*, edited by Chris Holmlund and Justin Wyatt. Routledge, 2005, pp. 141–53.

Rex, Cathy, and Shevaun E. Watson, editors. *Public Memory, Race, and Heritage Tourism of Early America*. Routledge, 2022.

Sanches, Manuela Ribeiro. "Memory, Authenticity, and (the Absence of) Ruins: Resonances between Werner Herzog and John Akomfrah." *Black Camera*, vol. 6, no. 2 (2015), pp. 94–111.

Searing, James F. "Aristocrats, Slaves, and Peasants: Power and Dependency in the Wolof States, 1700–1850." *The International Journal of African Historical Studies*, vol. 21, no. 3 (1988), pp. 475–503.

Sembene, Ousmane, director. *Ceddo*. Filmi Domirev, 1977.

Solomon, Frances-Anne, director. *I Is a Long Memoried Woman*. Leda Serene Films, 1990.

Swaminathan, Srividhya, and Steven W. Thomas, editors. *The Cinematic Eighteenth Century: History, Culture, and Adaptation*. Routledge, 2018.

Taylor, Clyde. "Black Cinema in the Post-aesthetic Era." *Questions of Third Cinema*, edited by Jim Pines and Paul Willemen. British Film Institute, 1989, pp. 90–110.

Temple, Christel N. "The Emergence of *Sankofa* Practice in the United States: A Modern History." *Journal of Black Studies*, vol. 41, no. 1 (2010), 127–50.

Thomas, Douglas H. "The Lingeer's Jihad: Challenging a Male-Normative Reading of African History." *History in Africa*, vol. 48 (2021), pp. 309–36.

Thomas, Steven W. "Cinematic Slavery: A Genealogy of Film from 1903 to 2020." *Slavery, Memory and Literature*, edited by Mads Anders Baggesgaard et al. Forthcoming 2025.

———. "Where Is African Cinema in Hollywood?" *Africa Is a Country*, November 3, 2023, https://africasacountry.com/2023/11/where-is-african-cinema-in-hollywood (last accessed November 15, 2024).

Thornton, John. *Africa and Africans in the Making of the Atlantic World, 1400–1800*. Cambridge UP, 1992.

Turner, Diane, and Muata Kamdibe. "Haile Gerima: In Search of an Africana Cinema." *Journal of Black Studies*, vol. 38, no. 6 (2008), 968–91.

Ukadike, Nwachukwu Frank. *Black African Cinema*. U of California P, 1994.

———. "Reclaiming Images of Women in Films from Africa and the Black Diaspora." *Frontiers: A Journal of Women Studies*, vol. 15, no. 1 (1994), pp. 102–22.

———. *Questioning African Cinema: Conversations with Filmmakers*. U of Minnesota P, 2002.

Zelizer, Barbie. *Remembering to Forget: Holocaust Memory through the Camera's Eye*. U of Chicago P, 1998.

12

Epistolary Writing and the Afterlife of Letters from a Woman of Color

Lisa Vandenbossche

In February of 2019, a letter written by Meghan Markle to her father, Thomas Markle, appeared in a series of articles in both print and online versions of the British newspaper the *Daily Mail*. Written in the wake of her wedding on May 19, 2018 to Prince Harry in St George's Chapel at Windsor Castle in the United Kingdom, the letter embodies sentimental epistolary tropes. Markle writes that her father's actions have "broken [her] heart in a million pieces" and pleads with him to "please stop lying, please stop creating so much pain, please stop exploiting [her] relationship with [her] husband" and to "please allow [them] to live their lives in peace" (C. Parker). This handwritten letter traveled as a physical document first from the United Kingdom to the Americas, then as a digital replica back to the U.K., where it found its way into the *Daily Mail,* both in physical print and ephemeral online editions. Through this movement, the letter went from material reality to digital imprint as it journeyed across national boundaries, through time and space, transforming from personal correspondence between Meghan Markle and her father into public discourse when Thomas Markle gave the letter to the *Daily Mail* in order to further his own self-interests and rehabilitate his public image. The publication of the letter set off events that captured the attention of British and American audiences alike, as both the British and American press documented its appearance and the subsequent aftermath.

On September 29, 2019, Markle took legal action against Associated Newspapers Limited (the parent company of the *Daily Mail*), arguing that the letter was private correspondence that was not meant for public consumption. These events culminated in a series of decisions by the British High Court that included payment of an undisclosed amount for copyright infringement and a court-ordered acknowledgment of the case published in the *Daily Mail*. The High Court Approved Judgment illustrates the ways in which Meghan Markle's legal argument was grounded in dual claims of privacy and copyright, citing that:

> the Letter disclosed her intimate thoughts and feelings; these were personal matters, not matters of legitimate public interest; she enjoyed a reasonable expectation that the contents would remain private and not be published to the world at large by a national newspaper; the defendant's conduct in publishing the contents of the letter was a misuse of her private information. (Royal Courts 2)

Because the contents of the letter are personal, Markle contends that she had the expectation, in sending it, that they mattered only to her and the recipient (her father), and thus would not be published. In doing so, she argues (and the court agrees) that a person's intimate thoughts and feelings are not matters of public interest, even if the author in question is a public figure. Thoughts and feelings thus enjoy legal protection against being made public without the consent of the writer.

Public attention to the publication of the letter and subsequent legal aftermath is due largely to the fact that Markle's husband, HRH Prince Harry, Duke of Sussex, is fifth in the line of succession to the British throne, and to her position as a mixed-race American actress who married into the British royal family.[1] As such, it is tempting to dismiss these events as otherwise insignificant, save for the public appetite surrounding their famous actors. This chapter, however, argues that we understand these events as echoing a much longer tradition of legal and public discourse surrounding sentimental epistolary writing by mixed-race, American, female characters, a tradition with origins in British colonialism and American material culture. We often think of these issues as being unique to our modern digital moment in which information moves through liminal spaces, challenging perceived control over narrative structure, authorial intention, and permanence. Linking the Markle court case with the anonymous 1808 novel *The Woman of Colour: A Tale*, however, calls attention to the ways in which these seemingly disparate geographic and temporal examples echo earlier questions of privacy, control, and even racialized difference that is inherent in the epistolary form.

---

[1] On March 31, 2021, Harry and Meghan stepped down as working royals and gave up their His/Her Royal Highness titles; however, Harry still remains fifth in line to the throne.

For those who study eighteenth-century writing, these events raise issues of privacy and gendered, racialized modesty tropes that reverberate across time and space, marking an ever-present past. Here I build on work done by Michael Warner, Susan Whyman, and Rachel Scarborough King, who trace the long history of letter writing into our present moment and modern media. Whyman and Warner both make convincing connections between letter writing and the rise of the novel in English and American literary traditions.[2] King more specifically offers a compelling argument for viewing the personal letter as a "bridge genre" that acts as "framing devices for communication across media" (6). King traces the evolution of the letter across the eighteenth century, arguing that in our modern, digital age "the letter has reemerged with a bridging function: in the form of email or text messaging, it has helped to normalize the global communications revolution in which constant connection is the assumed state of affairs" (18). Much as the letter worked as a frame device for early British novels, introducing readers to a new form of writing through a genre they were already familiar with reading, so too does the letter work as a frame device for the move from print to digital, offering a familiar form for reading content in a new medium.

While much has been made of the white, epistolary tradition in the eighteenth century as a driving force in the rise of the British novel,[3] far less attention has been paid to epistolary writing by Black women (real or fictional) in this same period. *The Woman of Colour* shares startling similarities with the contemporary echo that starts the chapter. Through a series of letters written by the fictional mixed-race heiress, Olivia Fairchild tells of her experience traveling from the Americas to England in order to marry her English cousin. After this marriage, it is revealed that her cousin is already married to a woman whom he thought dead. Upon her reappearance, Olivia is left a figurative "widow" who then returns to Jamaica to work as teacher and benefactress for the Black population—both enslaved and free. Like Markle, Olivia is the product of an interracial relationship between a Black woman and white man. Also, like Markle, Olivia's use of the epistolary genre becomes a means of framing the story

---

[2] Notably, these works focus largely on white letter writers, unlike the mixed-race Meghan Markle or Olivia Fairchild in *The Woman of Colour*.

[3] In *The Rise of the Novel*, Ian Watt views "familiar letter writing" as a "more unreserved expression of the writer's own private feelings" (176), and Michael McKeon in *The Origins of the English Novel* reads the epistolary form as a way of bringing realism and interiority into the novel form.

in her own voice, embodying the role of tragic mulatta, as readers become voyeurs into private correspondence that was ostensibly not written for public consumption, but has moved from domestic to public space upon publication. In language that is repeated in Markle's letter, Olivia's writing chronicles her growing disappointment in her father in the lead-up to her wedding and appeals to British legal systems that limit her power to act in her own interest.

In studying Markle's letter alongside *The Woman of Colour*, readers explore transhistorical connections in language, publication, and reception that draw these disparate examples into a single, epistolary tradition. Understanding these works as echoes of each other allows contemporary readers to see the ways in which modern discourse around celebrity, authorship, and privacy overlap with issues of race and gender that have roots in eighteenth-century writing and publication. Contemporary reactions to the publication of the letter and the subsequent court case offer readers critical insight into the very real prejudice faced by women of color—both past and present—who stray beyond the control of the white patriarchy in seeking to voice their own stories. When their private writings become public, Olivia and Markle are forced by editors to become bodies of public interest in service to the larger social good, often at a high personal cost to themselves. Thrust into roles as educators, their lives, and the narratives they tell about those lives, become the means by which audiences (both in the eighteenth and the twenty-first century) come to better understand the plight of marginalized, mixed-race women and are inspired to help lessen this plight. In exploring the ways in which these texts and their reception move from domestic to public space—at times against the wishes of those who author them—this chapter makes visible the often unseen and uncompensated labor that Olivia Fairchild, Meghan Markle, and countless women of color have been asked to do throughout time and continue to be asked to do to this day.

The Letter and High Court Judgment

Legal discourse around the Markle case centers on claims of privacy and copyright concerning the contents and publication of the letter, illustrating complex overlaps between transatlantic publication networks and contemporary legal systems. When Markle begins legal action against Associated Newspapers, she complains that "the Mail Articles involved a misuse of her private information, a breach of the defendant's duties under the data protection legislation, and an infringement of her copyright in the Letter" (Royal Courts 2). Markle's legal team argued that the letter was private correspondence that was not meant for public consumption. They contended that the letter "was correspondence about her private and family life, not her public profile or her work," and that, as the author of the letter, she held copyright over it and its contents (Royal Courts 2). Associated Newspapers denied these claims, countering that "the contents of the Letter were not private or confidential as alleged, and that the claimant had no reasonable expectation of privacy. Further or alternatively, any privacy interest she enjoyed was slight, and outweighed by the need to protect the rights of her father and the public at large" (Royal Courts 2). According to Associated Newspapers, Markle could not claim privacy because she had no expectation of it when she placed the handwritten letter in the mail to her father. Once received, the physical letter becomes the property of Thomas Markle, and Associated Newspapers' response maintains that Meghan Markle cannot claim privacy over her father's property. Furthermore, Associated Newspapers argues that the greater, public good outweighs the privacy claims of both parties. The act of physically placing the letter in the mail removes it (and in theory its contents) from the control of the sender. Associated Newspapers argues that the sender/creator thus relinquishes control over the content of the correspondence at the same time as they relinquish physical control of the material object.

Markle's legal team countered these claims by asserting claims of privacy and copyright. The court decision carefully takes readers through both of these threads in separate places in the decision. The privacy argument is framed in respect to content: "the Letter disclosed her intimate thoughts and feelings ... not matters of legitimate public interest; she enjoyed a reasonable expectation that the contents would remain private" (Royal Courts 2). While she may have given up physical control of the document upon mailing it, this does not mean that she gives up her right to privacy over the contents of the letter. The newspaper becomes an interloper into private thoughts as they move the contents of her writing from a private space to the public sphere upon publication, which exposes the thoughts and feelings to a reading audience for whom they were never intended. Copyright arguments run tandem with this argument and are articulated in terms of creation and ownership, rather than the relationship between letter writer and recipient. Markle's team contends "that the Letter is an original literary work in which copyright subsists ... and the Mail Articles infringed her copyright by reproducing in a material form, and issuing and communicating to the public, copies of a substantial part of the Electronic Draft and/ or the Letter" (Royal Courts 3). By this argument, Markle retains complete control over the letter—both in digital draft form and the material final document that was mailed to her father. Her copyright provides her, and her alone, the right to disseminate the information that is contained in the letter that she has created.[4] The epistolary form gives Markle control over its contents, and the personal, intimate nature of that unique creation of contents provides the letter with its right to privacy and copyright that the *Daily Mail* cannot violate in publication of the letter.

The High Court agreed with the statement of Markle's team, as events culminated in a series of decisions by the British High Court that included payment of an undisclosed amount for copyright infringement and a court-ordered acknowledgment of the case published in the *Daily Mail*. This "apology"[5] appeared on December 26, 2021, the day after Christmas, on the front page of the *Mail on Sunday*, directing readers to a short "article" inside the edition.[6] The message, scrolled along the bottom of the page, reads: "The Duchess of Sussex wins her legal case for copyright infringement against Associated Newspapers for articles published in *The Mail on Sunday* and posted on *Mail Online*—SEE PAGE 3" ("The Duchess of Sussex" 1). Inside the newspaper on page 3 there appears a small paragraph, under the header "The Duchess of Sussex," that acknowledges that the Duchess won her court case.[7] This blurb may seem like a small concession on behalf of the paper. It was in fact the least that they could do to meet the requirements that were laid out by the judgment. The significance is perhaps not the apology (or lack thereof), but rather the ruling

---

[4] While we typically think of copyright as being established by an author and their representatives through the formal publication of a work (often with a press), in court filings Markle's team argues that in this instance, copyright is established under the law by the nature of the contents of the work in question. The letter was never intended for press or publication, therefore that cannot be the basis of a copyright claim. The court documents refer to "the Letter" as a "unique literary work" and argue that copyright is conferred by this uniqueness. It is the originality (rather than its trip through a press) that "subsists" copyright and becomes the grounds for the High Court's requirement that Associated Newspapers Limited compensate the Duchess for violating her copyright.

[5] It has been characterized as an apology in various American and British news sources, yet the language itself simply acknowledges that the *Daily Mail* lost the court case, and never actually offers an apology for the publication of the letter itself.

[6] The date of December 26 is important in that it is Boxing Day in the United Kingdom. Printing the concession on a national holiday ensured that fewer people would be reading the newspaper on that day.

[7] The paragraph mentions the hearing and that the "[c]ourt found that Associated Newspapers infringed upon her copyright by publishing extracts of her handwritten letter" ("The Duchess of Sussex" 3).

itself that establishes Markle's right of ownership over her "thoughts and feelings" that cannot be made public without her consent. In doing so, the case upholds Markle's right to privacy because of the personal nature of the letter and the domestic ties between the letter writer and recipient. The private nature of the contents of the correspondence and the intimate and emotional relationship between Markle (writer) and her father (recipient), as proven through her writings to him and his texted responses to her and her husband, mean that the letter and its contents are not of enough public interest to allow for their being made available to a wider reading audience.

The Court of Public Opinion

The legal judgment handed down by the High Court is based on *content* and *use* of the letter in question. Conversely, public discourse in the aftermath of the publication and court case has focused on the *character* of its mixed-race author and her *intent* in writing the letter, illustrating complex overlaps between authorial intention and reception that are raised when private correspondence becomes public consumption. While the case might have been decided in favor of Markle in the courts, the court of public opinion remains more divided. In newspapers and on social media, countless news articles, online blogs, posts in public forums, and comment sections question if Markle, under the guise of private correspondence, created the original letter to draw attention to herself in order to gain public attention.

Much of the outcry around Markle's letter in British and American newspapers, gossip columns, and online sites like Reddit and Get Off My Internets centers on the intentionality of publication and the nerve of Markle to try to control the public discourse surrounding her and her family. Anonymous posters on these sites and others assert that Markle wrote and sent the letter with the intention of it being published, as a way of framing the story of her relationship between her and her father without the appearance of directly doing so. Several posters are upset about the calculations they think she made in order to get the letter published, calling her "manipulative" and referring to her as a "monster" (Lilithsarry). These posters are typically appalled that Markle is "calculating every word, every maneuver to cut the most against her daddy" (Lilthisarry). Interestingly, posters appear most disgruntled by the idea that Markle had the audacity to attempt to assert narrative control over the public recounting of her domestic, family affairs that was playing out in the media at the time. The assumption is often that "she wanted him to leak it so that she could cut him off " (savingrain). It is not the contents of the letter itself that these posters take exception to, but rather the assumption that the letter was written so that it might be intentionally leaked as a way of Markle controlling news publications about her and her relationship with her family. In this pushback, Markle is not the dutiful daughter that women are expected to be to their parents; she is a maneuvering "monster" whose actions are all the more horrible because they are directed at a white, male member of her family.

Markle's perceived ability to manipulate the narrative around her family is obvious to readers because of the materiality of the letter. A common thread in these posts focuses on the fact that the letter was handwritten, and not electronic, as evidence for intentionality and dishonor. Some posters are quick to point out that they were not fooled by her acting and "knew [when they] saw the numbers and the faux calligraphy that this was meant for public viewing" (GoldieLox9). Another poster contends that she "WANTED it to be leaked! So she gave legitimacy to the letter with her handwriting ... [because] she wanted the world to know how 'terrible' her father was" (eyenation). A third poster wonders, "if it was a 'personal and private letter,' [sic] why did she write it in her fauxligraphy? Especially with it so long?" (redseaaquamarine). For these commentators, Markle's guilt is proven by the genre that she uses and the materials with which she composes. These statements assume that the epistolary form, handwritten in cursive on physical paper, is intentionally used to further the manipulations of the letter writer, and it is this form that both enables the deceit and (to a careful, critical eye) exposes that deceit.[8]

This concern with control and authorial intent raises larger questions about the epistolary tradition and contradictions inherent in the genre that have a long history. Contemporary critics of the Duchess view Markle's ability (or at least attempt) to control the public perception of her domestic affairs through the use of letter writing as a bait and switch. They argue that she is using the rhetoric of privacy inherent in our modern understanding of the personal, handwritten letter to gesture toward privacy, while committing thoughts and feelings into a portable, permeant form that is able to be "leaked" for public consumption. Without realizing it, these detractors are pointing to a contradiction that is inherent to the epistolary form itself. Historically for writers, especially those who are often disenfranchised, or for narrators who are presented as such, this contradiction is the appeal of the form. It is the form of a letter, specifically a domestic letter between

---

[8] This argument also then assumes that these anonymous posters (and those who agree with them) are the only ones who are able to read and interpret Markle's choices correctly.

close confidants, which allows its author to address their audience directly, often with the stated expectation (whether genuine or not) of private reading and reception.

Privacy, Narrative Control, and *The Woman of Colour*

In the eighteenth century, letter writing moves from public business and governmental transactions, often performed by male secretaries and agents, to a writing trope increasingly defined by sentimentalized language of the heart and emotions of female writers who poured out domestic concerns for a close and personal confidant.[9] This reconceptualizing of the form was both encouraged and (in part) facilitated by eighteenth-century conduct books. As the novel gained prominence as a form, epistolary structure allowed fictional female letter writers to evoke modesty tropes and the assumption of privacy, while simultaneously committing to print the narration of private thoughts and feelings, along with personal histories. The form bestows a power upon the writer, along with presumed control over both the contents and the dissemination of those contents. The authors of letters in these novels and in non-fiction collections and published pamphlets are able to frame their stories directly for readers, allowing readers access to an interiority of the letter writer turned main character, whether that reader is the one intended by the letter writer or not.

The Woman of Colour capitalizes on the opportunities afforded by this epistolary form to give interiority to a mixed-race heroine, allowing English and American readers insight into an experience they otherwise would never gain, framed through domestic correspondence between the main letter writer (Olivia) and her governess (Mrs. Milbanke). In the novel, Olivia's eighteenth-century frustrations and sentiments echo Markle's twenty-first-century ones. Olivia's vexations with her father begin with his will, his interference in her domestic happiness, and her upcoming, arranged marriage. She evokes the sentimental as she laments:

> I see the generous intention of my father's will; I see that he meant at once to secure to his child a proper protector in a husband, and to place her far from scenes which were daily hurting her sensibility and the

---

[9] For more information on the long history of sentimental language and the increasing gendered dynamics of letter writing, see Janet Todd, *Sensibility: An Introduction*, and Elizabeth Heckendorn Cook, *Epistolary Bodies: Gender and Genre in the Eighteenth-Century Republic of Letters*.

pride of human nature! But ah! Respected Mrs. Milbanke! In guarding against these evils may he not have opened the way to those that are still more dangerous for your poor Olivia? (Anonymous 55)

In an effort to protect his mulatta child, the daughter of a woman who was once enslaved by him, Olivia's father uses British law to tie her inheritance to the stipulation that she marry her cousin. If she does marry her cousin, she will inherit her father's estate. If she chooses not to marry Augustus (or perhaps even more problematically, should he decide not to marry her), her fortune will revert to her father's brother and then his oldest son, of whom Olivia will become ward. Against her own wishes, Olivia is provided a new husband in a new land, as her father uses the British legal system surrounding inheritance to force her from Jamaica to England.

Time and time again, Olivia draws the reader's attention to the unusual form of her narrative, evoking both her act of writing and the transatlantic distance that produces it, regularly opening and ending letters with an emotional appeal to her recipient: "Mrs. Milbanke, I yet behold your tearful eye – I yet hear your fond adieu – I yet feel your fervent embrace! The recollection is almost insupportable; for the present, I lay down my pen!" (56). Or later as her emotions get the best of her, Olivia laments that she "feared that you would never again see the hand-writing of your Olivia. – I have feared that the attempt to portray my tale of sorrow would unnerve my brain" (136). Through the sentimental appeals of the letters, the novel draws attention to its own materiality. It reminds readers of the distance between the writer and the recipient of these letters, while simultaneously reinforcing the fact that readers are not the audience meant to bear witness to Olivia's passions. Referencing "hand-writing" evokes the physical object of the letter, both as Olivia strains to commit her emotions to paper by writing them down, and as she relinquishes control over the material documentation of her distress, when she sends the paper across the Atlantic in the hands of strangers. References to physical contact with Mrs. Milbanke highlight the missing physical relationship and oral communication for which the letter is standing in. Olivia's handwritten missives allow her to continue to feel the "fervent embrace[s]" of her friend who resides across the vast Atlantic space that the physical document will have to traverse in the absence of its writer.

It is the involuntary migration and distance between Jamaica and England that forces the epistolary structure, as Olivia's moving away from Mrs. Milbanke requires a written (rather than oral) correspondence. Olivia's correspondence takes shape over the course of the series of letters that she writes—first on the ship from Jamaica to England and later in various locations in England. She sends these letters back in packets, a unique form necessitated by transatlantic travel and the schedule of the ships that maintain it, which is outlined in detail by both Deven Parker in her article on precarity and correspondence in the novel and Lyndon Dominique in his introduction to the Broadview edition of the text. Unlike continental postal systems in which mail was picked up at regular intervals, the packet system required ships to transport letters across ocean spaces. Correspondents like Mrs. Milbanke and Olivia were forced to send their letters according to ship scheduling. Writers would leave letters "open," adding to them as time allowed, sealing them in time to deliver them to the departing ships. As a result, Olivia's narrative is chunked into a series of letters that conclude at irregular intervals, causing starts and stops along the way for readers. Letters are left in "continuation" until they are hurriedly concluded in order to make a departing ship. At times, the narrative starts and stops, leaving temporal gaps based around ships' schedules. Letters chronicling Olivia's disappointments along her journey to England, through marriage, its disillusion, and her embarking for a return to Jamaica, are then grouped into packets and sent to her governess, Mrs. Milbanke. As interlopers into the correspondence, readers get the narrative in the same irregular groupings.

As Olivia moves across the ocean and through English society, so too do the "intimate thoughts and feelings" about her reception as a mixed-raced woman in England and her hopes and dreams for acceptance in her new land and love in her new marriage. These written documents move in the opposite direction to Olivia, first from England to Jamaica and then back to England, in edited copy for publication. Yet, it is not Mrs. Milbanke, the absent governess, but rather us as readers who sit in as Olivia's audience. As Olivia imagines the physical presence of the "tearful eye" and "fervent embrace" of her missing friend, her emotions are poured out to us, a public reading audience, rather than being read by that friend (56). As the appended, imaginary dialogue "between the editor and a friend" at the end of the text tells readers, the letters have been formatted by the editor for "publication." As such, readers become voyeurs in this domestic correspondence. Olivia's letters are removed from their original audience and their original (albeit fictional) intentions. By the time we read them, the private letters have been made public to us, and in doing so, we (a reading public) invade the original private, domestic correspondence, much like the *Daily Mail* will centuries later invade Markle's letter to her father. Readers become voyeurs into this domestic relationship.

I am certainly not the first to suggest that the development of the narrative reflects Olivia's increasing control over her person and her story, as she elects to remain unmarried and return to her native country of Jamaica by novel's end. Victoria Barnett-Woods in particular offers a convincing analysis that suggests Olivia's return to Jamaica "maintains the difficult balance of feminine self-restraint and agentive thought" that is found throughout the work, as "her new self-declared social position as a 'widow,' frees her from the stipulations of her father's will" (622).[10] In tracing the history of transatlantic mail, however, Deven Parker argues that the material conditions of the packet system and the presence of an often-absent editor who interjects into the narrative at intervals, destabilizes the novel's form and complicates both the ending and the authority of its narrator, Olivia.[11] While Parker convincingly shows the ways in which these physical restrictions interrupt narrative continuity and a unified, unbroken plot line, I suggest that it is the letter frame that allows Olivia to speak directly to her audience, shaping her story's reception as she writes it.

In indulging the supposed requests of her friend for more information, Olivia structures her letters to include imagined reading preferences of her audience. As Rachael Scarborough King demonstrates, "the value of evoking letters was not primarily to trick readers into believing the texts were authentic or to disguise the author's true identity, but rather to guide readers on how to interpret this new kind of factious, ephemeral print" (King 9). And Olivia employs them for just this purpose. Time and again, Olivia references these preferences, writing things like: "You used to like my description of persons and characters as they struck my eye; and I the more readily indulge my pen in being minute. Yes! I will write what I think, my dear madam" (71). This scaffold allows her to tailor the content and structure of her narrative to meet the expectations of her readers, while she is simultaneously creating those expectations. In appealing to reading preferences, Olivia makes it seem as if she is responding to the expectations of readers. In reality, she is creating expectations, preparing us for the detailed character descriptions that we are about to wade through,

---

[10] This ending frees her from all obligations to marry and returns her inheritance back to her. Upon gaining the money, Olivia finds independence from white patriarchal control. She visibly asserts this independence in choosing to turn down an offer of marriage and return to Jamaica as a single woman intent upon using her education and fortune to better the lives of enslaved and free Black people in the colony.

[11] These interjections often reference missing letters, gaps in correspondence, and the difficulty of telling the full story of Olivia with missing documentation. The narrative reinforces the epistolary structure of the novel, as they draw a reader's attention to the physicality of the letter as a form.

conditioning our interactions with those she encounters throughout the text, and helping us to feel emotions alongside our heroine.

Just as Olivia draws her readers' attention to the epistolary form that she employs, she likewise seems to exert conscious control over the form as it is used by others. When her marriage to her cousin Augustus is proven fraudulent—because he is already married, and his first wife, who he assumed dead, reappears to reclaim her rightful place—the logistics of the deceit are confirmed through letters between Olivia and her sister-in-law that "produc[e] proofs of [the sister-in-law's] guilt" through written documentation of her crimes (169). It is through reading these letters that Olivia is able to understand the deceit that was perpetuated against her by those around her. The domestic correspondence of her sister-in-law provides evidence of the scheme and a narrative of how it unfolds. Olivia consciously does not include these letters in her own narration, telling Mrs. Milbanke, "[t]hese letters Augustus has transmitted for me for perusal. I cannot transcribe so black a scene of guilt! – neither can I transcribe Augustus's letter to myself" (169). Here readers hit the limit of the form as Olivia refuses to relinquish control over her narrative by transcribing the words of others. In refusing, Olivia firmly maintains control over the information that readers are privy to and does not give voice to those who sought to destroy her and her happiness. Readers are only able to gain insight into these characters, and their actions, through Olivia's narrative framing.

This private made public is a violation of the intimate thoughts of the letter writer; paradoxically, it is also how the author derives their power: over form, over narrative, and even over audience. The violation of privacy becomes the means of gaining agency, particularly for those who might not otherwise have it. This agency requires privilege, the privilege of an education that allows one to be able to write, and wealth that allows one the means to buy material objects to write on and with. Both Markle and Olivia enjoy this privilege, and it is (in part) this privilege that makes readers invested in each of their stories. Markle's court case is about being compensated for the agency that is wrested away from her by the *Daily Mail* when they moved her letter from private to public viewing without her consent. For Olivia, this move from private to public provides the means of retaking agency that is lost to her in her father's will and shaping the way that her readers understand the politics of race and gender in eighteenth-century England.

Narrating Racial Difference and *The Woman of Colour*

When her father requires in his will that Olivia travel to England to marry her cousin as a way of helping escape racial prejudice, readers recognize the miscalculation that he makes. Olivia's emotional response to imagining her reception in England in her early letters foreshadows the very real prejudice that her father should have anticipated she would face on the shores of England. Olivia writes from the ship that she "sometimes think[s], that had my dear parent left me in a decent competence, I could have placed myself in some tranquil nook of my native island and have been happily and usefully employed in meliorating the sorrows of the poor slaves who came within my reach . . . But my father willed it otherwise – Lie still, then, rebellious and repining heart" (56). Olivia's sentimental appeals to Mrs. Milbanke are also appeals to her absent father who has willed a future for her other than the one that she would choose for herself. While her father "meant at once to secure to his child a proper prosecutor in a husband, and to place her far from scenes which were daily hurting her sensibility and the pride of human nature," he underestimates Olivia's identification with who she terms her "kinsman" and the constant microaggressions—that at points become outright aggression—that she will face as a mixed-race woman in England (55). Olivia longs to make her home in Jamacia, at home with the "poor slaves" who might benefit from her religious instruction and benevolence, making her useful in ways that society will not allow her to be in England. Over the course of the novel, readers will see her go from dutiful daughter to disappointed wife to independent "widow," as she finally realizes the dream that she imagines in the first few pages.

Much of the analysis of the novel has thus rightly focused on questions of agency and autonomy as they intersect with race in Olivia's representations of herself, her reception in England, and her decision to return to Jamaica to "engage [her]self in ameliorating the situation, in instructing the minds – in mending the morals of our poor blacks," rather than marry and remain in England at the end of the narrative (188). Jennifer Reed notes that "Olivia Fairfield, the titular protagonist, is at once the stigmatized person, the source of the money, and the benevolent figure hoping to do good" (521). Olivia's mixed-race personage represents a conflict between the ideals of the white British lady who is celebrated in the homeland and the racial contamination of mixing of white and black blood in the colonies. Her colonial origins are literally written on her body through her mixed-race appearance. Lyndon Dominique views these contradictions as a triumph of representation for Olivia, reading the novel's epistolary form as one that "allows Olivia to control the way she represents her undeniably Negroid body" (*Imoinda's Shade* 248). Similarly, Melissa Adams-Campbell shows in her reconstructions of New World courtships that "Olivia's outsider position enables her to constantly compare and critique the supposedly more civilized British marriage system with the social norms of

Jamacia" (101). It is this position as outsider coupled with the epistolary form that positions Olivia to be a voice for colonial peoples, both as a representation of her race when she is in England and as a teacher and benefactress when she is back in Jamacia. From the onset of the novel, Olivia states her desire to return to her homeland, and fittingly the novel ends with her embarking on this very mission.

In the interim pages, Olivia documents for her friend Mrs. Milbanke her work in educating the people in England against racial prejudice. Time and time again, she serves as a model of superior education, superior reasoning skills, and superior religious morality for the characters who she encounters (and writes about) in England and for those of us interloping into her private, domestic correspondence. In making the private public, readers gain insight into Olivia's emotional response to acts of racial aggression that she encounters in England. If Olivia represents an "outside" position from which she is able to comment on these issues, through her private correspondence readers gain an inside view of racial prejudice in the homeland. According to the fictional "editor" of the work, this is why it is worth violating Olivia's privacy in publishing the letters. The editor says they choose to publish because "if [these pages] teach one *skeptical European* to look with a compassionate eye towards the *despised native of Africa* – then, whether Olivia Fairfield's be a *real* or an *imaginary* character, I shall not regret that I have edited the Letters of a *Woman of Colour!*" (189). The editor's argument is framed in terms of public interest, which Associated Newspapers Limited will similarly use to defend its actions in publishing a private letter by a mixed-race, female author two hundred years later.[12] The editor says that they do not regret making the contents of Olivia's letters public, because they have the potential to do public good. The knowledge contained in them is of public interest, as

---

[12] I am pointing here to the shared language between these two texts (separated by two hundred years) in defending the decision to publish. The sources each define "public interest" differently: both view public interest in terms of knowledge gained by readers. Associated Newspapers is suggesting that it is in the interest of the public to have knowledge of the inner workings of the British royal family, and publication of the letter is to further this knowledge and interest, not because it increases readers' sensibility for the plight of the mixed-race Markle, but because readers have a right to know the details of the lives of public figures like her. Markle notably is successful in arguing that access to the private correspondence of the royal family is not an actual "public interest." The editor of *The Woman of Colour* argues that knowledge of Olivia's life will improve the condition of peoples of African descent, which is in the interest of all peoples (i.e. the larger "public").

it might help readers to understand the plight of the mixed-race author and consequently be more sympathetic to all peoples of African descent. The fact that Olivia's private correspondence can do public good negates her right to privacy over them. As Olivia holds a mirror to the homeland, time and time again she is required to rise above race-baiting comments from both family and acquaintances in order to educate her readers about why these comments are a problem. In "teach[ing] one *skeptical European* to look with compassionate eye towards the *despised native of Africa*" (189), Olivia is forced to take on a tremendous amount of emotional labor on behalf of both the natives of Africa and white readers intruding into her personal correspondence.

Notably, two of the most significant instances of racial aggression happen in hallowed, British *domestic* spaces. The first takes place in the morning room as the family is relaxing at home, and Olivia's future nephew, George, is upset that Olivia's maid, the "nasty black woman[,] has been kissing me and dirtying my face" (78). It is not the physical contact that George is opposed to, but rather the contamination that he fears he will undergo from this contact because of Dido's race. George fears that the maid's blackness will rub off on him, making him "dirty" or impure and thus complicating his whiteness. Upon this outburst, Olivia is forced into the role of educator, teaching a lesson on religion and race as she explains, "the same God that made you made me . . . the poor black woman – the whole world – and every creature in it! . . . God chose it should be so, and we cannot make our skins white, any more than you can make yours black" (79). In showing the child that physical appearance cannot be transferred upon contact, Olivia makes an argument about racial contamination more generally. George's fear of contamination is proven false as Olivia shows that her blackness will not transfer to him. The threat is neutralized; her physical appearance will not impact his, and her very presence is one that is ordained by God. As Olivia evokes Christian religion, she shows how her color is a gift bestowed from the Creator that can (and should) coexist with George and his whiteness, even in England.

A second moment of overt racism takes place in an English ballroom— Olivia goes to pains to describe her first ball, because that is what she anticipates Mrs. Milbanke is interested in reading about. Olivia recounts (and thus relives) the painful events of the ball because "you will expect an account of the first English ball, which I have ever seen" (84). In educating Mrs. Milbanke about England, specifically the very British tradition of throwing and attending a ball, Olivia educates us as readers about racial prejudice within this institution. As she walks the ballroom, she notices that the men "eyed your Olivia, as if they had been admitted purposely to see the *untamed savage* at a shilling a piece" (85). While Olivia feels as if she is on display because her racial difference is marked on her face, it is those around her whose character she is making public for a reading audience. The men become the object to be dissected for readers, who are brought into sympathy with Olivia through her emotional appeals and sentimental language. We feel what she feels when she overhears two men eager to "have a stare at '*Gusty's* black princess,'" who then lament how much they "pity" Augustus because for them "one *hundred* thousand wouldn't be enough for the cursed sacrifice" of marrying Olivia (85). The epistolary form allows readers insight into this exchange through the eyes and emotions of Olivia. She narrates the events to Mrs. Milbanke as well as how they made her feel. Readers share disappointment along with Olivia and, as the novel progresses, we also join in her exhaustion in having to educate and re-educate those around her. As a mixed-race heroine, Olivia is forced to be exemplary in her actions, but it is in her thoughts where we can see the toll that this constant perfection takes on her.

As private descriptions of these experiences become public, Olivia's narrative offers readers insight into the "intimate thoughts" she has in reaction to constant provocation and the restraint that she is forced to exert to maintain her outward appearance of gentility. The private-made-public movement of the letters gives light to this larger struggle, bringing readers into a state of sympathy and understanding that otherwise might not have been possible. Olivia gains agency through the uncovering of her inner turmoil, as she articulates the impossible position she is put into as a mixed-race heiress without a firm place of belonging and with an identity in constant flux depending on social and geographic context. When her letters move from the domestic space to publication and then into public discourse, Olivia is able to use descriptions of the domestic to shape that same discourse. The domestic becomes the means of reaching and then shaping public perceptions of what we consider today to be political discourse—or at least identity politics.

These identity politics are made even more visible by the ending of the novel, when Olivia chooses to take her inheritance and return to Jamaica with the intention of using her wealth and education to better the plight of those she considers her community (enslaved and free Black women, men, and children) in the colony. In doing so, she turns her back on England and the white patriarchy that has failed her there, despite its best attempt to assert power over her. In rejecting an offer of marriage from Mr. Honeywell (an eligible, white, British gentleman) in favor of returning to the Black community that she left behind, Olivia herself moves from domestic to public space. She is no longer the object of white patriarchal protection that would confine her within an English domestic circle. Instead, she becomes the embodiment of personal sacrifice and public service—an example that her readers might look up to as a model for themselves. Her and her narrative have both realized the aspirations of the novel's editor, serving the public interest for the greater good of all.

Returning to the case of Meghan Markle that began this chapter, readers see the ways in which questions of privacy and public interest raised by *The Woman of Colour* echo into contemporary discourse around women (specifically mixed-race women) and writing today. In her 2022 tell-all book on the modern British royal family, Tina Brown suggests "Meghan's arrival . . . required an amped-up press strategy. Because she was a divorcee, an American, a woman of mixed race, and an actress, there were too many angles that could generate media mischief" (405). Yet interestingly, it was Markle's decision to revive the handwritten epistolary form that caused a stir in the press large enough to precipitate legal action from the Duchess. It was not a new strategy but one with roots dating back to the eighteenth century, writing in a physical form and genre with which readers have long been familiar, that became a focal point for British and American readers in the aftermath of the royal wedding. In appealing to her father through sentimental language sent via handwritten mail, Markle was participating in a long tradition of epistolary writing that has captivated a reading public and as such turned the private into the public with the rise of print culture.

As one reads through online comments and news coverage of Markle's letter, its publication, and the court judgment, it is difficult not to be struck by the outrage that posters feel over perception that Markle might be trying to control the narrative through the intentional writing and publication of a letter to her father. This outrage is then coupled with the anger that this attempt at control produced in some of those who were following the case. The British royal family is famously private, rarely allowing the public an unscripted view into their domestic lives and working to control their image in the press. Brown explains, "the culture of the Palace press department is almost never to comment on personal matters relating to the family. According to another Palace source, Meghan was told, 'We don't comment on private matters. Deal with it'" (418). Whether intentional or not, the publication of Markle's letter is a moment in which readers get insight into the domestic lives of one of its members, as told by that member. Understanding the intense, hate-filled commentary directed toward

Markle upon the Associated Newspapers Limited's publication of her letter allows readers to better realize Markle's experience as a highly visible, mixed-race woman living in twenty-first-century England. In bringing this commentary into conversation with *The Woman of Colour*, the ways in which Markle's story serves the public interest become clearer—not as Associated Newspapers incorrectly suggests the publication of the letter does, but rather as Olivia's editor hopes the publication of Olivia's letters will do. Reading the letter and the commentary published in response to it sharpens our sensibility for the plight of the author—it makes readers feel for Markle herself and better appreciate the prejudice faced by those like her, so that we are compelled to help alleviate it.

This critical insight that readers gain comes at a high personal cost for Markle, whose lawsuit rightfully condemns the paper's disregard for her privacy and agency in publishing a private correspondence without permission. One must wonder, though, what is so wrong about being able to tell one's own story? Readers of *The Woman of Colour* celebrate Olivia's attempt to wrest authority and agency from those who would seek to control her, her fortune, and her voice. Modern critical readings of the text may not agree on how much agency Olivia is able to exert, but they all seem to approve of her desire to control the events around her and of the telling of those events. Contemporary, nineteenth-century reviews of the novel also approved of Olivia as heroine, lamenting that "the poor heroine does not get a husband, for she is made very much to deserve one" ("The British Critic" 257). Another review applauded her style as "easy and unaffected" and complimented the "useful aim and good principles of the novel," thus making it "deserving of [their] commendation" ("The Monthly Review" 258). As the Markle case illustrates, twenty-first-century readers are uncomfortable with even the perception of a mixed-race woman attempting to use print to control public opinion of her private affairs, even if it turns out that the perception is not based in reality. Eighteenth-century readers appear more sympathetic to the plight of a mixed-race American letter writer, but perhaps it is Olivia's decision to leave England and return to serve fellow African descendants in the Americas that helps endear her to those reading at home, as she works on behalf of the public interest. While we like to think of progress as linear, reading these two texts and their reception alongside each other complicates this narrative of advancement across time. Like Olivia, Markle's father fails to protect her, and Markle finds herself with few options in England. While Markle does ultimately marry her British gentleman, she brings him with her upon her return to the Americas, as they both embark on lives of public service there. One is left to wonder if Markle's similar decision to relinquish her place in the British royal family and to leave England with Harry and her (eventual) children in order to live a life of philanthropy in America will help make her more popular in the eyes of a critical reading public.

Works Cited

Adams-Campbell, Melissa. *New World Courtships: Transatlantic Alternatives to Companionate Marriage*. Dartmouth College Press, 2015.

Anonymous. *The Woman of Colour: A Tale*. 1808. Reprint. Edited by Lyndon J. Dominique. Broadview Press, 2007.

Barnett-Woods, Victoria. "Models of Morality: The Bildungsroman and Social Reform in *The Female American* and *The Woman of Colour*." *Women's Studies*, vol. 45 (2016), pp. 613–23.

Brown, Tina. *The Palace Papers: Inside the House of Windsor—the Truth and the Turmoil*. Crown, 2022.

Cook, Elizabeth Heckendorn. *Epistolary Bodies: Gender and Genre in the Eighteenth-Century Republic of Letters*. Standford UP, 1996.

Dominique, Lyndon J. "Introduction." *The Woman of Colour*, edited by Lyndon J. Dominique. Broadview Press, 2007, pp. 11–42.

———. *Imoinda's Shade: Marriage and the African Woman in Eighteenth-Century British Literature, 1759–1808*. Ohio State UP, 2020.

eyenation. "New ANL court update: Meghan Markle deliberately used the word 'Daddy' in letter to TM to 'Pull at the heartstrings of the public.'" Reddit, https://www.reddit.com/r/SaintMeghanMarkle/comments/qqt69z/new_anl_court_update_meghan_markle_deliberately/ (last accessed November 15, 2024).

GoldieLox9. "New ANL court update: Meghan Markle deliberately used the word 'Daddy' in letter to TM to 'Pull at the heartstrings of the public.'" Reddit, https://www.reddit.com/r/SaintMeghanMarkle/comments/qqt69z/new_anl_court_update_meghan_markle_deliberately/ (last accessed April 20, 2022).

King, Rachael Scarborough. *Writing to the World: Letters and the Origins of Modern Print Genres*. Johns Hopkins UP, 2018.

Lilthisarry. "New ANL court update: Meghan Markle deliberately used the word 'Daddy' in letter to TM to 'Pull at the heartstrings of the public.'" Reddit, https://www.reddit.com/r/SaintMeghanMarkle/comments/qqt69z/new_anl_court_update_meghan_markle_deliberately/ (last accessed November 15, 2024).

McKeon, Michael. *The Origins of the English Novel, 1600–1740*. Johns Hopkins UP, 2002.

Parker, Charlie. "TOP MARKS Meghan Markle's Letter in Full: Read Explosive Message Duchess of Sussex Sent to Her Dad." *The Sun*, February 10, 2019, https://www.thesun.co.uk/news/8396792/meghan-markle-letter-read-dad-thomas/ (last accessed November 15, 2024).

Parker, Deven M. "Precarious Correspondence in *The Woman of Colour*." *Essays in Romanticism*, vol. 27, no. 2 (2000), pp. 135–51.

redseaaquamarine. "New ANL court update: Meghan Markle deliberately used the word 'Daddy' in letter to TM to 'Pull at the heartstrings of the public.'" Reddit, https://www.reddit.com/r/SaintMeghanMarkle/comments/qqt69z/new_anl_court_update_meghan_markle_deliberately/ (last accessed November 15, 2024).

Reed, Jennifer. "Moving Fortunes: Caribbean Women's Marriage, Mobility, and Money in the Novel of Sentiment." *Eighteenth-Century Fiction*, vol. 3, no. 3 (2019), pp. 509–28.

Royal Courts of Justice. *Sussex v Associated Newspapers Ltd*. Case No. IL-2019-000110, 11 Feb. 2021, High Court of Justice Chancery Division Business and Property Courts Intellectual Property Lists. www.judiciary.uk/wp-content/uploads/2022/07/Sussex-v-Associated-News-judgment-021221.pdf (last accessed November 15, 2024).

savingrain. "New ANL court update: Meghan Markle deliberately used the word 'Daddy' in letter to TM to 'Pull at the heartstrings of the public.'" Reddit, https://www.reddit.com/r/SaintMeghanMarkle/comments/qqt69z/new_anl_court_update_meghan_markle_deliberately/ (last accessed November 15, 2024).

"The British Critic (March 1818)." *The Woman of Colour*. 1808. Reprint. Edited by Lyndon J. Dominique. Broadview Press, 2007, p. 257.

"The Duchess of Sussex Wins Her Legal Case for Copyright Infringement against Associated Newspapers." *The Mail on Sunday*, December 26, 2021, pp. 1–3.

"The Monthly Review (June 1810)." *The Woman of Colour*. 1808. Reprint. Edited by Lyndon J. Dominique. Broadview Press, 2007, p. 258.

Todd, Janet. *Sensibility: An Introduction*. Metheun, 1986.

Warner, Michael. *The Letters of the Republic: Publication and the Public Sphere in Eighteenth-Century America*. Harvard UP, 1992.

Watt, Ian. *The Rise of the Novel*. U of California P, 1957.

Whyman, Susan. *The Pen and the People: English Letter Writers, 1660–1800*. Oxford UP, 2009.

Index

Abigail (character in *Turn*), 161
accuracy, 10, 18–19, 109, 114–17, 119, 177–8, 207–8, 210
Adams, Abigail, 166–7, 204–5, 212, 216, 220
Adams, John, 182, 216
Adams, John Quincy, 177–8, 202–4, 206, 209, 211–14, 217, *218*, 220–1
Adekeye, Toyin Ibrahim, 296; *see also Bigger than Africa*
aesthetics, 4, 86, 286
affect, 10–12
African cinema, 20, 252, 280–308
Akomfrah, John, 285, 303, 308; *see also Testament*
Alea, Tomás Gutiérrez, 281; *see also The Last Supper*
Alvitre, Weshoyot, 28, 34–6, 40, 44, 46, 55
Amazing Grace, 284; *see also* Apted, Michael
Amistad, 284; *see also* Spielberg, Stephen
Anglo-Saxon supremacy *see* white supremacy
anachronism, 140, 208, 276, 291

analysis, 2–4, 16, 18–21, 166–8
cinematic, 282, 297
comparative, 138, 148
counterfactual, 66–7, 80
diachronic and synchronic, 161–2
André, Major John, 161
anti-racism, 9, 18
Apted, Michael, 284; *see also Amazing Grace*
archive, 12–15, 26, 33, 85, 88–9, 95, 98–9, 112, 252, 256, 260, 281–4, 287, 307; *see also* Taylor, Diana
artifact, 2, 7, 11–12, 18–21, 41, 98–103, 159, 207
assimilation, 26, 70, 75–6, 80, 293
Associated Newspapers Limited, 312, 315–17, 326, 330
Daily Mail, 312–13, 317, 322–4
Atlantic slave trade, 96, 99–100, 270, 282–4, 288–90, 305
authenticity, 9, 16, 19, 49, 109, 113–17, 120, 126–7, 207–10, 224, 228, 237–40, 323
authority, 19, 46, 80, 114–14, 123, 141, 151, 178, 226, 235, 261–5, 289, 323, 330

autonomy, 19, 256, 270, 325
  bodily, 109–10, 132–54
  political, 168–9

back thenness, 133–7, 154
Baker, Kyle, 26, 85–94, 98–105
Balogun, Ola, 280, 285, 291, 296–7, 301–5, 308; *see also Black Goddess / A Deusa Negra*
Banks, Emily Scott, 205, 210, 213–22
Baptism of Pocahontas (Chapman), 5–7, 17
Barker, Joanne, 49, 51–2, 59
Berry, John, 281; *see also Tamango*
Bible, 45, 92, 116
Bigger than Africa, 296; *see also* Adekeye, Toyin Ibrahim
Bishop, Bridget, 135
Black Death, 68, 88
Black Goddess / A Deusa Negra, 252, 280, 283, 295–8, 301, 308; *see also* Balogun, Ola
Bloody Bloody Andrew Jackson, 177, 180–1, 189–98
body, 100, 141, 145, 147, 156, 164, 264, 266, 272, 274–6, 325
  violation, 90–4, 98, 150
Bogost, Ian, 70
book banning, 2
Bradford, Dorothy May, 120
Bradford, William, 120, 124
Brake, Justin, 50–2
Brant, Joseph (Haudenosaunee), 64
Brathwaite, Edward Kamau, 286
"British Critic, The," 330
British High Court, 312–18
Brubaker, Jack, 38
Bush, George H.W., 162

Cabral, Amílcar, 297, 299–300
Candomblé, 296
Capitol Rotunda, 5–7
cartoon, 32, 44–5, 86–7
Ceddo, 252, 280, 283, 286–90, 295–7, 300–8; *see also* Sembene, Ousmane
center-periphery visualization, 170
Chapman, John Gadsby *see Baptism of Pocahontas*
Cheer, Philomena, 161
Chilling Adventures of Sabrina, The, 133, 138
Christianity, 30–2, 237, 287–91, 298, 307, 327
Circle Legacy Center, 35–6, 55
City Upon a Hill (Winthrop), 4, 229
Civil War, The, 177, 180, 185–90
Clay, Henry, 204, 211
Clinton, Bill, 185, 191
Clinton, Hillary, 193
Clinton-Lewinsky Scandal, 181, 185
Cobra Verde, 283, 302; *see also* Herzog, Werner
Colescott, Robert, 84
Collingwood, R.G., 10, 96–7
colonialism, 7, 26, 38, 47, 58–9, 254, 295, 301, 304, 313; *see also* settler colonialism
colonization, 6, 17, 28, 37, 66, 69–70, 76, 79, 98, 109, 112, 126, 254
comics, 34, 85, 98, 101
consent, 18–19, 109–10, 132–55, 313, 318, 324
  affirmative, 136, 150
  Consent on Campus see Freitas, Donna
  declarative, 144, 150

Conestoga, 18, 25, 27–47, 58–9
Confederacy (Southern), 186–8;
    see also Haudenosaunee
Constitution of the United States, 17,
    32, 65–6
Contrast, The, 178, 224, 226–7,
    233–8, 243–4
copyright, 312–17
Cornplanter (Seneca), 64–5, 74
Corwin, Jonathan, 143–5
counterfactual history, 18, 25–6,
    66–71, 76, 79–82
covert and overt messages, 161, 164–7
critical fabulation, 33, 85, 101
critical race theory, 2
critical thinking, 134, 168–9
Cromer, Michael and Penney Clark, 43
Crucible, The, 143, 204, 219; *see also*
    Miller, Arthur
Culper Spy Ring, 161, 164, 170
Cultural Studies, 4
culture wars, 159, 190

Daisy Miller, 224, 233, 238
Dash, Julie, 298–9
Debord, Guy, 88
Declaration of Independence, 86–7,
    182, 294
decolonization, 29, 70, 74, 79, 286
DEI (Diversity, Equity, and
    Inclusion), 158; *see also* diversity
Deloria, Philip J., 207
Democratic Party Convention, 237
descendant communities, 18
devil, 74, 135, 139, 144–5, 149–53
Diegues, Carlos, 295; *see also Quilombo*
Dickinson, John, 182–3
discomfort, 28, 110, 133–7, 158, 172,
    180, 192

Disney+, 181, 197
diversity, 121, 148, 211, 280; *see also*
    DEI (Diversity, Equity, and
    Inclusion)
divisive concepts laws, 12, 19, 110,
    158, 160, 163–5, 172
*Dobbs v. Jackson Women's Health
    Organization*, 157
Douglass, Frederick, 187, 204–5,
    211, 214–15, 220
Du Bois, W.E.B., 286, 292, 294
Duchess of Sussex, 317–19, 329
Duke of Sussex, 313
Dunbar, John Raine, 32
dye *see* indigo

education, 3, 19, 70, 88, 90, 110,
    157, 277, 324, 326, 328
    legislation, 158
    women, 162–4, 165, 168–9
Egypt, 305–6
Eliza Pinckney (book), 254, 258–62
Elmina castle, 302
embodiment, 13, 15, 143, 153,
    215–17, 256–7, 329
emplotment, 102
enslaved people, 14–15, 86–103, 161,
    186–7, 251–6, 260–5, 269–77,
    282–307, 314, 321, 328
epistolary, 20, 251–2, 312–31
Equiano, Olaudah, 92
erasure, 36–9, 51, 55, 109, 126–7,
    181, 268
Estes, Nick, 66, 74
Evans, Richard J., 67

Fanon, Frantz, 288, 297, 300, 304–7
fantasy, 69, 79, 103, 115, 269, 273,
    276

fear, 4, 126, 158, 285, 327
Fear Street Part Three: 1666, 14, 19, 110, 132–54
Fédération Panafricaine des Cinéastes (FEPACI), 295
Feldman, Alexander, 209–10
feminism, 33, 162, 165–8, 172, 181, 216, 280, 300
Ferguson, Niall, 67, 79–80
FESTAC, 295, 305
fiction, 4, 11, 25, 28, 46, 59, 66, 103, 115, 210, 223, 227–8, 241, 258, 277
  restorative, 37–9
Floyd, George, 181, 197
forgetting, 12–13, 178, 225
Fort Worth, 202–5, 211, 214, 216–20
Francis 4, Lee, 28, 34–7, 42, 46, 55
Franklin, Benjamin, 27, 31–2, 65–6, 182–3, 227–30, 234, 241, 243–4, 260
Freitas, Donna, 137, 142
Fuentes, Marisa, 13–15, 33, 284

Gabriel, Teshome, 15, 286, 290, 294, 300, 304, 308
gender
  discrimination, 153
  misogyny, 45, 153, 232
  norms, 271
  roles, 110, 126, 135, 139, 153, 157, 159, 162, 169–72
  social construction, 157, 160
  southern identity, 251, 254, 256, 263
  types, 161
Georgia (state), 158, 165
  standards, 166

Gerima, Haile, 280, 283, 285, 291, 297–9, 301, 303; *see also Sankofa*
Getachew, Adom, 294
Get Off My Internets, 318
Ghana, 280, 296–7, 302–3, 307
God, 134–5, 145, 162, 164, 229, 239, 327
Godbeer, Richard, 132, 138
Good, Sarah, 135–46, 152–3
Good News From New England, 117, 120, 126
graphic novel, 12–13, 18, 25, 27–9, 32–44, 58–9, 84–5, 89–90, 92, 98, 102, 159
Gray, Thomas, 85, 89–90, 94, 102
griot, 297
Grinde Jr., Donald A., 65–6, 69–70, 75, 81
Gulley, Alison, 137
Gumbrecht, Hans Ulrich, 10–11, 114

Halbwachs, Maurice *see* memory
Halilu, Adamu, 280, 283, 305; *see also Shaihu Umar*
Hall, Rebecca, 26, 85–6, 95–103
Hamilton, Alexander 179, 194–6
Hamilton: An American Musical, 2, 10, 179–82, 189, 193–8, 204
Handsome Lake (Seneca), 74–7, 81
Harrison, William Henry, 71
Hartman, Saidiya, 14–16, 33, 100, 102, 282, 284, 288, 299, 303, 307
Hathorne, John, 140
Haudenosaunee, 16, 18, 25–6, 64–82
Hemings, Sally, 196
Herzog, Werner, 283, 302; *see also Cobra Verde*

heteronormativity, 148, 152
hierarchy, 33, 84, 102, 244
  gendered, 123, 135, 145
  social, 134, 235, 241
Hirsch, Jennifer and Shamus Khan, 136
historical
  drama, 178, 202–21
  erasure, 18
  imagination, 95–8
history
  as family legend, 259
  as myth, 84, 126, 192, 228–9, 258–61
  sentimentalization of, 252, 258
  and recovery work, 219, 251–2, 256–8, 277–8
Hobbamock, 111, 120, 125–6
Hopkins, Elizabeth, 120–4
Hondo, Med, 280, 283, 285, 291, 293, 294, 301, 303; *see also West Indies: the Fugitive Slaves of Liberty / West Indies ou les Nègres marrons de la liberté*
hooks, bell, 301–1
hot takes, 140
Hunter, John Dunn, 71
hypermediacy, 16–17

identity, 9, 161, 267, 290, 298–300, 323
  African, 300
  Black, 281, 284
  communal, 8
  gender, 19, 123, 158
  Indigenous, 48–56, 79
  politics, 328
  racial, 8, 143, 145

US national (American), 126, 178, 194, 223–46
ideology, 125, 127, 226, 229, 235, 262
I Is a Long Memoried Woman, 280, 301, 308; *see also* Solomona, Frances-Ann
immediacy, 16, 153
imperialism, 5, 20, 69, 77, 88, 126
Indigenous temporality *see* temporal sovereignty
indigo, 14, 251, 254–78
Indigo Girl, The (book), 254, 268–70
insurrection, 5, 89, 91, 95
Iroquois *see* Haudenosaunee
Islam, 75, 287–90
Israel Potter, 178, 226–8, 238, 240–6

Jackson, Andrew, 177, 180–1, 189–93, 198, 204, 211, 220
Jamaica, 314, 321–8
James, Henry *see Daisy Miller*
January 6, 2021 *see* insurrection
jazz, 288, 290–1, 296
Jefferson, Thomas, 39, 86–7, 196
Johanson, Bruce E., 65–6, 69–70, 81
JQA (play), 19, 177–8, 202–21

Kaya, 120–6
Kierkegaard, Søren, 87

Landsberg, Alison, 9–12, 112, 114
Last Supper, The, 281; *see also* Alea, Tomás Gutiérrez
Lenape, 27–59, 73–4
  Center, 28
  federally recognized, 28, 34–5, 38, 46–8, 52–7

Lenape (*cont.*)
  homelands, 47–8, 52, 54
  internment in Philadelphia, 31
  language, 42
  oral tradition (origin story), 38, 41, 44, 58
  Treaty of Shackamaxon, 41–5
  Tribal Nations, consultation (collaboration) for *Ghost River*, 29, 33, 37–9, 46, 54–8
  Turtle Island, 35, 39–40, 69
  wampum belt, 35, 41–3, 59
  William Penn and Tamanend, 41
  worldview, 42, 46
Leroux, Darryl, 49, 51–2
lesson plan, 110, 117, 159, 163, 166–72
letter writing *see* epistolary
LGBTQ+ rights, 158
Lincoln, Abraham, 187–8, 204–5, 211, 216–17, 220
Lind, Heather, 162–3
lingeer, 289–90
literacy, 85, 92–3
Logan, James, 27
Longfellow, Henry Wadsworth, 112, 126
Lost Cause, 181, 188–9

McNeill, William H., 67
Mann, Charles C., 65–6, 70, 81
marginalization, 109, 148–9
Markle, Meghan, 15, 252–3, 312–20, 322, 324, 329–31
Marxism, 281, 304
masculinity, toxic, 150
Massasoit, 111–12, 124–6
Mayflower, 109, 111–17, 121, 126–7

Megill, Allan, 67–8, 82
media, 3, 20, 50, 56, 70, 111, 232
  mass, 4, 9–13, 112
  material, 7
  new (contemporary), 16–19, 93, 109, 149, 154, 170, 314
  social, 21, 31, 162–3, 318
  visual, 2, 133, 138
memory
  collective (communal), 8, 303
  cultural, 3, 28, 112, 208
  essentialist, 185, 197, 304
  historical, 11, 82, 177, 180–1, 185, 193, 197–8, 281, 291, 297, 302, 307
  individual, 8, 15, 93
  On Collective Memory (Halbwachs), 8–9
  prosthetic, 9–12, 112
  public, 2, 7–13, 19, 21, 177, 252, 281, 284, 291, 294
  sanitized, 118, 127
  studies, 2, 7–12, 15
  unsanitized, 109, 118, 126
Micciche, Laura R., 165, 167, 172
Middle Passage, 86, 90–1, 97, 101, 297, 301
Miller, Arthur, 143, 204, 219; *see also Crucible, The*
Miranda, Lin-Manuel, 179, 194–7, 204
misogyny, 45, 153, 232, 257, 264
mob, 30–1, 36, 149–51
Mohawk, 64; *see also* Haudenosaunee
"Monthly Review, The," 330
Morrison, Toni, 99, 101–2
motherhood, 126, 157, 301
Murray, Judith Sargent, 110, 159–60, 162–8, 170–1

narrative, 35, 38, 40–4, 58–9, 86–94, 100–3, 110, 118, 143–51, 188, 193–5, 227, 240, 252–6, 260, 271, 275, 291, 330
   control, 320–4, 329
   of nationhood, 18, 66, 180, 268
   structure, 307, 313
National Geographic, 11, 109, 113–14, 117–21, 127
Nees, Heidi L., 207–8
Neolin (Lenape), 73–4, 77, 81
Netter, Louis and Oliver Gruner, 41
Nichols, Grace, 280, 302
Nigeria, 280, 283, 295, 305, 308
Nixon, Richard, 179, 181, 184–5
Nkrumah, Kwame, 292, 294, 302–3
non-conformity, 135
non-federally recognized claims to Native identity, 48, 52–4

Obama, Barack, 179, 181, 189–91, 193–4, 196–7, 245
Onondaga, 35, 64–5, 80–1; *see also* Haudenosaunee
"On the Equality of the Sexes" *see* Murray, Judith Sargent
oppression, 43, 70, 101, 149, 178, 226, 261, 281
origin stories, 35, 39–41, 44, 109, 126
Ousamequin *see* Massasoit
overseers, 271–2, 298

Palin, Sarah, 190–1
pamphlet war, 28–33
Pan-African, 100, 252, 280–6, 289–97, 302–7
paratext, 85, 90

Parkman, Francis S., 71
patriarchy, 19, 120–1, 123, 125, 135, 139, 145, 149, 163, 251, 254, 315, 328–9
   scripts, 142
Patterson, Orlando, 306
pedagogy, 1–2, 13, 19, 109–10, 206
   feminist, 165–7, 172
Pence, Mike, 195
Penn, William, 30–1, 37, 41, 59
Persuasive Games, 70
Pilgrims, 16, 111–12, 116, 118, 126
Pinckney, Eliza, 14, 20, 251, 254–78
plantation
   depiction in fiction, 257, 263–74
   myth, 261
   slavery, 261, 275, 296, 297
Plantation Patriot, 262–8, 271–2
Plymouth, 16, 99, 109, 111–28
politics, 1–5, 10, 17, 70, 84, 190, 193–4, 303
   anti-colonial, 280, 291, 295
   colonialist, 15, 160
   contemporary, 179, 189, 290
   gender, 257, 276
   identity, 284, 328
   racial, 282, 324
   representational, 208
   revolutionary, 44
Pontiac (Odawa), 29, 71–4
popular culture, 2–4, 10–11, 43, 81, 98, 133, 135–7, 159–60, 164, 168–70, 224
Posner, Aaron, 177–8, 202–21
power dynamics, 3, 119, 126, 274
Prentice Hall Literature, 166–7
presentification *see* Gumbrecht, Hans Ulrich

print culture, 85, 102, 329
Prince Harry (HRH), 312–13, 331
procedural rhetoric, 66–71, 76, 78–82
PROMESA, 197
public sphere, 4, 10, 31, 316
Public Theater, The, 189, 193
Puerto Rico, 181, 197
Puritanism, 4, 19, 123, 134–5, 138–9, 141–2, 146, 148, 152–3, 228–9

queerness, 134, 146, 148, 150, 158
Quilombo, 295; *see also* Diegues, Carlos

race, 2, 7, 15, 18, 26, 84–103, 119, 143, 158, 187, 190–6, 212, 257–69, 313–30
race-conscious casting, 181, 194–5
race shifting *see* Sturm, Circe
rape *see* sexual assault
Reagan, Ronald, 191
Reddit, 318
Red Jacket *see* Sagoyewatha
Reising, Russell, 133–4
remediation, 16–18, 92–4
repertoire *see* Taylor, Diana
reproductive rights, 2, 110, 157, 159, 162
Rex, Cathy and Shevaun Watson, 7–8, 21, 284
Richter, Daniel K., 28
Ridner, Judith, 45
Rifkin, Mark, 42
Rinderle, Katie, 158
Rise of Silas Lapham, The, 224, 233, 238
Robinson, Kim Stanley, 25, 68; *see also* *Years of Rice and Salt, The* (novel)

Roe v. Wade 157; *see also* *Dobbs v. Jackson Women's Health Organization*
Rose, Alexander, 160
Russo, Stephanie, 208

Sagoyewatha (Seneca), 68, 72, 77, 79–80
Saints & Strangers, 11, 16, 19, 109, 113–28
Salem, 1, 15, 19, 110
  witch crisis, 132–54, 204
Sankofa, 252, 280, 282, 297, *299*, 300–1, 305, 308; *see also* Gerima, Haile
Satan *see* devil
scenario *see* Taylor, Diana
secondary schools, 19, 110, 156–7, 159, 165
Second Continental Congress, 179, 182
Sembene, Ousmane, 280, 285–6, *288*, 289–91, 294–5, 300–4, 308; *see also* *Ceddo*
Seneca, 35, 38, 64, 72, 74; *see also* Haudenosaunee
Senegal, 280, 286–7, 289–90, 307
Senghor, Leopold Sédar, 290
settler-colonialism, 2, 5, 7, 9, 16–18, 25–6, 29–30, 32–3, 37–59, 65, 69
settler (colonial) time (linear temporality), 42–4, 58
Seven Years' War, 29–30
sex and sexuality, 110, 137, 142
  assault, 14–15, 133, 135–7, 150, 153–4, 162, 298, 301
sex/gender scripts, 4, 141–3, 151, 157
Sex Education (AMC), 19, 110, 156–7, 172

INDEX

Shaihu Umar, 280, 283, 305–6; see also Halilu, Adamu
Sharpe, Christina, 86
Shawnee Prophet *see* Tenskwatawa
Shippen, Peggy, 161
signifyin(g), 92–3
Silverman, David J., 57
Six Nations *see* Haudenosaunee
slave
   market, 96, 274
   narrative, 17, 84, 92
   revolt, 95, 97, 293
   trade, 15, 17, 92, 95–6, 99–102, 270, 280–305
slavery, 5, 7, 14, 84–103, 186–9, 254–78
   and memory, 12
   and violence, 15, 20
   films about, 15, 280–308
slut-shaming, 141
Society of Early Americanists, 1, 28
Solomon, Frances-Ann, 280, 303; see also *I Is a Long Memoried Woman*
South Carolina, 14, 251, 254–77
sovereignty, 5, 18, 25, 28, 37–9, 43–58, 64–82
speculation, 116
Spielberg, Stephen, 284; see also *Amistad*
Stage West, 202, 210–12, 215–19
stereotypes, 43–4, 84, 88, 98, 113, 120–1, 127–8, 193, 207, 300
Stodola, Zabelle, 1
storytelling, restorative (regenerative), 18, 25, 28, 37–47, 55–9, 94
Strong, Anna, 110, 161–70
Sturm, Circe, 49, 51
subservience, 120, 123

Sugden, John, 71, 74
Sullivan's genocidal campaign, 64, 66, 68, 72, 82
superheroism, 85, 92
Supreme Court (SCOTUS), 157
survivance, 18, 44, 46, 57–8; see also Vizenor, Gerald
Sussex v Associated Newspapers Ltd., 315–18

taboo, 135, 276, 285
talking book, 17, 92–4
TallBear, Kim, 49, 52
Tamango, 281; see also Berry, John
Taylor, Diana, 13–14, 159
Tea Party, 190–1
Tecumseh (Shawnee), 71–3
temporal sovereignty, 43–4
Tenskwatawa (Shawnee), 73–7, 81
Testament, 280, 283, 302, 308; see also Akomfrah, John
Texas, 19, 202, 205–6, 214, 219–21
theology, 134, 298
Tisquantum, 111, 124
Tituba, 1, 135, 143–5, 152
Third Cinema, 15, 20, 252, 281–2, 286, 294, 300, 303–4, 307
Town Destroyer *see* Washington, George
transatlantic
   Black solidarity, 291, 301
   epistolarity, 253
   mail, 323
   methodology, 20
   publication, 315
   slave trade, 15, 99, 270, 280, 282, 284, 286, 289, 305–6
   travel, 322

transhistorical
  connections, 1, 14, 252, 315
  methodology, 20–1, 159
  nexus, 3, 12, 41
  reimagining, 2
trans-Sahara, 280, 289, 305–6
trauma
  historical, 16, 44, 101
  psychological, 5, 301–2
Treaty of Canadaigua, 72
Trefry, Kate, 146
Treuer, David, 80–1
Tribal
  consultation, 29, 33, 37, 39, 54–8
  presses, 56–7
  specificity, 39
  sovereignty and representation, 54
Trump, Donald, 178, 181, 193, 197, 214, 219, 226, 232, 237, 245
Tuck, Eve, 79
Turner, Nat, 26, 85, 88–2, 94, 98, 101–2
Turn: Washington's Spies (AMC), 19, 110, 159

Union (Civil War), 186–8
usable past, 2–3, 7, 281, 283, 285

Van Engen, Abram, 4
video game(s), 3, 11, 16, 18, 21, 25, 66–70, 79, 159–72
Vietnam War, 180–4
violence, 7, 14–15, 17, 20–1, 251–2, 291, 301
  gun, 212
  police, 86
  settler colonial, 2, 13, 30–1, 37, 41, 44–5, 48, 52, 58–9, 192

sexual (gendered), 134–7, 142, 148–50, 153–4
slavery and, 95, 99, 254–5, 258, 264–6, 271, 273, 298
visuality, 85, 90, 93–4
Vizenor, Gerald, 44

Walker, Kara, 87
Walking Purchase, 27
Wallace, Anthony F.C., 73
Wampanoag, 19, 35, 111, 118–23
War of 1812, 71, 73
Warpath Campaign (Total War computer game series), 11, 16, 25–6, 68–82
Warrior, Robert, 45–6
Washington, George, 64–6, 79, 161, 166, 179, 194, 212–13, 219, 267
Washington's Spies: The Story of America's First Spy Ring see Rose, Alexander
Weaver, Jace, 45–6
West Indies: the Fugitive Slaves of Liberty / West Indies ou les Nègres marrons de la liberté, 252, 280, 283, 291, *293*, 296–7, 301, 305, 308; see also Hondo, Med
Wheatley Peters, Phillis, 270
white supremacy, 4–5, 7, 89, 94, 100, 102, 181, 186, 192–3, 197
Whitman, Walt, 235, 238–9
Winslow, Edward, 120, 126
witchcraft, 19, 110, 132–42, 152–4, 204
  on TV and film, 110, 142–52

Womack, Craig, 39, 45–6, 48–9
Woman of Colour, The, 252, 313–15, 320, 324–6, 329–30
women
  body, 19–20, 132, 134–53
  enslavers, 260–4, 276–7
  leading slave revolts, 88, 95–100
  representation, 109–30, 156–72, 109, 111–27
  womanhood, 156–72
Woodhull, Abraham (Abe), 161, 164
Woodhull, Mary, 161
Wynter, Sylvia, 15, 305–8

Yang, Wayne K., 79
"Yankee Doodle," 178, 230–3, 238–40
Years of Rice and Salt, The (novel), 68, 70–4, 77–8, 81–2; *see also* Robinson, Kim Stanley

Zunigha, Curtis, 28, 35, 40, 45–6, 54, 59

www.ingramcontent.com/pod-product-compliance
Lightning Source LLC
LaVergne TN
LVHW052015230825
819359LV00004B/121